Activities for Teaching Science as Inquiry

SIXTH EDITION

PEARSON

Merrill
Prentice Hall

Upper Saddle River, New Jersey
Columbus, Ohio

Activities for Teaching Science as Inquiry

ARTHUR A. CARIN (DECEASED)
Queens College

JOEL E. BASS
Professor Emeritus, Sam Houston State University

TERRY L. CONTANT
Sam Houston State University

Library of Congress Cataloging-in-Publication Data

Carin, Arthur A.
    Activities for Teaching science as inquiry/Arthur A. Carin, Joel E. Bass, Terry L.
Contant.—6th ed.
        p. cm.
    Includes bibliographical references and index.
    ISBN 0-13-118007-X
    1. Science—Study and teaching (Elementary)—Activity programs—Handbooks, manuals, etc.
I. Bass, Joel E. II. Contant, Terry L. III. Carin, Arthur A. Teaching science as inquiry.
IV. Title.
    LB1585.C267 2005
    373.3'5—dc22   2004003376

Vice President and Executive Publisher: Jeffery W. Johnston
Editor: Linda Ashe Montgomery
Editorial Assistant: Laura Weaver
Development Editor: Hope Madden
Production Editor: Mary M. Irvin
Production Coordination: Carlisle Publishers Services
Design Coordinator: Diane C. Lorenzo
Cover Designer: Ali Mohrman
Cover Images: Index Stock
Photo Coordinator: Kathy Kirtland
Production Manager: Pamela D. Bennett
Director of Marketing: Ann Castel Davis
Marketing Manager: Darcy Betts Prybella
Marketing Coordinator: Tyra Poole

Additional Credits: The *National Science Education Standards* boxes throughout the text were reprinted with
permission from *National Science Education Standards* by the National Academy of Sciences, courtesy of the
National Academies Press, Washington, DC.

This book was set in Goudy by Carlisle Communications, Ltd. It was printed and bound by Courier
Kendallville, Inc. The cover was printed by Coral Graphic Services, Inc.

Photo Credits: Scott Cunningham/Merrill: iii (bottom); Kenneth P. Davis/PH College: ii; Anthony Magnacca:
iii (top); Helen Bass: A-232.

Pearson Education Ltd.   Pearson Education Australia Pty. Limited
Pearson Education Singapore Pte. Ltd.   Pearson Education North Asia Ltd.
Pearson Education Canada, Ltd.   Pearson Educación de Mexico, S.A. de C.V.
Pearson Education—Japan   Pearson Education Malaysia Pte. Ltd.

10 9 8 7 6 5 4 3 2
ISBN: 0-13-118007-X

126217

Arthur A. Carin
1929–2003

I was first introduced to Arthur Carin while planning the revision of the seventh edition of this book. Awed by his longstanding reputation as a leading science educator, I wondered what kind of author I would find Dr. Carin to be—open to suggestions or resistant to change. Art was always open to new ideas and always excited to begin a new revision and improve the text. During our tenure together, I developed a great respect for Dr. Carin, knowing him to remain informed about science education research, still hungry to make a difference in the lives of teachers, and forever excited to be the one who turned a child's natural curiosity about the world into scientific adventure. He leaves this message.

> "I wish you much success as you experience the joy of seeing your students construct and broaden their science knowledge and grow in their appreciation of this marvelous world."

A few years before his death, we recognized Arthur Carin as one of our most highly esteemed and successful authors, a great presence for Merrill Education for over forty years. Even as it is hard to say good-bye, we who worked with Art continue to be humbled by his knowledge and leadership in the field of science education and are immensely grateful to have worked with such a giant. We miss you, Art.

Linda Montgomery
Senior Editor

Educator Learning Center:
An Invaluable Online Resource

Merrill Education and the Association for Supervision and Curriculum Development (ASCD) invite you to take advantage of a new online resource, one that provides access to the top research and proven strategies associated with ASCD and Merrill—the Educator Learning Center. At **www.EducatorLearningCenter.com** you will find resources that will enhance your students' understanding of course topics and of current educational issues, in addition to being invaluable for further research.

How the Educator Learning Center will help your students become better teachers

With the combined resources of Merrill Education and ASCD, you and your students will find a wealth of tools and materials to better prepare them for the classroom.

Research

- More than 600 articles from the ASCD journal *Educational Leadership* discuss everyday issues faced by practicing teachers.
- A direct link on the site to Research Navigator™ gives students access to many of the leading education journals, as well as extensive content detailing the research process.
- Excerpts from Merrill Education texts give your students insights on important topics of instructional methods, diverse populations, assessment, classroom management, technology, and refining classroom practice.

Classroom Practice

- Hundreds of lesson plans and teaching strategies are categorized by content area and age range.
- Case studies and classroom video footage provide virtual field experience for student reflection.
- Computer simulations and other electronic tools keep your students abreast of today's classrooms and current technologies.

Look into the value of Educator Learning Center yourself

A four-month subscription to Educator Learning Center is $25 but is FREE when used in conjuction with this text. To obtain free passcodes for your students, simply contact your local Merrill/Prentice Hall sales representative, and your representative will give you a special ISBN to give your bookstore when ordering your textbooks. To preview the value of this website to you and your students, please go to **www.EducatorLearningCenter.com** and click on "Demo."

Preface

THE RAPID ADVANCE of cognitive learning theories in the past few years has led educators to realize the need for students to be more actively engaged in their own construction of knowledge. This research tells us that an inquiry approach to science teaching motivates and engages every type of student, helping them understand science's relevance to their lives, as well as the nature of science itself.

Inquiry is both a way for scientists and students to investigate the world, and a way to teach. In this instructional environment, teachers act as facilitators of learning, guiding students in asking simple but thoughtful questions about the world and finding ways to engage them in answering their questions.

Inquiry incorporates the use of hands-on and process-oriented activities for the benefit of knowledge construction, while building investigation skills and habits of mind in students. Inquiry encourages students to connect their prior knowledge to observations and to use their observations as evidence to increase personal scientific knowledge and explain how the world works.

But is there a manageable way for new and experienced teachers to bring inquiry into their science classrooms?

Drawing on a solid understanding of inquiry with a teaching framework that builds in accountability for science content learning, and using inquiry-based activities, teachers can create and manage an engaging, productive science classroom. By integrating an inquiry approach, science content, the *National Science Education Standards* (NSES), and a bank of inquiry activities, the sixth edition of *Activities for Teaching Science as Inquiry* demonstrates a manageable way for new and experienced teachers to bring inquiry successfully into the science classroom.

The Inquiry Framework

In this edition we have taken the *National Science Education Standards* and the Learning Cycle's 5-E instructional model to create an inquiry framework for science teaching.

5-E Model

Each activity follows the 5-E model of instruction, which frames lesson activities in terms of engaging, exploring, explaining, elaborating, and evaluating. This Learning Cycle model reflects the NSES *Science as Inquiry Standards*, seamlessly integrating inquiry and the *Standards* to create a science teaching framework best suited for engaging students in meaningful science learning while providing accountability opportunities for teachers.

National Science Education Standards

Many years of work and research in the science education community have provided a coherent, research-based vision for a new era of science education. As a result, the *National Science Education Standards* were created to coordinate the goals and objectives for science instruction.

The activities in this edition will provide you with the opportunity to become familiar with the *National Science Education Standards*. Each activity is connected to a specific NSES *Content Standard* and to *Concepts and Principles* that support the Standard. In addition, the 5-E model which frames the activities reflects the NSES *Inquiry Standards*. This integrated application of the Standards highlights the importance of using them to inform curriculum and instruction.

Teaching Science as Inquiry

The activities have been reorganized to follow the NSES *Content Standards*, further developing new and experienced teachers' fluency with a *Standards*-based science classroom, and have been restructured to follow the 5-E instructional model, creating a manageable way to engage students in inquiry activities. The Activities for Teaching Science as Inquiry

- can be used to illustrate and expand on the science content, and model the 5-E lesson procedures, engaging students in constructivist inquiry;
- provide a comprehensive view of how the NSES *Science Content Standards* can be used to organize curriculum and inform instruction in elementary and middle school science;
- provide an interesting way for methods students to learn significant science content that will be important for them to know in teaching science;
- provide a way for students to prepare for the science portion of state certification exams; and
- become a bank of activities students can draw on in developing lesson plans to teach during their science methods courses and when they move into the schools as professional teachers.

Acknowledgments

To be meaningful, educational visions have to be practically implemented in teacher education and staff development programs, and most important, in our nation's classrooms. Our goal in writing and revising this textbook has been to present the new vision of science education and provide you with specific help, guidelines, and examples as you prepare to teach science in a new millennium.

The reviewers for the sixth edition of this text, as well as those who read and commented on the chapters in the fifth edition, have been very perceptive and insightful and have offered many comments and suggestions that, hopefully, have led to significant improvements. We acknowledge and express our gratitude to the following reviewers: Carol Brewer, The University of Montana; Rosemarie Kolstad, East Texas State University; Mark R. Malone, The University of Colorado; Richard H. Moyer, The University of Michigan—

Dearborn; Michael Odell, The University of Idaho; William A. Rieck, The University of Southwestern Louisiana; Joseph D. Sharpe, Tennessee Technological University; Leone E. Snyder, Northwestern College; M. Dale Streigle, Iowa State University; Dr. Phil Swicegood, Sam Houston State University; and Dana L. Zeidler, The University of South Florida—Tampa.

We thank editor Linda Montgomery at Merrill/Prentice Hall, who has provided substantive as well as editorial assistance throughout the writing and revision efforts. She has a great sensitivity to education issues, not only in science but in other specialized fields as well. We wish to acknowledge her contributions to this text and convey our appreciation to her.

We also wish to thank Hope Madden, our diligent and amenable development editor; Joan Lyon, copyeditor; Carlisle Communications, designer; Mary Irvin, production editor; and Emily Hatteberg, project coordinator at Carlisle Publishers Services.

From Art Carin

I am certain you will find this text a valuable resource as you become an even more competent, confident decision maker. I strongly encourage you to adapt the strategies in this text and appeal to you to apply the concepts in ways that are meaningful to you and your students. It is my hope that it will empower you to teach science confidently to your students in your unique classroom situations. I wish you much success as you experience the joy of seeing your students construct and broaden their science knowledge and grow in their appreciation of this marvelous world.

For their continued support and encouragement, I wish to personally thank my wife, Doris Terry, a former classroom teacher; my adult children, Jill, Amy, and Jon; and their respective spouses, Kevin, Rich, and Oberon. I appreciate the love and inspiration I continually get from my three wonderful grandchildren: Andy, a fine young man in high school; Becky, a beautiful, delightful student in first grade; and our newest addition, preschooler Scarlett who enjoys nature and learning about the world around her.

From Joel Bass

The real rewards for teachers come from the satisfaction of watching our students grow and change. But teaching is a two-way street. The pages in this book reflect a great deal that my own students have taught me about science, children, and teaching. Thanks to each and every one of you. Thanks also to my own teachers and colleagues for their guidance and friendship.

I would like to express my special appreciation for the support and encouragement of my wife, Helen. I am grateful to her for enlarging my own view of science and culture, particularly as it relates to American history. In our mutual quest to understand the first Americans, we have trudged down canyons, explored ancient ruins, gazed in wonder at rock art, meditated at sacred sites, and danced in tribal powwows. Our experiences in following the Lewis and Clark trail from Missouri to Oregon are reflected in Chapter 8 discussions. Helen, thanks for your continued love and care in the day-to-day life of balancing family, professional, and other concerns and responsibilities.

From Terry Contant

As a science educator, my favorite phrase is "I don't know, let's find out!" These words describe the fundamental nature of scientific endeavors, encourage the mutual learning that should take place in an ideal science classroom, and concisely sum up the essence of inquiry. I hope they also express your lifelong quest to understand how to be a great teacher. Inquiry is about questioning, planning, evaluating data, making connections, and communicating ideas. These activities are vital in both science and teaching. I encourage you to use this book as a resource as you apply inquiry approaches in your classroom and to your professional growth.

I want to thank my husband, Charlie, and my daughter, Heather, for helping me explore and discover the world around me as I grow personally and professionally. Whether stargazing, strolling on the beach, or petting the cats, sharing nature with my family is tremendously rewarding. Dinner discussions about current science discoveries on the news or what happened at school that day have stimulated my thinking about science education. Finding "good science fair projects" in everyday life is common in our home. I am also grateful to my parents and many teachers, colleagues, and students who have encouraged me to continue to "find out" throughout my life.

With sincere gratitude to all,

Art Carin
Joel Bass
Terry Contant

Contents

Activities for Teaching Science as Inquiry

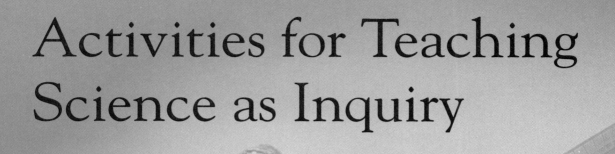

SECTION I
Teaching Inquiry Science Activities

NSES   *Inquiry is a set of interrelated processes by which scientists and students pose questions about the natural world and investigate phenomena; in doing so, students acquire knowledge and develop a rich understanding of concepts, principles, models, and theories. Inquiry is a critical component of a science program at all grade levels and in every domain of science. (National Research Council, 1996, p. 214)*

Terrariums offer a wonderful opportunity for children to investigate the world by questioning and hypothesizing, describing and classifying, manipulating and experimenting, inferring and predicting. Sharon Olson began a series of terrarium lessons with her second graders by asking: "What might you find on a forest floor?" As the class discussed this question, Ms. Olson held up the different materials the students suggested (soil, sand, leaves, seeds, fruit, plants, water, twigs, grass, and so on). She then told the students these were some of the things they would put in a container to make a home for living things. For the next few days, small groups of students built and investigated their own terrariums (Hosoume & Barber, 1994). Using readily available containers, such as large, plastic soda-water bottles (Ingram, 1993), the children arranged soil in the bottom of the containers, planted plants, sprinkled seeds, added moisture, and introduced earthworms and pill bugs to their new homes.

This scenario draws on activities described in this book. Here, you will find directions for more than 150 inquiry activities in physical science, life science, and earth and space science designed for elementary and middle school students. The activities presented here do not comprise a comprehensive science curriculum, but they do represent a large number of examples that will

1. provide you with concrete suggestions for teaching science as inquiry;
2. provide a bank of activities that you can draw on in teaching science as inquiry to children; and
3. help you connect science in the classroom to the *National Science Education Standards* in a very practical way.

You do not have to be a science specialist to engage your students in these activities, merely curious and willing to learn along with them.

Let us look more closely at what it means to teach science as inquiry.

When Scientists and Students Inquire

Science is an attempt to understand the natural world. Doing science can be as simple as one individual conducting field studies or as complex as hundreds of people across the world working together on a major scientific problem. Whatever the circumstances or level of complexity, scientists are likely to work from some common assumptions, have some common goals, and use some common procedures. When scientists inquire, they

- ask questions about objects, events, and systems;
- employ simple equipment and tools to make observations and measurements to obtain data and seek evidence;
- use accepted scientific concepts and principles to develop tentative explanations that make sense of collected evidence;
- make predictions to test explanations;
- blend logic and imagination;
- identify and avoid bias; and
- reach conclusions or *not* (American Association for the Advancement of Science (1993); Rutherford & Ahlgren, 1990, pp. 5–9; National Research Council, 1996, pp. 122–123).

Although what scientists do is a model for science instruction, because of developmental differences children may not be able to engage in inquiry as scientists do in professional communities. Thus, elementary and middle school science instruction occurs in a simplified form that enables children to participate with understanding (Lee, 2002).

The key ingredient in accommodating scientific inquiry to the level of children is the teacher, who plans, prepares, poses, presents, hints, prompts, questions, informs, guides, directs, scaffolds, tells, and explains—all in the context of children's hands-on engagement with the objects, organisms, and activities of the real world.

Phases of Inquiry Instruction

Inquiry instruction can be thought of in terms of five main components or tasks: *engage, explore, explain, elaborate,* and *evaluate.* You may recognize these five instructional phases as the components of the 5-E model of instruction. The roles of the teacher and the students are quite different in the 5-E model and the traditional textbook-oriented approach to science. See Tables I-1 and I-2 to identify these roles.

Engagement

Inquiry is initiated at the engagement phase. In this phase, teachers probe prior knowledge and conceptions (and misconceptions) of learners and generate a question to be investigated. Ideally, inquiry in the classroom should begin with authentic questions developed by students from their own experiences with objects, organisms, and events in the environment (American Association for the Advancement of Science, 1993, pp. 9–12). In classroom practice, teachers have to be prepared to provide guidance in forming initiating questions. Students learn from teachers how to ask good questions. Teachers can maintain the spirit of inquiry by focusing on questions that can be answered by collecting observational data, using available knowledge of science, and applying processes of reasoning (National Research Council, 1996, p. 189).

TABLE I-I   APPLYING THE 5-E INSTRUCTIONAL MODEL

Stage of the Instructional Model	What the TEACHER does	
	that is consistent with this model	that is inconsistent with this model
Engage	• Creates interest • Generates curiosity • Raises questions • Elicits responses that uncover what the students know or think about the concept/topic	• Explains concepts • Provides definitions and answers • States conclusions • Provides closure • Lectures
Explore	• Encourages students to work together without direct instruction from the teacher • Observes and listens to students as they interact • Asks probing questions to redirect students' investigations when necessary • Provides time for students to puzzle through problems • Acts as a consultant for students	• Provides answers • Tells or explains how to work through the problem • Provides closure • Tells students that they are wrong • Gives information or facts that solve the problem • Leads students step by step to a solution
Explain	• Encourages students to explain concepts and definitions in their own words • Asks for justification (evidence) and clarification from students • Formally provides definitions, explanations, and new labels • Uses students' previous experiences as the basis for explaining concepts	• Accepts explanations that have no justification • Neglects to solicit students' explanations • Introduces unrelated concepts or skills
Elaborate	• Expects students to use formal labels, definitions, and explanations provided previously • Encourages students to apply or extend the concepts and skills in new situations • Reminds students of alternative explanations • Refers students to existing data and evidence and asks: "What do you already know?" "Why do you think . . .?" (Strategies from Explore apply here also.)	• Provides definitive answers • Tells students that they are wrong • Lectures • Leads students step by step to a solution • Explains how to work through the problem
Evaluate	• Observes students as they apply new concepts and skills • Assesses students' knowledge and/or skills • Looks for evidence that students have changed their thinking or behaviors • Allows students to assess their own learning and group-process skills • Asks open-ended question, such as: "Why do you think . . .?", "What evidence do you have?", "What do you know about x?", "How would you explain x?"	• Tests vocabulary words, terms, and isolated facts • Introduces new ideas or concepts • Creates ambiguity • Promotes open-ended discussion unrelated to the concept or skill

Source: Teaching Secondary School Science, 7th ed., (p. 249), by Leslie Trowbridge and Rodger Bybee, © 2000, Merrill/Prentice Hall, Inc. Reprinted by permission of Pearson Education, Inc. Upper Saddle River, NJ.

TABLE I-2   APPLYING THE 5-E INSTRUCTIONAL MODEL

Stage of the Instructional Model	What the STUDENT does	
	that is consistent with this model	that is inconsistent with this model
Engage	• Asks questions, such as: "Why did this happen?", "What do I already know about this?", "What can I find out about this?" • Shows interest in the topic	• Asks for the "right" answer • Offers the "right" answer • Insists on answers or explanations • Seeks one solution
Explore	• Thinks freely, but within the limits of the activity • Tests predictions and hypotheses • Forms new predictions and hypotheses • Tries alternatives and discusses them with others • Records observations and ideas • Suspends judgment	• Lets others do the thinking and exploring (passive involvement) • Works quietly with little or no interaction with others (only appropriate when exploring ideas or feelings) • Plays around indiscriminately with no goal in mind • Stops with one solution
Explain	• Explains possible solutions or answers to others • Listens critically to one another's explanations • Questions one another's explanations • Listens to and tries to comprehend explanations offered by the teacher • Refers to previous activities • Uses recorded observations in explanations	• Proposes explanations from thin air with no relationship to previous experiences • Brings up irrelevant experiences and examples • Accepts explanations without justification • Does not attend to other plausible explanations
Elaborate	• Applies new labels, definitions, explanations, and skills in new, but similar, situations • Uses previous information to ask questions, propose solutions, make decisions, design experiments • Draws reasonable conclusions from evidence • Records observations and explanations • Checks for understanding among peers	• Plays around with no goal in mind • Ignores previous information or evidence • Draws conclusions from thin air • Uses in discussions only those labels that the teacher provided
Evaluate	• Answers open-ended questions by using observations, evidence, and previously accepted explanations • Demonstrates an understanding or knowledge of the concept or skill • Evaluates his or her own progress and knowledge • Asks related questions that would encourage future investigations	• Draws conclusions, not using evidence or previously accepted explanations • Offers only yes-or-no answers, memorized definitions, or explanations as answers • Fails to express satisfactory explanations in his or her own words • Introduces new, irrelevant topics

Source: *Teaching Secondary School Science,* 7th ed., (p. 248), by Leslie Trowbridge and Rodger Bybee, © 2000, Merrill/Prentice Hall, Inc. Reprinted by permission of Pearson Education, Inc. Upper Saddle River, NJ.

Exploration

The essence of science is to use whatever methods fit to gather evidence that can be used in making sense of the natural world. There are various types of investigations for scientists and children to use in doing science. Different types of questions call for different forms of investigation.

In the early grades, investigations are largely based on systematic description and classification of material objects and organisms (Lowery, 1997), such as we have seen in the terrarium lessons. Young children's natural curiosity motivates them to explore the world by manipulating and observing, comparing and contrasting, and sorting simple objects in their environment.

By grade 4 or 5, children begin to engage in experimental inquiry—posing questions, collecting information through experiments, and arriving at logical conclusions. Controlled experiments or fair tests can be very important parts of experimental investigations, especially in the upper elementary and middle grades. In controlled investigations, students manipulate one variable at a time, determine its effect on a responding variable, and control all other relevant variables. Carefully guided variations of experiments might also be introduced at earlier grades.

As students engage in these inquiry activities, they develop simple skills such as how to observe, measure, cut, connect, switch, pour, tie, hold, and hook. Beginning with simple instruments, they learn to use rulers, thermometers, watches, spring scales, and balance beams to measure important variables. Students learn to use magnifying lenses and microscopes to see finer details of objects and organisms. They may also begin to use computers and calculators in investigations (National Research Council, 2000).

Explanation

This phase of inquiry involves the interpretation of collected data. To interpret is to go beyond the data given and to construct inferences, make predictions, and build explanations that make sense of the world. Interpretations use reasoning processes to coordinate scientific knowledge and observational evidence to answer initiating questions.

In children's inquiry, teachers should refrain as much as possible from supplying information and providing explanations that children could attain on their own. Nevertheless, it is often necessary for teachers to directly teach terms and concepts, experimental procedures, and scientific principles. Although inquiry teachers may use expository methods to teach principles, the instruction always builds on children's recent activities, and what is learned is applied to new situations to assist the students in comprehending it.

Elaboration

If understanding is to be a result of inquiry, students must have opportunities to apply their new knowledge to new issues and problems (Bransford, Brown, & Cocking, 1999). In the elaboration phase, students identify additional questions to investigate, collect pertinent evidence, and connect their newly constructed knowledge to the evidence through such processes as classifying, relating, inferring, predicting, and explaining. Students communicate their investigations to one another and critique and analyze their work and the work of others. By applying their new knowledge in investigating new situations, students continually build understanding.

Evaluation

Evaluation in inquiry teaching involves use of assessment data to discover what students are learning (or not learning) and to provide feedback to modify lesson plans and teaching methods where needed. Continuous assessment through asking key questions, observing and judging the performances and products of students, and administering assessment tasks of various designs will help you probe your students' understanding, consider how misconceptions and alternative theories are affecting their learning, and determine how they are able to apply what they know in new situations.

Student participation is a key component of successful assessment and evaluation systems. If students are to participate successfully, they need to be clear about the objectives and criteria for good work, assess their own efforts in light of the criteria, and share responsibility in making judgments and taking action (Atkin, Black, & Coffey, 2001).

Teaching science as inquiry is especially compatible with a new type of assessment, called *performance assessment*. Performance assessment techniques make it possible to gather data on the processes of learning rather than just the outcomes, and to assess *how* students know rather than merely *what* they know. Performance assessments are often embedded in daily instruction, rather than administered at the end of the week or after a series of lessons.

All performance assessment tasks have a performance that can be observed or a work product that can be examined. Student performances might include measuring, observing, collecting and organizing data, constructing a graph, making a visual or audio presentation, participating in group discussion, presenting an oral defense of work, or presenting a how-to explanation of a procedure. Products presented for assessment could include data tables, graphs, models, reports, and oral or written explanations and problem solutions. Detailed scoring guides, such as checklists and rubrics, are developed and used with performance tasks to judge performance.

Characteristics of Inquiry Classrooms

At every step of inquiry instruction, learning takes place within classrooms characterized by student discourse, cooperative group activities, and teacher scaffolding.

Discourse

Children love to talk about their experiences. Inquiry science provides a rich context in which to develop language and thought (Rowe, 1973). Confronted with puzzling phenomena, and given some freedom to investigate, children work hard at expressing their experiences in language.

Just as communication among scientists is central in the construction of scientific knowledge, students learn by talking among themselves and writing about and formally presenting their ideas. Oral and written discourse focuses the attention of students on *what* they know, *how* they know it, and *how* their knowledge connects to the knowledge of other people, to other subjects, and to the world beyond the classroom (National Research Council, 1996, p. 36).

Teachers make students' ideas more meaningful by commenting and elaborating on them and asking students to clarify, expand, and justify their own emerging conceptions and those of others. Conversational partnerships with the teacher allow students to build on and use the teacher's thinking processes to support their own efforts to think in more flexible and mature ways.

Cooperative learning groups play a vital role in the learning community.

Cooperative Groups

Glenn T. Seaborg, 1951 Nobel Prize winner in chemistry and the principal investigator for GEMS (Great Explorations in Math and Science) at the Lawrence Hall of Science, reminds us that cooperation is the norm in science:

The PALS (Performance Assessment Links in Science) Website has collected many excellent performance assessment examples from the World Wide Web. Peruse the site at http://pals.sri.com/index.html.

In the case of all great "discoveries" it must be remembered that science is a group process. When we devise experiments and research today, we do so on the basis of an enormous body of knowledge contributed by people from all over the world over thousands of years. . . . Research effort is above all a team effort. (Seaborg, 1991)

In the context of inquiry instruction, cooperative learning is an important process that asks students to work together and support one another's learning. It entails students working collaboratively in small groups to

- consider a problem or assignment together;
- share limited supplies and science equipment;
- verbalize what they know and what they want to find out;
- plan investigations;
- collect and compare the data;
- consider the multiple viewpoints of group members; and
- propose group solutions to the problem.

Setting Up Cooperative Learning Groups (CLGs). Initially, you should assign students to teams because they tend to gravitate to friends only. For primary grade students, or older students who have not worked previously in CLGs, it is best to start with two students. As students acquire basic cooperative group skills, combine two groups of two as a working team. Generally, CLG teams of three or four are recommended once your classroom is comfortable and knowledgeable about the process.

When you form groups you will want to integrate students with various abilities, disabilities, and cultural backgrounds. Once you have established a cooperative group routine, keep teams together for at least 3 to 6 weeks so teammates have time to learn to work with each other. As a team builder, let each team choose its own name. After 3 to 6 weeks, change team membership, so students get to work with other students and learn the differences in team dynamics.

CLG Job Functions and Assignments. A specific job is assigned to each CLG team member. The names and functions are quite similar in all CLGs. The following are from Robert Jones's (1990) *Inquiry Task Group Management System:*

- *Principal investigator.* In charge of team operations including checking assignments, seeing that all team members can participate in activities, and leading group discussions. The principal investigator is also the one group member who communicates with the teacher when questions arise. This enables a more orderly atmosphere and limits the number of questions the teacher must respond to. Often groups can solve their own problems without consulting the teacher.
- *Materials manager.* Gets, inventories, and distributes materials to the team.
- *Recorder/reporter.* Collects and records data on lab sheets and reports results to whole class orally or in writing on class summary chart posted on chalkboard.
- *Maintenance director.* With the assistance of other team members, cleans up and returns materials and equipment to their appropriate storage space or container. Directs the disposal of used materials and is responsible for team members' safety.

An alternative set of cooperative group roles used in FOSS (Full Option Science System) activities is shown in Figure I-1.

CLG Job Badges. To enable easy identification of team members' jobs and responsibilities, students should wear job badges (see examples in Figures I-2 and I-3). Job badges will make it easier for students to remember their responsibilities and for you to spot students

Figure I-1 Cooperative group roles for FOSS (Full Option Science System) science activities.

- **Getters.** There are two Getters for each group. One (Getter 1) gets equipment from the materials station and the other (Getter 2) returns it.

- **Starter.** One person is the Starter for each task. This person makes sure that everyone gets a turn and that everyone has a chance to contribute ideas to the investigation.

- **Reporter.** The Reporter is the person who makes sure that everyone has recorded information on student sheets or in science journals. This is also the person who reports group data to the class or records it on the board or class chart.

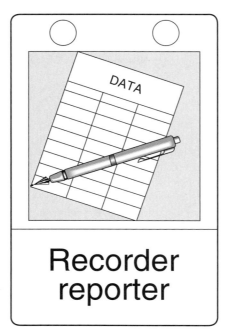

Figure I-2 Cooperative learning group (CLG) job badge.
Source: Reprinted by permission from Robert M. Jones, *Teaming Up! The Inquiry Task Group Management System User's Guide.* LaPorte, TX: ITGROUP, December 1990, 55.

Figure I-3 Cooperative learning group (CLG) job badge.
Source: Reprinted by permission from Robert M. Jones, *Teaming Up! The Inquiry Task Group Management System User's Guide.* LaPorte, TX: ITGROUP, December 1990, 43.

who should not be straying away from their group's space. Younger students will especially enjoy displaying an ID badge. As students get older, they may be reticent about wearing badges unless there is a level of sophistication to their design. You may liken the students' badges to the security badges that adults often wear in the workplace.

Scaffolding

In *scaffolding* student learning, the teacher supplies enough external support for students to be successful with the various inquiry tasks. The teacher might help learners at various steps in the inquiry process as they formulate the focus question for an investigation, plan and carry out procedures for data collection, and make sense of the data and answer the question posed. The younger the children and the less experience they have with scientific inquiry, the more scaffolding assistance they will probably need and the more structured the inquiry lessons will need to be.

To scaffold the learning process for students, teachers can (Grigorenko, 1998; Roehler & Cantlon, 1997) consider these types of assistance:

- start by making the learning task one that is challenging and interesting with an appropriate degree of novelty;
- if necessary, simplify the task so that the learner can manage it;
- facilitate student talk in small group and large group settings;
- ask meaningful questions at just the right time;
- lead students to clarify, elaborate, or justify their responses;
- supply necessary information or direct learners to appropriate sources;
- provide cues, prompts, and even direct instruction on needed concepts and principles;
- provide models of thinking processes; and
- provide external support, such as diagrams and concept maps, to aid students in making difficult connections.

An important task in the art of teaching is to know when to scaffold a student's learning and when to allow it to take its own course. Just as scaffolds in a building project are designed to be taken down when the building walls are strong, scaffolding support in teaching should be gradually removed or "faded" (Ormrod, 1999) as students develop science knowledge and inquiry processes. In the long run, students should develop their own self-regulated strategies to guide learning.

Planning for Inquiry Instruction

Thoughtful planning and organization is needed to prepare meaningful inquiry lessons. The science content you focus on will probably be dictated by your local or state curriculum guidelines. These guidelines will likely reflect the *National Science Education Standards*. That means that science content includes not only science knowledge but also essential inquiry skills and an understanding of the nature of science itself.

Once you have determined concepts and principles to be learned, find a series of activities, such as those in this book, that support investigations involving the science principles and concepts you want your students to understand. Be sure students have opportunities to experience, investigate, and think about phenomena so that they can begin to understand how science principles work in the world in which they live. Your lessons should enable students to learn how to form questions, design and conduct investigations, and use collected data and developing knowledge to answer the questions posed.

Getting Started with Inquiry Science

Now that you have selected lesson activities for students, how do you get started using inquiry in your science classroom? Here are some suggestions:

Step 1: Preparation. Prepare the inquiry activity for whole class or small group work.

- Arrange classroom furniture to facilitate inquiry and avoid excessive noise, movement, or confusion. Consider the furniture configuration illustrated in Figure I-4.
- Organize students into cooperative groups.
- Organize materials needed by teams in small boxes or bags, or on trays.

Figure I-4   Furniture arrangement for inquiry science.

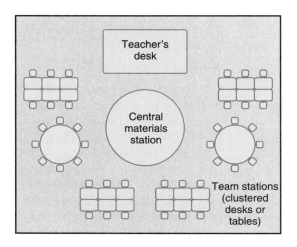

- Try out activities before they are introduced to students. By trying out activities beforehand, you can anticipate questions and ensure that the activity will work. Finding out in the middle of a lesson that you do not have enough materials or you cannot get the equipment to work properly can discourage you or your students.

Step 2: Engagement. Present an initiating activity designed to engage the students in pursuing the learning objectives.

- Keep the activity brief and open-ended.
- Ask or help the students ask specific key questions about the initiating activity.
- Ask questions to find out students' prior knowledge and conceptions or misconceptions.
- Tell students they will be exploring this and other related questions.
- Review general and specific safety procedures with students (see Figure I-5).
- Introduce or review pertinent activity information and cooperative group procedures such as, "When we begin, move quickly and quietly into your team. Stay with your team at all times. Speak softly, listen and respond to one another, and take turns. Concentrate on your assigned job."

Step 3: Distribution of Science Materials. Do not begin distributing materials until all of step 2 is completed. Then, have all the materials managers collect science materials from the central materials station and deliver them to each team station. This step can make or break the best-planned activity. Make certain that materials managers are reliable and know the specifics of their jobs before they begin!

Step 4: Exploration.

- As each team begins its work, move from team to team to ensure the proper distribution of materials has occurred and that teams have necessary materials and are proceeding safely.
- Be careful that you do not give away the "answer" during the exploration phase. Tell students very little about what can be expected to happen. You want students to make observations, discuss what they observe, and have a chance to make predictions or inferences from their observations. Otherwise, they are likely to discover exactly what you have told them they will discover. Part of the joy of exploring is not knowing what to expect!

1. Make certain you have the necessary science equipment and supplies in sufficient amounts to allow your students to participate in the lab activity. Have materials at a central workstation already set up with an adequate number of science materials and equipment for individual or group use.
2. Perform initial steps like boiling water, heating or cooling materials, and double-checking supplies before an activity begins.
3. If any chemicals are used, even diluted vinegar, make sure students wash up immediately following the activity.
4. Whenever possible, substitute plastics for all glassware. However, be certain when using heat that the plastics are able to withstand high temperatures. Whenever students use plastic bags, make sure the bags are too small to fit over their heads.
5. Avoid open flames in the classroom except under absolute necessity. Check your local school policies because the use of open flames in classrooms may be forbidden. Open flames should not be used in primary grade classrooms. Students should NEVER be allowed to use an open flame in any classroom activity. Candles and matches or a Bunsen burner should be used in teacher demonstrations only. If you must use an open flame, be sure a fire extinguisher is available and give instructions for its use.
6. Avoid the use of materials in your classroom that could cause serious damage to classroom facilities such as plaster of paris. Flushing excess plaster of paris powder down a sink drain can cause it to harden in the pipes. Check local guidelines before using any science materials to ensure you are aware of school policies regarding their use.
7. Avoid completely the use of electrical house current (110 volts) for student activities. Use dry cell batteries with students who are handling electrical equipment directly.
8. Assemble glass tubing and stoppers yourself and preferably before class. If possible and convenient, store glass tubing and connecting stoppers rather than disassembling and reassembling each time you need them.

Figure I-5   Guidelines for activity preparation and safety (additional safety suggestions are listed in Appendix G).

- Hold off on presenting science vocabulary. Do not give students the vocabulary words that will describe what they observe *before* they do the activity. Let students engage in the inquiry and experience the phenomena they observe. It is after exploration that science vocabulary will have more meaning for students.

Step 5: Explanation and Discussion of Results.

- Instruct reporter/recorders to post team results on a class summary chart visible to all. Conduct a discussion of the posted results. Then ask for students' conceptions of ideas and skills learned and discuss the similarities and discrepancies of team data.
- As students exchange their ideas, listen to how they have conceptualized what they think. Often, they will have developed erroneous beliefs about how something "works." Misconceptions are difficult to change. Simply pointing out alternative and naive conceptions will not generally change what students believe. There are several strategies you can employ to help students confront and reconsider their alternative conceptions:
  a. Ask questions that challenge students' current beliefs.
  b. Present phenomena that students cannot adequately explain within their existing perspectives.
  c. Engage students in discussions of the pros and cons of various explanations.
  d. Point out, explicitly, the differences between students' beliefs and "reality."
  e. Show how the correct explanation of an event or phenomenon is more plausible or makes more sense than anything students themselves can offer (Ormrod, 1999; Roth & Anderson, 1988).

- Although the child must do the interpretation work, teachers must be ready to assist in the process. During the explanation phase of inquiry, it is appropriate for teachers to supply vocabulary terms, invent relevant concepts and principles, and give hints and even complete explanations to children. But always follow this principle: Tell only after student inquiry.

Step 6: Elaboration. Suggest questions and activities that allow students to apply what they have learned to new and novel situations. Principal investigators then lead their teams in inquiring into the new questions. Follow up with appropriate class discussion. Also, have students extend their learning with readings, worksheets, Internet research, or other individualized reinforcement of concepts and principles being learned.

Step 7: Evaluation. Vary your methods for assessing understanding of individual team members and the group as a whole. Performance tasks and traditional assessment items could be used. Assess student understanding in every phase of your inquiry teaching. For example, determine:

- What information do students know about an activity before they begin exploration? What facts, concepts, and principles are mentioned?
- How well are students able to use the materials provided for the exploration activities? Do they discuss their observations? Are students able to provide reasons for their observations? Do they relate their observations to the initiating questions?
- Do students use their data to make predictions? How well were students able to provide reasons for their predictions? Are the reasons plausible?
- Are students providing plausible explanations for their observations? Are the students' reasons becoming more detailed? Do students provide more than one reason for their explanations?

Step 8: Team Cleanup. Maintenance directors, with the assistance of team members, arrange materials so they can be easily reused, return all supplies to designated areas, and ensure that work areas are cleaned. Note that cleanup is a team effort.

Using the Science Activities in This Book

The activities in this book are set within the context of specific **National Science Education Standards**. **Objectives** are given to provide specific focus for instruction, learning, and assessment, and to help tie the inquiry activities to the standards. **NSES Concepts and Processes** related to the *Science Standards* are also given. **Materials** needed for the lesson are specified, and a series of **activities** with an implied sequence is provided. The activities are keyed to specific phases of the **5-E Model.**

The science activities in the book focus on children raising questions about and exploring the natural world, learning concepts and principles and using them with observational evidence to make sense of natural phenomena, and developing inquiry procedures and abilities. The activities represent a bank of resources to use in developing your own inquiry lessons.

The activities are intended to be used flexibly as you design inquiry lessons. Feel free to add or subtract from them. Some activities are conducive for cooperative groups and some for teacher demonstrations. Activities that might be better done as teacher demonstrations are so marked.

The most important element in these inquiry activities is that students can discover the joy and wonder of science. And so can you. Have fun!

Many exciting science programs for children have been developed across the years (see Appendix K). Type acronyms such as FOSS, GLOBE, GEMS, AIMS, STC, and BSCS into a search engine such as Google to identify sources from groups that have long been recognized for their outstanding contributions to science education. You will find a variety of relevant and motivating activities for your classroom use.

REFERENCES

American Association for the Advancement of Science. (1993). *Benchmarks for science literacy*. New York: Oxford University Press.

Atkin, J. M., Black, P., & Coffey, J. (Eds.). (2001). *Classroom assessment and the national science education standards*. Washington, DC: National Academy Press.

Bransford, J. D., Brown, A. L., & Cocking, R. R. (Eds.). (1999). *How people learn: Brain, mind, experience, and school*. Washington, DC: National Academy Press.

Grigorenko, E. L. (1998). Mastering tools of the mind in school (Trying out Vygotsky's ideas in classrooms). In R. J. Sternberg & W. M. Williams (Eds.), *Intelligence, instruction, and assessment*. Mahwah, NJ: Erlbaum.

Hosoume, K., & Barber, J. (1994). *Terrarium habitats*. Berkeley: Great Explorations in Math and Science (GEMS), Lawrence Hall of Science, University of California.

Ingram, M. (1993). *Bottle biology*. Madison: Bottle Biology Project, Department of Plant Pathology, College of Agricultural and Life Sciences, University of Wisconsin.

Jones, R. M. (1990, December). *Teaming up! The inquiry task group management system user's guide*. LaPorte, TX: ITGROUP.

Lee, O. (2002). Promoting scientific inquiry with elementary students from diverse cultures and languages. In W. C. Secada (Ed.), *Review of research in education* (Vol. 26, pp. 23–69). Washington, DC: American Education Research Association.

Lowery, L. F. (Ed.). (1997). *Pathways to the science standards: Elementary school edition*. Arlington, VA: National Science Teachers Association.

National Research Council. (1996). *National science education standards*. Washington, DC: National Academy Press.

National Research Council. (2000). *Inquiry and the national science education standards: A guide for teaching and learning*. Washington DC: National Academies Press.

Ormrod, J. (1999). *Human learning*. Upper Saddle River, NJ: Merrill/Prentice Hall.

Roehler, L. R., & Cantlon, D. J. (1997). Scaffolding: A powerful tool in social constructivist classrooms. In K. Hogan & M. Pressley (Eds.), *Scaffolding student learning: Instructional approaches and issues*. Cambridge, MA: Brookline Books.

Roth, K., & Anderson, C. (1988). Promoting conceptual change learning from science textbooks. In P. Ramsden (Ed.), *Improving learning: New perspectives*. London: Kogan Page.

Rowe, M. B. (1973). *Teaching science as continuous inquiry*. New York: McGraw-Hill.

Rutherford, F. J., & Ahlgren, A. (1990). *Science for all Americans*. New York: Oxford University Press.

Seaborg, G. T. (1991, Fall/Winter). Some thoughts on discovery. *GEMS Network News*. Berkeley: Lawrence Hall of Science, University of California, p. 5.

Trowbridge, L., & Bybee, R. (2000). *Teaching secondary school science* (7th ed.). Upper Saddle River, NJ: Merrill/Prentice Hall.

SECTION II

Physical Science Activities

NSES   Science as Inquiry Standards

All students should develop abilities to

- ask questions about objects, organisms, and events in the environment;
- plan and conduct simple investigations;
- use appropriate tools and techniques to gather and interpret data;
- use evidence and scientific knowledge to develop explanations; and
- communicate investigations, data, and explanations to others.

Based on the *National Science Education Standards*, this section presents physical science activities that involve the investigation of matter, forces, sound, heat, light, magnetism, and electricity. Through engaging in these activities, children develop a better understanding of how the physical world works. At the same time, they develop their abilities to inquire—to ask questions about the world around them, to investigate and gather data, and to use their observations as evidence to construct reasonable explanations for the questions posed.

Each activity in the section is organized according to the 5-E model of instruction, which draws on the *Science as Inquiry Standards* (see box). In following the 5-E approach to instruction, teachers guide students to:

Engage. Ask a question to initiate inquiry about objects, organisms, and events in the natural world.

Explore. Plan and conduct simple investigations to collect relevant data.

Explain. Use data to construct knowledge and generate interpretations, including descriptions, classifications, predictions, and explanations, that make sense of the world and answer their questions.

Elaborate. Investigate new problems and questions to extend concepts and principles.

Evaluate. Demonstrate knowledge, understanding, and ability to use inquiry strategies through formal and informal assessments.

Although the activities in this section may be used individually, most of them are arranged sequentially to provide a comprehensive view of the phenomena, concepts, and principles of each topic.

I. PROPERTIES OF MATTER

The simple activities on properties of matter included here enable children to exercise their natural curiosity as they manipulate, observe, and classify common objects and materials in their environment and continue to form explanations of the world. Consistent with the *National Science Education Standards,* topics studied include properties of material objects, and the nature of solids, liquids, and gases (air).

A. PROPERTIES OF MATERIAL OBJECTS

▶ *Science Background*

All material objects may be described by their unique properties. By dynamically investigating properties of different objects, children can function much as research scientists do. They will learn to question, observe, classify, design and perform experiments, collect and analyze data, explain, and test explanations. In the process, they will begin to acquire a level of understanding of the world compatible with their own levels of development.

NSES   **Science Standards**

All students should develop an understanding of

- properties of objects and materials (K–4).
- changes of properties in matter (5–8).

Objectives for Students

1. Define *property* as a characteristic of an object—something you can see, touch, hear, smell, or taste.
2. Use simple equipment and tools that extend the senses to gather data about properties of objects and materials.
3. Develop descriptions and classifications of objects according to their properties.
4. Use description and classification to identify the most significant properties of buttons and how different properties of buttons might be related.

NSES   **Concepts and Principles**

Activities 1 and 2 address these fundamental concepts and principles related to the *Science Standards:*

- Objects have many observable properties (K–4).
- Objects are made of one or more materials (K–4).
- Properties can be used to separate or sort a group of objects or materials (K–4).

1. HOW ARE BUTTONS ALIKE AND DIFFERENT? (K–2)

Materials

For each group:

- Collection of 20 to 30 buttons differing in many ways, including color, shape, number of holes, and material from which they are made
- One small tray to hold buttons or other objects to be observed and grouped

Safety Precautions

Caution the students not to put the buttons or other small objects in their mouths, ears, nostrils, or eyes.

ENGAGE: ASK A QUESTION ABOUT OBJECTS, ORGANISMS, OR EVENTS IN THE ENVIRONMENT.

a. With the children in a large group, hold up an object, such as a ball. Ask: *What can you tell me about this object? Yes, it is a ball, but what else can you tell me about it? What is its shape, its color, its texture?*

   Discuss with children the various words that can be used to describe the object. Tell the children that, in science, the term *property* means the characteristics of objects—things you can observe with your senses or with instruments like magnifying lenses and stethoscopes that extend your senses. Discuss other uses of the word *property* with the children.

EXPLORE: PLAN AND CONDUCT SIMPLE INVESTIGATIONS TO COLLECT RELEVANT DATA.

b. Organize children into cooperative groups. Give each small group of children about 20 different buttons on a tray.

   Ask: *How many properties of these buttons can you name? What do we have to do to discover the properties of an object?*

   Tell children to observe the buttons and describe them to one another. Using a gamelike format similar to "I Spy," allow each child to describe a button in sufficient detail (without touching it or otherwise designating it) for the other children in the small group to pick it out. Characteristics to be described might include the button's color, its shape, its texture, the material it is made from, the number of holes it has, and other properties.

EXPLAIN: USE DATA TO GENERATE INTERPRETATIONS, INCLUDING DESCRIPTIONS, CLASSIFICATIONS, AND EXPLANATIONS.

c. Gather children as a whole class and ask: *What are the properties of the buttons you have observed?*

   On the board, make a list of each of the properties identified by the children.[1]

2. WHAT ARE SOME DIFFERENT WAYS YOU CAN GROUP BUTTONS? (K–2)

Materials

Button collections
Button bingo cards
Collection of fabric swatches, samples of wood panels or tiles, or pieces of metal

ENGAGE: ASK A QUESTION ABOUT OBJECTS, ORGANISMS, OR EVENTS IN THE ENVIRONMENT.

a. Ask: *How can you group your buttons? How many different ways can you find to group them?*

EXPLORE: PLAN AND CONDUCT SIMPLE INVESTIGATIONS TO COLLECT RELEVANT DATA.

b. Tell the children to sort their buttons into groups based on the properties of the buttons. For example, children might have collections of red buttons, blue buttons, green buttons, and multicolored buttons.

---

[1]For a delightful introduction to properties of buttons, see *The Button Box* by Margarette S. Reid (illustrated by Sarah Chamberlain), New York: Dutton Children's Books, 1990.

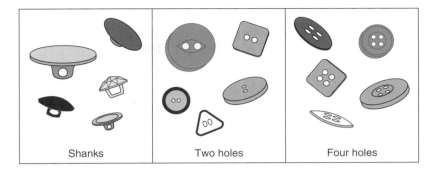

Shanks   Two holes   Four holes

As children sort their buttons, circulate among them and ask such questions as: *How are the buttons in this group alike? How are they different from one another?*

c. Show the children how to classify their buttons according to two stages. For example, in the first stage of classification they may get a class of all red buttons. In the second stage of classification, they may group the red buttons into two groups, such as round and not round. Thus, they end up with a group of red buttons that are round and a group of red buttons that are not round.

d. Let two cooperative groups come together. Members of one group should study the button classification system of the other group and guess the basis of the classification.

Ask: *How did you sort the buttons? How are the buttons in one group alike? How are they different from one another?*

EXPLAIN: USE DATA TO GENERATE INTERPRETATIONS, INCLUDING DESCRIPTIONS, CLASSIFICATIONS, AND EXPLANATIONS.

e. Ask: *What are buttons for? How are buttons used?* Answers might relate to the function of buttons to fasten garments or the ornamental nature of buttons. *What properties of buttons relate to how they work? What properties of buttons relate to their ornamental use?*

Building on children's observations and descriptions, guide them to suggest and explain that buttons are fasteners. They attach to garments in different ways, and they hold garments together in different ways. Investigating how different buttons are designed to be attached to garments and to hold garments together is a good way to extend the concepts studied.

How could you help children understand what scientists do?

f. Ask: *Why do scientists classify things? What is the purpose of classification?* Through discussion, bring out the advantage that through classification, we can simplify our thinking by dealing with a few groups rather than many individual elements. Also, explain that it is through classification of properties of buttons that we begin to identify their most significant properties. These include how buttons are attached to garments, how they function as fasteners, how they are ornamental, and so on.

ELABORATE: EXTEND CONCEPTS, PRINCIPLES, AND STRATEGIES TO NEW PROBLEMS AND QUESTIONS.

g. Give each group a pile of objects containing fabric swatches, samples of wood paneling or tile (obtained from a decorating store), pieces of metal, and so on. Give each group an envelope with several index cards, each stating a different basis for grouping. A pair of children take a card and group the objects on the basis of the property or properties stated. The other children must guess the basis of the grouping. Use singular properties such as "red" objects, "rough" objects, "metal" objects, or "cloth" objects. Also, place multiple properties on some cards, such as "rough and red." Challenge children to do a multistage classification of the materials based on the two properties.

Additionally, challenge children to create their own cards with their own desired multiple properties and to group materials according to the properties.

h. Prepare several different 9-square (3 by 3) button bingo cards, with button properties named in each square. As in the diagram, include single properties such as red, round, two-holed, wooden, and cloth. Also include some multiple-property squares, such as red and round, or two-holed and plastic.

RED	RED AND ROUND	NOT RED
CLOTH	ROUND	WOODEN
NOT ROUND	TWO HOLES AND PLASTIC	TWO HOLES

SAMPLE BUTTON BINGO CARD

i. Pass a button bingo card facedown to each pair of children. Give each pair several bingo tokens. Draw buttons from a bag of buttons. Call on children to name different properties of each button you draw. Instruct the children that they are to place a token in each square on their cards that contains a property named. Circulate among the children and interact with them about their understanding of the meaning of properties and classification. If you use a competitive group structure, winners might be the children who are able to correctly place three tokens in a row, column, or diagonally, or the children who are able to place the most tokens on their button bingo card. (You may think of other ways to play button bingo to give students additional practice at observing and classifying properties, and recognizing classification systems.)

B. PROPERTIES OF LIQUIDS

▶ *Science Background*

Students can conduct simple investigations with water that can be explained through use of an abstract model. In the model of water developed through the activities in this section, water consists of tiny particles or droplets. These particles of water are attracted to each other. Scientists refer to this force of attraction as *bonding*. For children, water drops are *sticky* or *grabby*.

Because water drops are sticky, water can heap up in a cup much more than first expected. Water at the surface of a filled cup attracts new water drops as they are added to the cup. Eventually, as the water being added heaps up too much, its weight causes it to overcome the stickiness of water and it flows over the edge of the cup.

As they develop new understandings of liquids, students also continue to develop their abilities to inquire.

 NSES   Science Standards

All students should develop an understanding of

- properties of objects and materials (K–4).
- changes in properties in matter (5–8).

Objectives for Students

1. Use simple apparatus and tools to gather data and extend the senses.
2. Describe the behavior of water and other liquids under various conditions.
3. Use observational evidence and a model of the bonding of liquid particles to explain the behavior of water and other liquids under different conditions.

 NSES   Concepts and Principles

Activities 1–8 address these fundamental concepts and principles related to the *Science Standards*:

- Materials can exist in different states—solid, liquid, and gas (K–4).
- Objects (such as liquids) have many different properties (K–4).

1. HOW MUCH WATER CAN HEAP UP IN A CUP? (2–4)

Materials

For activities 1–8, supply a kit of the following materials for each group:

- Two 30 ml medicine cups
- Beaker for water
- Magnifying lens
- Two medicine droppers (use identical droppers for the whole class)
- 6-inch squares of aluminum foil, wax paper, and plastic wrap
- 30–45 regular size paper clips

For the teacher:

- Small container of liquid dishwashing soap
- Toothpicks

Safety Precautions

Caution the students not to taste any liquid substances. When children work with water, provide table coverings, such as newspapers, and plenty of paper towels to absorb spills. Clean up spills promptly.

ENGAGE: ASK A QUESTION ABOUT OBJECTS, ORGANISMS, OR EVENTS IN THE ENVIRONMENT.

a. Pouring water from the beaker, students should fill the cup completely full of water until some overflows. When the children's cups seem completely filled, ask: *How many drops of water from a medicine dropper do you think you can add to your filled cup before it overflows?* Tell the children to make a prediction and record it before they carry out the activity.

EXPLORE: PLAN AND CONDUCT SIMPLE INVESTIGATIONS TO COLLECT RELEVANT DATA.

b. Tell your students to hold the medicine dropper about 2 cm above the cup as in the diagram. Slowly drop water into the cup, counting the number of drops needed for the water to overflow. As they count drops, students should observe the shape of the surface of water in the cup and what happens to water drops as they are added to the cup. Instruct them to bend down so that they are eye level with the 30 ml cup when they observe it. Show students how to use a magnifying lens (magnifying glass) to enhance their observations.

Allow reporters for cooperative groups to chart predictions and actual counts on the chalkboard or a transparency. Note and discuss variations in the data. If you think there is too much variation among groups, you might ask the groups to repeat their investigation under more common procedures.

EXPLAIN: USE DATA TO GENERATE INTERPRETATIONS, INCLUDING DESCRIPTIONS, CLASSIFICATIONS, AND EXPLANATIONS.

c. Ask: *How many drops did you add before the water spilled over the edge of the cup? How does your tested result compare with your prediction? How would you describe the shape of the water above the rim of the cup? What happens to each drop of water as it hits the surface of water in the cup? What happens to the last drop added to the cup, the one that makes the water overflow?*

d. Ask: *What is the property of water that makes it tend to heap up in a cup? That is, what keeps the water from overflowing as water drops are added?*

As children discuss possible answers to these questions, begin to develop a mental model of water, with water consisting of particles or drops that are all attracted to one another. Lead children to understand that water heaps up in medicine cups and does not overflow because water particles bond to, stick to, or grab on to one another. This simple model of liquids anticipates and lays a foundation for the introduction of atomic and molecular forces in later grades. If the children mention atoms and molecules of water (H_2O), listen but do not pursue the idea at this time. Rather, continue to focus on the notion that water is made up of tiny droplets that attract one another.

ELABORATE:
INVESTIGATE NEW
PROBLEMS AND QUESTIONS
TO EXTEND CONCEPTS AND
PRINCIPLES.

e. As an extension, ask: *How many drops of water do you think you can place on the surface of a clean penny? Can you add more drops to the head or tail of a penny?*

Lead children to make and record predictions, and then to design and conduct investigations to answer their questions. Chart the results on the board and discuss the results.

2. HOW MANY PAPER CLIPS CAN YOU ADD TO A CUP OF WATER? (2–4)

ENGAGE: ASK A
QUESTION ABOUT OBJECTS,
ORGANISMS, OR EVENTS IN
THE ENVIRONMENT.

a. Using the beaker, students should fill the 30 ml cup completely full of water again. Ask: *How many paper clips do you think you can add to the water in the cup before it flows over the rim?* Tell the children to make and test a prediction.

EXPLORE: PLAN
AND CONDUCT SIMPLE
INVESTIGATIONS TO
COLLECT RELEVANT DATA.

b. Tell students to gently slide regular-size paper clips one at a time into the water in the cup and count the number of paper clips needed to make the water flow over the rim. Chart results on the board and discuss similarities and differences.

EXPLAIN: USE DATA
TO GENERATE
INTERPRETATIONS,
INCLUDING DESCRIPTIONS,
CLASSIFICATIONS, AND
EXPLANATIONS.

c. Ask: *How do your predictions compare with actual results? Why do you think so many paper clips could be added to the cup before the water overflowed?* Students should explain that the water did not overflow at first because of the attractive forces between water droplets.

How could you help
children understand
what scientists do?

d. As children carry out these investigations of water, occasionally emphasize to them that they are *doing* science and *being* scientists. They are asking questions, gathering evidence, building a model of water drops, and using their model to construct explanations of what they see.

3. CAN YOU GET A PAPER CLIP TO "FLOAT" ON TOP OF WATER? WHY DOES THE PAPER CLIP NOT SINK? (2–4)

ENGAGE: ASK A
QUESTION ABOUT OBJECTS,
ORGANISMS, OR EVENTS IN
THE ENVIRONMENT.

a. Ask: *What can you do to make a paper clip "float" on the surface of water? If you push the paper clip down, will it bob back up?*

EXPLORE: PLAN
AND CONDUCT SIMPLE
INVESTIGATIONS TO
COLLECT RELEVANT DATA.

b. Allow students to try to make a paper clip stay on the top of water in a medicine cup or glass. To accomplish this task, bend a second paper clip so that a cradle is formed (see diagram). Place the other paper clip on the cradle and lower it into the water as in the diagram. The paper clip should stay suspended on top of the water.

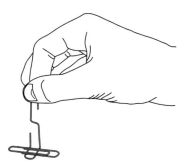

Use wire cradle to place another
paper clip on water.

EXPLAIN: USE DATA AND SCIENCE KNOWLEDGE TO GENERATE INTERPRETATIONS, INCLUDING DESCRIPTIONS, CLASSIFICATIONS, AND EXPLANATIONS.

Ask: *Why does the paper clip stay suspended on the top of the water? Is the paper clip floating?* Tell students that to explain why the paper clip "floated," we must connect observations to our model of water. Lead students to understand that because of the attractive forces among water drops, the surface of the water acts like a skin. The paper clip does not float in the water, like boats do, but is supported by water's skinlike effect. The paper clip rides on the top of the water's skin. If you push the paper clip down in the water, it breaks the skin and goes to the bottom of the container and will not bob back up. Scientists refer to the skinlike effect of water as *surface tension.*

ELABORATE: INVESTIGATE NEW PROBLEMS AND QUESTIONS TO EXTEND CONCEPTS AND PRINCIPLES.

c. Ask: *How do some bugs walk on water?* Explain that similar to the paper clip, a water strider is able to walk on the "skin" at the surface of the water.

4. WHAT DOES SOAP DO TO THE SKINLIKE EFFECT OF WATER? (2–4)

ENGAGE: ASK A QUESTION ABOUT OBJECTS, ORGANISMS, OR EVENTS IN THE ENVIRONMENT.

a. Ask: *How can we break or overcome the skinlike effect of water?*

EXPLORE: PLAN AND CONDUCT SIMPLE INVESTIGATIONS TO COLLECT RELEVANT DATA.

b. Tell students to use a beaker to fill the 30 ml cup completely full of water again. Tell them to add drops of water to the cup until it is about ready to flow over the rim. Take two toothpicks. Dip one of the toothpicks in a container of liquid dishwashing soap. Go from group to group, touching the end of the clean toothpick and then the soapy end of the other toothpick to the surface of the water in the cups.

EXPLAIN: USE DATA TO GENERATE INTERPRETATIONS, INCLUDING DESCRIPTIONS, CLASSIFICATIONS, PREDICTIONS, AND EXPLANATIONS.

c. Ask: *What did you see happen?* (The water flowed over the rim of the cup.) *What do you think was on the second toothpick? Why do you think the water flowed over the rim of the cup when it was touched with the soapy toothpick? Why did we use two toothpicks, a clean one and a soapy one?* (This is a controlled experiment. Using two toothpicks, a clean one and a soapy one, shows that it was not the toothpick, but what was on it that caused the water to overflow.)

d. Through discussion, lead the students to apply the model of water drops, adding the idea that soap tends to break the bonds that water drops have for one another. When the bonds are broken, the weight of the water allows it to flow over the rim of the cup.

5. WHAT HAPPENS TO WATER DROPS ON DIFFERENT SURFACES? (2–4)

ENGAGE: ASK A QUESTION ABOUT OBJECTS, ORGANISMS, OR EVENTS IN THE ENVIRONMENT.

a. Ask: *Do water drops look and act the same on different kinds of surfaces? How could we investigate to find out?*

EXPLORE: PLAN AND CONDUCT SIMPLE INVESTIGATIONS TO COLLECT RELEVANT DATA.

b. Provide each group small squares (about 15 cm by 15 cm) of wax paper, aluminum foil, and plastic wrap. Tell students to use a medicine dropper to place three or four drops of water on the wax paper. Ask: *How would you describe the shape of the water drops?*

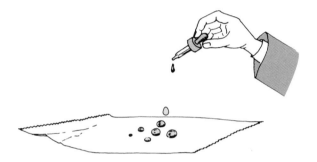

c. Tell students to push the drops of water around with a pencil point. Ask: *What happens to the drop when you push on it with a pencil point? What happens when you push several drops near each other?*

d. Tell them to investigate and compare what water drops look like and what they do on each of the three surfaces—wax paper, aluminum foil, and plastic wrap (see diagram). Provide magnifying lenses to enhance student observations.

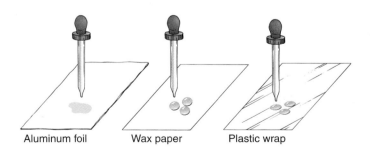

Aluminum foil   Wax paper   Plastic wrap

Ask: *What is the smallest size drop you can make? What is the largest size drop you can make? On which of the three surfaces does water heap up the most? spread out the most? What is the shape of water drops on wax paper? on aluminum foil? on plastic wrap?*

EXPLAIN: USE DATA AND SCIENTIFIC KNOWLEDGE TO GENERATE INTERPRETATIONS, INCLUDING DESCRIPTIONS, CLASSIFICATIONS, AND EXPLANATIONS.

e. Ask: *Why do you think the drops were heaped up on wax paper and spread out on aluminum foil?*

Using *evidence* from the children's investigations, invent (directly teach) the terms *cohesion* and *adhesion*. The bonding of a material to the same kind of material is known as **cohesion.** Water drops cohere to one another. The attraction of one material for another material is called **adhesion.** Adhesive tape bonds to different kinds of material, such as skin. Add the notions of cohesion and adhesion to the model of water drops bonding to one another.

Help children understand that the adhesive attraction between water and aluminum foil is greater than the adhesive attraction between water and wax paper. Thus, water drops can bead up more on wax paper because they do not have to overcome a great adhesive force for the surface.

ELABORATE: EXTEND CONCEPTS, PRINCIPLES, AND STRATEGIES TO NEW PROBLEMS AND QUESTIONS.

f. Ask: *Do you think it would be easier to use a toothpick to lead a drop of paper around on wax paper or on aluminum foil? Why do you think so? Try it and see. What differences do you observe for the two surfaces? Why do you think these differences happen?*

Guide children to plan and conduct an investigation and to use their data to answer these questions. With your assistance, children should reason that because there is greater adhesion (greater stickiness) between aluminum foil and water than between wax paper and water, it is harder to lead a drop of water around on aluminum foil than on wax paper. The aluminum foil grabs on to the drop more than the wax paper does.

NSES   **Concepts and Principles**

Activity 6 also addresses these fundamental concepts and principles related to the *Science Standards:*

• Forces will cause changes in the speed or direction of an object's motion (5–8).

6. WHEN THE SURFACES ARE SLANTED, WILL WATER DROPS RUN DOWN FASTER ON WAX PAPER, PLASTIC WRAP, OR ALUMINUM FOIL? (3–5)

ENGAGE: ASK A QUESTION ABOUT OBJECTS, ORGANISMS, OR EVENTS IN THE ENVIRONMENT.

a. Ask: *When the surfaces are slanted, on which surface will water drops slide or roll down fastest? What could you do to find out?*

EXPLORE: PLAN AND CONDUCT SIMPLE INVESTIGATIONS TO COLLECT RELEVANT DATA.

b. Help students plan a *controlled experiment (fair test)* to determine on which surface the water drops run down more quickly (see the diagram). They might, for example, control the slant of the surface and vary the type of surface (aluminum foil, plastic wrap, or wax paper).

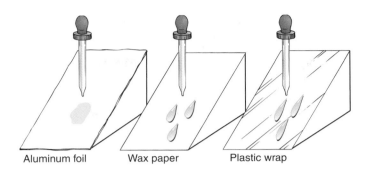

Aluminum foil   Wax paper   Plastic wrap

EXPLAIN: USE DATA TO GENERATE INTERPRETATIONS, INCLUDING DESCRIPTIONS, CLASSIFICATIONS, AND EXPLANATIONS.

c. Ask: *Why do you think the water drops ran more quickly down the wax paper ramp?* With your assistance, children should explain that water drops do not adhere or stick to wax paper as much as they do to aluminum foil and plastic wrap. Thus, the water drops ran down the wax paper ramp more quickly.

7. HOW DO THE COHESIVE AND ADHESIVE BONDS OF DIFFERENT LIQUIDS COMPARE? (2–4)

ENGAGE: ASK A QUESTION ABOUT OBJECTS, ORGANISMS, OR EVENTS IN THE ENVIRONMENT.

a. Ask: *Do water drops and drops of other liquids look and act the same on different surfaces?*

EXPLORE: PLAN AND CONDUCT SIMPLE INVESTIGATIONS TO COLLECT RELEVANT DATA.

b. Using a clean medicine dropper, the teacher should place a few drops of alcohol on the aluminum foil, wax paper, and plastic wrap of each group. Students should then place water drops near the alcohol drops on the surfaces and compare the properties of the two liquids on each surface. For example, tell students to compare the sizes of water drops and alcohol drops on the different surfaces, compare how small drops of each kind cohere to form larger drops, or try to lead water drops and alcohol drops around with a toothpick. Provide magnifying lenses to enhance students' observations.

Safety Precautions

Only the teacher should have access to the container of alcohol.

EXPLAIN: USE DATA TO GENERATE INTERPRETATIONS, INCLUDING DESCRIPTIONS, CLASSIFICATIONS, AND EXPLANATIONS.

c. Ask: *Does alcohol or water have stronger internal bonding forces? What is your evidence?* Lead the students to notice that water drops bead up more on each surface than alcohol drops. Help them infer that because water drops bead up more, they must have stronger internal bonds than alcohol drops, that is, water drops are more cohesive.

How could you help
children understand
what scientists do?

d. Ask: *What does it mean to explain something? How do scientists make up explanations? How do they know their explanations are correct?*

     Through discussion, lead children to understand that to explain an event means to use observations and science knowledge to show that the event is reasonable and could be expected to occur. Explain that scientific explanations are guesses about the way things are. They can be altered with new observations and new scientific knowledge.

8. WHY DO SEVERAL STREAMS OF WATER COHERE INTO ONE STREAM? (2–4)

ENGAGE: ASK A
QUESTION ABOUT OBJECTS,
ORGANISMS, OR EVENTS IN
THE ENVIRONMENT.

a. About 2 cm apart as shown in the diagram, puncture four very small holes in a horizontal line about 2 cm from the bottom of a 1 gallon plastic jug. Put masking tape over the holes.

    Note: Do not make the holes too large. Also, be sure the holes are very close together.

    Ask: *What do you think will happen when water is poured into this container and the masking tape is removed?*

      How many jets of water will you get coming out of the holes in the bottom of the plastic jug?

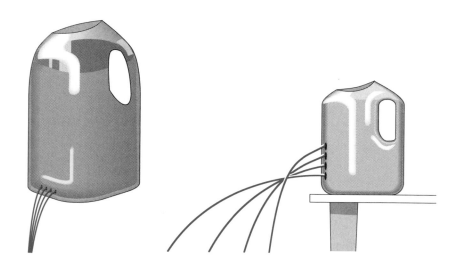

EXPLORE: PLAN
AND CONDUCT SIMPLE
INVESTIGATIONS TO
COLLECT RELEVANT DATA.

b. This activity might be conducted as a teacher demonstration with students assisting. Hold the jug over a sink or large tub, pour water into the jug, and remove the tape.

    Ask: *What do you observe?*

    Tell students to pinch the four jets of water together just as if they were going to pinch someone.

EXPLAIN: USE DATA
TO GENERATE
INTERPRETATIONS,
INCLUDING DESCRIPTIONS,
CLASSIFICATIONS, AND
EXPLANATIONS.

c. Ask: *What do you observe? Why do you think this happened?*

Lead students to use the water drop model and the concept of cohesion (the bonding of water drops) to explain why the four streams of water cohered into one stream.

C. PROPERTIES OF SOLIDS: OOBLECK

▶ *Science Background*

Investigating and describing the properties of oobleck can be a fascinating task for students grades 1–8. Oobleck is the name given to a special mixture of cornstarch, water, and food coloring that has some unique properties. The substance flows like liquid when you pour it, but keeps its shape like a solid when you hit it hard and fast. Many substances, like syrup and cooking oil, become more viscous and flow more easily when they are heated and less viscous when they are cooled. Oobleck is one of a number of puzzling *non-Newtonian* fluids that get more viscous when they are stirred or pressed.

You may have recognized the name oobleck from the Dr. Seuss children's book, *Bartholomew and the Oobleck*. In this little tale, a strange green rain falls from the sky. The properties of this green rain—Oobleck—cause quite a mess in the kingdom. Other books that treat this substance or its variations include *Horrible Harry and the Green Slime* by Suzy Kline and *The Slimy Book* by Babette Cole. You may want to read one or more of these books with your class in language arts as you investigate oobleck in science, focusing as you read about the properties of materials.

Information, recipes, and activities related to oobleck are excerpted from the GEMS teacher's guide, *Oobleck: What Do Scientists Do?* by Cary L. Sneider (Lawrence Hall of Science, University of California at Berkeley).

NSES Science Standards

All students should develop an understanding of

• properties of objects and materials (K–4).
• changes in properties in matter (5–8).

Objectives for Students

1. Conduct simple investigations to determine the properties of oobleck.
2. Describe properties of oobleck and compare them with various properties of solids and liquids.
3. Explain how their investigations of oobleck are like what scientists do when they investigate.

NSES Concepts and Principles

Activity I addresses these fundamental concepts and principles related to the *Science Standards*:

• Objects have many observable properties (K–4).
• Materials can exist in different states—solid, liquid, and gas (K–4).

···

1. WHAT ARE THE PROPERTIES OF OOBLECK? (1–6)

Materials

Four boxes cornstarch
Food coloring
Plastic bowls

Preparation

About 2 hours before class add 15 drops of food coloring to 4 1/4 cups of water. Pour the light green water into a large bowl and add four boxes of cornstarch and another 2 1/2 cups of water. Swirl and tip the bowl to level the mixture, then set the bowl aside.

Safety Precautions

- Oobleck is strange but is safe to handle.
- However, oobleck can be quite messy. Have plenty of newspaper around for children to use as a surface to work on. Impress on the children that part of doing science is to maintain a clean, orderly laboratory for investigating. Thus, they must be actively responsible for the cleanliness of their own work area.
- To protect their clothing, let the children wear large shirts over their regular clothes, as in art. Or give the children "lab coats" made of plastic grocery sacks with armholes and a neck hole cut in the bottom.
- Do not put oobleck down the sink as it will clog the drain. If oobleck falls on the floor, scoop most of it up and mop up the remainder with a damp sponge. If it falls on a carpet area, scoop up what you can, then vacuum after it dries.

ENGAGE: ASK A QUESTION ABOUT OBJECTS, ORGANISMS, OR EVENTS IN THE ENVIRONMENT.

a. Remind the children that a *property* is a characteristic of something that can be seen, heard, smelled, or felt by the senses or detected by instruments, such as magnifying lenses, that extend the senses.

Tell the children that you have a very strange substance that you will call oobleck, after the Dr. Seuss story, *Bartholomew and the Oobleck.* Ask: *What are the properties of oobleck? What can you do to find out?*

EXPLORE: PLAN AND CONDUCT SIMPLE INVESTIGATIONS TO COLLECT RELEVANT DATA.

b. Tell children they are to play the role of scientists in investigating the properties of this strange substance. Instruct them to write down as many properties of oobleck as they can discover, but to put a star by the two or three properties they think are most important.

c. Pour about a cup of oobleck into plastic bowls, give a bowl to each cooperative group, and let the fun begin. Some properties children might observe include:

It is gooey, sticky, and green; you can throw it like a ball; it is soft when you move your hand through it slowly, and hard when you move your hand fast; it dries out when left on paper for more than 10 seconds.

EXPLAIN: USE DATA TO GENERATE INTERPRETATIONS, INCLUDING DESCRIPTIONS, CLASSIFICATIONS, AND EXPLANATIONS.

d. Ask cooperative group reporters to write on the chalkboard one property their group has found. Continue until all properties have been exhausted. Place a star beside the two or three properties the children think are most distinctive for oobleck.

e. Show the children a solid object and a liquid in a container.

Ask: *What are the main properties of these two things?* Discuss whether oobleck is best classified as a liquid (flowing easily and taking the shape of its container) or a solid (maintaining its shape). Discuss whether oobleck should be called a solid or a liquid— or do we need a third category?

How could you help children understand what scientists do?

f. Ask the students to identify and list the ways they acted like scientists during their investigation of oobleck. In their lists they might include asked questions, talked, searched, planned, used magnifying lenses, experimented, recorded, explained, discussed, argued, defined, criticized, changed ideas, decided, asked more questions.

Discuss with students how what they did fits within these more formal statements in the *National Science Education Standards* of what scientists do when they inquire:

- Ask a question about objects, organisms, and events in the environment.
- Plan and conduct an investigation, using simple equipment and tools to gather data and extend the senses.
- Use data to construct descriptions, classifications, and explanations.
- Communicate investigations and explanations.

Ask students to give specific examples of what they did that is like one or more of these processes of scientists.

D. PROPERTIES OF SOLIDS: MYSTERY POWDERS

▶ *Science Background*

Investigating the physical and chemical properties of materials forms the basis for an exciting inquiry for children. This set of activities involves the study of four common white powders: granulated sugar, table salt, baking soda, and cornstarch. At first, it seems hard to distinquish among the powders; they appear to have closely similar properties. But when observed through a magnifying lens, an instrument that extends the sense of sight, the powders are found to be quite distinctive. Further, chemical tests reveal that the white powders react differently from one another when drops of water, iodine, and vinegar are added to them.

When given a mystery mixture of two powders, children use magnifying lenses and chemical indicator tests to identify the powders in the mixture. In the process of investigating the powders, children function as research scientists as they observe, design and perform chemical tests, and collect, record, analyze, and explain data. They also add to their own understanding of our fantastically diverse world.

NSES   **Science Standards**

All students should develop an understanding of

- properties of objects and materials (K–4).
- changes in properties in matter (5–8).

Objectives for Students

1. Use simple tools and instruments that extend the senses to gather data.
2. Carry out chemical indicator tests to determine how different powders react with water, iodine, and vinegar.
3. Accurately record and analyze data.
4. Use data to draw conclusions.

NSES Concepts and Principles

Activities 1 and 2 address these fundamental concepts and principles related to the *Science Standards:*

- Objects have many observable properties (K–4).
- Materials can exist in different states—solid, liquid, and gas (K–4).
- Substances react chemically in characteristic ways with other substances (5–8).

1. WHAT ARE THE DISTINGUISHING PROPERTIES OF COMMON WHITE POWDERS? (3–6)

Materials

For each pair of students:

- Small quantities of salt, granulated sugar, baking soda, and cornstarch
- Medicine droppers
- Plastic spoons
- Plastic wrap
- Magnifying lenses
- Safety goggles
- Small containers of water, vinegar, and iodine

Safety Precautions

- Students should wear safety goggles for these investigations with powders.
- Caution children not to taste any of the powders or liquids and to wash their hands after they test each powder.
- Do not put powders in the sink as they may clog drains.

ENGAGE: ASK A QUESTION ABOUT OBJECTS, ORGANISMS, OR EVENTS IN THE ENVIRONMENT.

a. Ask: *How are sugar and salt different? How are they alike? If you have several white powders, how can you tell them apart?*

Tell the students they will be doing chemical tests, acting like scientists (e.g., forensic chemists) to see what happens when different indicators (water, vinegar, and iodine) are added.

Show students the prepared data table and conclusion sheet and how to enter data in it. Explain that the data table provides a record of observations and experiments that we can refer to later. If necessary, remind students how to use a magnifying lens to extend the sense of sight.

Using a Magnifying Lens

To observe an object through a magnifier or magnifying lens, hold the magnifier close to the object, look through the magnifier at the object, then lift the magnifier toward your eye, stopping when the object begins to blur.

Many science classrooms have magnifiers with three lenses. The large lens usually provides a twofold magnification, the medium-sized lens provides a sixfold magnification, and the small lens an eightfold magnification. To provide increased magnification, two or even three magnifiers can be fitted together and used as a single magnifier.

DATA TABLE AND CONCLUSIONS FOR INVESTIGATING WHITE POWDERS

Observations	Powder 1 Granulated Sugar	Powder 2 Table Salt	Powder 3 Baking Soda	Powder 4 Cornstarch
Visual (Magnifying Glass)				
Water Test				
Iodine Test				
Vinegar Test				
Conclusions:				

EXPLORE: PLAN AND CONDUCT SIMPLE INVESTIGATIONS TO COLLECT RELEVANT DATA.

b. *Visual Observation.* Instruct students to use a magnifying lens to visually observe each powder, and to write down their observations on the data table.

c. *Preparation.* Give each group of students a sheet of plastic wrap. The plastic wrap will serve as a tray for their investigations. Show them how to place white powders in a row on the plastic wrap. Data will be recorded on the data table.

d. *Water Tests.* Students should place a small spoonful of each powder in a row on top of the plastic wrap. They should then add several drops of water and mix with a toothpick to see what happens. Observations should be recorded in the data tables.

e. *Iodine Tests.* Instruct students to place a small spoonful of each powder in a row on top of the plastic wrap. Then, they should add a drop or two of iodine to each powder and write down the results in their data tables. Caution the students to be careful! Iodine can stain hands and clothing.

f. *Vinegar Tests.* Students should place a small spoonful of each powder in a row on top of the plastic wrap. They should then add a drop or two of vinegar to each powder and write down the results in their data tables.

EXPLAIN: USE DATA TO GENERATE INTERPRETATIONS, INCLUDING DESCRIPTIONS, CLASSIFICATIONS, AND EXPLANATIONS.

g. *Compare.* Discuss the properties of the five powders that have been revealed through the different chemical tests. Help students to compare the results of their tests with the class master chart of properties of white powders. If necessary, ask students to repeat tests to see what happens.

PROPERTIES OF WHITE POWDERS

Observations	Powder 1 Granulated Sugar	Powder 2 Table Salt	Powder 3 Baking Soda	Powder 4 Cornstarch
Visual (Magnifying Glass)	White crystals	White box-shaped crystals	Fine white powder	Fine yellowish white powder
Water Test	Dissolves in water	Dissolves in water	Turns milky water	Makes water cloudy
Iodine Test	Turns yellow with iodine	No reaction with iodine	Turns yellow orange with iodine	Turns red, ends black with iodine
Vinegar Test	Dissolves in vinegar	No reaction with vinegar	Fizzes with vinegar	Gets thick, then hard with vinegar

2. HOW CAN YOU DETERMINE THE IDENTITY OF A MYSTERY POWDER?(3–6)

Materials

Flour
Materials from Activity 1
Mixtures of flour and one of the original white powders for each pair of students

ENGAGE: ASK A QUESTION ABOUT OBJECTS, ORGANISMS, OR EVENTS IN THE ENVIRONMENT.

a. Ask: *If you had a mixture of powders, how could you find out what is in the mixture?*

EXPLORE: PLAN AND CONDUCT SIMPLE INVESTIGATIONS TO COLLECT RELEVANT DATA.

EXPLAIN: USE DATA TO GENERATE INTERPRETATIONS, INCLUDING DESCRIPTIONS, CLASSIFICATIONS, AND EXPLANATIONS.

How could you help children understand what scientists do?

b. Give each pair of students small samples of a mixture of two white powders, flour, and one of the original white powders.
　　Ask: *What powders are these?* Challenge children to determine if each powder is one they have encountered previously, and if so, which one. (Children would not have studied the properties of flour.) Ask: *What is the evidence for your conclusions?*

c. Let students present and discuss their procedures and their conclusions. Ask students to explain the basis for their conclusions.

d. Lead a discussion about how the children's activities in these investigations are like those of scientists. Ask: *What are some of the ways you have acted as scientists in this investigation of powders?* Common activities of children and scientists might include asking questions, talking, searching, planning, using magnifying lenses, experimenting, recording, explaining, discussing, arguing, defining, criticizing, exchanging ideas, deciding, asking more questions.

e. Students should throw away plastic wrap and toothpicks, return powders and test supplies to teacher-designated spot, clean and dry anything dirty—including their hands. Caution students not to put any of the powders in the sink since they can clog drains.[2]

E. PROPERTIES OF AIR

▶ *Science Background*

Although we cannot see, taste, smell, hear, or feel air (if we reach out our hand to grab it), we know that air is a real substance because of the way it interacts with objects that we can see.
　　Through the following activities, discussion, and expository teaching you will help the students begin to develop an understanding of these principles about air:

▶ *Principles about Air*

1. Air, like solids and liquids, is a real material substance (made up of particles too small to see).
2. Bubbles in water indicate the presence of air.
3. Air exerts pressure; it can press or push on things.
4. We live at the bottom of an ocean of air that exerts a great pressure on all things on the surface of the earth.
5. Objects tend to be moved from regions of high air pressure toward regions of low air pressure.
6. Air tends to exert more pressure when it is heated; it exerts less pressure when it is cooled.

Together, these principles can be used to *explain evidence* gathered about a wide variety of phenomena. The principles are appropriate for students from about grades 3 or 4 (ages 9–10 or older), provided the children have had plenty of opportunities to lay a foundation for the principles by raising questions, investigating, and trying out their explanations.

---

[2]More information on these activities on white powders can be found at these Internet sites: http://www.csulb.edu/~lhenriqu/mysterypowder.htm, http://etc.sccoe.kiz.ca.us/i98/ii98units/cross/mystery/text/powders.html, http:/eduref.org/ cgi~bin/printlessons.cgi/virtual/lessons/science/chemistry/chm0200.html.

Science Standards

All students should develop an understanding of

- properties of objects and materials (K–4).
- changes in properties in matter (5–8).

Objectives for Students

1. Investigate and describe natural events related to air and air pressure.
2. Demonstrate and describe evidence for each of the principles about air and air pressure.
3. Use observational evidence and the principles about air to explain what happens in various investigations and phenomena.

NSES **Concepts and Principles**

Activity I addresses these fundamental concepts and principles related to the *Science Standards*:

- Materials can exist in different states—solid, liquid, and gas (K–4).
- Objects (such as gases) have many different properties (K–4).

1. WHAT DO KITES NEED TO FLY? (2–4)

Materials

Plastic, such as that used by dry cleaners, to cover the kite
Small pieces of wood to form the kite supports
String, transparent tape or glue, and cloth for the tail

Safety Precautions

- Caution children about flying kites near power lines. Point out that they should never use wire instead of string to fly a kite because of the danger involved if the wire hits a power line.
- Also warn children of the danger of putting plastic wrapping over their heads or on their faces.

ENGAGE: IDENTIFY A TECHNOLOGICAL PROBLEM.

a. *Note:* This activity is about technology—about human designs and constructions— rather than about the natural environment.

Ask: *What is a kite? How are kites designed? How can we make kites? What will we need?*

EXPLORE: DESIGN AN APPROACH TO SOLVE THE PROBLEM AND IMPLEMENT THE APPROACH.

Encourage students to plan in small groups how they are going to make their kites before they construct them. Guide them in discussing what they know about air and how it might affect how kites fly and how they should be built. After they have done this, you might bring in some books on kites. Discuss the role of the tail and how it helps to stabilize the kite.

b. Assist groups as they plan and build their kites. Perhaps have a kite available to serve as a model.

EXPLAIN: TEST THE PROBLEM SOLUTION.

c. Arrange for students to fly their kites.

Ask: *How do kites provide evidence that air is a real material substance?*

NSES **Concepts and Principles**

Activities 2–9 address these fundamental concepts and principles related to the *Science Standards:*

- Objects have many observable properties (K–4).
- Materials can exist in different states—solid, liquid, and gas (K–4).

2. IS AIR A REAL MATERIAL SUBSTANCE LIKE SOLIDS AND LIQUIDS? (1–4)

Materials

For Activities 2–9:

Large syringes   Soda straws
Several medicine droppers   Potato
Containers for water

▶ *Teaching Suggestions*

We suggest that you use Activities 2–9 as teacher demonstrations in inventing and developing principles about air. Emphasize that these principles are based on evidence and are useful in explaining phenomena and predicting outcomes. The demonstrations might then be made available later to your students, perhaps at learning stations.

ENGAGE: ASK A
QUESTION ABOUT OBJECTS,
ORGANISMS, OR EVENTS IN
THE ENVIRONMENT.

a. Show the children three plastic food storage bags, one filled with a solid (such as sand), a second with water, and a third with air. Ask: *What is in each bag?*

After children discuss the contents of each bag, ask: *How do you know what is in each bag? What is your evidence?*

Some children may say that air is in the third bag. Ask: *Since you cannot see, hear, feel (if you place your hand in the bag), smell (if you open the bag), or taste what's in the bag, how do you know that air is really in the bag?*

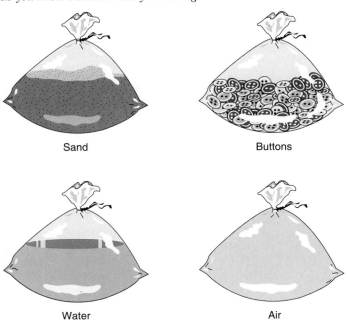

Sand   Buttons

Water   Air

b. Discuss the meaning of the term *evidence* (observations that we can use to support conclusions). Use the term in story form, such as:

> Two boys came out of the house and noticed that the driveway was wet. One boy said, "It has rained." The other boy said, "No, my Dad washes his car every Saturday."

What *evidence* might have supported the first boy's conclusion? What was the implied conclusion of the second boy? What evidence might have supported the second boy's conclusion?

EXPLORE: PLAN AND CONDUCT SIMPLE INVESTIGATIONS TO COLLECT RELEVANT DATA.

c. Lead students to note that although we cannot see air, evidence for the existence of air comes from many activities, such as activities with medicine droppers and syringes.

Place a medicine dropper or a syringe underwater. Squeeze the bulb of the medicine dropper or push in on the plunger of the syringe. Ask: *What do you observe? How can you explain what you see?*

EXPLAIN: USE DATA TO GENERATE INTERPRETATIONS, INCLUDING DESCRIPTIONS, CLASSIFICATIONS, AND EXPLANATIONS.

d. Use this activity to introduce and develop these two principles about air:

Principle 1. Air is a real material substance. Although we cannot observe air directly, we can observe its effects as it interacts with other materials.

Principle 2. Bubbles in water indicate that air is present. The bubbles are filled with air.

ELABORATE: EXTEND CONCEPTS, PRINCIPLES, AND STRATEGIES TO NEW SITUATIONS AND QUESTIONS.

e. Ask: *What other evidence can you think of to show that air is a real material substance?* Through discussion, help your students come up with many examples involving interactions with air, such as wind, rustling of leaves in a tree, paper airplanes, kites, balloons, your breath on a cold morning, or a dropped sheet of paper floating down to the floor.

3. HOW DOES AIR INTERACT WITH WATER? (1–4)

ENGAGE: ASK A QUESTION ABOUT OBJECTS, ORGANISMS, OR EVENTS IN THE ENVIRONMENT.

a. Ask: *Can air and water be in the same space?*

EXPLORE: PLAN AND CONDUCT SIMPLE INVESTIGATIONS TO COLLECT RELEVANT DATA.

b. Push an "empty" glass straight down into a container of water. Ask: *What do you observe? How can you explain what you see?*

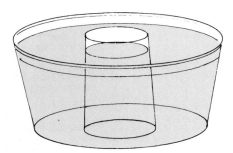

Excerpts from a video of a teacher demonstrating the "crumpled paper in the glass" activity at grade 1 is available on the Virtual Classroom in Chapter 2 of the Companion Website for this book: http://www.prenhall.com/carin.

c. Tilt the glass while it is underwater. Ask: *What do you observe? Why do you think this happens?*

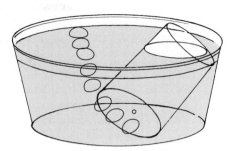

EXPLAIN: USE DATA TO GENERATE INTERPRETATIONS, INCLUDING DESCRIPTIONS, CLASSIFICATIONS, AND EXPLANATIONS.

d. Through discussion, lead students to apply the principle that air is a real material substance. Air keeps the water from coming into the glass. Although the glass looks empty, we infer that it contains air.

e. Ask: *Why were bubbles seen in the water when the glass was tilted?*

Through discussion and direct instruction, help students use Principle 2 to explain that bubbles show that air is escaping into the water from the glass.

4. HOW CAN AIR KEEP WATER OUT OF A CONTAINER? (1–4)

ENGAGE: ASK A QUESTION ABOUT OBJECTS, ORGANISMS, OR EVENTS IN THE ENVIRONMENT.

a. Crumple up a paper towel in the bottom of a dry, empty glass. Push the glass mouth down into a large container of water so that it is completely submerged. Ask: *What do you observe? Why do you think that the paper towel remains dry?*

EXPLAIN: USE DATA TO GENERATE INTERPRETATIONS, INCLUDING DESCRIPTIONS, CLASSIFICATIONS, AND EXPLANATIONS.

b. Help students use Principle 1 to explain what they see in this demonstration. Air is a real material substance that keeps water from coming up into the glass and wetting the paper towel. Tell the students that large, air-filled, inverted containers, called **diving bells,** have been used in underwater work for centuries. Ask: *Why does water not come into a diving bell when it is submerged?*

ELABORATE: EXTEND CONCEPTS, PRINCIPLES, AND STRATEGIES TO NEW PROBLEMS AND QUESTIONS.

c. Push an empty glass mouth down into a large container of water until it is completely submerged. Tilt the glass so that it fills with water. Ask: *How can you use a straw to replace the water in the glass with air? When you have emptied the glass of its water using the straw, how can you use the straw to replace the air in the glass with water again?*

EXPLAIN: USE DATA TO GENERATE INTERPRETATIONS, INCLUDING DESCRIPTIONS, CLASSIFICATIONS, AND EXPLANATIONS.

Your students will need Principle 1 to explain their observations. When air is blown into the glass through the straw, it replaces the water in the glass. When the air is removed through the straw, the water comes back in.

5. HOW CAN YOU USE A SYRINGE TO FEEL AIR PRESSURE? (3–5)

ENGAGE: ASK A
QUESTION ABOUT OBJECTS,
ORGANISMS, OR EVENTS IN
THE ENVIRONMENT.

a. With the plunger pulled part of the way out of a small- to medium-sized syringe, plug the opening of the syringe with your finger. Try to push the plunger in. Ask: *What do you observe? Why do you think the plunger of the syringe is so hard to push in?*

EXPLAIN: USE DATA
TO GENERATE
INTERPRETATIONS,
INCLUDING DESCRIPTIONS,
CLASSIFICATIONS, AND
EXPLANATIONS.

Use Principle 1 to help students understand that when you push in on the plunger, the air presses back. This demonstration is another type of evidence that air is a real material substance. The demonstration also shows that air can exert pressure. Building on this experience and the children's discussion of it, teach (invent) Principle 3.

Principle 3. Air exerts pressure; it can press or push on things.

Concepts and Principles

Activities 6–8 also address these fundamental concepts and principles related to the *Science Standards:*

- The position and motion of objects can be changed by pushing or pulling. The size of the change is related to the strength of the push or pull (K–4).
- Unbalanced forces will cause changes in the speed or direction of an object's motion (5–8).

6. HOW DOES A MEDICINE DROPPER WORK? (3–5)

ENGAGE: ASK A
QUESTION ABOUT OBJECTS,
ORGANISMS, OR EVENTS IN
THE ENVIRONMENT.

a. Ask: *What do you have to do to get water up into a medicine dropper?*

EXPLORE: PLAN
AND CONDUCT SIMPLE
INVESTIGATIONS TO
COLLECT RELEVANT DATA.

b. Dip a medicine dropper into a container of water and fill the medicine dropper with water. Ask: *What did you see happen? What did I do to get water into the medicine dropper? Why do you think the water rose into the medicine dropper?*

EXPLAIN: USE DATA
TO GENERATE
INTERPRETATIONS,
INCLUDING DESCRIPTIONS,
CLASSIFICATIONS, AND
EXPLANATIONS.

c. Your students will likely say that the water was "sucked" into the medicine dropper. Help the students understand that, even though the term is commonly used, *suction* is a misconception; liquid is not pulled into the dropper by suction.

Ask: *What do you do to get water to come into the medicine dropper?* (You dip the tube of the medicine dropper in water, squeeze the bulb, release it, and water comes into the medicine dropper tube.) *What happens to the air in the medicine dropper tube when you squeeze it?* (Some air comes out of the tube.) Ask: *What happens when you pull up on the plunger?*

Lead the children to understand that when you squeeze air out of the tube, there is less air in the tube. When you release the tube underwater, the reduced number of air particles left exert less air pressure. Through discussion, lead the students to understand Principles 4 and 5.

Principle 4. We live at the bottom of an ocean of air that exerts a great pressure on all things on the surface of the earth.

Principle 5. Objects tend to be moved from regions of high air pressure toward regions of low air pressure.

Use Principles 4 and 5 to help children understand that the greater air pressure of the atmosphere pushes water up into the medicine dropper when we have removed air from it.

An understanding that water is pushed (rather than pulled) into the medicine dropper comes only gradually for students. The younger the students, the more partial and fragmented the explanation is likely to be and the more scaffolding support they will need to achieve optimal understanding.

ELABORATE: EXTEND CONCEPTS, PRINCIPLES, AND STRATEGIES TO NEW PROBLEMS AND QUESTIONS.

d. Ask: *In what ways might a syringe be like a medicine dropper? How do you think a syringe works to get air up into the dropper?* Help students to see that the two systems are similar. When you pull up on the syringe plunger, the air in the plunger tube has more space and less pressure. Since there is less air pressure in the syringe than before, the pressure of the atmosphere surrounding us then pushes down on the surface of the water, forcing some liquid up into the syringe.

....

7. HOW DOES A SODA STRAW WORK? (3–5)

ENGAGE: ASK A QUESTION ABOUT OBJECTS, ORGANISMS, OR EVENTS IN THE ENVIRONMENT.

a. Ask: *How does a soda straw work?*

EXPLORE: PLAN AND CONDUCT SIMPLE INVESTIGATIONS TO COLLECT RELEVANT DATA.

b. Use a clean soda straw to draw liquid up out of a container.

Ask: *In what ways is a soda straw like a medicine dropper? Using what you know about how water comes up into medicine droppers and syringes, how do you think water comes up through soda straws and into your mouth when you drink through a straw? How do you think the air pressure in the soda straw is reduced enough for atmospheric pressure to push liquid up into the straw?*

EXPLAIN: USE DATA TO GENERATE INTERPRETATIONS, INCLUDING DESCRIPTIONS, CLASSIFICATIONS, AND EXPLANATIONS.

c. Lead students to arrive at the explanation that when you drink through a straw, you expand your lungs and some air comes out of the straw into your lungs. Because some air went out of the straw, there is now less air and lower air pressure in the straw. The atmospheric pressure—remember, we live at the bottom of an ocean of air—pushes on the liquid surface, forcing some liquid up through the straw and into your mouth.

ELABORATE: EXTEND CONCEPTS, PRINCIPLES, AND STRATEGIES TO NEW PROBLEMS AND QUESTIONS.

d. Using a straight pin, put a tiny hole in a soda straw above the liquid line. Try drinking liquid through the straw. Ask: *What do you observe? Why do you think this happens?*

How could you help
children understand
what scientists do?

e. Ask: *What do scientists do when they explain something?* Through discussion, lead students to understand that when scientists explain an event, they connect observations
and scientific concepts and principles in a reasonable way to make sense of the observations. When scientists propose an explanation, they appeal to scientific knowledge
and observational evidence to support their explanation. Children should check their
explanations against scientific knowledge, experiences, and observations of others.

8. HOW CAN YOU PUSH A SODA STRAW THROUGH A POTATO? (3–5)

ENGAGE: ASK A
QUESTION ABOUT OBJECTS,
ORGANISMS, OR EVENTS IN
THE ENVIRONMENT.

a. Ask: *Can you push a soda straw through a potato?*

EXPLORE: PLAN
AND CONDUCT SIMPLE
INVESTIGATIONS TO
COLLECT RELEVANT DATA.

b. Place a potato on a table and ask a student to hold it. Raise the straw about 5 inches
above the potato and then quickly and forcibly stick the potato, as shown in (a) in the
diagram.
   Ask: *What happened?*

c. Repeat step *b* but this time hold your thumb over the end of the straw as you stick the
potato, as shown in diagram (b).
   Ask: *Why is this different from before?*

EXPLAIN: USE DATA
TO GENERATE
INTERPRETATIONS,
INCLUDING DESCRIPTIONS,
CLASSIFICATIONS, AND
EXPLANATIONS.

d. Explanation: The first straw usually bends and only partially penetrates the potato.
The second straw does not bend and goes through the potato. Blocking the straw end
traps and compresses the air inside the straw, creating greater air pressure. Some of the
potato is forced into the straw, further increasing the air pressure.

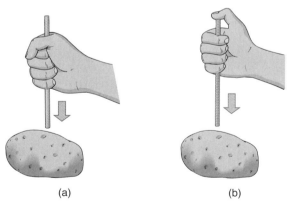

(a)   (b)

9. HOW CAN YOU DEMONSTRATE THAT AIR EXPANDS WHEN IT IS HEATED? (1–4)

ENGAGE: ASK A
QUESTION ABOUT OBJECTS,
ORGANISMS, OR EVENTS IN
THE ENVIRONMENT.

a. Ask: *What can we do to change the shape of a soap bubble on the mouth of a container?*

EXPLORE: PLAN AND CONDUCT SIMPLE INVESTIGATIONS TO COLLECT RELEVANT DATA.

b. Squirt some liquid soap into a large container of water with a wide opening at the top. Stir the water. Dip the open end of a test tube, medicine vial, or small juice can into the soapy water so that a soap film forms across the end of the container. Challenge students to get the soap film to expand. One way to get the soap film to expand is for students to wrap their hands around the container (without squeezing) so that their hands cover as much of the container as possible.
    Ask: *What do you observe?*

c. Get a soap bubble on a small container, such as a test tube or medicine vial. Put the container in a bucket of ice. Ask: *What happens to the soap bubble?*

EXPLAIN: USE DATA TO GENERATE INTERPRETATIONS, INCLUDING DESCRIPTIONS, CLASSIFICATIONS, AND EXPLANATIONS.

d. Ask: *Why did the soap bubble expand when you held the container in your hands? Why did the soap bubble go down into the container when you placed the container in ice?*
    Through their explorations, the students should note that when they hold the container in their hands, the soap film expands, becomes dome-shaped, and eventually pops. Lead students to understand Principle 6:
    Principle 6. Air tends to exert more pressure when it is heated; it exerts less pressure when it is cooled.
    The students' hands warmed the air in the small container, the air pressure in the container was increased, and the air expanded. When the container is in ice, the air in the container cools and its pressure is reduced. The outside air pressure then forces the soap bubble into the container.

ELABORATE: EXTEND CONCEPTS, PRINCIPLES, AND STRATEGIES TO NEW PROBLEMS AND QUESTIONS.

e. Obtain a very large can, such as a vegetable can from the school cafeteria. Get a soap film on a large can. Let several students wrap their hands around it to see if they can get the soap film to expand. Ask children to describe what they see and to explain why it happens.

II. MOTION AND FORCES

An object's motion can be described by noting how its position changes over time. To change the motion of an object—to start it moving or stop it, to speed it up or slow it down—a force is needed. An object continues in motion, in a straight line, unless interfered with by some outside force—some push or pull on the object. In most cases of moving objects on the earth, frictional forces act to slow objects down and eventually stop them.

There are many different kinds of forces in addition to frictional forces, such as the mechanical forces exerted by simple machines, gravitational forces, magnetic forces, static electric forces, and the bonding forces between water molecules. A force may be direct, as when we push on a lever arm, or it may be indirect, as when a magnet pulls on a piece of iron from a distance.

The study of simple forces at grades K–4 provides concrete experiences on which a more comprehensive study of forces and motion may be based in grades 5–8 and 9–12.

A. FRICTIONAL FORCES

▶ *Science Background*

Friction is the result of an interaction between a moving object and the surface on which it moves. Students' everyday experience is that friction causes all moving objects to slow down and stop. Through experiences in which friction is reduced (by a lubricant or through the use of wheels), students can begin to see that a moving object with no friction would continue to move indefinitely.

    Science Standards

All students should develop an understanding of

• motions and forces (5–8).

Objectives for Students

1. Design and conduct an investigation to demonstrate the friction present as an object moves across a level surface.
2. Ask questions about friction and describe frictional effects as an interaction between an object and a surface.
3. Explain how wheels and lubricants can reduce friction.

    Concepts and Principles

Activity I addresses these fundamental concepts and principles related to the *Science Standards:*

• The position and motion of objects can be changed by pushing or pulling (K–4).
• The size of the change is related to the strength of the push or pull (K–4).

1. WHAT IS FRICTION? HOW CAN FRICTION BE REDUCED? (3–6)

Materials

Screw hook
Block of wood
Rubber bands
Ruler
Sheets of coarse sandpaper
Five or six round pencils

ENGAGE: ASK A QUESTION ABOUT OBJECTS, ORGANISMS, OR EVENTS IN THE ENVIRONMENT.

a. Ask: *How can you measure the effects of friction?*

EXPLORE: PLAN AND CONDUCT SIMPLE INVESTIGATIONS TO COLLECT RELEVANT DATA.

b. Students should carry out these investigation procedures in cooperative groups.
   1. Turn the screw hook into the end of a block of wood. Attach a rubber band (or a spring scale) to the hook.
   2. With the rubber band on your finger, lift the block into the air and measure the stretch with a ruler, as in diagram (a). Design a data table and record your measurement in it.

3. Position the block on a table with the rubber band extended, as in diagram (b). Now drag the block on the table and measure the rubber band's stretch once the block begins to move. Record your measurements.

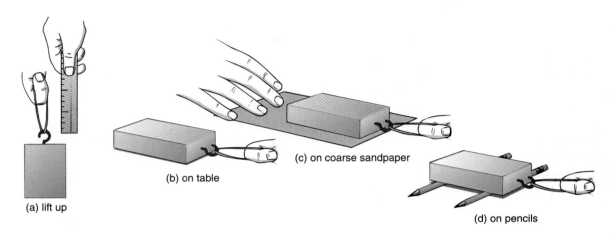

(a) lift up

(b) on table

(c) on coarse sandpaper

(d) on pencils

4. Repeat the procedure in step 3, this time with sandpaper beneath the block, as in diagram (c). Ask: *What change do you observe in the stretch of the rubber band when the block is dragged on the table and on sandpaper? What is the cause of the increase in force needed to move the object on sandpaper?* Introduce the concept of friction. Friction is a force opposing motion that results when two surfaces slide across one another.

5. Now place two round pencils underneath the block and drag it across the table, as in diagram (d). Measure the stretch of the rubber band just after the block begins to move. Ask: *What happens to the stretch of the rubber band this time? Why? In what way do wheels help objects to move?* Explain that wheels reduce friction.

6. Older students might repeat the activity using a spring scale.

EXPLAIN: USE DATA TO GENERATE INTERPRETATIONS, INCLUDING DESCRIPTIONS, CLASSIFICATIONS, AND EXPLANATIONS.

c. Invite students to present their procedures and findings. Ask: *How does the surface on which the block slides affect the force to move it? What is friction? How do wheels reduce the force needed to move a block across a table?*

B. EQUAL-ARM BALANCES

▶ *Science Background*

An equal-arm balance is a system consisting of a crossbar pivoted in the center and weights that can be placed at different positions on each side of the bar, as is shown in the diagram. The amount of each weight and its distance from the central pivot point are the relevant factors in determining balance.

Homemade balances can be constructed for the following activities, but if at all possible, students should use commercial plastic balances, often referred to as "math balances." The Invicta Math-Balance, sold by Delta Education and other equipment companies, is an excellent tool for studying balancing from kindergarten through middle school. Addresses for equipment companies are given in Appendix C.

Science Standards

All students should develop an understanding of

- motions and forces (5–8).

Objectives for Students

1. Use these qualitative rules to predict and explain balance on an equal-arm balance:
   - *Symmetry rule*. Equal weights at equal distances will balance [see diagram(a)].
   - *Relational rule*. Heavier weights close in can balance lighter weights farther out [see diagram (b) and diagram (c)].
2. Demonstrate and explain that balance occurs when the products of weights and distances on one side of the pivot equal the product of weights and distances on the other side of the pivot.

 Concepts and Principles

Activity I prepares students to learn these fundamental concepts and principles related to the *Science Standards*:

- Unbalanced forces will cause changes in the speed or direction of an object's motion (5–8).

1. WHAT FACTORS AFFECT THE EQUILIBRIUM OF AN EQUAL-ARM BALANCE? (3–6)

Materials

Equal-arm balance for each pair of students

ENGAGE: ASK A QUESTION ABOUT OBJECTS, ORGANISMS, OR EVENTS IN THE ENVIRONMENT.

a. Ask: *What affects the balance of an equal-arm balance scale? How can you predict accurately whether a balance will be level?*

EXPLORE: PLAN AND CONDUCT SIMPLE INVESTIGATIONS TO COLLECT RELEVANT DATA.

b. Distribute balances to your students. Try to obtain enough balances so that two, or no more than three, children work together on their own balance. If balances are limited, you may wish to set up stations that children can work at during the day.

Give the children the following balance problems, one at a time. Allow ample time for students to work on each problem and discuss their findings, before giving the next one. Be noncommittal about patterns they may discover.

1. Place two weights at the second peg from the center on the left side. Leaving the left side always the same, find at least three different ways to balance the crossbar by adding weights to a peg on the other side. (You can use as many weights as necessary, but be sure to add weights to only one peg at a time on the right side, not to two or three pegs.) Use drawings, words, or data columns to show what you did. Tell your teacher what you did to balance the crossbar.

2. Start with two weights on the left side at the third peg from the center. Find at least four ways to balance the crossbar. (Remember, you can use as many weights as necessary, but be sure to add weights to only one peg on the right side, not to two or three pegs.) Write down what you did and show your work to your teacher.

3. Start with four weights at the third peg on the left side. How many ways can you find to balance the crossbar? (Remember to add weights from only one peg at a time on the other side.)

4. Set up your own combinations of weights and distances on one side of the balance and use your developing knowledge to predict what might be done to the other side to produce balance.

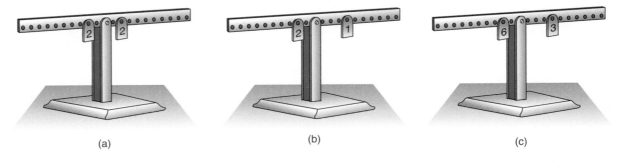

(a)   (b)   (c)

EXPLAIN: USE DATA TO GENERATE INTERPRETATIONS, INCLUDING DESCRIPTIONS, CLASSIFICATIONS, AND EXPLANATIONS.

c. Ask: *What did you do to balance the crossbar? Can you find patterns in the different ways you found to balance the crossbar? How can you test to determine if the pattern you found is a general one, applying in all cases?*

   Through discussion, lead your students to understand the following balance patterns or rules:

   • *Symmetry rule.* Equal weights at equal distances will balance [see diagram (a)].
   • *Relational rule.* Heavier weights close in can balance lighter weights farther out [see diagram (b) and diagram (c)].

   Both of these rules are qualitative, nonnumerical rules. They are understood by children from ages 8 or 9, but they may not be stated explicitly.

d. At some point, older students (from ages 10 or 11) may understand the use of formal mathematics to coordinate weights and distances. Challenge students to work with their data from step *b* to find a mathematical rule for the balance, a rule involving doing something with the actual numbers.

   The mathematical rule for the balance is:

$$(W_L) \times (D_L) = (W_R) \times (D_R)$$

where W = weights, D = distances, L = left side, and R = right side of the balance. Thus, the product of the weight and distance on one side is equal to the product of weight and distance on the other side.

   Lead older children to try this rule for themselves, using the data from different trials. If the crossbar is balanced, the products of the weights and distances on the left side will always equal the products on the right side for each of these three cases.

   Interestingly, this rule applies even if weights are placed on more than one peg on each side. Then, the sum of the weights times distances on one side must equal the sum on the other side.

C. LEVERS

▶ *Science Background*

The rules governing equal-arm balances are important in science because they also apply to the operation of levers. A lever system has a crossbar, pivoted at a fulcrum. Using a small effort force far out from a fulcrum, a person can lift a heavy load (or move a resistance) that is nearer the fulcrum. At the lower grades, students can use the symmetry and relational rules of the equal-arm balance to explain and predict actions of a lever. Middle school students might use the balance equation to predict how much force is needed to lift a load of a given weight when the distances involved are known.

Levers have been classified as first-, second-, and third-class levers, depending on the relative placement of the fulcrum, effort force, and resistance or load. But the goal in teaching children about levers is not that they be able to identify the type of lever. Rather, the focus should be on descriptive and relational thinking. Students should learn to identify the fulcrum, load, load arm, effort, and effort arm for a variety of levers and explain how their physical arrangement in a particular lever affects the effort force needed to lift a given load. Students should be able to consistently demonstrate and explain that through the use of a lever, a small effort force far from the fulcrum can lift a heavy load that is near the fulcrum.

NSES   **Science Standards**

All students should develop an understanding of

• motions and forces (5–8).

Objectives for Students

1. Identify the fulcrum, effort force, and load/resistance of different kinds of levers.
2. Explain how a lever is like an equal-arm balance.
3. Demonstrate and explain that a small effort force far from the fulcrum can lift or move a large load near the fulcrum.

NSES   **Concepts and Principles**

Activities 1 and 2 prepare students to understand these fundamental concepts and principles related to the *Science Standards:*

• Unbalanced forces will cause changes in the speed or direction of an object's motion (5–8).

---

1. WHAT IS A LEVER? HOW COULD YOU USE ONE? (2–6)

Materials   Large stone or other heavy object
                             Half-meter stick or 50 cm board

ENGAGE: ASK A QUESTION ABOUT OBJECTS, ORGANISMS, OR EVENTS IN THE ENVIRONMENT.

a. Tell students a story about two girls that were climbing a mountain. A rock slide deposited a large boulder on the leg of one of the girls. The boulder was too heavy to lift directly. What might her companion do to lift the boulder enough so that the girl could get her leg free?

Ask: *What do you think the second girl could do to help free her friend?*

EXPLORE: PLAN AND CONDUCT SIMPLE INVESTIGATIONS TO COLLECT RELEVANT DATA.

b. Lead students to consider getting a tree limb, finding something to use as a fulcrum (pivot), and then using the tree limb to lift the boulder enough for the girl to get her leg free. Model the situation in the classroom using a heavy box to represent the boulder, a half-meter stick for the lever arm, and a book as the pivot.

EXPLAIN: USE DATA TO GENERATE INTERPRETATIONS, INCLUDING DESCRIPTIONS, CLASSIFICATIONS, PREDICTIONS, AND EXPLANATIONS.

c. Ask: *Where was the load (or resistance) for this lever? Where was the fulcrum? Where was the force applied?*

Lead students to understand that a lever can be used to lift a heavy load, if the force on the lever is much farther from the fulcrum than the load is.

2. HOW IS A LEVER LIKE A BALANCE? (3–6)

ENGAGE: ASK A QUESTION ABOUT OBJECTS, ORGANISMS, OR EVENTS IN THE ENVIRONMENT.

a. Make sure that students have studied the equal-arm balance, following procedures similar to those in the previous section of these activities. Ask: *How is a lever like an equal-arm balance?* Ask the students to identify the fulcrum, effort, and resistance on a balance and on a lever.

EXPLORE: PLAN AND CONDUCT SIMPLE INVESTIGATIONS TO COLLECT RELEVANT DATA.

b. Instruct the students to design an investigation to determine how much effort they must exert at different distances on one side of the balance/lever to lift weights at specific positions on the other side. For example, using the balance as a lever, they might place a load of 8 weights at a distance of 10 units from the fulcrum and note that the farther from the pivot/fulcrum they apply the effort force, the easier it is to lift the load. Through this activity, students can experience directly the great amount of effort force needed to move a heavy load when the effort force is much nearer to the fulcrum than is the load.

EXPLAIN: USE DATA TO GENERATE INTERPRETATIONS, INCLUDING DESCRIPTIONS, CLASSIFICATIONS, AND EXPLANATIONS.

c. Ask: *How does the balance and lever principle apply to a seesaw?*

If possible, take your students to a playground seesaw. Or make a classroom seesaw by placing a solid 2 inch by 6 inch board about 6 to 8 feet long on another board under it to act as a pivot. Let the children investigate how a smaller child far out from the pivot of the seesaw can balance a larger child nearer to the fulcrum.

D. INCLINED PLANES

▶ *Science Background*

An inclined plane or ramp can be used as a simple type of machine to reduce the force needed to move an object up to a given height.

NSES **Science Standards**

All students should develop an understanding of

• motions and forces (5–8).

Objectives for Students

1. Describe and demonstrate how an inclined plane can be used to reduce the force needed to move an object up to a given height.
2. Name and describe examples of inclined planes in everyday life.

NSES **Concepts and Principles**

Activity I provides a foundation for students to understand these fundamental concepts and principles related to the *Science Standards*:

• Unbalanced forces will cause changes in the speed or direction of an object's motion (5–8).

---

1. WHAT IS AN INCLINED PLANE? HOW CAN YOU USE IT? (3–6)

Materials

Smooth board, 4 feet long
Block with screw eye in one end or a rubber band wrapped around it
Spring scale

ENGAGE: ASK A
QUESTION ABOUT OBJECTS,
ORGANISMS, OR EVENTS IN
THE ENVIRONMENT.

a. Ask: *What happens to the force needed to move an object up an inclined plane when the angle of the plane is increased?*

EXPLORE: PLAN
AND CONDUCT SIMPLE
INVESTIGATIONS TO
COLLECT RELEVANT DATA.

b. Lead students to plan and conduct an investigation similar to this one.
    1. Use the spring scale to find the weight of the block by lifting it straight up as shown in the diagram. Repeat this several times and find the average reading on the scale. Record the average weight.
    2. Take the 4-foot board and place two or three books under one end so that end of the board is raised about 10 cm. Place the block with the screw eye in it on the inclined board as shown in the diagram. Slip the hook of the spring scale through the eye of the block.
    3. Slowly and evenly pull the scale and block up the board.
    4. Record the amount of force needed to pull the block up the board and the height of the plane. Do this several times and record your observations. Using the data obtained, determine the average force required to pull the weight.

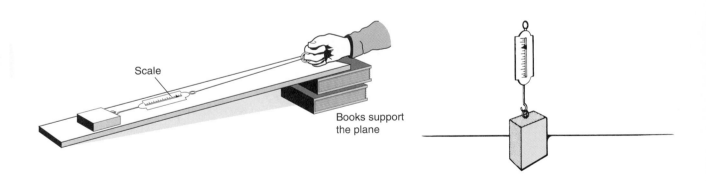

Scale

Books support
the plane

Ask: *How much force is required to pull the block up each plane? Is the force to move the block up the plane greater than, equal to, or less than the weight of the block? Why?*
    5. Repeat the activity but this time make the inclined plane steeper by changing the number of support books so that the end of the board is about 20 cm high.
    6. Again, find the average force needed to pull the weight up the board.

EXPLAIN: USE DATA
TO GENERATE
INTERPRETATIONS,
INCLUDING DESCRIPTIONS,
CLASSIFICATIONS, AND
EXPLANATIONS.

c. Ask: *How do the forces to move the block up the two inclined planes compare? How is the force needed different when lifting the block straight up than when pulling the block up the board? Why?*

Guide students to understand that inclined planes are used for moving objects that are too heavy to lift directly. An inclined plane is a simple type of machine. Because of the slant of the plane, a smaller force is needed to move an object up an inclined plane than to lift it straight up the same height.

Ask: *What generalization can you make about the amount of force required to move a block as an inclined plane becomes steeper? What is the advantage of having a long inclined plane rather than a short inclined plane if both planes are the same height?*

ELABORATE: EXTEND
CONCEPTS, PRINCIPLES,
AND STRATEGIES TO NEW
PROBLEMS AND
QUESTIONS.

d. Ask: *Why do roads not go straight up and down mountains?*

Which of the following examples is an inclined plane?
   a. wheelchair ramp   d. stairway
   b. hill   e. vertical cliff
   c. gangplank   f. head of an ax
       Where are there examples of inclined planes in the school or on the school campus?

E. PULLEYS

▶ *Science Background*

A pulley also can be used as a simple type of machine to reduce the force needed to lift an object to a given height.

NSES   **Science Standards**

All students should develop an understanding of

• motions and forces (5–8).

Objectives for Students

1. Describe and demonstrate how pulleys can be used to reduce the force needed to lift an object to a given height.
2. Name and describe examples of pulleys in everyday life.

NSES   **Concepts and Principles**

Activities 1 and 2 prepare students to understand these fundamental concepts and principles related to the *Science Standards:*

• Unbalanced forces will cause changes in the speed or direction of an object's motion (5–8).

1. WHAT IS A MOVABLE PULLEY, AND HOW CAN YOU USE IT? (3–6)

Materials

Ring stand and clamp for attaching pulleys
Two single pulleys
String for the pulley
Spring scale
100 g weight
50 g weight
Meterstick

ENGAGE: ASK A
QUESTION ABOUT OBJECTS,
ORGANISMS, OR EVENTS IN
THE ENVIRONMENT.

a. Ask: *What is a pulley? How do pulleys work? How can pulleys help us lift heavy objects?*

EXPLORE: PLAN
AND CONDUCT SIMPLE
INVESTIGATIONS TO
COLLECT RELEVANT DATA.

b. Lead students to conduct this investigation.
1. Obtain a ring stand and a clamp for attaching a pulley, a single pulley, some string, a spring scale, and a 100 g weight. Assemble your equipment as shown in the diagram.
    Ask: *How much do you think you will have to pull on the scale to raise the 100 g weight?*

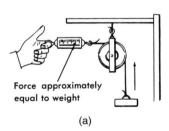

Force approximately
equal to weight

(a)

2. Pull on the scale and raise the 100 g weight. Record the force needed to raise the weight.
3. Repeat this activity several times and record each measurement.
    Ask: *What do you think will happen when you use two pulleys to raise the 100 g weight?*
4. In addition to the equipment you have, obtain a second pulley and a 50 g weight. Assemble your equipment as shown in the diagram.
5. Pull the 50 g weight and record your observations.
6. Remove the 50 g weight and attach the spring scale to the free end of the string, as shown in the following diagram.
    Ask: *How much force do you think the scale will show when you raise the 100 g weight?*

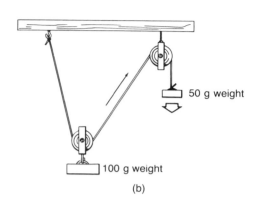

(b)

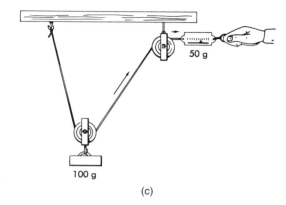

(c)

7. Raise the weight by pulling on the scale. Ask: *How much is the reading on the scale when you raise the weight?* Repeat the activity several times and record each measurement. Ask: *Why is there an advantage in using this type of pulley system?*

EXPLAIN: USE DATA TO GENERATE INTERPRETATIONS, INCLUDING DESCRIPTIONS, CLASSIFICATIONS, AND EXPLANATIONS.

c. Ask: *From your investigation, what can you generalize about pulley systems?* Design a pulley system to lift a piano weighing 300 pounds. Draw a sketch of that pulley system.

▶ *Teaching Background*

As you can see from the activities, more pulleys reduce the amount of force needed to lift a heavy weight. Actually, it is not the number of pulleys, but the number of ropes or strings pulling against the resisting weight that makes a difference. In diagram (a), one string pulls upward and the force needed to lift the block is the same as the weight of the block. In diagram (b), two strings pull upward against the load/block and the force needed to lift the load is one-half its weight. If four strings in a pulley arrangement pulled upward, how much force you would need to exert to lift the block (one-fourth the weight of the block).

2. HOW CAN A PULLEY ARRANGEMENT HELP YOU USE A SMALL FORCE TO OVERPOWER A LARGE FORCE? (4–6)

Materials

Two 1 3/4 inch dowel rods, about 36 inches long
20 feet of 1/2 inch nylon rope

Safety Precautions

Since a large force will be involved, make sure the dowel rods are short and very strong. Safe dowel rods can be cut from a shovel handle purchased from a hardware or building supply store.

ENGAGE: ASK A QUESTION ABOUT OBJECTS, ORGANISMS, OR EVENTS IN THE ENVIRONMENT.

a. Ask: *How can we design a pulley system out of dowel rods and a rope so that a small force can overcome a very large force?*

EXPLORE: PLAN AND CONDUCT SIMPLE INVESTIGATIONS TO COLLECT RELEVANT DATA.

b. Tie a strong loop in one end of the rope and loop it over one of the dowel rods. With one person holding one dowel rod in both hands and a second person holding the other dowel rod in both hands, pass the rope back and forth over the dowel rods about 4 times as in the illustration.

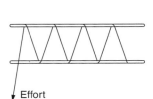

Effort

With a pulley arrangement, a small effort force can overcome a large resistance force.

c. Select four large volunteers and let them hold on to the ends of the dowel rods, with two against two in a tug-of-war. Let a smaller person pull on the free end of the rope.

EXPLAIN: USE DATA TO GENERATE INTERPRETATIONS, INCLUDING DESCRIPTIONS, CLASSIFICATIONS, AND EXPLANATIONS.

d. Ask: *What happens? Why?* (The force of the smaller person draws the two larger persons together. The rods and rope make up a pulley system with several pulleys. If the rope is looped four times over the rods, there are eight ropes pulling on a dowel. The smaller person will have to pull with one-eighth of the force of the four students trying to hold the rods apart. The effect of this pulley system is very dramatic.)

F. BERNOULLI'S PRINCIPLE

▶ *Science Background*

When air rushes over a surface, it has the effect of reducing the air pressure on that surface. This cause-and-effect relationship is called Bernoulli's principle, for Daniel Bernoulli (1700–1782), an important Swiss mathematical scientist who first described the relationship.

As an example of the application of this principle, take a strip of paper and hold it between your lips, with the long edge of the paper trailing down. Blow across the top of the paper. Because of the air rushing over the top surface of the paper, the air pressure on the top of the paper is reduced. The air pressure on the bottom of the paper, which has not changed, is now larger and pushes the paper strip upward.

Bernoulli's principle is the principle of flight. Wings of planes are designed so that as the plane is propelled through the air, air moves faster over the top of the wing than the bottom of the wing. This results in a lower air pressure on the top wing surface, and the air pressure on the bottom of the wing surface can then support the weight of the plane and hold it aloft.

Several activities that illustrate Bernoulli's principle are presented in this section. The activities may take a lot of practice from you and your students to get them to work appropriately.

 Science Standards

All students should develop an understanding of

• motions and forces (5–8).

Objectives for Students

1. State Bernoulli's principle and use it to analyze a rushing air situation.
2. Use Bernoulli's principle to explain what happens in various rushing air demonstrations.

 Concepts and Principles

Activities 1–4 address this fundamental principle related to the *Science Standards*:

• Unbalanced forces will cause changes in the speed or direction of an object (5–8).

1. WHAT IS BERNOULLI'S PRINCIPLE? HOW CAN YOU USE A PIECE OF PAPER TO INVESTIGATE IT? (4–6)

Materials

Notebook paper
Drinking straw

ENGAGE: ASK A QUESTION ABOUT OBJECTS, ORGANISMS, OR EVENTS IN THE ENVIRONMENT.

a. Conduct this demonstration for students.
   1. Obtain a piece of paper about 8 inches by 8 inches.
   2. Make a fold 1 inch wide along one side of the paper. Make another 1 inch fold on the opposite side as indicated in the diagram.
   3. Place the paper on a flat surface, with the folds acting as legs to hold the paper up.
      Ask: *What do you think will happen if I blow through a straw under this folded paper?*

4. Using a drinking straw, blow a stream of air under the paper.

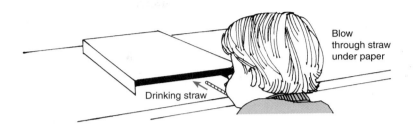

Blow through straw under paper

Drinking straw

EXPLORE: PLAN AND
CONDUCT SIMPLE
INVESTIGATIONS TO
COLLECT RELEVANT DATA.

b. Provide paper and straws to students and allow them to repeat the demonstration.

EXPLAIN: USE DATA
TO GENERATE
INTERPRETATIONS,
INCLUDING DESCRIPTIONS,
CLASSIFICATIONS, AND
EXPLANATIONS.

c. Ask: *What do you notice about the way the paper moves?* (The center of the paper moves down.)
   How did the air move under the paper when you blew under it? (The air was moving in a stream under the paper.)
   What can you infer about why the paper went down in the center? Guide students to understand that air pressure pushed the paper down.
   Would the air pressure be greater on the top of the paper or on the bottom of the paper? Help students understand that the air pressure would be greater on the top if the paper was pushed down by the air pressure.
   Why is the air pressure lower on the bottom of the paper? Invent Bernoulli's principle: When air rushes over a surface, the air pressure on that surface is reduced. Make sure that the students can use Bernoulli's principle, along with their observational evidence, to explain the example.

2. HOW CAN YOU USE A PIECE OF PAPER IN ANOTHER WAY TO INVESTIGATE BERNOULLI'S PRINCIPLE? (3–6)

ENGAGE: ASK A
QUESTION ABOUT OBJECTS,
ORGANISMS, OR EVENTS IN
THE ENVIRONMENT.

a. Ask: *If you were to hold a strip of paper by each corner and blow across the top of the paper, what would happen to the paper? Why do you think so?*

EXPLORE: PLAN
AND CONDUCT SIMPLE
INVESTIGATIONS TO
COLLECT RELEVANT DATA.

b. Assist students to conduct this investigation.
   1. Obtain a strip of paper about 3 inches by 11 inches.
   2. Along the 3 inch side, hold the upper left corner of the strip with your left hand and the upper right corner with your right hand.

3. Blow hard across the top of the paper (see diagram).

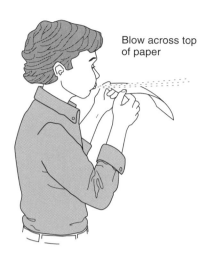

Blow across top
of paper

EXPLAIN: USE DATA TO GENERATE INTERPRETATIONS, INCLUDING DESCRIPTIONS, CLASSIFICATIONS, AND EXPLANATIONS.

c. Ask: *What happens to the paper while you are blowing across it?*
    Why does the paper move in this direction? Where does the air move faster, over the top of the paper or the bottom of the paper? Why do you think so?
    Lead students to apply Bernoulli's principle to explain why the paper strip moves upward. The air pressure was reduced as air rushed over the top of the paper. The greater air pressure under the paper pushed the paper upward, overcoming the gravitational forces that tend to bend the paper downward.

ELABORATE: EXTEND CONCEPTS, PRINCIPLES, AND STRATEGIES TO NEW SITUATIONS AND QUESTIONS.

d. Discuss these questions with the class:
    1. *Why is it unwise to stand close to the edge of a platform as a moving train is coming?*
    2. *How does Bernoulli's principle apply to flying planes?*
        If a plane is moving fast enough, the upward pressure on the wings is enough to support the weight of the plane. The plane must keep moving to stay aloft. If the plane's engines cut out in midair, it would glide down immediately.
    3. Look at the following diagram of an airplane wing. *Is the air moving faster at A or B? Why?*
    4. *How do wing slopes vary and why?*

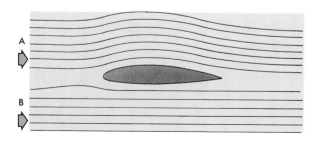

A

B

3. HOW CAN YOU USE A BOTTLE AND A PIECE OF PAPER TO INVESTIGATE BERNOULLI'S PRINCIPLE? (3–6)

Materials   Pop bottle

ENGAGE: ASK A QUESTION ABOUT OBJECTS, ORGANISMS, OR EVENTS IN THE ENVIRONMENT.

a. Ask: *Using what you know about the effects of rushing air on air pressure, what do you think will happen to a wad of paper placed in the opening of a pop bottle if you blow across the bottle opening? Will the paper go into the bottle or come out of the bottle? Make a prediction. Explain your reasoning.*

EXPLORE: PLAN AND CONDUCT SIMPLE INVESTIGATIONS TO COLLECT RELEVANT DATA.

b. Guide students to conduct this investigation.
    1. Wad a small piece of paper so it is about the size of a pea (about 0.5 cm diameter).
    2. Lay the pop bottle on its side.
    3. Place the small wad of paper in the opening of the bottle, next to the edge of the opening. (See diagram.)
    4. Blow across the opening in front of the bottle. Make sure you bend down so that you are level with the bottle.

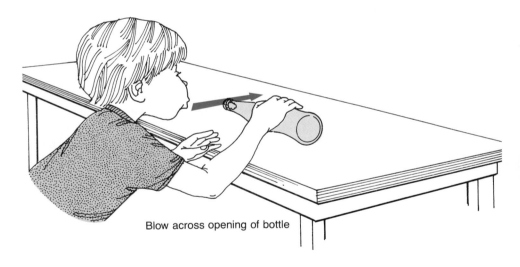

Blow across opening of bottle

EXPLAIN: USE DATA TO GENERATE INTERPRETATIONS, INCLUDING DESCRIPTIONS, CLASSIFICATIONS, AND EXPLANATIONS.

c. Ask: *What happens to the wad of paper?* (It moves out of bottle.)
    Why is the wad of paper forced to do that?
    What do you infer about the air pressure in the bottle and the air pressure at the opening of the bottle when you blow across it? (Air pressure in the bottle is greater.)

ELABORATE: EXTEND CONCEPTS, PRINCIPLES, AND STRATEGIES TO NEW PROBLEMS AND QUESTIONS.

d. Ask: *What do you think will happen if you place a wad of paper in the opening of a pop bottle (as before) and blow directly into the bottle?*
    1. Blow hard directly into the bottle as shown.
    2. Record your observations.
        What do you conclude from your observations?

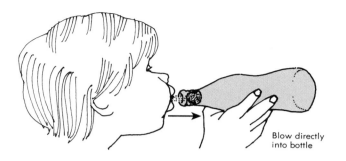

Blow directly
into bottle

....

4. HOW CAN YOU USE A FUNNEL AND PING-PONG BALL TO INVESTIGATE BERNOULLI'S PRINCIPLE? (3–6)

Materials

Ping-Pong ball
Thistle tube or funnel

ENGAGE: ASK A
QUESTION ABOUT OBJECTS,
ORGANISMS, OR EVENTS IN
THE ENVIRONMENT.

a. Ask: *What will happen to a Ping-Pong ball if it is placed in the large end of a thistle tube or funnel and you blow through the small end of the thistle tube or funnel?*

EXPLORE: PLAN
AND CONDUCT SIMPLE
INVESTIGATIONS TO
COLLECT RELEVANT DATA.

b. Let children observe as you perform this investigation.
   1. Hold the Ping-Pong ball in the wide, larger opening of the thistle tube or funnel, put your mouth on the other end, and blow with a long, steady breath. (See diagram.) *Hint:* Get a deep breath before you put your mouth on the tube end to blow.
   2. While blowing hard and steady through the tube end of the funnel, let go of the Ping-Pong ball.
   3. Tell students to record their observations.

Safety Precautions

Wash the funnel or thistle tube with soap and hot water before this activity. Do the activity only as a teacher demonstration.

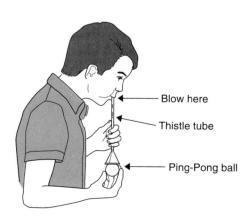

Blow here

Thistle tube

Ping-Pong ball

EXPLAIN: USE DATA
   TO GENERATE
   INTERPRETATIONS,
   INCLUDING
   DESCRIPTIONS,
   CLASSIFICATIONS, AND
   EXPLANATIONS.

c. Ask: *What happens to the ball? Why does the ball spin around in the thistle tube or funnel?*

G. PENDULUMS

▶ *Science Background*

Students typically identify three variable factors that might affect the rate of swing of a pendulum: the weight of the pendulum bob, the angle at which it is released, and the length of the pendulum string. Determining which factors are indeed relevant requires that students conduct controlled investigations in which one factor at a time is varied and its effect on the rate of swing of the pendulum is determined, while the other two variables are controlled or left unchanged.

   Surprisingly, only the length affects the rate of swing. Varying the weight of the pendulum bob or the angle at which the pendulum is released has no effect on its rate of swing.

NSES   Science Standards

All students should develop an understanding of

- the position and motion of objects (K–4).
- motion and forces (5–8).

Objectives for Students

1. Demonstrate procedures for measuring the rate of a pendulum's swing.
2. Design controlled experiments to test hypotheses about factors that might affect the speed of a pendulum.
3. Record, analyze, and draw accurate conclusions from data.
4. Construct and make predictions from graphs of data from pendulum investigations.

NSES   Concepts and Processes

These pendulum activities address these fundamental concepts and principles that underlie the stated standards:

- Changes in systems can be quantified through measurement (5–8).
- Mathematics is essential for accurately measuring change (5–8).
- Rate involves comparing one measured quantity with another measured quantity (5–8).

(National Research Council, 1996, p. 118)

---

1. WHAT IS A PENDULUM? (5–8)

Materials

Watch with a second hand for each group, or clock with a second hand for the whole class
Paper clips
Pennies
Ball of string
Tongue depressors or pencils (to support the pendulums)
Masking tape (to tape the pendulum support to a desk)

Preparation

- Tie a paper clip to one end of several pieces of long string and insert one or more pennies into each paper clip to make the pendulum bobs (as in the drawing). Wedge the string into the slit of a tongue depressor as in the drawing. Students can adjust the length of string as needed by sliding it along the notch of the tongue depressor.

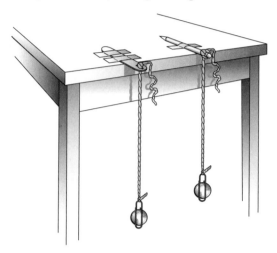

- Determine where teams of students can set up pendulums that can swing freely. To support the pendulums, students should tape or hold the tongue depressor or the pencil securely on the edge of a table.

ENGAGE: ASK A QUESTION OR PRESENT A PROBLEM TO INITIATE INQUIRY.

a. Show students a pendulum using the paper clip and pennies as a pendulum bob and a tongue depressor as a support. Start the pendulum swinging. Ask: *How does a pendulum move? How many ways can you think of to change the motion of the pendulum?* Write these two questions on the board or on chart paper.

    Allow students time to talk with partners or classmates about answers to the questions.

EXPLORE: GUIDE STUDENTS TO PLAN AND CONDUCT SIMPLE INVESTIGATIONS.

b. Help each team of students construct and find a place to support their pendulum. Invite students to explore with their pendulums. Ask: *What can you find out about the motion of a pendulum?*

EXPLAIN: ASSIST STUDENTS TO DEVELOP CONCEPTS, PRINCIPLES, MODELS, AND EXPLANATIONS.

c. After about 10 minutes of open exploration, stop students and ask them what they have discovered. After students share some ideas, invite them to suggest questions they might investigate.

2. WHAT FACTORS MIGHT AFFECT THE RATE OF SWING OF A PENDULUM? (5–8)

ENGAGE: ASK A QUESTION OR PRESENT A PROBLEM TO INITIATE INQUIRY.

a. Ask: *Do all pendulums swing at the same rate, or do some swing slower or faster? How can you measure how fast a pendulum swings?* (Lead the students to count the number of swings in 15 seconds. Explain that this is called the rate of swing of the pendulum. Define a swing as one complete back-and-forth cycle.)

Ask: *How can you get a pendulum to swing faster or slower (more or fewer swings in 15 seconds)?*

b. After some discussion, ask students to focus on these three separate, measurable *variables* that might make a pendulum swing faster or slower:
1. Length of the pendulum
2. Weight or number of pennies that make up the pendulum bob
3. Angle at which the pendulum is released

EXPLORE: GUIDE STUDENTS TO PLAN AND CONDUCT SIMPLE INVESTIGATIONS.

c. Instruct students to write down a separate question about each variable (e.g., How does the rate change when the weight of the pendulum bob is changed?). Then tell them to design and conduct controlled experiments to answer the questions they have asked.
d. Monitor students' experiments and provide assistance with the procedures, logic, and data interpretation for controlled experiments. Ask the students to record what they do and what they find out.
e. When students have had ample time to explore, help the class to standardize the way they measure weight, length, angle, and rate (number of back-and-forth swings in 15 seconds). At this time you should be ready to introduce the use of a data table like the one illustrated to help students organize their investigations, keep track of their data, and interpret their data to form conclusions.

PENDULUM DATA TABLE

Does length affect the rate of swing of a pendulum?		Does weight affect the rate of swing of a pendulum?		Does the release angle affect the rate of swing of a pendulum?	
What variable did you manipulate?		What variable did you manipulate?		What variable did you manipulate?	
What variables did you control?		What variables did you control?		What variables did you control?	
What responding variable did you measure?		What responding variable did you measure?		What responding variable did you measure?	
Length of Pendulum	Rate (number of swings in 15 seconds)	Weight of Pendulum (number of pennies)	Rate (number of swings in 15 seconds)	Angle of Pendulum Release	Rate (number of swings in 15 seconds)
20 cm		1		small	
40 cm		2		medium	
60 cm		3		large	
What can you conclude about length and rate of swing?		What can you conclude about weight and rate of swing?		What can you conclude about the angle of release and rate of swing?	

This data table is not only a place for students to record measurements so they can remember them but also a "think sheet" that facilitates the planning and conducting of investigations, guides the students in recognizing relationships, and assists them in drawing conclusions.

EXPLAIN: ASSIST STUDENTS TO DEVELOP CONCEPTS, PRINCIPLES, MODELS, AND EXPLANATIONS.

f. Instruct students to use their data to answer their questions about the factors that affect the rate of a pendulum.

If students have changed more than one variable at a time (for example, changing length and weight together), discuss with them the importance of experimental design. Ask: *Why must you change only one variable at a time when investigating? Why must other variables be kept constant?* (So you can be sure which of the variables really made a difference.)

Guide students to use their data to arrive at these conclusions:
1. The rate of swing decreases as the length of the pendulum increases.
2. The rate of swing is not affected by changes in the weight of the pendulum bob.
3. The rate of swing is not affected by changes in the angle of release.

ELABORATE: PRESENT PROBLEMS AND ASK QUESTIONS TO EXTEND CONCEPTS AND PRINCIPLES.

Students often have great difficulty in controlling variables while experimenting. For a dramatic example, see the video clip and essay about designing pendulum investigations for seventh grade students in Chapter 3 of the Companion Website: http://www.prenhall. com/carin.

g. Using data from the whole class and an overhead transparency of a grid (or a computer graphing program or spreadsheet and LCD projector), show students how to construct a graph of *rate* versus *length* for pendulums. Rate (the number of swings in 15 seconds) should be graphed on the *y* axis (vertical axis). Length should be graphed on the *x* axis. Explain that scientists conventionally graph the *independent* variable (the variable deliberately *manipulated*) on the *x* axis and the *dependent* variable (the variable responding to the deliberate manipulation) on the *y* axis.

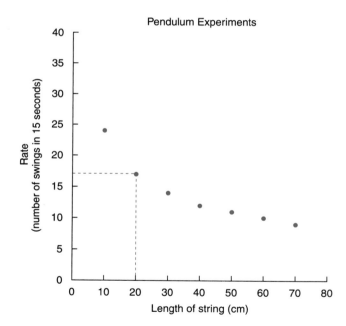

1. Explain to students that the graph visually depicts the *pattern of changes* in rate that occur when the length of the pendulum is changed.
2. Ask students how they can use the data tables and graph to predict future events as well as indicate their observations and arrive at conclusions.
3. Once they have recorded the number of swings per 15 seconds for string lengths of 20 cm, 40 cm, and 60 cm, for example, lead students to use the pattern of change represented by the graph to predict the rate for a pendulum length that is between two measured lengths (30 cm or 35 cm, for example) and the rate for a pendulum length that is greater than any length shown on the graph (an 80 cm pendulum, for example).

4. Ask students to test their predictions by making pendulums of the designated lengths and measuring the rate of swing for each one (the number of swings in 15 seconds).

Encourage students to notice pendulums in the world around them. Grandfather clocks, swings, and trapezes are all forms of pendulums.

EVALUATE: USE FORMAL AND INFORMAL MEANS TO ASSESS STUDENTS' KNOWLEDGE, UNDERSTANDING, AND INQUIRY SKILLS.

1. Performance assessment task for cooperative learning groups:
   - Instruct students to create a pendulum that swings from one extreme to the other in one second (7.5 complete back-and-forth swings in 15 seconds).
   - Encourage students to try to predict the appropriate length. (*Note:* A 100 cm pendulum is needed.) Students can use data from their previous investigations and gather additional data as needed. Remind students of the data tables and graph created previously.
   - Develop and use a rubric to assess levels of group performance in solving the task.
2. Assessment task for individuals:
   - Ask students to explain in writing: *How would you adjust a grandfather clock that was running too fast? too slow?* (Students should realize that the pendulum must be lengthened for the clock to slow down and shortened for the clock to run faster.)
   - You might develop and use a rubric to assess levels of individual performance in solving the task.

III. SOUND

Sound is an important part of our lives, enabling us to communicate with one another, be alert to different situations, and enjoy music and the sounds of the world around us. The simple activities included here enable children to begin to understand the basic physics of sound. Consistent with the *National Science Education Standards*, topics studied include sources of sounds, how sounds travel, and detectors of sound.

A. SOURCES OF SOUND

▶ *Science Background*

Sounds are produced when objects vibrate or move back and forth rapidly. An object that produces sound is called a sound source. Many different objects can generate sounds. For example, musical instruments produce sound when some part of them is made to vibrate.

Characteristics such as pitch and loudness allow us to distinguish one sound from another. Pitch is determined by the frequency, or rate of a vibration of sound. Humans can ordinarily hear pitches between about 15 Hz (15 vibrations per second) and 20,000 Hz. Dogs and cats can hear frequencies as high as 30,000 Hz. Ultrasound refers to high-pitched sounds beyond the range of human hearing. Physicians rely on the penetrating power of ultrasound to see inside the human body and examine internal organs or check the development of babies.

NSES   **Science Standards**

All students should develop an understanding of

- position and motion of objects (sound) (K–4).

Objectives for Students

1. Define *vibration* as the back-and-forth movement of an object.
2. Demonstrate, describe, and explain the generation of sound by various vibrating sources.
3. Define *pitch* as how high or low a sound is. Demonstrate, describe, and explain how the pitch of a sound may be varied.
4. Define *loudness* as the amount, amplitude, or intensity of sound. Demonstrate, describe, and explain how the loudness of a sound may be increased.

 Concepts and Principles

Activities 1–8 address these fundamental concepts and principles related to the *Science Standards:*

- Sound is produced by vibrating objects (K–4).
- The pitch of a sound can be varied by changing the rate of vibration (K–4).

1. HOW ARE SOUNDS PRODUCED? (2–4)

Materials

Craft sticks

ENGAGE: ASK A QUESTION ABOUT OBJECTS, ORGANISMS, OR EVENTS IN THE ENVIRONMENT.

a. Ask: *How can you use a craft stick to create sounds?*

EXPLORE: PLAN AND CONDUCT SIMPLE INVESTIGATIONS TO COLLECT RELEVANT DATA.

b. Instruct students to hold a 15 cm craft stick firmly against a desk with one hand. With the other hand, they should pluck the overhanging part of the stick, causing it to vibrate.

EXPLAIN: USE DATA
TO GENERATE
INTERPRETATIONS,
INCLUDING DESCRIPTIONS,
CLASSIFICATIONS, AND
EXPLANATIONS.

c. Ask: *What is meant by vibration? Which part of the craft stick vibrates and produces sound?*

2. WHAT AFFECTS THE PITCH AND LOUDNESS OF A SOUND? (2–4)

Materials

Craft sticks

ENGAGE: ASK A
QUESTION ABOUT OBJECTS,
ORGANISMS, OR EVENTS IN
THE ENVIRONMENT.

a. Ask: *How can you create sounds of different pitches with a craft stick?*

EXPLORE: PLAN
AND CONDUCT SIMPLE
INVESTIGATIONS TO
COLLECT RELEVANT DATA.

b. Challenge students to produce a high-pitched sound by vibrating the stick and to produce a low-pitched sound by vibrating the stick.

EXPLAIN: USE DATA
TO GENERATE
INTERPRETATIONS,
INCLUDING DESCRIPTIONS,
CLASSIFICATIONS, AND
EXPLANATIONS.

c. Ask: *What is meant by the pitch of a sound? How can you change the pitch of a vibrating craft stick? Does the craft stick vibrate faster or slower when more of it hangs over the edge of a desk?*

3. HOW IS SOUND PRODUCED BY A TUNING FORK? (2–4)

Materials

Tuning forks
Wood blocks
Container of water

Safety Precautions

To protect tuning forks from damage, strike them only against a wood surface or the sole of your shoe or with a rubber mallet to produce vibrations and sounds.

ENGAGE: ASK A
QUESTION ABOUT OBJECTS,
ORGANISMS, OR EVENTS IN
THE ENVIRONMENT.

a. Ask: *What is a tuning fork? How does a tuning fork produce sounds?*

EXPLORE: PLAN AND
CONDUCT SIMPLE
INVESTIGATIONS TO
COLLECT RELEVANT DATA.

b. Instruct students to observe while you conduct this demonstration:
1. Hold the tuning fork by its stem.
2. Strike a wood block or sole of your shoe crisply with the tip of one of the fork tines.
3. Bring the fork near your ear and listen. Strike the fork again and lightly touch the tip of one of the fork tines to the surface of the water in a container.

EXPLAIN: USE DATA
TO GENERATE
INTERPRETATIONS,
INCLUDING DESCRIPTIONS,
CLASSIFICATIONS, AND
EXPLANATIONS.

c. Ask: *What vibrates in producing sound from a tuning fork? What is your evidence that the fork tines are vibrating?*

4. HOW IS SOUND PRODUCED WHEN YOU TALK OR SING? (2–4)

ENGAGE: ASK A
QUESTION ABOUT OBJECTS,
ORGANISMS, OR EVENTS IN
THE ENVIRONMENT.

a. Ask: *When you talk or sing, what part in your body vibrates to produce the sound?*

EXPLORE: PLAN
AND CONDUCT SIMPLE
INVESTIGATIONS TO
COLLECT RELEVANT DATA.

b. Have students place their fingers on their voice box or larynx near the bottom of their throats. Tell them to buzz like a bee.

EXPLAIN: USE DATA
TO GENERATE
INTERPRETATIONS,
INCLUDING DESCRIPTIONS,
CLASSIFICATIONS, AND
EXPLANATIONS.

c. Ask: *What did you feel in your voice box when you buzzed like a bee? What vibrates in your throat to produce sounds?*
    Help students understand that inside your throat is a voice box or larynx. When you buzz, speak, or sing, air passes across the voice box, causing it to vibrate and produce sounds.

5. HOW IS SOUND PRODUCED BY A DRUM? (2–4)

Materials

Cylindrical container
Puffed rice or wheat cereal
Large balloon or sheet rubber
Strong rubber band
Drumstick or pencil with eraser

ENGAGE: ASK A
QUESTION ABOUT OBJECTS,
ORGANISMS, OR EVENTS IN
THE ENVIRONMENT.

a. Ask: *What vibrates in a drum to produce sound?*

EXPLORE: PLAN AND CONDUCT SIMPLE INVESTIGATIONS TO COLLECT RELEVANT DATA.

b. Stretch a large balloon or piece of sheet rubber over the open end of a cylindrical container, such as an oatmeal container. Place a rubber band around that end to hold the rubber sheet securely in place. This makes a simple drum. Sprinkle puffed rice or wheat cereal on the drumhead. Tell students to tap the drumhead softly with a drumstick or eraser end of a pencil and observe what happens. Then tell them to hit the drumhead harder and watch the cereal and observe the sound produced.

EXPLAIN: USE DATA TO GENERATE INTERPRETATIONS, INCLUDING DESCRIPTIONS, CLASSIFICATIONS, AND EXPLANATIONS.

c. Ask: *What part of a drum vibrates to produce sound? What is your evidence? What is meant by loudness? How do you vary the loudness of a drum?*

6. HOW IS SOUND PRODUCED BY A BANJO? (2–4)

Materials

Rubber bands of varying lengths and thicknesses
Small, open box or plastic cup

ENGAGE: ASK A QUESTION ABOUT OBJECTS, ORGANISMS, OR EVENTS IN THE ENVIRONMENT.

a. Ask: *What vibrates to produce sound in a stringed musical instrument, such as a banjo?*

EXPLORE: PLAN AND CONDUCT SIMPLE INVESTIGATIONS TO COLLECT RELEVANT DATA.

b. Tell students to make banjos by stretching rubber bands of varying lengths and thicknesses over a small box or plastic cup. Pluck the rubber bands to produce sounds.

EXPLAIN: USE DATA TO GENERATE INTERPRETATIONS, INCLUDING DESCRIPTIONS, CLASSIFICATIONS, AND EXPLANATIONS.

c. Ask: *What part of a rubber band banjo vibrates to produce sound? What is your evidence?* Many good activities on sound concern musical instruments. Rather than focusing on music or on band instruments, keep the focus on what is vibrating to produce the sound in each instrument. Studies in the physics of sound will lay a good foundation for musical training on the fundamentals of music, how specific band instruments are played, and how they work.

d. Ask: *What do you think might affect the pitch of the sound from a banjo?* Instruct students to investigate how the pitch of a sound is varied on a rubber band banjo by varying the tension and thickness of the rubber bands. Ask: *What two variables can you change to vary the pitch of a rubber band banjo? How do you vary the loudness of the banjo?*

ELABORATE: USE DATA TO GENERATE INTERPRETATIONS, INCLUDING DESCRIPTIONS, CLASSIFICATIONS, AND EXPLANATIONS.

e. Ask: *How can you vary the pitch of the sound produced by a stringed musical instrument, such as a guitar or ukulele?* Allow students to investigate how strings of differing thickness produce different pitches in guitars, ukuleles, or other stringed instruments. Demonstrate how the tension of a string can be varied to produce high- and low-pitched sounds with a guitar or other stringed instrument.

▶ *Teaching Background*

Each time a guitar player plucks a guitar string, it starts to vibrate. The rate of vibration determines the pitch of the string. Guitars have strings of differing thickness. Thinner strings vibrate more quickly and produce higher-pitched sounds than thicker ones. Strings under greater tension also vibrate more quickly and produce higher pitches than strings under less tension. The musician uses the tuning knobs on the guitar to adjust the tension of the strings. As she increases the tension of a string, that string vibrates more rapidly and the pitch gets higher. As she decreases the tension of a string, the string vibrates more slowly and the pitch gets lower.

Source: Full Option Science System, *Physics of Sound.* Lawrence Hall of Science, University of California, Berkeley.

7. HOW CAN YOU MAKE A DRINKING STRAW FLUTE? (2–4)

Materials

Drinking straws
Scissors

ENGAGE: ASK A QUESTION ABOUT OBJECTS, ORGANISMS, OR EVENTS IN THE ENVIRONMENT.

a. Ask: *What is a flute? How is sound produced in a flute? How can you vary the pitch of a sound produced by a flute?*

EXPLORE: PLAN AND CONDUCT SIMPLE INVESTIGATIONS TO COLLECT RELEVANT DATA.

b. Give each student a drinking straw. Have students use scissors to cut a V-shape at the end of the straw and pinch it closed to produce a reed.

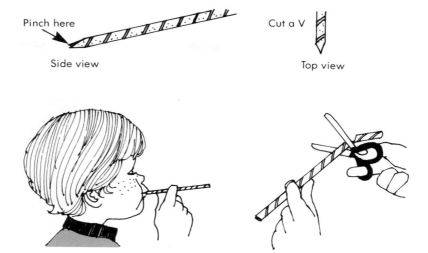

Have students blow on the "V" cut into the straw flute to produce a sound. (*Note:* They will need to experiment to get the proper lip vibration.) Now, have students cut the straw into different lengths and blow on the straw flute to get different pitches.

EXPLAIN: USE DATA TO GENERATE INTERPRETATIONS, INCLUDING DESCRIPTIONS, CLASSIFICATIONS, AND EXPLANATIONS.

c. As you circulate among students, or when you return to a whole class structure, ask: *What part of a straw flute vibrates to produce a sound? What can you vary to change the pitch of a straw flute? How do you think clarinets, oboes, and saxophones produce sounds?*

8. HOW CAN YOU MAKE A POP-BOTTLE PIPE ORGAN? WHAT AFFECTS THE PITCH OF THE SOUND PRODUCED BY A POP BOTTLE? (2–4)

Materials   At least eight identical glass pop bottles

ENGAGE: ASK A QUESTION ABOUT OBJECTS, ORGANISMS, OR EVENTS IN THE ENVIRONMENT.

a. Blow across a pop bottle that is about three-fourths full of water so that a sound is produced from the bottle. Ask: *How could you vary the pitch of the sound coming from the bottle?*

EXPLORE: PLAN AND CONDUCT SIMPLE INVESTIGATIONS TO COLLECT RELEVANT DATA.

b. Fill eight identical pop bottles with varying amounts of water. Blow across the open ends of the bottles. Arrange the bottles to play a simple tune.

EXPLAIN: USE DATA
TO GENERATE
INTERPRETATIONS,
INCLUDING DESCRIPTIONS,
CLASSIFICATIONS, AND
EXPLANATIONS.

c. Ask: *What part of a pop bottle vibrates to produce sound? How is the air in the pop bottle made to vibrate? What can you vary to change the pitch of a pop bottle? How do you think pipe organs and horns produce sounds?*

▶ *Teaching Background*

In a pipe organ, air is blown across the bottom opening of a metal pipe. The air in the pipe then vibrates to produce a sound. The pitch of the sound depends on the length and thickness of the pipe. Shorter pipes produce higher-pitch sounds.

When a musician blows air into the mouthpiece of a horn, the air in the open column of the horn vibrates and produces sounds. The pitch of the sound produced in a horn depends on the length and volume of the air column.

B. TRANSFER OF SOUND

▶ *Science Background*

Sound moves away from a source through a material medium. Air, water, and solids are all good media for carrying sound. Sounds travel through media in waves that are analogous to waves at the seashore. Sound cannot travel through a vacuum because there are no particles to vibrate and carry the sound waves. When sound waves bounce off some solid object in the distance, they return to the source as echoes.

Sound travels through air at about 760 miles per hour (1 mile in 5 seconds). In contrast, light travels at 186,000 miles per second. Traveling much slower than light, the sound of the thunder which was produced simultaneously with lightning reaches your ears a few seconds after you see a flash of lightning.

NSES   Science Standards

All students should develop understanding of

- position and motion of objects (sound) (K–4).
- transfer of energy (5–8).

Objectives for Students

1. Define *medium* as the material substance through which sound travels from a vibrating source to a receiver. Demonstrate and describe how sound travels through solid, liquid, and gas media.
2. Demonstrate properties of water waves. Describe how sound travels through different media in waves that are analogous to water waves.

3. Demonstrate and describe ways that sound can be directed and amplified.
4. Describe and explain echoes as the reflection of sound waves.

NSES   Concepts and Principles

Activities 1 and 2 prepare students to understand these fundamental concepts and principles related to the *Science Standards*:

- Energy is transferred in many ways (5–8).
- Vibrations in materials set up wavelike disturbances that spread away from the source. Sound waves and earthquake waves are examples. These and other waves move at different speeds in different materials (*Benchmarks for Science Literacy*, 6–8).

1. DOES SOUND TRAVEL THROUGH AIR, SOLIDS, AND LIQUIDS? (2–4)

Materials

Lengths of garden hose
Metersticks
Pieces of metal or rocks
Bucket

ENGAGE: ASK A QUESTION ABOUT OBJECTS, ORGANISMS, OR EVENTS IN THE ENVIRONMENT.

a. Ask: *How does sound travel? Does sound travel through all kinds of materials? Can sound travel through the air in a garden hose? Does sound travel through solids? Does sound travel through water?*

EXPLORE: PLAN AND CONDUCT SIMPLE INVESTIGATIONS TO COLLECT RELEVANT DATA.

b. Have students listen to sounds through straight and curving lengths of garden hose. Make sure all of the water is drained out of the hose.
c. Have students work in pairs. One student should hold a meterstick to her ear. The partner should scratch the other end of the stick with a pencil. Repeat the activity with the meterstick held away from the ear a few centimeters.

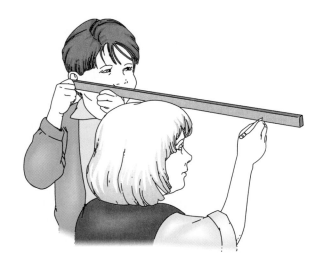

d. Obtain a large bucket of water. Ask students to take two pieces of metal or two rocks and hit them together under the water. Then, tell them to hit the objects together out of water.

EXPLAIN: USE DATA TO GENERATE INTERPRETATIONS, INCLUDING DESCRIPTIONS, CLASSIFICATIONS, AND EXPLANATIONS.

e. Ask: *How does the garden hose demonstration show that sound travels through air?*
   What do you hear through the meterstick? How do you think the sound of the pencil travels through the meterstick?
   What did you hear when you hit the objects together underwater? Was the sound louder or softer when you hit the objects together out of the water?
   Which seemed to be a better conductor of sound: the solid meterstick, air, or water?

2. HOW IS THE MOVEMENT OF SOUND LIKE WAVES ON WATER? (2–4)

Materials

Dominoes
Large dishpan or other container

ENGAGE: ASK A QUESTION ABOUT OBJECTS, ORGANISMS, OR EVENTS IN THE ENVIRONMENT.

a. Ask: *How does sound travel through a material? Does sound travel like a water wave, or like a pulse along a line of dominoes?*

EXPLORE: PLAN AND CONDUCT SIMPLE INVESTIGATIONS TO COLLECT RELEVANT DATA.

b. Instruct students to drop a pebble or other small object into a large dishpan of water and observe what happens. Tell students to place a cork in the water and observe how it interacts with the water wave. Also tell them to notice how the pulses from the disturbance interact with the walls of the container.

c. Ask: *What happens to a curving line of dominoes when you push the first one down?*
   Tell students to take 10 dominoes and stand them up on end in a straight row. Push the first domino over so that a chain reaction causes all the dominoes to fall.

EXPLAIN: USE DATA TO GENERATE INTERPRETATIONS, INCLUDING DESCRIPTIONS, CLASSIFICATIONS, AND EXPLANATIONS.

d. Ask: *What do you observe about water waves? What happens to the cork?* (Rather than moving along with the wave, it bobs up and down.) *How does the water wave interact with the walls of the container?* (The water wave reflects off the walls.)

e. Ask: *What travels along the row of dominoes? Is it a domino or a pulse caused by the first domino?*
   How might the action of the dominoes be like waves traveling through water? (In both cases, pulses travel.)
   How is the pulse traveling along the line of dominoes different from the water wave? (The domino chain reaction is a single pulse; the disturbance at the source of a water wave sends out many pulses coming one after the other.)

f. Ask: *How might the action of dominoes be like sound traveling through a solid, liquid, or air?* (Both sound and the domino pulse are created by an initial disturbance and travel along or through a material.)
   Does sound travel more like a pulse along a line of dominoes or more like a wave from a disturbance in water? Why do you think so? How is the reflection of a water wave like a sound echo?

C. RECEIVERS OF SOUND

▶ *Science Background*

Receivers are instruments that detect sound. Sound is one of the many forms of energy. Our ears are marvelously designed receivers of sound that are tuned to keep us in touch with much of our environment.

 NSES   Science Standards

All students should develop an understanding of

- position and motion of objects (sound) (K–4).

Objectives for Students

1. Explain how the outer ear and megaphone are similar in gathering incoming sound signals.
2. Explain that in receiving sound, a detector in the receiver is set in vibration by the incoming sound signals.
3. Identify and describe the operation of the sound detectors in the human ear and a stethoscope.
4. Compare the ear as a receiver of sound with the eye as a receiver of light.

 NSES   Concepts and Principles

Activity I addresses these fundamental concepts and principles related to the *Science Standards*:

- Energy is transferred in many ways (5–8).
- Sound is a form of energy (5–8).

1. HOW CAN SOUNDS BE HEARD BETTER? (2–4)

Materials

Stethoscope
Megaphone
Listening tube

ENGAGE: ASK A QUESTION ABOUT OBJECTS, ORGANISMS, OR EVENTS IN THE ENVIRONMENT.

a. Ask: *What part of your body detects sounds? How is your ear specially designed to receive and detect sounds?*

EXPLORE: PLAN AND CONDUCT SIMPLE INVESTIGATIONS TO COLLECT RELEVANT DATA.

b. Roll a piece of poster board into a cylinder and fasten it on both ends with paper fasteners. Have students use the listening tube to listen to faint sounds.

c. To make a megaphone, curl a fan-shaped piece of cardboard into a cone. Fasten the cone with three brass fasteners. Ask students to place the small end of the megaphone to their ears and listen to the faint whispers of partners some distance away from them.

d. Ask students to tap their fingers together and listen to the sound. Have them tap their fingers together again and listen to the sound through a stethoscope. Then, have them tap their fingers underwater and listen to the sound without and with a stethoscope.

Safety Precautions

- Help students to clean earpieces of stethoscopes with alcohol and cotton swabs before using them.
- Caution students not to damage the diaphragm of a stethoscope by striking it against hard objects.

EXPLAIN: USE DATA TO GENERATE INTERPRETATIONS, INCLUDING DESCRIPTIONS, CLASSIFICATIONS, AND EXPLANATIONS.

Ask: *How do listening tubes enable sounds to be heard better?*

Ask: *How does the megaphone enhance hearing? How is a megaphone similar to the outer ear?*

Ask: *How does the stethoscope work? How does a stethoscope enable you to hear soft sounds better?*

Ask: *In what ways do the rolled cylinder, the megaphone, and the stethoscope extend the sense of hearing?*

▶ *Teaching Background*

A sound receiver must be able to detect sound pulses that reach it. The ear is a sound receiver. The outer part of the ear collects sound much like the large end of a megaphone when it is used as a listening tube. When sound energy strikes the eardrum, vibrations are set up which initiate the hearing process.

A stethoscope has a diaphragm that vibrates when sound strikes it. Faint sounds can be detected by the diaphragm. The sounds are then conducted from the diaphragm down the air-filled tubes to the ear. In a similar way, a telephone mouthpiece has a diaphragm that vibrates when sound energy strikes it. In a telephone, the vibrations in the diaphragm are converted electromagnetically to electrical energy. Electrical energy is then conducted from one telephone along telephone wires or from a series of towers to another telephone.

D. SOUND CHALLENGES: HOMEMADE TELEPHONES

NSES   Science Standards

All students should develop an understanding of

• position and motion of objects (sound) (K–4).

Science and Technology Standards

Students should also develop

• abilities of technological design, including the ability to
  a. identify a simple problem of human adaptation in the environment;
  b. propose a solution;
  c. implement proposed solutions;
  d. evaluate a product or design; and
  e. communicate a problem, design, and solution (K–4).

Objectives for Students

1. Construct homemade telephones.
2. Explain the operation of a homemade telephone, using the concepts of vibrating source, conducting material, and receiver.
3. Design and carry out investigations to determine the best type of materials for a homemade telephone.
4. Demonstrate abilities of technological design.

NSES   Concepts and Principles

Activities 1 and 2 address these fundamental concepts and principles related to the *Science Standards*:

• Sound is produced by vibrating objects (K–4).
• Energy is transferred in many ways (5–8).
• Sound is a form of energy (5–8).

1. CAN SOUND TRAVEL THROUGH A STRING? (2–4)

Materials   Spoon
                                 String

ENGAGE: ASK A
QUESTION ABOUT OBJECTS,
ORGANISMS, OR EVENTS IN
THE ENVIRONMENT.

a. Ask: *Can sound travel through a long string?*

EXPLORE: PLAN
AND CONDUCT SIMPLE
INVESTIGATIONS TO
COLLECT RELEVANT DATA.

b. Loop a length of string around a spoon. Try to tie the spoon at about the middle of the string. Hold the two ends of the string in your ears. Bend over so the spoon hangs freely. Have your partner gently strike the spoon with another spoon.

EXPLAIN: USE DATA
TO GENERATE
INTERPRETATIONS,
INCLUDING DESCRIPTIONS,
CLASSIFICATIONS, AND
EXPLANATIONS.

Ask: *What do you observe? What is your evidence that the string is a good conductor of sound?*

ENGAGE: IDENTIFY A
SIMPLE PROBLEM OF
HUMAN ADAPTATION IN
THE ENVIRONMENT.

2. HOW CAN YOU MAKE A DEMONSTRATION TELEPHONE? (2–4)

Materials   String, wire, nylon fishing line
                                 Cups of various kinds (Styrofoam, waxed cardboard, plastic, large, small)
                                 Nail, paper clips, toothpicks

ENGAGE: ASK A
QUESTION ABOUT OBJECTS,
ORGANISMS, OR EVENTS IN
THE ENVIRONMENT.

a. Ask: *How can you design a "telephone" that will enable you to communicate across some distance using a string as a medium?*

EXPLORE: DESIGN AND
IMPLEMENT AN APPROACH
TO THE PROBLEM.

b. Show students how to construct a homemade telephone using plastic cups. In advance, use a small nail to punch a hole in the bottom of each cup. Tell pairs of students to cut a 20 foot (6 or 7 meter) length of string and thread the ends into cups. Tell them to tie a paper clip around each end to hold the string firmly in place inside the cup. Instruct them to try out their homemade telephones with their partners.

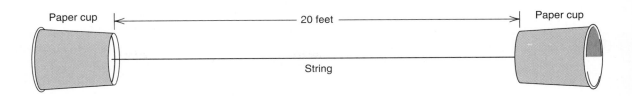

Paper cup ⟵————— 20 feet —————⟶ Paper cup

String

EVALUATE: EVALUATE THE PROBLEM SOLUTION.

c. Challenge students to improve the quality of their homemade telephones by investigating the effects of different string or wire media, different types of cups, and different ways to hold the string or wire against the bottom of the cups. Tell students to come up with standard ways to test their telephones so they can decide which parts are most effective.

EXPLAIN: USE DATA TO GENERATE INTERPRETATIONS, INCLUDING DESCRIPTIONS, CLASSIFICATIONS, AND EXPLANATIONS.

Ask: *What is the original source of sound for your telephones? What is set in vibration in the mouthpiece of the telephone? What is the conductor of sound? How is the sound detected at the other end of the telephone?*

▶ *Teaching Background*

A homemade telephone is a human-constructed product that connects well to scientific principles. Many concepts introduced in the activities on sound are used in this activity. The voice of one partner sets particles of air in vibration. The cup/mouthpiece of the string telephone is then set in vibration. The sound energy produced by the vibrating cup is conducted along the string to the other cup. Thus, the second cup is set in vibration. This vibrating cup sets the air in vibration, producing sound. The sound is then carried to the ear. Designing, constructing, and evaluating homemade telephones provides a good introduction to the technological design cycle.

IV. TEMPERATURE AND HEAT

▶ *Science Background*

Heat, like light, sound, and electricity, is a form of energy. Energy is one of the few concepts in science that children talk about accurately before they can define it. Children's ideas about energy—getting "quick energy" from a candy bar or turning off lights so as not to "waste energy"—may be imprecise but are reasonably close to the concept of energy that we want children to learn (*Benchmarks for Science Literacy*, American Association for the Advancement of Science, 1993, p. 81).

Technically, energy is the ability to do work. More intuitively, something has energy if it can bring about a change in another object or in itself. Heat can bring about many changes. For example, it can change the state of a substance from liquid to gas (evaporation) or from solid to liquid (melting); it can change the temperature of a substance; it can cause most things to expand; and it can change the rate of a reaction, such as how fast a substance dissolves. Changes in temperature give us an indication of how much heat energy has been transferred into or out of a system, but heat and temperature are not the same thing. This is a distinction that is complex and hard for children to understand. Children do not need to know precise definitions of energy, heat, and temperature to investigate them. These can come later in secondary school.

There are many sources of heat in our everyday lives—lights, radios, television sets, motors, computers, friction, and even people. Heat can be transferred or spread from an energy source to an energy receiver by conduction when things are in contact, by radiation across space, or in air and liquids through convection currents. Heat is transferred from the sun to the earth by radiation. Heat energy carried by ocean currents has a strong influence on climate around the world. Weather is also a product of the transfer of heat energy from solar radiation into and out of the earth's atmosphere.

 Science Standards

All students should develop an understanding of

- light, heat, electricity, and magnetism (K–4).
- transfer of energy (5–8).

Objectives for Students

1. Name and describe sources of heat and activities that produce heat.
2. Design, conduct, and interpret experiments to determine the effects of heat on the dissolving time of substances.
3. Describe what happens in the transfer of heat by radiation, conduction, and convection. Give examples of each.
4. Design, conduct, and interpret experiments to determine the effects of the color of a material on the amount of radiated heat absorbed by the material.
5. Design and conduct experiments to determine the final temperature of water mixtures.
6. Explain that heat flows from warmer substances to cooler substances until an equilibrium temperature is reached.

 Concepts and Principles

Activities 1 and 2 address these fundamental concepts and principles related to the *Science Standards*:

- Heat can be produced in many ways, such as burning, rubbing, or mixing one substance with another (K–4).

1. WHAT MAKES THINGS GET HOTTER? (K–5)

Materials

6 inch piece of wire coat hanger
Mineral oil
Brass button
Wool cloth
Piece of metal
Pencil eraser
Notebook paper
Ice cubes
Newspapers or paper towels
Miscellaneous magazines

ENGAGE: ASK A QUESTION ABOUT OBJECTS, ORGANISMS, OR EVENTS IN THE ENVIRONMENT.

a. Ask: *What happens when you bend a wire rapidly or rub your hands together rapidly?*

EXPLORE: PLAN AND CONDUCT SIMPLE INVESTIGATIONS TO COLLECT RELEVANT DATA.

b. Bend a 6 inch piece of wire hanger back and forth 10 times as shown. Quickly touch the wire at the point where you bent it.
    Ask: *What do you feel?* (The wire got hotter.) *What do you think will happen if you bend the wire more times, for example, 20, 25, 30, 35 times?* (Each time the wire gets hotter.)

Safety Precautions

Try out this activity first to find out how many bends will make the wire too hot for students to touch.

c. Rub your hands together very fast and hard. Ask: *What do you feel?* (Heat.) Now rub different things together and quickly touch them to your upper lip or the tip of your nose (sensitive parts of your body): brass button on a piece of wool, metal on paper, pencil eraser on paper, and so on.

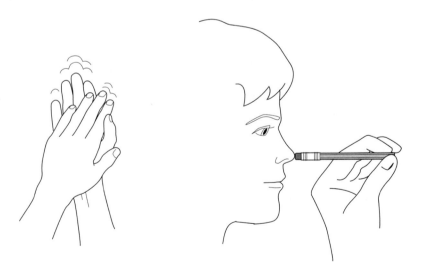

EXPLAIN: USE DATA TO GENERATE INTERPRETATIONS, INCLUDING DESCRIPTIONS, CLASSIFICATIONS, AND EXPLANATIONS.

d. Ask: *What did you observe in each case? How was heat produced in these two investigations?*
    Guide students to understand that bending things and rubbing things produces heat.

ELABORATE: EXTEND
CONCEPTS, PRINCIPLES,
AND STRATEGIES TO NEW
PROBLEMS AND QUESTIONS.

e. Try rubbing your hands together again, but put a few drops of oil or water on your hands first. Ask: *How do you think the second rubbing will feel different from the first rubbing?* Ask: *What did you observe? Why do you think it happened?*

2. HOW CAN YOU HEAT UP THE SAND IN A JAR? (3–6)

Materials

Baby food jar with screw top
Sand
Thick towel
Thermometer

ENGAGE: ASK A
QUESTION ABOUT OBJECTS,
ORGANISMS, OR EVENTS IN
THE ENVIRONMENT.

a. Ask: *What do you think will happen to the sand in a baby food jar if you shake it many times?*

EXPLORE: PLAN
AND CONDUCT SIMPLE
INVESTIGATIONS TO
COLLECT RELEVANT DATA.

b. Fill a baby food jar three-fourths full of sand, screw on the jar top, and then wrap it with a thick towel. Each person should take a turn doing the following things:

1. Measure the initial temperature of the sand, then shake the sand vigorously for 5 minutes.
2. Measure the temperature of the sand.
3. Write your findings on a record sheet like the one shown.

Person	Minutes of Shaking	Temperature in °C
1	5	
2	10	
3	15	
4	20	
5	25	

4. Pass the jar to the next person.
5. When everyone has had a turn, compare the temperature of the sand from the first to the last reading.
6. How were they different? (The temperature was higher after each shaking.)
7. Set up a graph like the one shown, then graph the data from the record sheets.

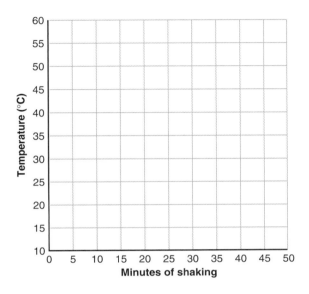

EXPLAIN: USE DATA TO GENERATE INTERPRETATIONS, INCLUDING DESCRIPTIONS, CLASSIFICATIONS, AND EXPLANATIONS.

c. Ask: *What did you observe? What do your data indicate? What was the source of the heat energy in the sand?* Explain that shaking something is a form of energy (mechanical energy; kinetic energy). Heat is also a form of energy. When you shook the sand, the energy of the sand's motion was transferred to heat energy when the sand grains struck one another and the glass. The heat energy in the sand caused its temperature to go up.

ELABORATE: EXTEND CONCEPTS, PRINCIPLES, AND STRATEGIES TO NEW PROBLEMS AND QUESTIONS.

d. Discuss these questions with the class:
    1. Why do you rub a match against the side of a matchbox?
    2. Why do matches not catch fire while sitting in a matchbox?
    3. When you bend a wire back and forth several times, why does it get warm?
    4. When you put two pencils together and rub them back and forth several times, what happens to your hands?
    5. A person tried to strike a match against a piece of glass to light it. The match would not light. Why?
    6. If you feel the tires of your car before you take a trip and then just after you get out of the car, they will not feel the same. How do you think they will differ? How would you explain the difference?
    7. A person was chopping wood with an ax. After chopping very hard for about 10 minutes, she felt the ax. How do you think the ax felt and why?

NSES Concepts and Principles

Activity 3 serves as preparation for learning these fundamental concepts and principles related to the *Science Standards*:

• Energy is a property of many substances and is associated with heat (5–8).

3. WHAT ARE SOME SOURCES OF HEAT? (K–5)

ENGAGE: ASK A QUESTION ABOUT OBJECTS, ORGANISMS, OR EVENTS IN THE ENVIRONMENT.

a. Ask: *What do we mean by a source of heat? Are sweaters or mittens sources of heat?* (No.) *Why are we "warm" under the covers on a cold night?* Conduct a brainstorming session on sources of heat. To initiate the following activity, ask: *What happens to an ice cube held in your hand?*

EXPLORE: PLAN AND CONDUCT SIMPLE INVESTIGATIONS TO COLLECT RELEVANT DATA.

b. Hold an ice cube in your hand over newspapers or paper towels. (*Note:* From experience, it is recommended that young students go to the bathroom before and after this activity!)

　　　Ask: *How does your hand feel with the ice cube in it?* (Cold.) *What is happening to the ice cube?*

c. Leave an ice cube in a nearby dish and notice the difference between this ice cube and the one in your hand.

EXPLAIN: USE DATA TO GENERATE INTERPRETATIONS, INCLUDING DESCRIPTIONS, CLASSIFICATIONS, AND EXPLANATIONS.

d. Ask: *What differences did you observe between the ice cube in your hand and the one in the dish? Why do you think the ice cube in your hand melted more?* (Your hand is a source of heat. Heat from your hand melts the ice cube faster than heat from the room melts the ice cube in the dish.)

Ask: *Which received heat—your hand or the ice cube you held?* (Ice cube; heat moved from hand to ice.)

Ask: *How is this the same as when you pour a warm soft drink over ice cubes?* (The warm drink gets cooler as heat moves from the drink to the ice.)

ELABORATE: EXTEND CONCEPTS, PRINCIPLES, AND STRATEGIES TO NEW PROBLEMS AND QUESTIONS.

e. Students in grades 3–5 could go on a "heat source hunt" in school and at home. Look for sources of heat, places where heat is produced (school or home heater or furnace, oven and stove, toaster, microwave oven, sunshine through windows, electric motors, car engines). List these places in a booklet or chart and illustrate them with magazine or computer pictures. Then, use these three questions to organize your list of heat producers:
   • Where did you see it?
   • What was the source of heat?
   • What was the receiver of heat, that is, what was heated?

Safety Precautions

Caution students not to touch heat-producing appliances or other hot objects.

NSES   **Concepts and Principles**

Activity 4 addresses these fundamental concepts and principles related to the *Science Standards:*

• Most change involves energy transfer (5–8).

4. HOW DOES HEAT AFFECT THE DISSOLVING TIME OF SUBSTANCES? (3–6)

Materials

Six baby food jars or clear plastic tumblers
Sugar cubes
Colored cinnamon candies or jelly beans
Tea bags
Pencils
Two Pyrex or tin pans

ENGAGE: ASK A QUESTION ABOUT OBJECTS, ORGANISMS, OR EVENTS IN THE ENVIRONMENT.

a. Ask: *How does heat affect the dissolving time of substances? What could you do to find out?*

EXPLORE: PLAN AND CONDUCT SIMPLE INVESTIGATIONS TO COLLECT RELEVANT DATA.

b. Lead students to plan and conduct a controlled experiment to determine the effect of heat on dissolving time. Students could set up two sets of three containers of water as follows:
   1. Fill six baby food jars or plastic drinking glasses with water to within 2 cm of the top and let them stand until the water is room temperature.
   2. Slowly lower a sugar cube into each of two containers, a few cinnamon candies or jelly beans into two more, and a tea bag into the other two. (See diagram.) Set up two sets of three containers with sugar, cinnamon candies, and tea bags.

3. Place one set of containers in ice-cold water in a pan and the other set in a pan of very hot water.

4. Observe the two sets of containers and make records of what is seen every 10 minutes.

EXPERIMENT: Substances dissolving with stirring

Pencil as stirrer

Sugar solution (colorless)

Colored cinnamon candies (lightly colored)

Tea solution (deep brown)

EXPLAIN: USE DATA TO GENERATE INTERPRETATIONS, INCLUDING DESCRIPTIONS, CLASSIFICATIONS, AND EXPLANATIONS.

c. Ask: *In which containers do you think the materials will dissolve first? Why?*

From the experiment, you can conclude that heat affects dissolving time. The hotter the liquid, the faster a substance dissolves. This investigation uses the strategy of controlled experimenting. If you think your students are ready, you might introduce the concept of variables. The temperature of the water is the manipulated variable (independent variable) and dissolving time is the responding variable (dependent variable). All other conditions are controlled, such as the type of container, the amount of water, and whether or not you stir the water.

NSES

Concepts and Principles

Activities 5–7 address these fundamental concepts and principles related to the *Science Standards*:

• Energy is transferred in many ways (5–8).

5. WHAT AFFECTS THE TEMPERATURE CHANGE OF WATER HEATED BY RADIATION? (3–6)

Materials

Three tin cans of same size
Small can of shiny white paint
Small can of dull black paint
Two small paintbrushes
Styrofoam covers for cans
Three thermometers
Lamp with 150 to 300 watt bulb

ENGAGE: ASK A QUESTION ABOUT OBJECTS, ORGANISMS, OR EVENTS IN THE ENVIRONMENT.

a. Ask: *If something is left in sunlight, does its color affect how hot it gets? How could you investigate to find out?*

EXPLORE: PLAN AND CONDUCT SIMPLE INVESTIGATIONS TO COLLECT RELEVANT DATA.

b. Guide students to plan and conduct a controlled experiment to determine the effect of color on heating in sunlight. These activities may be done in cooperative groups. For immature or unruly children, the teacher should demonstrate these activities.
  1. Obtain three identical-sized cans and remove all labels. Paint one can dull black and another can shiny white; leave the third can unpainted, shiny metal.
  2. Fill each can with the same amount of regular tap water.
  3. Put a Styrofoam cover on each can and insert a thermometer through each cover.
  4. Set the cans in direct sunlight or at equal distances from a 150 to 300 watt light bulb. (See diagram.)
  5. Prepare a table for data collection and record the temperature of the water in each can at 1-minute intervals. (Do not move the thermometers when you record the temperature each time.)

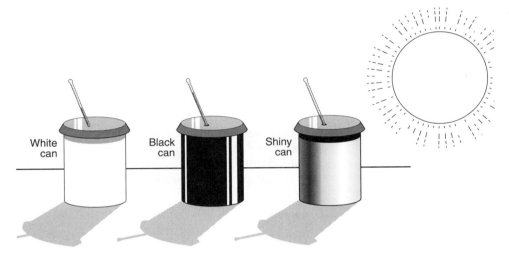

EXPLAIN: USE DATA TO GENERATE INTERPRETATIONS, INCLUDING DESCRIPTIONS, CLASSIFICATIONS, AND EXPLANATIONS.

c. Ask: *What happens to the water temperature in the three different cans after being in the sun or near light bulbs for a while? If there are different temperatures, how would you explain that?* Explain that radiation is the transfer of heat across space, such as the transfer of heat energy from the sun to earth. Lead students to understand that the shiny surface of the unpainted can and the shiny white paint reflect radiant energy, whereas the dull black paint absorbs most of the radiant energy.

ELABORATE: EXTEND CONCEPTS, PRINCIPLES, AND STRATEGIES TO NEW PROBLEMS AND QUESTIONS.

d. Ask: *How would you relate the unequal heating in the tin cans to different land and water surfaces of the earth?* Guide students to understand that dark patches of ground absorb more radiant energy than do shiny water surfaces or lighter-colored land surfaces. The unequal heating of the earth contributes to climate and weather changes.

e. Ask: *What color space suits do astronauts wear? Why?*

6. HOW IS HEAT TRANSFERRED THROUGH CONVECTION? (3–6)

ENGAGE: ASK A QUESTION ABOUT OBJECTS, ORGANISMS, OR EVENTS IN THE ENVIRONMENT.

a. Ask: *Where do you think the warmest and coolest spots are in your classroom? Try this activity to see if you can find the answer.*

EXPLORE: PLAN AND CONDUCT SIMPLE INVESTIGATIONS TO COLLECT RELEVANT DATA.

b. Guide students to plan and conduct this investigation.
1. As far away as possible from the room's source of heat, tape three thermometers to a wall at these places: near the ceiling, halfway up the wall, and near the floor.
2. Make a chart of the thermometer readings once an hour for 1 day.
3. Using the data collected, graph the temperature on the y axis (vertical axis) and time on the x axis (horizontal axis).
4. From your data and graph, answer these questions:
   Which thermometer consistently had the highest temperatures? the middle temperatures? the lowest temperatures? Why do you think the temperatures were different?

EXPLAIN: USE DATA TO GENERATE INTERPRETATIONS, INCLUDING DESCRIPTIONS, CLASSIFICATIONS, AND EXPLANATIONS.

c. Explain to students that **convection** is the transfer of heat by the movement of either a gas (air) or a liquid (water). When the air in the room is heated, it expands and becomes lighter per given volume. The lighter air then rises as heavier air settles under it. This rising and falling is called a **convection current.**

ELABORATE: EXTEND CONCEPTS, PRINCIPLES, AND STRATEGIES TO NEW PROBLEMS AND QUESTIONS.

d. Ask: *When you see "wiggly lines" rising from a blacktop parking lot on a sunny day, how is this the same as the convection current in our classroom? Why does a "cloud" fall down from a freezer that is above a refrigerator when you open the freezer door? Why does smoke usually rise up a chimney? Under what conditions would smoke come into the house through the fireplace opening? Why would a pinwheel start to spin if put over a lit light bulb?*

NSES   Concepts and Principles

Activity 7 also addresses these fundamental concepts and principles related to the *Science Standards*:

• Heat can move from one object to another by conduction (5–8).

---

7. HOW IS HEAT TRANSFERRED THROUGH CONDUCTION? (4–6)

Safety Precautions

Because of the use of an open flame from a candle, you should demonstrate all or part of this activity yourself.

Materials

Candle
Matches
Nine thumbtacks
Tripod stand
One 4 3/4 inch square of aluminum foil
Silver or steel knife
4 inch length of copper tubing

ENGAGE: ASK A QUESTION ABOUT OBJECTS, ORGANISMS, OR EVENTS IN THE ENVIRONMENT.

a. Ask: *What do you think will happen to tacks that have been attached with wax to a strip of aluminum foil, to a silver or steel knife, and to a copper tube when the tips of these metals are heated?*

EXPLORE: PLAN AND CONDUCT SIMPLE INVESTIGATIONS TO COLLECT RELEVANT DATA.

b. Demonstrate the following activity for your students:
    1. Obtain a 4 3/4 inch square of aluminum foil, a candle, a match, and nine tacks.
    2. Roll the aluminum foil tightly.
    3. Light the candle. Drip some wax onto three tacks and the aluminum foil rod so the tacks stick to the foil.
    4. Obtain a tripod stand, a silver knife, and a 4 inch length of copper tubing.
    5. Stick three tacks each to the knife and to the copper tubing as you did with the foil.
    6. Place the foil, knife, and copper tubing on a tripod stand as shown in the diagram. Heat the tips of each of these with a candle flame. Have students observe and record what happens.

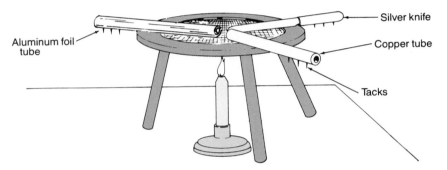

Aluminum foil tube · Silver knife · Copper tube · Tacks

EXPLAIN: USE DATA TO GENERATE INTERPRETATIONS, INCLUDING DESCRIPTIONS, CLASSIFICATIONS, AND EXPLANATIONS.

c. Ask: *Why did the tacks not all fall at the same time? How do you think the heat affected the three metals?*
    Guide students to understand that heat is conducted from a heat source through materials. Heat is conducted through different materials at different rates. Heat is always conducted from hotter to cooler areas.

ELABORATE: EXTEND CONCEPTS, PRINCIPLES, AND STRATEGIES TO NEW PROBLEMS AND QUESTIONS.

d. The following questions relate to radiation, convection, or conduction of heat energy. Tell students to answer each question and to explain or give the evidence for their answers.
    1. When you stand in front of a fireplace and only the front of you is warmed by the fire, how is the heat transferred?
    2. How does heat energy come from the sun to the earth?
    3. What colors are more likely to absorb heat?
    4. Why do people generally wear lighter-colored clothes in the summer?
    5. In the can experiment, what kind of energy did the black surface absorb?
    6. How was the heat transferred from the black surface to the thermometer?
    7. Why is it desirable to have a copper-bottomed tea kettle?
    8. Why would you not want a copper handle on a frying pan?
    9. What metals conduct heat well?

10. What advantage would there be in having a white car rather than a black car?
11. What advantage might there be to having a lighter-colored roof on a house rather than a darker-colored roof?
12. Why would you prefer to put a hot dog on a stick rather than on a wire to cook the hot dog over a campfire?

 NSES **Concepts and Principles**

Activity 8 addresses these fundamental concepts and principles related to the *Science Standards*:

- Heat moves in predictable ways, flowing from warmer objects to cooler ones, until both reach the same temperature (5–8).

8. WHAT AFFECTS THE FINAL TEMPERATURE OF A WATER MIXTURE? (3–6)

Materials

Styrofoam cups (at least 250 ml)
Graduated cylinder or measuring cup
Thermometers
Stirring spoon

ENGAGE: ASK A QUESTION ABOUT OBJECTS, ORGANISMS, OR EVENTS IN THE ENVIRONMENT.

a. Ask: *What happens to the temperature of bath water when you add hot water to cold water? Does the amount of hot water and cold water matter? How could you predict the new temperature when hot and cold water are mixed?*

EXPLORE: PLAN AND CONDUCT SIMPLE INVESTIGATIONS TO COLLECT RELEVANT DATA.

b. Tell students to plan an investigation to determine the final temperature when hot and cold water are mixed. Students could plan and conduct the following activity in cooperative groups:
1. Pour the following volumes of water at the indicated temperatures into separate Styrofoam cups:
   · 100 ml of hot water
   · 100 ml of cold water
   · 50 ml of hot water
   · 50 ml of cold water
   · 150 ml of hot water
   · 150 ml of cold water
2. Measure and record the temperature of the 100 ml samples of water in a copy of the prepared data table (see illustration). If possible, make all temperature measurements in degrees Celsius.
3. In a third cup, carefully mix and stir the two 100 ml samples of water.
4. When the temperature of the mixture stops changing, measure and record the final temperature.
5. Repeat steps 2, 3, and 4 for the following mixtures:
   · 150 ml of hot water and 50 ml of cold water
   · 150 ml of cold water and 50 ml of warm water

TEMPERATURE OF WATER MIXTURES

	Amount of Water in Each Container	Initial Temperature of Water	Final Temperature of Mixture
Mixture 1	100 ml		
	100 ml		
Mixture 2	150 ml		
	50 ml		
Mixture 3	50 ml		
	150 ml		
Mystery Mixture			Predicted _____ Measured _____

c. Instruct cooperative group recorders to record their data on the class master data table.

EXPLAIN: USE DATA TO GENERATE INTERPRETATIONS, INCLUDING DESCRIPTIONS, CLASSIFICATIONS, AND EXPLANATIONS.

d. Ask: *Do you see a pattern to your final temperature for different mixtures?* Lead students to notice that if the volumes of two samples of water are the same, the final temperature will be halfway between the two initial temperatures. If the volumes of the two samples are different, the final temperature will be nearer the initial temperature of the larger sample.

ELABORATE: EXTEND CONCEPTS, PRINCIPLES, AND STRATEGIES TO NEW SITUATIONS AND QUESTIONS.

e. Tell students you are going to give them a new water mixing problem, but they will need to predict the final temperature before they mix the water samples and take data.

f. Prepare a large container of cold water at near freezing temperature (but with no ice). Prepare another large container of water at room temperature. Give materials managers a cup of cold water and a cup of room temperature water.

g. Instruct groups they are going to mix 175 ml of cold water with 50 ml of warm water. Ask groups to make a prediction of the final temperature and then to conduct the investigation. Predictions do not need to be exact. For example, a group may just predict that the final temperature will be halfway between the temperatures of the two samples or very near the temperature of the larger sample.

h. Instruct recorders to record the predicted and final temperatures of their mixtures on a class chart. Invite students to present and discuss their predictions, the basis of the predictions, and the final temperatures obtained.

Explain that the final temperature of a mixture depends on both the initial temperatures and amounts of the samples. When a large volume of water is mixed with a smaller volume of water, the final temperature will be nearer the initial temperature of the large volume. There are actually mathematical ratios here that can be dealt with at upper grades.

How could you help
children understand
what scientists do?

i. Ask: *What have you done in this investigation that is like what scientists do?*

Lead students to understand that they have formulated a problem, planned and conducted an investigation, used a thermometer and graduated cylinder to collect data, recorded data in a table, interpreted the data and formed an explanation for experimental results, and tested the explanations through a prediction. These are some of the things scientists do.

V. LIGHT

▶ *Science Background*

Visible light is a form of energy. Along with gamma rays, X-rays, microwaves, and radio waves, light is one of the many forms of electromagnetic radiation. Light is produced by the actions of electrons. Light can be modeled as a wave motion, something like water waves on a still surface. In empty space, light travels at a speed of 186,000 miles per second.

Because our eyes are light detectors, light is an especially important part of our lives, enabling us to see the world around us. We see objects when light that is either emitted or reflected from an object reaches our eyes. Further, light is the energy source for photosynthesis and the growth of plants which sustain both human and animal life. Thus, light is essential for life.

A. SOURCES AND RECEIVERS OF LIGHT

NSES   Science Standards

All students should develop an understanding of

• light, heat, electricity, and magnetism (K–4).

**Objectives for
Students**

1. Distinguish between sources and reflectors of light.
2. Identify and describe human-constructed sources of light (e.g., light bulbs) and natural sources of light (e.g., the sun).
3. Explain that our eyes are detectors of light and that we can "see" an object only if light is emitted or reflected from the object.
4. Identify materials that are transparent, translucent, and opaque, and explain what we "see" when each of these materials is placed over an object.

NSES   Concepts and Principles

Activities 1 and 2 address these fundamental concepts and principles related to the *Science Standards:*

• Light interacts with matter by transmission (including refraction), absorption, or scattering (including reflection) (5–8).
• To see an object, light from that object—emitted by or scattered from it—must enter the eye (5–8).

1. HOW DO WE SEE THINGS? (1–5)

Materials
Flashlights
Shoe box

Safety Precautions

As they study light, impress on students the importance of protecting their eyes at all times. Students should never look directly into the sun or any other bright light source. Also, they should never look into a laser light source nor shine a laser toward someone else.

ENGAGE: ASK A QUESTION ABOUT OBJECTS, ORGANISMS, OR EVENTS IN THE ENVIRONMENT.

a. Darken the room and write this statement on the chalkboard: "We cannot see without light." Tell students to read what you have written. Illuminate the sentence with a flashlight and tell students to read it. Ask: *How does light enable us to see things?*

EXPLORE: PLAN AND CONDUCT SIMPLE INVESTIGATIONS TO COLLECT RELEVANT DATA.

b. Cut two small holes in a shoe box, one for students to look into the box and the other to illuminate the inside of the box with a flashlight. Place an object in the box, cover the flashlight hole, and put the top on the box. Tell students to look into the box and describe the object. Illuminate the object with the flashlight and tell students to describe the object again.

c. Build a small electric circuit consisting of a bulb in a bulb holder, a battery in a battery holder, a switch, and wires. Place the circuit inside another shoe box with only one hole cut in the end of it. Arrange the circuit so the switch is outside the box and place the top on the box. Tell students to look into the box and describe the objects in it. Tell them to activate the switch and describe the objects again.

EXPLAIN: USE DATA TO GENERATE INTERPRETATIONS, INCLUDING DESCRIPTIONS, CLASSIFICATIONS, PREDICTIONS, AND EXPLANATIONS.

d. Ask: *How did light enable you to see the statement on the chalkboard? How did the flashlight enable you to see the object in the shoe box?* (Lead students to understand that we see things only when light from them reaches our eyes. Light from the flashlight reflected from the object to our eyes, enabling us to see it.) *Why were you able to see the bulb in the box?* (Lead students to apply the idea that we see things only when light from them reaches our eyes. Light coming from the bulb reached our eyes and enabled us to see it. Explain that there are natural sources of light, such as a flame, and artificial, human-constructed sources of light, such as the light bulb.) *Why are you able to see the sun? Why are you able to see the moon? What objects/things can you see in the classroom or outside now? What enables you to see these objects? Which sources of light are natural and which are artificial?* Fill in a chart like the one illustrated for the different rooms in your house.

▶ *Teaching Background*

Emphasize that we can see things only if light emitted or reflected from them reaches our eyes. The eye is a receiver of light, like the ear is a receiver of sound.

Room	Light source	Artificial or natural light

2. WHY CAN WE SEE CLEARLY THROUGH SOME MATERIALS AND NOT OTHERS? (K–2)

Materials

Transparent materials (clear plastic wrap, clear glass)
Translucent materials (wax paper, cloudy plastic)
Opaque materials (paper, cardboard)

ENGAGE: ASK A QUESTION ABOUT OBJECTS, ORGANISMS, OR EVENTS IN THE ENVIRONMENT.

a. Allow students to examine a small object placed underneath a sheet of wax paper or a piece of cloudy plastic. Ask: *What do you see? Why is the object not easily seen?*

EXPLORE: PLAN AND CONDUCT SIMPLE INVESTIGATIONS TO COLLECT RELEVANT DATA.

b. Give each group of students some samples of transparent, translucent, and opaque materials. Ask the students to place one kind of material at a time over a printed page. For each material, have students fill in a chart with one of these choices: (1) can see through it easily; (2) can see through it but not very clearly; (3) cannot see through it.

Transparent   Translucent   Opaque

EXPLAIN: USE DATA TO GENERATE INTERPRETATIONS, INCLUDING DESCRIPTIONS, CLASSIFICATIONS, PREDICTIONS, AND EXPLANATIONS.

c. Ask: *How does light interact with each of the different materials you used in the investigation?* Guide students to understand that light is transmitted through transparent media, such as air, water, and glass. Translucent objects transmit some light, but absorb some of the light energy. Opaque objects absorb all of the light energy striking them. We see things only if light reflected from them or passing through them strikes our eyes. A transparent object transmits light to our eyes; translucent objects transmit only a portion of the light from an object to our eyes; opaque objects absorb light so that none of the light is transmitted to our eyes.

B. HOW LIGHT TRAVELS

▶ *Science Background*

Light travels in straight lines until it is absorbed, reflected, or refracted by an object. Unlike sound, light cannot ordinarily bend around corners.

NSES   Science Standards

All students should develop an understanding of

• light, heat, electricity, and magnetism (K–4).

Objectives for Students

1. Demonstrate that light travels in straight lines unless it is absorbed, refracted, or reflected by an object.
2. Compare the speed of light to the speed of sound.

NSES   Concepts and Principles

Activities 1 and 2 address these fundamental concepts and principles related to the *Science Standards*:

• Light travels in straight lines until it strikes an object (K–4).

....

1. WHAT TYPE OF PATH DOES LIGHT TAKE AS IT TRAVELS? (1–4)

Materials

Flashlight or projector
Index cards
Hole puncher or pointed object (pencil)
Modeling clay
Wax paper

ENGAGE: ASK A QUESTION ABOUT OBJECTS, ORGANISMS, OR EVENTS IN THE ENVIRONMENT.

a. Tell a child to stand behind a barrier or just outside the classroom so that she can be heard but not seen. Instruct the child to speak softly. Ask: *Can you hear her talking? Can you see her? Why can you hear someone talking when the person is out of sight?*

EXPLORE: PLAN AND CONDUCT SIMPLE INVESTIGATIONS TO COLLECT RELEVANT DATA.

b. Holding three or four index cards together, punch a 1/4 inch (7 mm) hole in the center of each card. Stand each card up in a lump of modeling clay. Instruct students to space the cards about 30 cm apart and to arrange them in such a way that light from a flashlight passes through the center hole in each of the cards.

EXPLAIN: USE DATA
TO GENERATE
INTERPRETATIONS,
INCLUDING DESCRIPTIONS,
CLASSIFICATIONS,
PREDICTIONS, AND
EXPLANATIONS.

c. Ask: *What must you do to the holes in the index cards if light is to pass through them? Do you think that light travels along a straight or curved pathway? What is your evidence, or why do you think so? Can light travel around an opaque object? Can sound travel around an opaque object? How can you test your inference about how sound travels?*

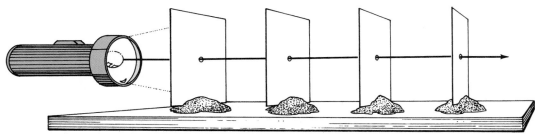

2. HOW ARE SHADOWS FORMED? (1–4)

ENGAGE: ASK A
QUESTION ABOUT OBJECTS,
ORGANISMS, OR EVENTS IN
THE ENVIRONMENT.

a. Have students observe their own shadows. Tell students to make some change so that their shadows are smaller or larger, lighter or darker. Point out shadows in the room, in the school building, and outside. Ask: *How are shadows formed?*

EXPLORE: PLAN
AND CONDUCT SIMPLE
INVESTIGATIONS TO
COLLECT RELEVANT DATA.

b. Place an object between a light source (flashlight or projector) and a screen (such as a white wall). Let students form shadows on the screen.

c. Have students make puppets from cardboard. Make a screen out of a heavy cardboard frame and wax paper. Place the puppet between the flashlight and the screen. Shine a flashlight on the puppet so that a shadow is formed on the screen as shown in the diagram.

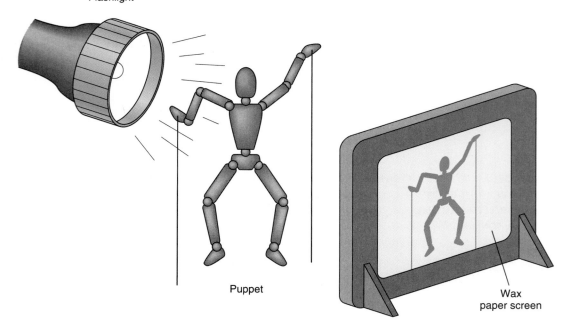

Flashlight

Puppet

Wax
paper screen

EXPLAIN: USE DATA TO GENERATE INTERPRETATIONS, INCLUDING DESCRIPTIONS, CLASSIFICATIONS, PREDICTIONS, AND EXPLANATIONS.

d. Ask: *How are shadows formed? What is the relationship (physical alignment) between the light source, opaque object, and screen when a shadow is formed? What can you do to make a shadow smaller or larger? How do shadows illustrate that light travels in straight lines until it is absorbed by an object?*

ELABORATE: EXTEND CONCEPTS, PRINCIPLES, AND STRATEGIES TO NEW SITUATIONS AND QUESTIONS.

e. Ask: *How is a lunar eclipse related to shadows? What is the light source for a lunar eclipse? What object forms a shadow on the moon?*

▶ *Teaching Background*

Shadows are formed when light from a source strikes the edge of an opaque object, with some light being absorbed and some light moving past the object in a straight line. The object casting the shadow is between the light source and the screen. Shadows can be enlarged by moving the object nearer the light source. Shadows are made smaller when the object is moved farther from the light source.

   When teaching about light and shadows, you may wish to discuss lunar phases and eclipses. Lunar phases are not related to the earth's shadow. Lunar eclipses occur when the sun, earth, and moon are aligned. For a lunar eclipse, the earth blocks some sunlight, and a shadow of the earth falls on all or part of the moon. A solar eclipse also occurs when the sun, earth, and moon are perfectly aligned, but shadows are not involved. During a solar eclipse, all or a portion of the sun appears dark because the moon blocks the light.

C. LIGHT REFRACTION

▶ *Science Background*

Light ordinarily travels in straight lines, but it bends or refracts when it passes at an angle into a clear material, such as glass, plastic, or water. Lenses use the property of refraction to form images of objects. A magnifying lens bends the light coming from an object so that we see the object larger than it actually is. A lens can also be used to form an image of an object on a screen.

NSES **Science Standards**

All students should develop an understanding of

• light, heat, electricity, and magnetism (K–4).

Objectives for Students

1. Describe the refraction or bending of light rays passing through water, clear plastic, or glass.
2. Use knowledge of refraction to explain different light phenomena.
3. Define *magnifying power* and relate it to the curvature of a lens.
4. Define *image* and describe the image of an object formed on a screen.

| **NSES** | **Concepts and Principles** |

Activities 1–3 address these fundamental concepts and principles related to the *Science Standards:*

- Light travels in straight lines until it strikes an object (K–4).
- Light can be reflected by a mirror, refracted by a lens, or absorbed by the object (K–4).

1. WHAT IS REFRACTION? (3–6)

Materials

For the teacher:

- Glass
- Pencil
- Opaque cylindrical container such as a large butter tub
- Coin
- Modeling clay

For each group:

- Flashlight
- Black rubber or plastic comb
- Two cylindrical jars of different diameters

ENGAGE: ASK A QUESTION ABOUT OBJECTS, ORGANISMS, OR EVENTS IN THE ENVIRONMENT.

a. Place a pencil in a glass of water so that half of it is in water and half of it out of water. Ask: *What do you see? Why does the pencil seem distorted?*

EXPLORE: PLAN AND CONDUCT SIMPLE INVESTIGATIONS TO COLLECT RELEVANT DATA.

b. Provide each group with a flashlight, a comb, and two cylindrical jars of very different diameters. Show them how to form rays of light by laying the flashlight on a white poster board and shining the flashlight through the comb. Instruct students to follow these directions:
   1. Fill a jar almost full of water, place it in the path of the rays, and observe what happens.
   2. Repeat the procedure with the other jar.
   3. Record your observations. Include any differences you observed.

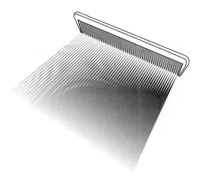

EXPLAIN: USE DATA TO GENERATE INTERPRETATIONS, INCLUDING DESCRIPTIONS, CLASSIFICATIONS, PREDICTIONS, AND EXPLANATIONS.

c. In a large group, invite students to discuss their procedures and observations.

Ask: *What did you observe? What differences did you observe in the effects of the two jars? Which jar, the larger or smaller diameter one, bent the light rays more and caused them to converge nearer to the jar?* Lead students to recognize that the smaller jar, which had the greater curvature of its surface, caused the most bending of the light rays.

Explain that light rays are bent when they pass into and out of a clear material, such as water, plastic, or glass. The bending of light rays is called *refraction*.

Ask: *Why do you think the pencil appeared distorted in the glass of water?* Lead the students to understand that the water bent or refracted the light rays coming from the pencil, causing it to appear distorted.

ELABORATE: EXTEND CONCEPTS, PRINCIPLES, AND STRATEGIES TO NEW SITUATIONS AND QUESTIONS.

d. Invite students to observe the following demonstration and use their knowledge of light to explain what happens.

1. Obtain an opaque, cylindrical container (such as a margarine "tub") that is about 15 cm deep and 15 cm across.
2. Use a small amount of clay or some transparent tape to anchor a coin to the bottom of the container, in the very center.
3. Ask students to stand above the container so that they can see the coin. Then direct them to move back slowly, still looking at the coin, until the coin just disappears from view.
4. With the students fixed in place and the coin just out of sight, gradually pour water into the container, taking care that the coin is not moved by the water.
5. As the water level in the container rises, the coin appears to gradually float into view.

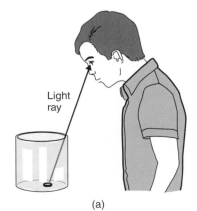
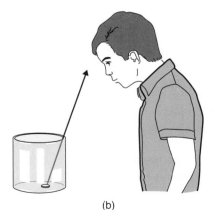
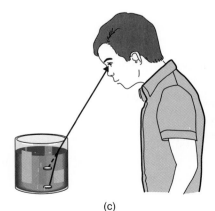

Light ray

(a)　　　　　　　　　　　(b)　　　　　　　　　　　(c)

e. Ask: *What did you see?* (The coin floated into view.) *Why do you think it happened?* Through discussion, lead students to apply their knowledge of light rays to form this explanation.

> Light rays coming from the coin refract or bend when they pass from the water into the air. Because they have been refracted or bent, the light rays from the coin can then reach our eyes, even though we are not in a direct line of sight with it. Since light ordinarily travels in straight lines, we think the light reaching our eyes comes from high in the water, making the coin seem like it floated upward.

2. WHAT IS A MAGNIFIER? HOW DOES IT WORK? (3–6)

Materials

For each group:

- Two or more cylindrical, glass jars or jugs of different diameters
- Magnifying lenses, including at least two lenses of different magnifying power
- Clear plastic sheets, such as transparency sheets (sandwich bags might be substituted)
- Dropper

ENGAGE: ASK A QUESTION ABOUT OBJECTS, ORGANISMS, OR EVENTS IN THE ENVIRONMENT.

a. Obtain two cylindrical, glass jars of different diameters. Fill them with water within a few centimeters of the top. Allow students to look through each jar of water at some small writing. You can place the jars on a tray and carry them around the room for all students to see. Ask: *What do you see? Do you see the same thing through each jar? Which jar makes things appear larger? Why do you think the jars of water magnify? What other things will magnify?*

EXPLORE: PLAN AND CONDUCT SIMPLE INVESTIGATIONS TO COLLECT RELEVANT DATA.

b. Arrange students in small groups of three or four. Provide each group a clear plastic sheet, a dropper, and a small container of water. Tell students to place different-sized drops of water on the plastic sheet and to look through the drops at some very small writing. Ask: *What do you see through drops of different sizes? Do different-sized drops magnify differently?* (*Note:* Very small drops provide greater magnification.) Tell students to record their observations on a record sheet or in their science journals.

c. Provide at least two magnifiers of different magnifying power to each group. If necessary, show students how to use the magnifiers. Lead students to examine writing and different objects through each of the magnifying lenses. Lead students to compare the magnifying lenses. Ask: *How are your magnifying lenses different? What makes lenses have different magnifying power?*

EXPLAIN: USE DATA TO GENERATE INTERPRETATIONS, INCLUDING DESCRIPTIONS, CLASSIFICATIONS, PREDICTIONS, AND EXPLANATIONS.

d. Invite students to share their observations.

Explain that what your students see through a lens is called an *image*. Lenses fool our eyes; we think the light comes from the image, when it really comes from the object and only appears to come from the image. The lens bends or *refracts* the light, making it appear to come from the image.

Define the *magnifying power* of a lens as the number of times bigger it can make an object appear or how many times bigger the image is than the object. Ask: *Which jar had a greater magnifying power?* (The smaller one.) *Which water drop had a greater magnifying power?* (The smaller one.) *Why do you think this is so?* Guide students to understand that the smaller jar and smaller water drops have a greater curvature. Light is refracted or bent more when the surface at which refraction is occurring is curved more. The magnifying power of a magnifier depends on how much the surface of the magnifier is curved. The greater the curvature, the greater the magnifying power.

e. Ask: *Which magnifying lens had a greater magnifying power? Did that lens have a greater curvature?* If lenses are of the same diameter, the lens with greater curvature will be the one that is thicker in the middle.

ELABORATE: EXTEND CONCEPTS, PRINCIPLES, AND STRATEGIES TO NEW SITUATIONS AND QUESTIONS.

f. Challenge students to measure the magnifying power of each of their magnifying lenses. This might be done by examining a millimeter scale through a lens to determine the number of times bigger an image appears than the object.[3]

3. WHAT DO LENSES DO IN CAMERAS? (3–6)

Materials

For the class:

- Lamp with 40 to 75 watt bulb

For each group:

- At least two lenses of different magnifying power

ENGAGE: ASK A QUESTION ABOUT OBJECTS, ORGANISMS, OR EVENTS IN THE ENVIRONMENT.

a. Ask: *Where have you seen lenses? What things have lenses in them?* List students' answers on the board. Students might suggest eyeglasses, contact lens, the eye, microscopes, telescopes, projectors, binoculars, cameras, and other instruments.

Ask: *What do lenses do in cameras? How do they work?*

EXPLORE: PLAN AND CONDUCT SIMPLE INVESTIGATIONS TO COLLECT RELEVANT DATA.

b. Arrange students in groups. Provide two lenses of different magnifying power to each group. Show students how to support a lens vertically by taping it to the bottom of a Styrofoam cup. Remove the shade from the lamp and place the lamp in the room so that all groups have an unobstructed view of it.

---

[3]Adapted and modified from *More than Magnifiers*, one of more than 75 teacher's guides in the Great Explorations in Math and Science (GEMS) series, available from the Lawrence Hall of Science, University of California at Berkeley. For more information, visit their website at www.lhsgems.org.

Provide these instructions to students:

1. Tape each of the two lenses to the bottom of cups. Label the cups and lenses A and B.
2. Place lens A, supported by a cup, on the table so that it faces the lamp.
3. Fold a white sheet of paper along two opposite edges so it will stand up.
4. Place the sheet of paper behind the lens and move it back and forth until you see an image of the lamp on the paper.

5. Measure and record the distance from the lens to the image on the paper.
6. Ask: *Is the image inverted or right side up?* (Inverted.) *Is the image of the lamp larger or smaller than the lamp itself?* (Smaller.) Record your answers on a record sheet or in your science journal.
7. Repeat the procedures for lens B. Is the image formed on the paper inverted or right side up? Is the image larger or smaller than the lamp?
8. Which lens, A or B, formed a larger image? For which lens, A or B, was the lens closer to the paper screen?

EXPLAIN: USE DATA TO GENERATE INTERPRETATIONS, INCLUDING DESCRIPTIONS, CLASSIFICATIONS, PREDICTIONS, AND EXPLANATIONS.

c. In a large group, invite students to discuss their procedures and observations.

Ask: *Why do you think the images formed of the lamp were inverted?* Draw the following diagram to show how light rays from the top of the lamp are bent or refracted by the lens and converge so that the lamp is upside down.

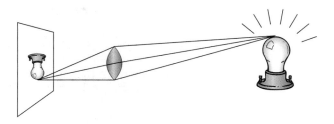

ELABORATE: EXTEND CONCEPTS, PRINCIPLES, AND STRATEGIES TO NEW SITUATIONS AND QUESTIONS.

d. Ask: *How are lenses used in cameras? What do the lenses do? Do you think the images formed in cameras are right side up or upside down? Are they larger or smaller than the object forming the image?*

Draw on the board the illustration of a camera and lens showing an image formed on a film. Explain that some of the light coming from the bulb strikes the lens. The light is bent and converges on the film so that the image is small and upside down. The film is coated with a light-sensitive chemical. When the film is developed, the image of the bulb is clearly seen.[4]

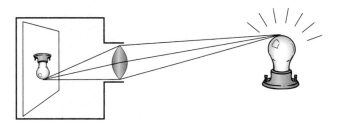

D. LIGHT REFLECTION

▶ *Science Background*

Reflection, the bouncing of light rays, follows a pattern that can be discovered through investigations. Light reflects from a smooth, plane surface in such a way that the angle at which it strikes the surface is equal to the angle at which it reflects from the surface. Mirrors are excellent examples of reflecting surfaces. As a consequence of reflection, images can be seen in mirrors. In a flat, plane mirror, an image is symmetric with the object forming the image, but the image is reversed.

[4]Adapted and modified from *More than Magnifiers*, one of more than 75 teacher's guides in the Great Explorations in Math and Science (GEMS) series, available from the Lawrence Hall of Science, University of California at Berkeley. For more information, visit their website at www.lhsgems.org.

NSES Science Standards

All students should develop an understanding of

- light, heat, electricity, and magnetism (K–4).

Objectives for Students

1. Describe the reflection of light off reflecting surfaces.
2. Describe images in mirrors as symmetric with objects, but reversed.
3. State and apply the rule that an image is formed deep within mirrors at a distance equal to the distance of the object in front of a mirror.

NSES Concepts and Principles

Activities 1–3 address these fundamental concepts and principles related to the *Science Standards*:

- Light travels in straight lines until it strikes an object (K–4).
- Light can be reflected by a mirror, refracted by a lens, or absorbed by the object (K–4).

1. WHAT ARE IMAGES IN MIRRORS LIKE? WHAT IS MEANT BY MIRROR SYMMETRY? (1–4)

Materials

Mirrors
Pictures of butterflies, flowers, and other things that might show symmetry

ENGAGE: ASK A QUESTION ABOUT OBJECTS, ORGANISMS, OR EVENTS IN THE ENVIRONMENT.

a. Ask: *What does the image in a mirror look like? Is your face reversed in a mirror? Is your face symmetric? Is the left side of your face identical to the right side? Is a butterfly symmetric? Is the left side of a butterfly like the right side? What letters of the alphabet are symmetric?*

EXPLORE: PLAN AND CONDUCT SIMPLE INVESTIGATIONS TO COLLECT RELEVANT DATA.

b. Allow children to examine their own images in mirrors. Show children how to use a mirror to explore the symmetry of different objects and patterns:
1. Find an axis you think divides the object symmetrically.
2. Place a plane mirror along that axis.
3. Look at the image of one-half of the object in the mirror and compare it with the other half of the object.

c. Provide students an activity sheet with all of the letters of the alphabet displayed in block lettering. Tell students to use a mirror to identify all of the axes of symmetry for each letter. For example, ask: *Does the letter* **A** *have an axis of symmetry? How many axes of symmetry can you find for an* **H**?

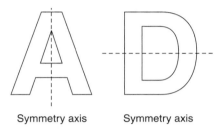

Symmetry axis   Symmetry axis

EXPLAIN: USE DATA TO GENERATE INTERPRETATIONS, INCLUDING DESCRIPTIONS, CLASSIFICATIONS, PREDICTIONS, AND EXPLANATIONS.

d. Ask: *What does the mirror image of your face look like?* Lead students to realize that the image of an object is reversed in a mirror. Ask: *What is meant by symmetry? Where is the axis of symmetry for a butterfly? Does the left side of the butterfly differ from the right side? What letters of the alphabet show symmetry?* Discuss with the students the axis or axes of symmetry of each letter of the alphabet.

2. HOW DOES LIGHT REFLECT FROM A MIRROR? (3–6)

Materials

Flashlight
Cardboard
Transparent tape
Mirrors

Preparation

Make a light-ray source by obtaining a stiff cardboard shield about the diameter of a flashlight, cutting a slit in the shield, and attaching the shield over the lens of a strong flashlight with transparent tape. A light ray is formed when light from the flashlight passes through the slit.

ENGAGE: ASK A QUESTION ABOUT OBJECTS, ORGANISMS, OR EVENTS IN THE ENVIRONMENT.

a. Ask: *Is there a pattern in the way light reflects from a mirror?*
b. Lay the flashlight source on a white poster board so you can see the light ray on the board. Attach a small, plane mirror to a block of wood with a rubber band. Put the mirror in the path of light. Tell children to mark a spot on the poster board and to orient the mirror so that the reflected ray hits the spot. Instruct the students to initially

use trial and error to align the mirror so that the reflected light ray hits the desired spot. Gradually, the students should make and test predictions of how the mirror should be aligned to direct the reflected light ray to the spot.

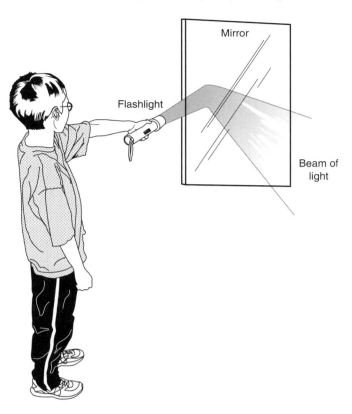

EXPLAIN: USE DATA TO GENERATE INTERPRETATIONS, INCLUDING DESCRIPTIONS, CLASSIFICATIONS, PREDICTIONS, AND EXPLANATIONS.

c. Ask: *How does light reflect from a mirror? What pattern did you detect about how light reflects? How did you know how to align a mirror to make a reflected light ray hit a desired spot?* Lead students to understand that the angle formed between a reflected light ray and a mirror is the same as the angle between the incident light ray and the mirror.

3. WHERE ARE THE IMAGES FORMED IN REFLECTING SURFACES? (4–6)

Materials

Light sources
Empty glass aquarium

ENGAGE: ASK A QUESTION ABOUT OBJECTS, ORGANISMS, OR EVENTS IN THE ENVIRONMENT.

a. Place a candle upright in an aluminum pie pan in front of an empty aquarium. Place a second candle inside the aquarium. Light the first candle. Allow students to stand behind the lit candle and to look into the aquarium. Ask: *What do you see? Do you see an image of the candle and candle flame inside the aquarium? Where is the image?*

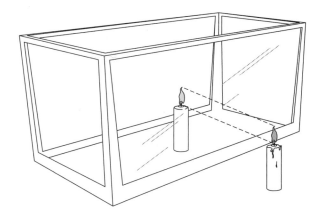

b. Locate a plate glass door within the school. Allow students to explore their own images formed within the door. If students do not come up with this idea, suggest that one person (the image partner) stand on the other side of the door right on top of the image of another person (the object partner). Provide metersticks and ask students to measure, record, and compare the object distance and image distance.

c. Ask: *What did you observe about the image of the candle flame?* (If the candle inside the aquarium is positioned correctly, the image of the flame can be seen right on top of the second candle, so that the second candle appears to be lit.) *What did you observe about your image in the door?* (The image was the same size as the object, but was reversed.) *How did the object distance compare to the image distance?*

E. LIGHT AND COLOR

Color is a response of the human eye to different frequencies of visible light. The color spectrum includes red, orange, yellow, green, blue, indigo, and violet. White is a combination of all colors. An object appears black when all colors are absorbed by it. The color of an object depends on the colors absorbed and reflected. A red object, for instance, will appear red because it reflects mostly red and absorbs other colors of light.

1. WHAT IS WHITE LIGHT? (K–4)

Materials

Prism
Sheet of heavy, white cardboard
Scissors
Felt markers or crayons
String

ENGAGE: ASK A
QUESTION ABOUT OBJECTS,
ORGANISMS, OR EVENTS IN
THE ENVIRONMENT.

a. Obtain a prism. Place the prism in the path of a strong beam of light as indicated in the diagram.

Ask: *What do you see? What happened to the white light when it passed through the glass prism? What colors do you see?*

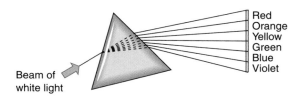

EXPLORE: PLAN AND
CONDUCT SIMPLE
INVESTIGATIONS TO
COLLECT RELEVANT DATA.

b. Challenge students to construct color wheels by following these directions:
   1. Cut out a circle about 10 cm in diameter from stiff cardboard.
   2. Divide the circle into three pie-shaped sections.
   3. Use felt markers or crayons to color each section a different color.
   4. Punch two small holes about a centimeter apart in the center of the cardboard circle.
   5. Pass a string about 60 cm long through the two holes; tie the free ends of the string forming a loop.
   6. Hold the loop by the ends and turn the cardboard color wheel many times, twisting the string as you go.
   7. Pull the two ends of the string suddenly and watch the color wheel spin. What do you see? What colors do you observe as the color wheel is spinning?
c. Let different groups color their color wheel sections differently. Have groups compare what they see with different color wheels.

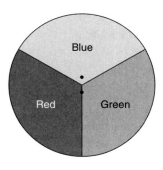

EXPLAIN: USE DATA TO GENERATE INTERPRETATIONS, INCLUDING DESCRIPTIONS, CLASSIFICATIONS, PREDICTIONS, AND EXPLANATIONS.

d. Invite students to report on their procedures and findings related to their color wheels.

Ask: *What did the prism do to the light?* (It separated white light into different colors.) *What did the color wheel do to the light?* (It combined different colors to form a white color.)

Lead students to understand that white light is produced by the combination of several different colors. A prism breaks white light into its constituent parts. A color wheel combines different colors, forming white.

F. A LIGHT CHALLENGE: PINHOLE CAMERA

▶ *Science Background*

A pinhole camera can be used to illustrate what happens in a regular camera. In a pinhole camera, light passes through a small hole in the end of a box and forms an inverted image on a wax paper screen. In a real camera, light is focused by a lens and forms an inverted image on a strip of film.

NSES Science Standards

All students should develop understanding of

- light, heat, electricity, and magnetism (K–4).

Objectives for Students

1. Construct a pinhole camera and demonstrate how it works to form an image.
2. Describe the pathway of light as it passes through a hole in the end of a pinhole camera and forms an inverted image on a wax paper screen in the camera.

NSES Concepts and Principles

Activity I addresses these fundamental concepts and principles related to the *Science Standards*:

- Light travels in straight lines until it strikes an object (K–4).

1. HOW CAN YOU MAKE A PINHOLE CAMERA? (3–6)

ENGAGE: ASK A QUESTION ABOUT OBJECTS, ORGANISMS, OR EVENTS IN THE ENVIRONMENT.

a. Ask: *How does a camera work? How can you make a type of camera that illustrates how a camera works? How does a camera use light?*

EXPLORE: PLAN AND CONDUCT SIMPLE INVESTIGATIONS TO COLLECT RELEVANT DATA.

b. Follow these directions to construct a pinhole camera. Students might construct and demonstrate their own pinhole cameras, or the teacher might make one and allow students to use it.
   1. Obtain a shoe box.

2. Cut a hole about 4 cm square in the end of the box. Cover the hole with a larger square of aluminum foil using transparent tape. Using a sharpened pencil, punch a small, clean hole in the center of the aluminum foil.
3. Cut a flap about 3 cm by 5 cm in the other end of the box to use as a window to see into the box.
4. Cut a heavy piece of corrugated cardboard the same size as the end of the box to use as a screen. Cut a rectangular hole in the cardboard, leaving about 2 cm on each side. Tape wax paper over the hole to form a screen.
5. Attach the screen to a small block of wood so that it can stand upright inside the box.
6. Stand the screen upright in the box. Place the lid securely on the box.
7. Point the pinhole in the aluminum foil at a bright object such as a lamp bulb. Look at the screen through the window in the box. Describe and record what you see on the screen. What is the size of the image? Is the image upright or inverted?
8. Point the pinhole camera at other things and report what you see. Record your observations on a record sheet or in your science journal.

EXPLAIN: USE DATA TO GENERATE INTERPRETATIONS, INCLUDING DESCRIPTIONS, CLASSIFICATIONS, PREDICTIONS, AND EXPLANATIONS.

Ask: *What did you see on the pinhole camera screen when you looked at the lamp? Did you see an image of the bulb? How large was the image compared to the bulb? Was the image upright or inverted? How was the image formed in the pinhole camera? How is a pinhole camera like a real camera?*

Use the following diagram to help students understand how the image is formed on the screen in a pinhole camera. Light from the top of the bulb travels in a straight line, passes through the pinhole, and strikes the screen, forming an inverted image.

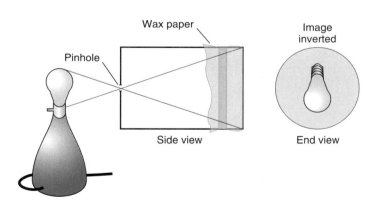

VI. MAGNETISM

▶ *Science Background*

The *National Science Education Standards* emphasize that, through the study of its history and nature, students should begin to understand science as a human endeavor. The study of magnetism is a very good place for students to examine the long history of science and technology. As you guide students in learning about magnetism, provide them with interesting information about the history of the topic and make appropriate biographies and other books and resources available to them.

William Gilbert's book on magnetism is readily available as part of Volume 28 of the Great Books Series published by the Encyclopedia Britannica and found in many libraries.

More than 2,000 years ago, people knew that bits of a certain kind of rock, today called magnetite, would stick to iron objects. It was later discovered that when a piece of magnetite was placed on a cork floating in water, the cork would turn until the magnetite lined up in a north-south direction (as determined from observations of the North Star). Around a thousand years ago, this phenomenon was applied in the development of the magnetic compass. Because the magnetite could *lead* a person by indicating directions, it came to be known as a *lodestone (loadstone)* or *leading stone*.

Four hundred years ago, William Gilbert, an English physician, wrote a book titled *On the Loadstone and Magnetic Bodies*. It was the first important work in physical science published in England. Gilbert's book provides the first written account of numerous experiments on magnetism, experiments which can be readily carried out in elementary and middle school science today. Gilbert argued for a new method of knowing, dedicating his book to those "ingenuous minds, who not only in books, but in things themselves look for knowledge."

In the activities in this section, we will explore the following concepts, most of which were also set out by William Gilbert:

Some of the concepts and activities in this section are adapted from a FOSS (Full Option Science System) grade 3–4 unit on *Magnetism and Electricity*.

- Objects containing iron stick to a magnet.
- Magnets come in many sizes and shapes.
- Magnetism can occur naturally, or it can be induced in objects containing iron.
- All magnets, regardless of their size or shape, have two places, called poles, where magnetic forces are greatest.
- When two magnets are brought together, like poles repel (push one another apart), while unlike poles attract (pull one another together).
- The magnetic field around a magnet can be mapped by a compass or iron filings. The greater the distance from the pole of a magnet, the less the magnetic force.
- Magnetic forces act through most materials, although the magnetic interaction decreases with the thickness of the materials.
- The earth acts like a large bar magnet is buried within it, with an S-pole near the north geographic pole and an N-pole near the south geographic pole.
- The earth's magnetic poles are today almost a thousand miles from the geographic poles. (Gilbert assumed, erroneously, that the magnetic poles and geographic poles coincided.)

A. MAGNETS AND MAGNETIC MATERIALS

NSES Science Standards

All students should develop an understanding of

- light, heat, electricity, and magnetism (K–4).

Objectives for Students

1. Identify materials that interact with magnets.
2. State that magnets come in many sizes and shapes.
3. Demonstrate that only objects containing iron stick to magnets.
4. Demonstrate that magnetism will act through most materials.

NSES	**Concepts and Principles**

Activities 1 and 2 address these fundamental concepts and principles related to the *Science Standards* and *Benchmarks for Science Literacy*:

- Magnets attract each other and certain kinds of other materials (K–4).
- Magnets can be used to make things move without touching them (K–2).

1. HOW DOES A MAGNET INTERACT WITH DIFFERENT OBJECTS? (1–4)

Materials

For each group:

- Assortment of magnets, including bar magnets, U-shaped magnets, ring magnets, disc magnets, and other magnets
- Bag of assorted magnetic materials (objects containing iron, such as paper clips and most screws and nails) and nonmagnetic materials (such as wood, plastic, and paper objects, and non-iron metallic objects, such as aluminum nails, most soda cans, and brass fasteners)

Safety Precautions

- Keep computer disks, audio- and videocassettes, and credit cards away from magnets, as magnets can destroy information on them. Also, keep magnets away from computer and television screens and antique watches, as magnetism can damage them.
- Magnets must be treated with care so as not to destroy their magnetic effects. Magnets can be destroyed by dropping them, extreme heat, or storing two magnets of the same type together.

ENGAGE: ASK A QUESTION ABOUT OBJECTS, ORGANISMS, OR EVENTS IN THE ENVIRONMENT.

a. Give each student a magnet. Without pointing out what it is or calling it a magnet, tell students to find out how the object interacts with the things within reach of their seats. Explain that when things interact, they do something to one another. Many possible interactions may be observed, but the key one is that some objects stick to a magnet. Provide the term *magnet* as the name of the object the students have investigated.

Ask: *What other magnets have you seen or used? What were their shapes? What were they used for?*

   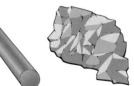

| Bar | V-shaped | U-shaped | Horseshoe | Cylindrical | Lodestone | Doughnut-shaped |

EXPLORE: PLAN AND CONDUCT SIMPLE INVESTIGATIONS TO COLLECT RELEVANT DATA.

b. Ask: *What kinds of things will stick to magnets?*

Give each small group of students a bag of assorted magnetic and nonmagnetic materials. Instruct students to sort the objects into two piles, according to which objects they predict will stick to a magnet and which will not. When groups have made their predictions, give them magnets and ask them to test each object.

EXPLAIN: USE DATA
TO GENERATE
INTERPRETATIONS,
INCLUDING DESCRIPTIONS,
CLASSIFICATIONS, AND
EXPLANATIONS.

c. Ask: *How accurate were your predictions? Were you surprised by any objects you tested?* (Students might mention the aluminum nail or the brass fastener.) *Are there any metal objects in the things-that-don't-stick pile? What do you think is the difference between the metal objects in the will stick and won't stick piles?*

▶ *Teaching Background*

Iron is the only common kind of metal that magnets stick to. Magnets will not stick to such metals as aluminum, copper, and brass. Magnets stick to steel because steel is mostly iron.

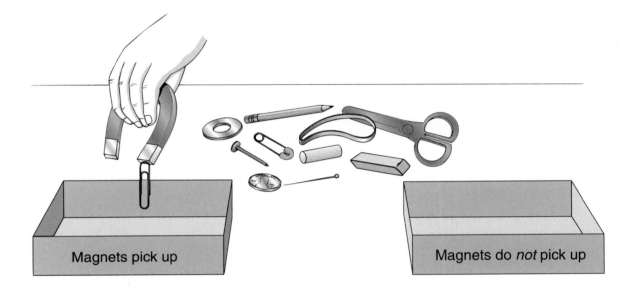

Magnets pick up

Magnets do *not* pick up

ELABORATE: EXTEND
CONCEPTS, PRINCIPLES,
AND STRATEGIES TO NEW
PROBLEMS AND
QUESTIONS.

d. Ask students to explore the room to determine which objects interact with magnets. Place "NO MAGNETS HERE!!" signs on computers, computer and television screens, computer disks, and audio- and videocassettes. Caution students not to bring magnets near these objects, because magnets can damage them.

e. Ask: *Which objects interacted with the magnet? Which objects in the room contain iron? What is your evidence? Did some objects, such as painted objects, turn out to contain iron when you thought they would not?*

2. CAN MAGNETS INTERACT WITH OBJECTS THROUGH DIFFERENT MATERIALS? (1–4)

Materials

Magnets
Paper clips

ENGAGE: ASK A
QUESTION ABOUT OBJECTS,
ORGANISMS, OR EVENTS IN
THE ENVIRONMENT.

a. Ask: *Will magnets work through books and other materials?*

EXPLORE: PLAN AND CONDUCT SIMPLE INVESTIGATIONS TO COLLECT RELEVANT DATA.

b. Ask students to investigate if a magnet will attract a paper clip through different materials. Students should try a sheet of paper, cardboard, plastic tumblers, glass jars, aluminum foil, a tin can, and a sheet of steel, such as the walls of a filing cabinet.

EXPLAIN: USE DATA TO GENERATE INTERPRETATIONS, INCLUDING DESCRIPTIONS, CLASSIFICATIONS, AND EXPLANATIONS.

c. Ask: *What kinds of things did you find that magnetic forces act through?*

ELABORATE: EXTEND CONCEPTS, PRINCIPLES, AND STRATEGIES TO NEW PROBLEMS AND QUESTIONS.

d. Challenge students to investigate how many pages of a book magnets can act through.

▶ *Teaching Background*

Magnetic forces act through most materials, although the magnetic interaction decreases with the thickness of the materials.

B. MAGNETIC INTERACTIONS

NSES Science Standards

All students should develop an understanding of

• light, heat, electricity, and magnetism (K–4).

Objectives for Students

1. Define the terms *force*, *attract*, and *repel* and apply them to the interactions between two magnets.
2. Demonstrate procedures for mapping magnetic fields.
3. State in their own words the meanings of the terms *pole*, *north-seeking* or *north pole*, and *south-seeking* or *south pole*.
4. Demonstrate a procedure for identifying the north and south poles of magnets.
5. State and demonstrate that like poles of magnets repel and unlike poles attract.

NSES Concepts and Principles

Activities 1–5 address these fundamental concepts and principles related to the *Science Standards* and *Benchmarks for Science Literacy*:

• Magnets attract each other and certain kinds of other materials (K–4).
• Magnets can be used to make things move without touching them (*Benchmarks*, K–2).

1. WHAT HAPPENS WHEN TWO MAGNETS INTERACT? (2–4)

Materials

For each group:

* Three or four ring magnets

ENGAGE: ASK A QUESTION ABOUT OBJECTS, ORGANISMS, OR EVENTS IN THE ENVIRONMENT.

a. Ask: *How do two magnets interact with each other?*

EXPLORE: PLAN AND CONDUCT SIMPLE INVESTIGATIONS TO COLLECT RELEVANT DATA.

b. Give each pair or small group of students three or four ring-shaped magnets. Ask the students to find out what happens when magnets interact. Allow time for exploration. If necessary, challenge students to try
* using one magnet to move another magnet without the two magnets touching; and
* placing several ring magnets over a pencil in different ways to see what happens.

EXPLAIN: USE DATA TO GENERATE INTERPRETATIONS, INCLUDING DESCRIPTIONS, CLASSIFICATIONS, PREDICTIONS, AND EXPLANATIONS.

c. Ask: *What did you do to test how the magnets interact? What did you find out about how the two magnets interact?* Building on the children's activities, use discussion and expository teaching to help them understand the terms *attract*, *repel*, and *force* to describe magnetic interactions.
* When two magnets or a magnet and an object come together, we say they attract.
* When two magnets push apart, we say they repel.
* A force is a push or a pull. We can see some forces, such as when you push someone in a swing. Some forces, such as magnetic forces, are invisible and act without direct contact between objects.
* Magnets can attract or repel each other. When two magnets come together, there is a force of attraction. When two magnets push apart, there is a force of repulsion.

2. HOW DO THE ENDS (POLES) OF TWO MAGNETS INTERACT WITH EACH OTHER? (2–6)

Materials

Bar magnets
Masking tape

ENGAGE: ASK A QUESTION ABOUT OBJECTS, ORGANISMS, OR EVENTS IN THE ENVIRONMENT.

a. Place masking tape over the ends of bar magnets so the N-pole and S-pole designations are obscured. Provide each group with three identical bar magnets with taped ends. Ask: *Can you find a way to determine which ends of the magnets are the same?*

EXPLORE: PLAN AND CONDUCT SIMPLE INVESTIGATIONS TO COLLECT RELEVANT DATA.

b. The students should arrive at the idea that if the ends of two magnets are the same, then they interact in the same way with the end of the third magnet. For example, if the ends of two magnets both attract one end of a third magnet, the ends of the first two magnets are the same. Tell children to use red and blue crayons to designate the like ends of the three magnets. (*Note:* Do not introduce the terms *magnetic pole* and *north* and *south magnetic poles* yet. They will be introduced through later investigations.)

EXPLAIN: USE DATA TO GENERATE INTERPRETATIONS, INCLUDING DESCRIPTIONS, CLASSIFICATIONS, AND EXPLANATIONS.

c. Ask: *Now that you know which ends of the magnets are like and which are unlike, can you find a pattern or rule in how like and unlike ends of magnets interact?*
   Through exploration, discussion, and expository teaching of new concepts, make sure that students understand this rule:
   - When two magnets are brought together, like poles repel (push one another apart), while unlike poles attract (pull one another together).

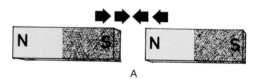

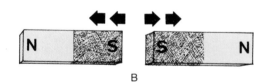

Ask the students to try out their rule with other types of magnets, such as ring-shaped magnets.

3. WHAT ARE MAGNETIC FORCE LINES? (2–6)

Materials

Magnets
Iron filings
Food storage bags

Preparation

Sprinkle iron filings into a large, transparent, food storage bag so that a thin layer covers about three-fourths of the area of one side of each bag. Prepare a bag for each cooperative group of students.

ENGAGE: ASK A QUESTION ABOUT OBJECTS, ORGANISMS, OR EVENTS IN THE ENVIRONMENT.

a. Ask: *How will a magnet interact with the material in this storage bag?*

EXPLORE: PLAN AND CONDUCT SIMPLE INVESTIGATIONS TO COLLECT RELEVANT DATA.

b. Ask students to explore what happens when a magnet touches or is brought near a storage bag. Explain that a magnetic field is the region around a magnet that interacts with other magnets or with magnetic materials. Iron filings can be used to map the magnetic force lines in the field of a magnet. Give students these instructions:

  - Spread an iron filings bag out flat on your desk. Tap the bag lightly so that the iron filings are evenly distributed. Slide a bar magnet under the bag. Tap the bag again so that the iron filings move about. (See the diagram.)
  - Draw a diagram of the magnet's field as shown by the iron filings.

  - Experiment with the field around two magnets placed end to end a few centimeters apart so that the magnets attract. Experiment with the field around two magnets placed end to end a few centimeters apart so that the magnets repel.

EXPLAIN: USE DATA TO GENERATE INTERPRETATIONS, INCLUDING DESCRIPTIONS, CLASSIFICATIONS, AND EXPLANATIONS.

c. Ask: *What did you observe about the magnetic field around a single bar magnet? What did you observe about the magnetic field for attracting bar magnets? What did you observe about the magnetic field for repelling bar magnets?*

d. Explain that all magnets have two regions where the magnetic interaction with other magnets or magnetic materials is strongest. These regions are called *poles*. Point out that the concentration of iron filings is greatest at the poles of the magnets.

4. HOW DOES A MAGNET INTERACT WITH THE EARTH, AND WHAT ARE NORTH-SEEKING AND SOUTH-SEEKING POLES OF A MAGNET? (2–6)

Materials

Ring magnets
String
Compasses

ENGAGE: ASK A
QUESTION ABOUT OBJECTS,
ORGANISMS, OR EVENTS IN
THE ENVIRONMENT.

a. Ask: *How can you use a magnet to tell directions?*

EXPLORE: PLAN AND
CONDUCT SIMPLE
INVESTIGATIONS TO
COLLECT RELEVANT DATA.

b. Suspend a bar magnet by a string from a nonmagnetic support as in the diagram. Note the directions the ends of the bar magnet point. Compare the directions pointed to by the bar magnet and the directions indicated by a compass. How does the bar magnet interact with a second bar magnet? (See the following diagram.)

EXPLAIN: USE DATA
TO GENERATE
INTERPRETATIONS,
INCLUDING DESCRIPTIONS,
CLASSIFICATIONS, AND
EXPLANATIONS.

c. Ask: *What happens to the suspended bar magnet?* Lead students to compare the directions pointed to by the magnet and the directions indicated by the compass.

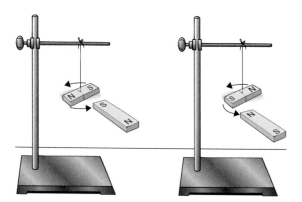

- One end of the magnet points toward the north (as indicated by the compass) and is called a north-seeking pole, or simply a north pole. The other pole of the magnet is a south-seeking pole or south pole.
- Our suspended magnet acts like a compass. The main part of a compass is a small permanent magnet attached to a pivot at the bottom of the compass.
- North and south are defined geographically by the rotational axis of the earth and astronomically by observations of the fixed North Star. The projection onto earth of a line drawn between us and our North Star, Polaris, will be within a degree of true, geographic north.
- The interaction between the earth and magnets can be explained in terms of a model in which the earth acts like it has a large bar magnet buried within it. Contrary to expectations, the earth's S-pole is near the north geographic pole and attracts the N-poles of magnets. The earth's N-pole is near the south geographic pole and attracts the S-poles of magnets.
- The earth's magnetic poles are nearly a thousand miles from the geographic poles. Thus, a compass may point several degrees away from true north.

5. HOW CAN YOU MAKE A MAGNET? (2–6)

Materials

For each group:

- Steel needle
- Bar magnet
- Cork
- Plastic bowl of water

ENGAGE: ASK A QUESTION ABOUT OBJECTS, ORGANISMS, OR EVENTS IN THE ENVIRONMENT.

a. Ask: *How can you make a compass?*

EXPLORE: PLAN AND CONDUCT SIMPLE INVESTIGATIONS TO COLLECT RELEVANT DATA.

b. Obtain a steel needle, a magnet, a cork (substitute a flat piece of Styrofoam), and a plastic bowl with a few centimeters of water in it. Holding the magnet in one hand and the needle in the other, stroke the needle about 25 times in one direction with the magnet.

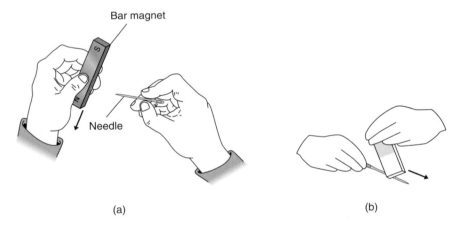

(a)   (b)

c. Float the cork in the water, and lay the needle on it.
    Ask: *What happens to the needle and the cork?* Rotate the needle and cork 90 degrees and then release it. *What happens to the needle-cork system when you release it?*

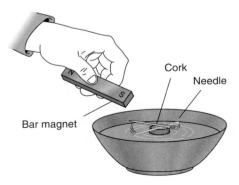

d. Bring the magnet near the needle on the cork. Ask: *What happens to the needle and cork now?*

EXPLAIN: USE DATA TO GENERATE INTERPRETATIONS, INCLUDING DESCRIPTIONS, CLASSIFICATIONS, PREDICTIONS, AND EXPLANATIONS.

e. Ask: *What is your evidence that stroking the needle magnetized it? What made the needle move when it was first placed on the cork? How is this like a compass? How can you make a compass? Which pole of the needle is the N-pole? What is your evidence?*

VII. ELECTRICITY

A. STATIC ELECTRICITY

▶ *Science Background*

More than 2,000 years ago, the Greeks were aware that when amber, a resinous substance, was rubbed with a cloth, the amber was able to attract small bits of straw. The Greek word for amber is electron, so the phenomenon came to be called electricity. In his book on magnetism, published in 1600, William Gilbert carefully distinguished between magnetism, which occurred naturally, and electricity, which had to be induced by friction. Gilbert also reported investigations showing that not only amber, but many other substances—including diamond, sapphire, opal, glass, sealing wax, and sulphur—demonstrated electric qualities when rubbed.

Benjamin Franklin, the American statesman and scientist, investigated electric phenomena in the 1700s. Franklin found that things could be not only attracted by electric forces but also repelled. Franklin proposed that the attracting and repelling forces of static electricity resulted from two kinds of electrical "fluids," which he called positive and negative fluids.

NSES   Science Standards

All students should develop an understanding of

- light, heat, electricity, and magnetism (K–4).

Objectives for Students

1. Describe electrostatic investigations and identify materials that can interact electrostatically.
2. Describe ways electrostatic interactions are different from magnetic interactions.
3. Explain in their own words what is meant by electrical charge and how objects become electrically charged.
4. State and demonstrate evidence for the electrostatic force rule: Like charged bodies repel; unlike charged bodies attract.
5. Demonstrate and explain what is meant by electrostatic induction.
6. Apply the model of electrostatic interaction to explain evidence from electrostatic investigations.

Concepts and Principles

Activities I and 2 address these fundamental concepts and principles related to the *Science Standards* and *Benchmarks*:

- The position or motion of an object can be changed by pushing or pulling (K–4).
- The size of the change is related to the strength of the push or pull (K–4).
- Without touching them, a material that has been electrically charged pulls on all other materials and may either push or pull other charged materials (*Benchmarks*, 3–5).

1. HOW CAN YOU DEMONSTRATE STATIC ELECTRIC FORCES? (3–6)

Materials

Plastic or acetate sheet
Plastic rulers
Hard rubber comb or resin rod
Wool cloth
Balloons
Paper towels
Paper clips
Flour
Salt
Thread
Bits of paper

ENGAGE: ASK A QUESTION ABOUT OBJECTS, ORGANISMS, OR EVENTS IN THE ENVIRONMENT.

Moisture in the air can interfere with electrostatic effects. Thus, electrostatic investigations are best done on a cool, dry day.

EXPLORE: PLAN AND CONDUCT SIMPLE INVESTIGATIONS TO COLLECT RELEVANT DATA.

a. Have students rub a clear acetate sheet with a rough paper towel. (Coarse paper towels from restrooms work well.) Instruct them to bring the rubbed acetate near a pile of tiny bits of torn paper and observe what happens. Experiment to see what other materials interact with the acetate sheet. Try such materials as paper clips, bits of aluminum foil, flour, salt, cotton and nylon thread, and wood shavings from a pencil sharpener.
   Ask: *What did you observe in the investigation? Why do you think it happened?*

b. Rub a hard rubber comb or resin rod with a wool cloth. Try to pick up flour with the rubbed comb or rod. Ask: *What do you observe?*

Resin rod or
hard rubber comb

Flour

c. Tie a 1 meter string around the mouth of an inflated balloon. Vigorously rub the inflated balloon with a piece of wool. Investigate to determine what materials interact with the balloon.

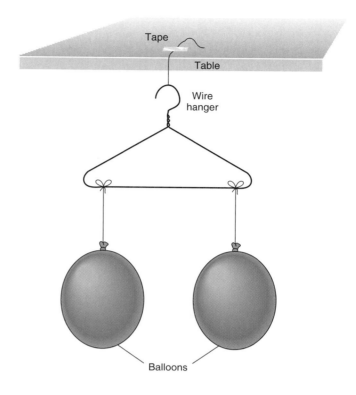

Tape

Table

Wire
hanger

Balloons

d. Inflate a second balloon. Tie a 1 meter string around the mouth of the balloon. Vigorously rub the two balloons with wool. Suspend the two balloons by their strings from a support as in the diagram and investigate how they interact with each other.

EXPLAIN: USE DATA TO GENERATE INTERPRETATIONS, INCLUDING DESCRIPTIONS, CLASSIFICATIONS, AND EXPLANATIONS.

e. Ask: *What did your rubbed balloon attract? Why do you think it happened? In what ways is this investigation similar to your previous investigation? Which materials did the ruler pick up? What materials did the balloon attract?*

f. Ask: *What happened when the two rubbed balloons were brought near one another? What kind of force did you observe, attraction or repulsion?*

g. Introduce the notions of positive and negative electric charges and electrical forces. Help the students relate each part of the explanation to some part of their investigation.
   1. There are two kinds of electric charges in all materials: positive charges and negative charges.
   2. In ordinary substances, positive charges and negative charges are balanced. These substances are electrically neutral.
   3. When some materials are rubbed together, the friction causes the materials to acquire electrical charges.
   4. Two electrically charged substances can interact.
   5. An electrically charged substance can interact with a neutral substance by a process called *induction*.

2. HOW CAN I DEMONSTRATE POSITIVE AND NEGATIVE ELECTRICAL CHARGES? (2–6)

Materials

Transparent tape (one roll for each cooperative group)

ENGAGE: ASK A QUESTION ABOUT OBJECTS, ORGANISMS, OR EVENTS IN THE ENVIRONMENT.

a. Stick a 20 cm strip of transparent tape (A) to a wooden tabletop. Press the tape down well with your fingers, leaving 2 or 3 cm loose as a handle. Very carefully, peel the tape away from the table. Attach one end of the tape to the end of a pencil. Test to see if the tape will pick up bits of paper. (Try to bring only the nonsticky side of the tape near the paper.)

Ask: *How does the strip of tape affect bits of paper? Why do you think this interaction took place? What is your evidence that the tape was charged? Were the bits of paper charged?* (No. The paper had not been rubbed.)

EXPLORE: PLAN AND CONDUCT SIMPLE INVESTIGATIONS TO COLLECT RELEVANT DATA.

b. Charge a second 20 cm strip of tape (B) by sticking it to the tabletop and peeling it away as before. Hang the strip of tape (B) to a wooden pencil or dowel. Bring it near the first strip of tape (A) to see how they interact.

EXPLAIN: USE DATA TO GENERATE INTERPRETATIONS, INCLUDING DESCRIPTIONS, CLASSIFICATIONS, AND EXPLANATIONS.

c. Ask: *How do the two strips of tape interact?* (They repel one another.) *Do you think the two strips of paper carry like or unlike charges?* (Like.) *What is your evidence?* (We did the same thing to each strip of tape.) *What can you conclude: Do like charged substances attract or repel?* (Repel.)

d. Stick a third 20 cm strip of tape (C) to the table, leaving a 2 to 3 cm handle. Stick a fourth strip of tape (D) on top of tape strip C, again leaving a handle. Press them down well. Remove the two tape strips, still stuck together, from the table. Run the tape strips over your lips or over a water pipe. Now carefully peel the two strips of tape apart. Investigate to see how they interact with one another. Also investigate to see how each of these two tape strips (C and D) interact with tape strip A.

Ask: *What did you observe?* (The tape strips attracted one another.) *Did tape strips C and D have like charges?* (They must not have had like charges because they did not repel one another.)

Explain that when tape strips C and D were peeled apart, they acquired opposite charges. Add these principles to the explanation in the previous activity:

- Unlike charged materials attract one another.
- Like charged materials repel one another.

B. CURRENT ELECTRICITY

▶ *Science Background*

In the section on static electricity, you learned that objects can be charged positively (more protons than electrons) or negatively (more electrons than protons). You also learned that like charged materials repel one another, while unlike charged materials attract.

Current electricity refers to a movement of electrical charge along a conducting path. Electrical energy is produced in a battery and converted to heat, light, or motion in an electrical component such as a light bulb or a motor. For energy to be transferred to an electrical component, there must be a complete conducting path—a complete circuit—from the battery along conducting wires through the electrical component and back to the battery along conducting wires.

If two or more electrical components are aligned so that current flows from one to the next, the circuit is a series circuit. If the components are arranged so that each is in an independent circuit, then the circuit is a parallel circuit. A switch is a device that breaks or opens a circuit so that it is not a continuous path and current cannot flow through it.

NSES **Science Standards**

All students should develop an understanding of

- light, heat, electricity, and magnetism (K–4).

Objectives for Students

1. Demonstrate and explain through words and drawings how to make a bulb light in various ways, given one or two batteries, one or two bulbs, and one or two wires.
2. State, explain, and demonstrate the complete circuit rule:
   For a bulb to light,
   - the bulb must be touched on the side and the bottom;
   - the battery must be touched on both ends; and
   - there must be a complete circuit or continuous path along the wires and through the battery and bulb.
3. Explain in their own words what a conductor is and how to test a material to determine if it is an electrical conductor.
4. Identify and construct series circuits and use the complete circuit rule to explain why the other bulbs in a series circuit go out when one bulb is removed from its holder.

5. Identify and construct parallel circuits and use the complete circuit rule to explain why the other bulbs in a parallel circuit stay lit when one bulb is removed from its holder.

6. Demonstrate a switch and use the complete circuit rule to explain how it works.

 Concepts and Principles

Activities 1–6 address these fundamental concepts and principles related to the *Science Standards:*

- Electricity in circuits can produce light, heat, sound, and mechanical motion (K–4).
- Electrical circuits require a complete conducting loop through which an electric current can pass (K–4).
- Electrical circuits provide a means of transferring electrical energy to produce heat, light, sound, mechanical motion, and chemical changes (5–8).

1. HOW CAN YOU CONSTRUCT A CIRCUIT IN WHICH A BULB LIGHTS? (2–6)

Materials

For each student, at least:

- One flashlight bulb
- One battery (1.5 volt D-cell)
- One 15–25 cm wire

(Students initially need their own materials but will later combine materials with one or more other students.)

Safety Precautions

Discussing safe habits to use with electricity is a must.

- Caution children not to experiment with anything but 1.5 volt flashlight batteries (D-cells) and flashlight bulbs. There is no danger of electrical shock from these batteries.
- Children should wear safety goggles to protect their eyes from the sharp ends of the copper wires used in the activities.
- Children should never experiment with the electricity from wall sockets or from car batteries.
- Do not use electrical appliances near water; for example, do not use a hair dryer near a water-filled sink.
- When you pull an electrical cord out of a wall socket, grasp it by the plug and pull firmly.

ENGAGE: ASK A QUESTION ABOUT OBJECTS, ORGANISMS, OR EVENTS IN THE ENVIRONMENT.

a. Give each child a small flashlight bulb, a length of wire, and a 1.5 volt D-cell. (*Note:* A 1.5 volt D-cell is commonly referred to as a battery, although batteries actually have multiple cells.) Ask: *Can you make the bulb light?* The question might be posed as part of a story about some hikers who lost their flashlight in a dark cave. One hiker had an extra battery, another had an extra bulb, and a third had a wire. *Can you help them light the bulb so they can get out of the cave?*

b. The story provides a focus for the activities of the children. Let the children work to light the bulb. Some children may take 20 minutes or longer to light the bulb. Resist the temptation to step in and "teach" them how to light the bulb. Encourage them to keep trying on their own. As they succeed, the children develop confidence in their own abilities to learn about electrical circuits.

As each child lights the bulb, ask: *Can you find another way to light the bulb?* Students may experiment by placing the bulb on its side or on the other end of the battery. If two or more children want to cooperate at this point, let them. More hands may be helpful. Be accepting and reinforcing of the children's efforts.

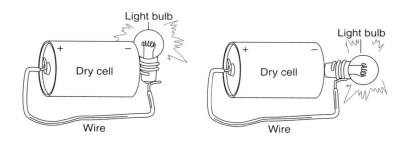

c. Give each pair of children a second wire. Ask: *Can you make the bulb light using two wires?* Children may simply twist the two wires together and make one wire of them. If so, ask: *Can you use two wires to light the bulb without the bulb touching the battery?*

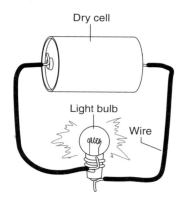

Lighting a bulb without it touching the battery.

d. Ask children, individually, to draw pictures of what they did to light the bulb with one battery and one wire. Look at the children's drawings carefully to see if they have observed that the electrical path (circuit) is a continuous or complete one.

Also ask them to draw a picture of what they did to light the bulb using two wires, with the bulb not touching the battery.

e. Ask the children to explain their drawings to you and to one another. Look at the drawings carefully to see if the wires touch the bulb on the bottom and the side.

Ask: *What two places must you touch a bulb for it to light? Where must the battery be touched?*

Referring to actual circuits and drawings, children should state, explain, and write the complete circuit rule:

For a bulb to light,

- the bulb must be touched on the side and the bottom;
- the battery must be touched on both ends; and
- there must be a continuous path through the battery, bulb, and wires.

ELABORATE: EXTEND CONCEPTS, PRINCIPLES, AND STRATEGIES TO NEW PROBLEMS AND QUESTIONS.

f. Instruct children to do Prediction Sheet 1. It is a good idea to cut this activity sheet into two parts and hand out the second part after the first part is completed. The children should make a prediction for each frame (*Will the bulb light?*) and then experiment to test their prediction (*Try it and see.*). When the children have completed the prediction sheet, go back over it with them. (*Will this one light? Why won't it light? What could you do to get it to light?*)

As children predict, test, and explain, they have the opportunity to use and develop better understanding of the complete circuit rules.

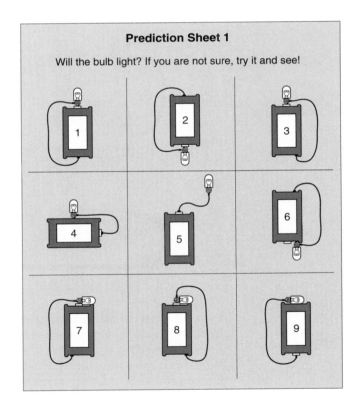

Prediction Sheet 1

Will the bulb light? If you are not sure, try it and see!

---

2. WHAT HAPPENS WHEN THERE IS MORE THAN ONE BULB OR BATTERY, OR A MOTOR IN A CIRCUIT? (2–6)

Materials

Batteries, bulbs, wires
Bulb holders
Small 1.5 volt electric motors

ENGAGE: ASK A QUESTION ABOUT OBJECTS, ORGANISMS, OR EVENTS IN THE ENVIRONMENT.

a. Instruct the children to explore different arrangements of batteries and bulbs. Ask: *What happens when you try two bulbs? Try two batteries. Can you use three batteries and two bulbs? Does the orientation of the batteries matter?*

EXPLORE: PLAN AND CONDUCT SIMPLE INVESTIGATIONS TO COLLECT RELEVANT DATA.

Let children explore and discover. Children may discover that when batteries are placed end-to-end (in series), a positive terminal of one battery must be connected to the negative terminal of an adjacent battery.

Safety Precautions

Do not allow children to experiment with more than three batteries. More batteries can result in burned-out bulbs.

Ask: *What happens to the bulbs when you use more than one battery?* (The bulbs get brighter.)

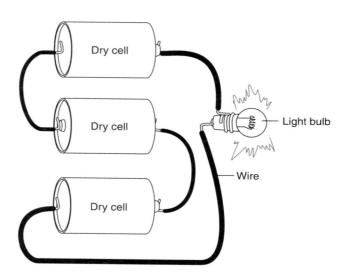

b. As the children try different arrangements, the need for a "bulb holder" arises. Give the children bulb holders and demonstrate how to use them in building one, two, and three bulb circuits.
c. Provide each group with a small electric motor (available from Radio Shack). The motors have two wires coming from them. Challenge the groups to connect the motor to a battery and observe what happens. Place a plastic or wooden propeller on the motor shaft and observe what happens.

Ask: *How could a motor be used to do useful work? Where around your home or school can you find electric motors being used?* (Fans, washing machines, hair dryers, blenders, vacuum cleaners, air conditioners, etc.)

Wire a motor in a circuit with a bulb in a bulb holder. You may need to give the motor shaft a little spin to start the motor whirring. Ask: *What happens to the bulb when the motor starts turning? What happens to the bulb when the motor stops turning?*

EXPLAIN: USE DATA
TO GENERATE
INTERPRETATIONS,
INCLUDING DESCRIPTIONS,
CLASSIFICATIONS, AND
EXPLANATIONS.

d. Ask: *Can you trace the complete circuit path for each circuit you have built?* Help the children see that the bulb holder is constructed so that one part of it is connected to the metal side of a bulb and another part is connected to the bottom base of the bulb. The terminals of the bulb holder are then connected to the battery. So the bulb holder is doing the same thing the children were doing with their hands when they made the bulb light. The bulb holders provide a complete circuit path for the electricity.

3. WHAT IS A SERIES CIRCUIT? (3–6)

ENGAGE: ASK A
QUESTION ABOUT OBJECTS,
ORGANISMS, OR EVENTS IN
THE ENVIRONMENT.

a. Show the children the accompanying circuit illustration. Ask them to build the circuit using their materials.

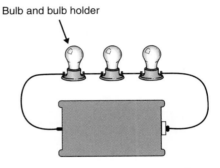

Bulb and bulb holder

    Tell the children that electricians, scientists, and engineers call this circuit a *series circuit* because the bulbs are lined up in a series and electricity flows from bulb to bulb.

EXPLORE: PLAN
AND CONDUCT SIMPLE
INVESTIGATIONS TO
COLLECT RELEVANT DATA.

b. Ask: *What will happen to the other bulb in a series circuit if one of the bulbs is removed from its holder? Try it and see.* (The other bulb will go out.)

EXPLAIN: USE DATA
TO GENERATE
INTERPRETATIONS,
INCLUDING DESCRIPTIONS,
CLASSIFICATIONS, AND
EXPLANATIONS.

c. Ask: *Why did the other bulb not light?* The children should tell you that the continuous path was broken when the bulb was removed.

4. WHAT IS A PARALLEL CIRCUIT? (3–6)

ENGAGE: ASK A
QUESTION ABOUT OBJECTS,
ORGANISMS, OR EVENTS IN
THE ENVIRONMENT.

a. Show the children the accompanying circuit illustration and ask them to build it.

Bulb and bulb holder

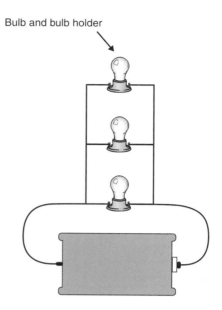

This circuit is called a parallel circuit because there are parallel paths through the bulbs for the electricity. Each bulb is part of an independent circuit with the battery.

EXPLORE: PLAN AND CONDUCT SIMPLE INVESTIGATIONS TO COLLECT RELEVANT DATA.

b. Ask: *What will happen to the other bulb if one of the bulbs is removed from its bulb holder? Try it and see.*

EXPLAIN: USE DATA TO GENERATE INTERPRETATIONS, INCLUDING DESCRIPTIONS, CLASSIFICATIONS, AND EXPLANATIONS.

c. Ask: *What happened to the other bulbs when you removed one? Why did it happen?* The students should observe and explain that the other bulb stays lit because it is still part of a continuous path with the battery.

ELABORATE: EXTEND CONCEPTS, PRINCIPLES, AND STRATEGIES TO NEW PROBLEMS AND QUESTIONS.

d. Ask: *How are the electrical circuits in the classroom wired, series or parallel? If one light burns out, will the others light?* Through discussion, lead children to understand that electrical circuits in the classroom are wired in parallel. If the lights in the room are off, the TV or computers will still work. If one light bulb (or bank of lights) is out, the others still work.

You might discuss strings of Christmas tree or holiday lights at this point. Most strings of lights sold today are wired in parallel. If one bulb burns out, the others still light. If the bulbs were in series, if one bulb burned out, none of the others would light. You would have to test each one of them to determine which one needed to be replaced.

5. WHAT ARE CONDUCTORS AND NONCONDUCTORS? (3–6)

Materials

Batteries
Bulbs
Wires
Bulb holders
Diverse array of conducting and nonconducting materials made from paper, cloth, wood,
plastic, and metals of different kinds

ENGAGE: ASK A
QUESTION ABOUT OBJECTS,
ORGANISMS, OR EVENTS IN
THE ENVIRONMENT.

a. Ask: *Do all things conduct electricity? Are some materials better conductors of electricity than others?*

EXPLORE: PLAN
AND CONDUCT SIMPLE
INVESTIGATIONS TO
COLLECT RELEVANT DATA.

b. Make available to each cooperative group a diverse array of conducting and nonconducting materials. Instruct students to use the test circuit illustrated to find out which materials will and which will not conduct electricity. Place the test object (made of metal, cloth, wood, plastic, etc.) between the bare ends of the two pieces of wire. If the bulb lights, the material is a conductor. Ask: *What types of materials did you find are the best conductors?* (Metals.)

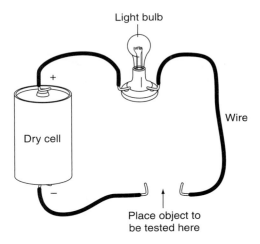

Light bulb

Wire

Dry cell

Place object to
be tested here

EXPLAIN: USE DATA TO
GENERATE INTERPRETATIONS,
INCLUDING DESCRIPTIONS,
CLASSIFICATIONS, AND
EXPLANATIONS.

c. Through discussion lead children to understand that some materials will conduct electricity. Others will not. Materials that conduct electricity well are called *conductors*. Materials that do not conduct electricity well are called *insulators* or *nonconductors*.

6. WHAT IS A SWITCH AND HOW DOES IT WORK? (2–6)

Materials

Heavy cardboard
Brass paper fasteners
Paper clips

ENGAGE: ASK A QUESTION ABOUT OBJECTS, ORGANISMS, OR EVENTS IN THE ENVIRONMENT.

a. Ask: *What does a switch do? How does a switch work? How can you make a switch?*

EXPLORE: PLAN AND CONDUCT SIMPLE INVESTIGATIONS TO COLLECT RELEVANT DATA.

b. Ask your students to make an electrical "switch" using a 10 cm by 10 cm piece of corrugated cardboard, two brass paper fasteners, and a paper clip, as in the illustration. Tell them to connect the switch into an electric circuit as shown.

EXPLAIN: USE DATA TO GENERATE INTERPRETATIONS, INCLUDING DESCRIPTIONS, CLASSIFICATIONS, AND EXPLANATIONS.

c. Ask: *What happens when the switch is open (with the paper clip not touching the second fastener)? What happens when the switch is closed (with the paper clip touching the second fastener)?*

The children should note that when the switch is closed, a complete circuit is formed and the bulb lights. When the switch is open, the circuit is broken and the bulb does not light. Take time for children to identify and talk about the electrical switches in the classroom.

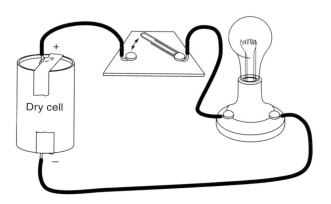

Dry cell

C. ELECTROMAGNETS

▶ *Science Background*

All magnetism is the result of moving electrical charges. When current flows in a wire, a magnetic field is set up. If the wire is placed over a compass, the magnetic field of the wire interacts with the magnetic field of the compass needle, causing it to deflect. Since the earth's magnetic field affects the compass needle strongly, the needle may deflect only a small amount. More coils of wire increase the magnetic effects of the current. When the current is less, which occurs when a bulb is wired into the circuit, the resulting magnetic field produced will also be less.

Even permanent magnets are the result of electrical currents. In the case of permanent magnets, the current is the result of the movement of electrons within the atoms of the iron from which the magnets are made.

 NSES   Science Standards

All students should develop an understanding of

• light, heat, electricity, and magnetism (K–4).

Objectives for Students

1. Describe interactions between compass needles and current-carrying wires.
2. Construct an electromagnet.
3. Design and conduct an experiment to determine the effects of variables such as the type of core, number of loops of wire, and amount of current on the strength of an electromagnet.
4. Explain the cause of electromagnetic effects.

 NSES   Concepts and Principles

Activities 1–3 address these fundamental concepts and principles related to the *Science Standards* and *Benchmarks:*

• Electricity in circuits can produce heat, light, sound, and magnetic effects (K–4).
• Electric currents and magnets can exert a force on each other (*Benchmarks*, 6–8).

1. HOW DO COMPASS NEEDLES INTERACT WITH CURRENT-CARRYING WIRES? (4–6)

Materials

Batteries
Bulbs
Wires
Iron nails or rivets
Switches
Paper clips

ENGAGE: ASK A QUESTION ABOUT OBJECTS, ORGANISMS, OR EVENTS IN THE ENVIRONMENT.

a. Instruct students to take a 50 cm length of wire and stretch it out on a table. Lay a compass over the wire as in the diagram. Orient the wire so the compass needle is perpendicular to the wire. Connect one end of the wire to one of the terminals of a D-cell. Quickly touch the other end of the wire to the other terminal of the D-cell and then disconnect it. Observe what happens to the compass needle. Move the wire so it points in different directions. Quickly connect and disconnect the wire to the D-cell.

Safety Precautions

Since there is no light bulb or other resisting component in the circuit in this investigation, it is a "short" circuit. You must connect and disconnect the short circuit quickly so that the wire does not get too hot and the D-cell is not drained of electrical energy.

EXPLAIN: USE DATA TO GENERATE INTERPRETATIONS, INCLUDING DESCRIPTIONS, CLASSIFICATIONS, AND EXPLANATIONS.

b. Ask: *What did you observe in this investigation?* (The compass needle moved.) *Why do you think this happened? What is your evidence that the electric current in the wire produced some magnetism?*

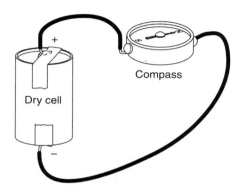

Compass

Dry cell

ELABORATE: EXTEND CONCEPTS, PRINCIPLES, AND STRATEGIES TO NEW PROBLEMS AND QUESTIONS.

c. Tell students to obtain a wire about 50 cm long and to wrap five loops of the wire around a compass as in the diagram. Leave the ends of the wire long enough to connect to a D-cell. Quickly connect and disconnect the wire to a single D-cell. Ask: *What did you observe?* (The compass needle deflected more than before.)

Why do you think this happened? What evidence can you state that a magnetic interaction took place? Was the effect stronger or weaker than in the first investigation? What is your evidence that the electric current in the loops of wire produced some magnetism?

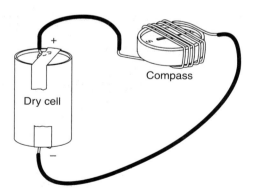

Compass

Dry cell

2. WHAT IS AN ELECTROMAGNET, AND HOW CAN YOU MAKE ONE? (3–6)

ENGAGE: ASK A QUESTION ABOUT OBJECTS, ORGANISMS, OR EVENTS IN THE ENVIRONMENT.

a. Show children an electromagnet. Demonstrate how it can attract small objects like paper clips. Ask: *How can we make an electromagnet?*

EXPLORE: PLAN
AND CONDUCT SIMPLE
INVESTIGATIONS TO
COLLECT RELEVANT DATA.

b. Give students these directions:
1. Obtain a D-cell, a large iron nail or rivet, a 50 cm length of insulated (enameled) copper wire, some iron filings in a plastic bag, and some paper clips.
2. Wrap the nail around the wire about 50 times as shown in the diagram.
3. Place the nail on the bag of iron filings.
4. Scrape the insulation off the two ends of the wire. Connect one end of the wire to one of the terminals of the D-cell.
5. Holding the other end of the wire along the insulated portion, touch the bare end of the wire to the other terminal of the D-cell for only a few seconds. Move the nail around on the plastic bag and observe how it interacts with the iron filings.
6. Repeat the activities using paper clips rather than iron filings to observe electromagnetic effects.

Safety Precautions

Do not let the wire and terminal remain in contact for more than a few seconds because

- intense heat builds up, and you could get a burn through the insulation; and
- the electrical energy in the battery will be used up quickly.

EXPLAIN: USE DATA
TO GENERATE
INTERPRETATIONS,
INCLUDING DESCRIPTIONS,
CLASSIFICATIONS, AND
EXPLANATIONS.

c. Ask: *What happens to the iron filings and the paper clip when the circuit is completed (or when the wire is touched to the battery)? What happens to the iron filings and the paper clip when the circuit is broken (or when the wire is removed from the battery)? What is the evidence that the nail became a magnet temporarily?*

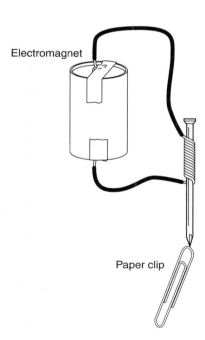

Electromagnet

Paper clip

d. Explain that when a loop of wire is placed around an iron object and current runs through the wire, the object becomes an electromagnet. The electromagnetic effect is suddenly reduced when current no longer runs through the wire.

3. HOW CAN YOU INCREASE THE STRENGTH OF AN ELECTROMAGNET? (3–6)

ENGAGE: ASK A QUESTION ABOUT OBJECTS, ORGANISMS, OR EVENTS IN THE ENVIRONMENT.

a. Ask: *What determines the strength of an electromagnet?* Through discussion, generate the hypothesis that the strength of an electromagnet might be increased by
   - increasing the number of wire loops around the iron object; or
   - increasing the current (or increasing the number of D-cells).

EXPLORE: PLAN AND CONDUCT SIMPLE INVESTIGATIONS TO COLLECT RELEVANT DATA.

b. Tell students to design and conduct a controlled experiment to determine how the number of coils of wire around the nail or rivet affects the strength of the electromagnet. Measure the strength of the electromagnet by how long a chain of paper clips it can pick up. Use 20 coils, 40 coils, and 60 coils of wire.

c. Ask: *What is the responding variable in this experiment?* (Number of paper clips lifted.) *What is the manipulated variable in the experiment?* (Number of loops of wire around the nail.) *What variables have you controlled in this experiment?* (Type of wire; number of batteries; length of wire.)

EXPLAIN: USE DATA TO GENERATE INTERPRETATIONS, INCLUDING DESCRIPTIONS, CLASSIFICATIONS, AND EXPLANATIONS.

d. Instruct students to display their data in a graph like the one shown here. Tell them to use the graph to predict how many paper clips the electromagnet can hold with 50 coils of wire and 80 coils of wire. Instruct students to test their predictions.

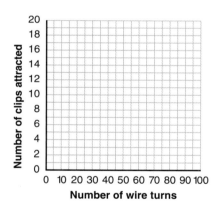

e. Ask: *What were your predicted and tested amounts of paper clips attracted to the electromagnet?*

SECTION III
Life Science Activities

Life is a complex, exciting, and mysterious subject for inquiry. Children should have the opportunity to develop a deep and personal appreciation for the variety and wonder of life. Children are naturally curious about the diversity of life around them. Studying characteristics of plants and animals and of their habitats also provides a very good context for students to develop inquiry skills. Investigations in life science might involve

1. asking different kinds of questions that suggest different kinds of scientific investigations;
2. observing and describing plants and animals;
3. classifying plants and animals (insects, fish, birds, mammals) according to their properties;
4. investigating plant and animal life cycles;
5. planning and carrying out investigations that show the function of different parts/structures of plants and animals;
6. investigating how different habitats or environments enable the needs of plants and animals to be met; and
7. investigating how the activities of people bring about changes in the environment.

As students learn more and more about plants, animals, and the environment, they become better prepared to assume responsibility for the well-being of living things on our planet.

Investigation Journals. Life science activities provide an excellent context for students to learn how to keep good records of investigations. Records may be kept in student observation journals, or you may want for students to keep their records on pages you prepare. Decorate prepared record pages with clip art designating the function of each part of the journal.

Here is a suggested format for student investigation journals and examples of a child's journal entries from a seed germination experiment.

<table>
<tr><td colspan="3" align="center">My Investigation Journal</td></tr>
</table>

1. **Key Question**	• *Is moisture needed for seeds to sprout?*
2. **My Investigation**	• *We put a sponge in a bowl of water and sprinkled grass seeds on it. We put grass seeds on a dry sponge. We watched the seeds for several days.*
3. **My Prediction**	• *I think the dry seeds won't grow but the moist ones will.*
4. **What Happened**	

Day	What I Observed on the Wet Sponge	What I Observed on the Dry Sponge
1	• *Nothing is happening.*	• *Nothing is happening.*
2	• *Nothing.*	• *Nothing.*
3	• *Some sprouts are coming up on the moist sponge.*	• *Nothing.*
6	• *There was lots of grass on the moist sponge but nothing growing on the dry one.*	• *Nothing.*

5. **What I Concluded**	• *Seeds need moisture to sprout.*

I. CHARACTERISTICS OF ORGANISMS

Children can begin to sense the astounding variety of living things on our planet as they investigate seeds, plants, insects, and birds.

A. SEEDS

▶ *Science Background*

Amazingly, seeds contain the ingredients of life. A living seed may lie dormant for years until it is awakened by just the right conditions. To begin the **germination** or sprouting process, seeds need moisture, air, and moderate temperatures.

Seeds typically have very hard **seed coats** that keep water from penetrating them. Thus, they will germinate more quickly after being soaked or scarified to allow water inside the seeds. Within every viable seed lives a tiny **embryo plant,** complete with leaf, stem, and root parts. When the seed begins to germinate, a temporary food supply, stored within the **cotyledons** of the seeds, nourishes the growing embryo. Eventually, as the leaves develop, the plant will obtain its energy for growth and survival from sunlight through the process of **photosynthesis.**

NSES   **Science Standards**

All students should develop an understanding of

- characteristics of organisms (K–4).
- structure and function in living systems (5–8).
- life cycles of organisms (K–4).
- organisms and their environments (K–4).

Objectives for Students

1. Recognize the wide variation in seeds and where seeds are found.
2. Identify and describe different parts/structures of seeds (seed coats, cotyledons, embryo plants) and describe the functions of each.
3. Define *germination* and describe the sequence of events in the germination of a seed.
4. Ask questions about seeds that can be answered through investigations.
5. Design and carry out descriptive, classificatory, and experimental investigations to gather information for answering questions about seeds.
6. Use simple equipment and tools to gather data and extend the senses.
7. Through investigations, identify basic conditions for seed germination: air, water, and moderate temperature.
8. Use evidence from investigations and science knowledge to answer questions about seeds, construct explanations, and make predictions.

 Concepts and Principles

Activities 1–4 address or provide preparation for learning these fundamental concepts and principles related to the *Science Standards* or *Benchmarks for Science Literacy*:

- Some animals and plants are alike in the way they look and the things they do, and others are very different from one another (K–2).
- A great variety of living things can be sorted into groups in many ways using various features to decide which things belong to which group (3–5).
- Features used for grouping depend on the purpose of the grouping (3–5).
- Each plant or animal has different structures that serve different functions in growth, survival, and reproduction (K–4).

1. WHAT IS INSIDE A BEAN POD? (K–4)

Materials

Bean pods
Plastic knives
Assortment of fruits

Large bag of pea pods
Paper plates

ENGAGE: ASK A QUESTION ABOUT OBJECTS, ORGANISMS, OR EVENTS IN THE ENVIRONMENT.

a. Distribute two bean pods to each small group. Ask: *What are the properties of the bean pod? What do you observe inside the bean pod?* Introduce or review the term *property* as a characteristic of an object or something you can observe about an object using your senses.

EXPLORE: PLAN AND CONDUCT SIMPLE INVESTIGATIONS TO COLLECT RELEVANT DATA.

b. Distribute a plastic knife to each group. Provide instructions on safe use of the plastic knife. Challenge students to use the knives to open their bean pods. Encourage students to use all of their senses, except taste, to observe the inside of the bean pod. They should observe color, texture, size, shape, and other features.

EXPLAIN: USE DATA TO GENERATE INTERPRETATIONS, INCLUDING DESCRIPTIONS, CLASSIFICATIONS, PREDICTIONS, AND EXPLANATIONS.

c. Ask: *What observations did you make? What are the properties of what is inside the bean pods?* List the students' observations on the board. Discuss the various observations with them. Tell students that the pod is the part of the plant that holds the seeds, and the scientific term for that part of the plant is the fruit. Explain that although in everyday language we call bean pods *vegetables*, in scientific terms they are *fruits*.

2. WHERE ARE SEEDS FOUND? HOW ARE SEEDS ALIKE AND DIFFERENT? (K–2)

Materials

Paper plates
Plastic knives
Variety of fresh fruits (Children might be encouraged to bring a fruit from home.
Tomatoes, apples, corn on the cob, apples, cherries, cantaloupes, and bell peppers
make interesting fruits for children to observe.)

ENGAGE: ASK A
QUESTION ABOUT OBJECTS,
ORGANISMS, OR EVENTS IN
THE ENVIRONMENT.

a. Ask: *Are there seeds in each of these fruits? How many seeds are in each of the fruits? How
can we find out?*

EXPLORE: PLAN
AND CONDUCT SIMPLE
INVESTIGATIONS TO
COLLECT RELEVANT DATA.

b. Distribute paper plates and several fruits to each group. Tell children to use their plastic knives to cut their fruits open. They should find and observe the seeds in each one.

EXPLAIN: USE DATA TO
GENERATE INTERPRETATIONS,
INCLUDING DESCRIPTIONS,
CLASSIFICATIONS, AND
EXPLANATIONS.

c. Ask: *Did you find seeds in your fruit? How many seeds did you find? What are the properties of the seeds? How are they similar? How do they differ?*

ELABORATE: EXTEND
CONCEPTS, PRINCIPLES,
AND STRATEGIES TO NEW
SITUATIONS AND
QUESTIONS.

d. Tell the students to take turns sorting the seeds on the paper plates. Ask: *How have you
sorted the seeds?* Allow groups to describe and explain how they sorted the seeds. Lead
students to compare and contrast the different ways they have sorted the seeds and to
discuss the best ways to sort them.

3. HOW DO SEEDPODS VARY? (K–4)

Materials

Large number of pea pods
Paper plates

ENGAGE: ASK A
QUESTION ABOUT OBJECTS,
ORGANISMS, OR EVENTS IN
THE ENVIRONMENT.

a. Ask: *Do all pea pods have the same number of peas?*

EXPLORE: PLAN AND
CONDUCT SIMPLE
INVESTIGATIONS TO
COLLECT RELEVANT DATA.

b. Give two pea pods to each pair of students. Tell students to open the pods, count the
number of peas in each pod, and put the peas and pods on their paper plates.

EXPLAIN: USE DATA TO GENERATE INTERPRETATIONS, INCLUDING DESCRIPTIONS, CLASSIFICATIONS, PREDICTIONS, AND EXPLANATIONS.

c. Ask: *Who found the most peas in their pods?* Record this number on the chalkboard. Also ask: *Who found the least number of peas in their pods?* Record this number on the board. Let each group report the number of peas they found in their pods.

d. Construct a histogram showing the numbers of peas in the different pods. Have one student from each pair come to the chalkboard and place an X above the numbers that correspond to the number of peas in each of their two pods. Ask: *What does the graph (histogram) show? What does it tell about peas and pods? If you open another pea pod, what might be the most likely number of peas in the pod? Why do you think so?* Discuss the notion of predictions and how predictions are based on collected evidence.

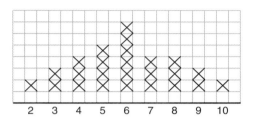

Give each pair another pea pod, and tell them to make predictions about the number of peas in each pod. Tell them to open the pea pods to test their predictions. Ask: *How accurate were your predictions? Why were your predictions so accurate (or so inaccurate)?*

ELABORATE: EXTEND CONCEPTS, PRINCIPLES, AND STRATEGIES TO NEW PROBLEMS AND QUESTIONS.

e. Ask: *Do you think there is a relationship between the number of peas in a pod and the length of the pod? How would you investigate to find out?* Carry out an investigation to see if the number of peas in a pod is related to the length (centimeters) of the pod. Display class data in a line graph (number of peas in a pod on the *y* axis; length of the pod in centimeters on the *x* axis). Use the graph to make predictions about the number of peas in pods of different lengths. Discuss the use of graphs to display data from investigations and to make predictions. Discuss how science can enable students to put mathematical skills, such as graphing, to work.

f. Ask: *How do other things in nature vary? How do dogs vary? What are some ways that children vary?*

4. WHAT ARE THE PROPERTIES OF SEEDS? (K–4)

Materials

Assortment of seeds, perhaps from old seed packets
Magnifying lens

ENGAGE: ASK A QUESTION ABOUT OBJECTS, ORGANISMS, OR EVENTS IN THE ENVIRONMENT.

a. Give each group an assortment of 10 to 15 seeds. Ask: *How are the seeds alike? How are they different? How many different kinds of seeds do you have? What are the properties of each seed?*

EXPLORE: PLAN AND CONDUCT SIMPLE INVESTIGATIONS TO COLLECT RELEVANT DATA.

b. Students should be encouraged to notice and talk about the color, shape, size, and texture of each kind of seed. Provide magnifying lenses to each group to better observe details.

    For very young children, include other small objects with the seed assortments, such as marbles, small pebbles (gravel), jelly beans, and other small pieces of candy. As children observe and talk about their collection, discuss what is living and what is not living. Caution children not to place small objects in their mouths, noses, or ears.

c. Invite students within small groups to play "I'm thinking of . . ." with their assortment of seeds. One child describes a particular seed or a type of seed and the other children try to figure out which one is being described.

EXPLAIN: USE DATA TO GENERATE INTERPRETATIONS, INCLUDING DESCRIPTIONS, CLASSIFICATIONS, PREDICTIONS, AND EXPLANATIONS.

d. Ask: *What characteristics do seeds seem to have in common? What makes a seed a seed? How can you tell a seed from a nonseed?*

 NSES   Concepts and Principles

Activities 5–7 address these fundamental concepts and principles related to the *Science Standards:*

- Each plant or animal has different structures that serve different functions in growth, survival, and reproduction (K–4).
- Plants and animals have life cycles that include being born, developing into adults, reproducing, and eventually dying. The details of this life cycle are different for different organisms (K–4).

---

5. WHAT DOES THE INSIDE OF A SEED LOOK LIKE? (K–4)

Materials

Lima bean seeds
Magnifying lenses

ENGAGE: ASK A QUESTION ABOUT OBJECTS, ORGANISMS, OR EVENTS IN THE ENVIRONMENT.

a. Ask: *What do you think the inside of a seed looks like?* Discuss possibilities.

EXPLORE: PLAN AND CONDUCT SIMPLE INVESTIGATIONS TO COLLECT RELEVANT DATA.

b. Give each pair or group of students four lima bean seeds, one-half cup of water, and a magnifying lens. Have them place two seeds in the water for 24 hours and observe them regularly. After 24 hours, ask: *How have the seeds in the water changed? How are the soaked seeds different from the unsoaked seeds?* (They are larger.) *Why are the soaked seeds larger?* (They have soaked up water.)

c. Ask: *What do you think was happening inside the seed?* Have students carefully peel the outer coat from one of the seeds and examine it with the magnifying lens. Show students how to pull the coatless seed in half with a fingernail. Ask: *What does the inside of the seed look like? What are the distinctive parts of a seed?* Tell students to draw a picture of the inside of the seed. Ask students to compare their drawings with the illustration.

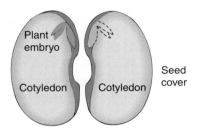

EXPLAIN: USE DATA TO GENERATE INTERPRETATIONS, INCLUDING DESCRIPTIONS, CLASSIFICATIONS, PREDICTIONS, AND EXPLANATIONS.

d. Provide names for the main parts of the bean seed: *seed coat* or cover; *cotyledon* or the meaty, pulpy part of the seed; and the *embryo,* the "beanie baby" with its embryo leaves, stem, and root.

6. HOW MUCH WATER CAN A BEAN SEED SOAK UP? (K–4)

Materials

Unsoaked lima bean seeds
Lima bean seeds that have been soaked overnight
Balances
1 g weights
Plastic containers

ENGAGE: ASK A QUESTION ABOUT OBJECTS, ORGANISMS, OR EVENTS IN THE ENVIRONMENT.

a. Ask: *If the seeds are soaking up water, how can we find out how much water they are holding?* Through discussion, arrive at the possibility of weighing the seeds before and after they have been soaked to gather data on how much water seeds can soak up.

EXPLORE: PLAN AND CONDUCT SIMPLE INVESTIGATIONS TO COLLECT RELEVANT DATA.

b. Provide each group 10 unsoaked bean seeds and a plastic container. Tell students to use a balance to find the mass of their 10 bean seeds and to record their measurements in the data table:

DATA TABLE

Mass of 10 soaked bean seeds _____

Mass of 10 unsoaked bean seeds _____

How much water did the bean seeds soak up? _____

c. Instruct students to add water to the container to a level of about 1 cm above the bean seeds. Set the bean seeds aside for 24–48 hours to soak up water. Allow students to add water to their containers if necessary during this time. After the bean seeds have soaked, tell students to use a balance to determine the mass of the soaked seeds and to record this measurement in the data table.

EXPLAIN: USE DATA TO GENERATE INTERPRETATIONS, INCLUDING DESCRIPTIONS, CLASSIFICATIONS, PREDICTIONS, AND EXPLANATIONS.

d. Ask: *How much water did the bean seeds absorb?* Lead students to subtract the before-soaking measurement from the after-soaking measurement to determine how much water the seeds soaked up. Enter the difference in the data table.

e. Ask: *How does the amount of water soaked up compare to the initial mass of the bean seeds? Is it larger, much larger, smaller, much smaller, or about the same? Why do you think water is important in the sprouting of the dry seeds?*

How could you help children understand what scientists do?

f. Explain that scientists use mathematics in all aspects of scientific inquiry. Ask: *How did we use mathematics in this activity?* (Measuring, putting data in a table, subtracting, comparing.) Discuss that a practical value of mathematics is using it to answer questions in science. *Mathematics is the language of science.*

....

7. WHAT HAPPENS TO SEEDS WHEN THEY GERMINATE? (K–4)

Materials

A 7 inch by 8 inch (quart size) plastic storage bag for each child
Paper towels
Stapler
Lima bean seeds
Ruler or centimeter-gram cubes

ENGAGE: ASK A QUESTION ABOUT OBJECTS, ORGANISMS, OR EVENTS IN THE ENVIRONMENT.

a. Ask: *What are some things we do with seeds?* When students suggest that we plant them, ask: *What happens to seeds when they are planted?* Explain that if we plant the seeds in the soil, we cannot see what happens to them underground. Tell them we will place the seeds in a plastic bag and observe what happens for a few days.

EXPLORE: PLAN AND CONDUCT SIMPLE INVESTIGATIONS TO COLLECT RELEVANT DATA.

b. Give each child a 7 inch by 8 inch (quart size) plastic storage bag. Show students how to line the inside of the bag with a paper towel. Place four or five staples along the bottom portion of the bag about 4 to 5 cm (2 inches) from the bottom. Place a lima bean seed above each staple inside the bag, as in the illustration. Gently pour water into the bag, being careful not to dislodge the seeds (the water should bulge slightly at the bottom of the bag to about a finger's thickness). There should be enough water to keep the seeds moist, but the seeds should not rest in water. Some of the seeds will germinate within 24–48 hours. Others may take longer.

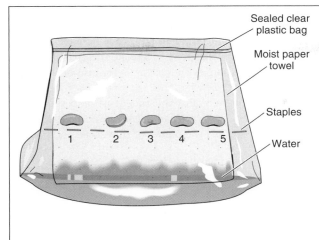

Sealed clear plastic bag

Moist paper towel

Staples

Water

- Line a 7 inch by 8 inch (quart size) sealable, transparent storage bag with a moist paper towel.
- Place six staples across the bag about 4 to 5 cm from the bottom, as shown in the diagram.
- Position each seed to be germinated above one of the staples.
- The seeds may be presoaked for about 24 hours.
- Gently pour water from a small container into the bag, being careful not to dislodge the seeds (the water should bulge slightly at the bottom of the bag to about a finger's thickness).

The water will soak the paper towel and keep the seeds moist. The staples keep the seeds from lying in the water at the bottom of the bag. The transparent bag allows the seeds and roots to be observed.

c. Children should observe their germinating seeds and developing plants regularly for 2 weeks or more, recording daily in their investigation journals or on a prepared chart any changes in color, length, shape, texture, special features, and so on.

d. This investigation is a good one to promote careful measurement. Tell students to use a ruler or centimeter-gram cubes (plastic cubes which are 1 cm on a side and interlock) to measure the length of the stem and root each day and to record the measurements in a chart. The chart should show length in centimeters for each day observed. The measurement data can then be displayed in a graph, which provides a picture of growth.

At lower grade levels, rather than measuring with a ruler, students can cut a green strip of paper to the length of the stem and a brown strip of paper to the length of the root. If the strips of paper are attached to a time line, such as a calendar, with the green strip above the line and the brown strip below, a visual display of growth over 2 or 3 weeks can be seen.

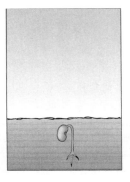

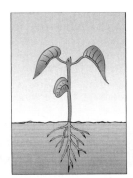
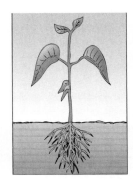

EXPLAIN: USE DATA TO GENERATE INTERPRETATIONS, INCLUDING DESCRIPTIONS, CLASSIFICATIONS, PREDICTIONS, AND EXPLANATIONS.

e. From their observational data, you want children to discover the sequence of growth changes for the beans from day to day—to learn that the root appears first and grows downward, that the stem is connected to the root and grows upward carrying the bean seed with it, and that leaves grow on the stems. To make the growth sequence clear, ask students to make drawings of changes they observe for one of their germinating bean seeds.

f. In addition to observing the sequence of growth, students should also learn to recognize the seed coat, cotyledons, and embryo plant of seeds, and the root, stems, and leaves of the developing plants. Provide the names of these seed and plant parts.

NSES Concepts and Principles

Activity 8 addresses these fundamental concepts and principles related to the *Science Standards*:

- Each plant or animal has different structures that serve different functions in growth, survival, and reproduction (K–4).

---

8. WHAT IS THE FUNCTION OF EACH SEED PART IN THE GROWTH OF THE PLANT? (3–6)

Materials

Transparent storage bags
Paper towels
Soaked bean seeds

ENGAGE: ASK A QUESTION ABOUT OBJECTS, ORGANISMS, OR EVENTS IN THE ENVIRONMENT.

a. Ask: *What are the parts of a seed? How do different parts of a seed change during germination? Which part of the seed do you think grows into a plant? How could we investigate to find out?* Lead children to observe that a lima bean seed has two cotyledons (it is a dicot), with the embryo embedded in one of them. Lead them to consider trying to germinate a cotyledon by itself, an embryo plant and cotyledon, an embryo plant by itself, and a whole lima bean, and to observe what happens.

EXPLORE: PLAN AND CONDUCT SIMPLE INVESTIGATIONS TO COLLECT RELEVANT DATA.

b. Assist children to set up a germination bag (as in Activity 7) containing
   1. one cotyledon by itself;
   2. one cotyledon with an embedded embryo plant;
   3. an embryo plant by itself; and
   4. a whole lima bean.

Allow the students to observe their germination bags for several days, keeping records on their observations. *Note:* Open the bags daily for 15 minutes to prevent mold formation. Add just enough water to keep the paper towel slightly moist.

EXPLAIN: USE DATA TO GENERATE INTERPRETATIONS, INCLUDING DESCRIPTIONS, CLASSIFICATIONS, PREDICTIONS, AND EXPLANATIONS.

c. Ask: *Which of the seed parts, if any, started to grow? Why do you think that is so? Which parts did not grow at all? What do you conclude from your investigation about what seed parts are necessary for seed germination and growth into a plant? (Only the whole seed and the one cotyledon and embryo produced growth.) What do you think the role of the embryo was in sprouting? What do you think the role of the cotyledon was? Why do seeds not germinate (sprout) if the embryo is removed? Why do seeds not germinate if the cotyledon is removed?*

 Concepts and Principles

Activity 9 expands on these fundamental concepts and principles related to the *Science Standards:*

- Organisms have basic needs. Plants require air, water, nutrients, and light (K–4).
- Organisms can survive only in environments in which their basic needs are met (K–4).

9. WHAT CONDITIONS ARE NEEDED FOR SEEDS TO GERMINATE OR SPROUT? (3–6)

Materials

Lima bean seeds
Radish seeds
Transparent storage bags
Paper towels
Stapler

ENGAGE: ASK A QUESTION ABOUT OBJECTS, ORGANISMS, OR EVENTS IN THE ENVIRONMENT.

a. Ask: *What do seeds need to germinate?*

EXPLORE: PLAN AND CONDUCT SIMPLE INVESTIGATIONS TO COLLECT RELEVANT DATA.

b. Ask: *How could we find out?* Lead children to suggest an investigation to determine if light is needed for seed germination. In the investigation, the same kinds of seeds are placed in two germination bags. One bag is placed in a well-lit place; the other in a very dark place. Ask: *What is the manipulated variable?* (The amount of light.) *What is the responding variable?* (The germination of the seeds.) *What variables should be controlled?* Emphasize that to be a controlled investigation, the moisture in each bag and its temperature have to be the same.

c. Let groups of children set up the investigation and observe the seeds for about 2 weeks, being careful not to expose the dark seeds to the light. Tell students to keep their observational records in a chart like the one illustrated.

Seed name and amount	Date planted	Germination date Predicted	Germination date Actual	Germination conditions	Number of seeds germinated

d. Ask: *What did you observe? What do you conclude?* (That light is not necessary for seed germination. After all, seeds germinate underground in the dark.)

e. Ask: *Are there other factors that affect the germination of seeds? How could we determine the range of temperatures that seeds can tolerate and still sprout?* Lead the students to plan a controlled investigation using two germination bags, with one bag placed in the refrigerator and one in a warm, dark place. Discuss the responding variable (growth), the manipulated variable (temperature), and the variables to be controlled (amount of light, kinds of seeds, amount of water, etc.). Ask: *If one bag is placed in a refrigerator, why would the other one need to be in a "dark" place?*

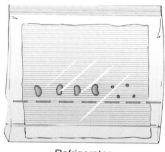

Refrigerator

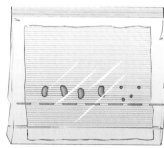

Dark cabinet

f. Tell students to place three lima bean seeds and three radish seeds in two separate plastic germination bags. Have students carry out the controlled investigation they planned. Put one bag in a cool, dark place (e.g., inside a refrigerator) and one bag in a warm, dark place (e.g., inside a cabinet). Make sure the two bags have the same amount of moisture and light.

g. Instruct students to observe the two bags regularly for about 2 weeks and to record their observations in their chart (like the one in the previous illustration). *Note:* Open the bags daily for about 15 minutes to prevent the formation of mold. Also, keep the paper towels just slightly moist.

h. After 2 weeks of observations, ask: *How do the seeds in the two bags compare? How were the conditions for the two bags different? What do you think is the effect of temperature on germination (sprouting)? Why do you think so? What is your evidence?*

NSES   **Concepts and Principles**

Activity 10 addresses these fundamental concepts and principles related to the *Science Standards:*

- All animals depend on plants (K–4).
- Some animals eat plants for food (K–4).

10. WHAT SEEDS DO WE EAT? (K–4)

ENGAGE: ASK A
QUESTION ABOUT OBJECTS,
ORGANISMS, OR EVENTS IN
THE ENVIRONMENT.

a. Ask: *What seeds or seed products do we eat?*

EXPLORE: PLAN
AND CONDUCT SIMPLE
INVESTIGATIONS TO
COLLECT RELEVANT DATA.

b. Hold a classroom "seed feast." Provide a variety of seeds for children to eat. Consider some of the seeds and seed products in the accompanying chart for the seed feast.

Safety Precautions

Make sure children are not allergic to any food you provide for them to eat, such as peanuts.

EXPLAIN: USE
DATA TO GENERATE
INTERPRETATIONS,
INCLUDING DESCRIPTIONS,
CLASSIFICATIONS,
PREDICTIONS, AND
EXPLANATIONS.

c. Using the chart, conduct a discussion of the various seeds and seed products we eat. Emphasize that rather than the cotyledons providing food for the seeds to germinate and begin growth, they are providing food energy for our survival and growth.

SEEDS AND SEED PRODUCTS WE EAT

Food	Seed or Seed Product
Peas	seeds (and fruit)
Beans	seeds (and fruit)
Corn	seeds
Rice	seeds
Peanuts	seeds
Sunflower seeds	seeds
Chocolate	made from seeds of cacao plant
Coffee	made from seeds of coffee plant
Vanilla	made from seeds of orchid
Cumin (spice)	made from cumin seeds
Flour	made from wheat, barley, or other grass seeds
Pretzels	made from flour
Bread	made from flour
Tortillas	made from flour or corn
Breakfast cereals	made from the seeds of grasses including wheat, rye, oats, and barley

Source: Adapted from National Gardening Association, 1990. *GrowLab.* National Gardening Association, Burlington, VT.

B. PLANTS

▶ *Science Background*

Biologists classify organisms on the basis of their structures and behaviors. Most organisms can be classified as plants or animals. Each plant or animal has different structures that serve different functions in growth, survival, and reproduction. All organisms have basic needs. Plants need light, air, water, and nutrients. Animals need air, water, and nutrients. Plants and animals can survive only in environments in which their needs are met. Roots absorb water and nutrients through small root hairs. Water and nutrients are carried from the roots to the leaves through small tubes, called capillaries, that are inside the stem. Plants get their energy for survival and growth directly from sunlight through a process called photosynthesis. Animals live by consuming the energy-rich foods initially synthesized by plants.[1]

NSES Science Standards

All students should develop an understanding of

- characteristics of organisms (K–4).
- structure and function in living systems (5–8).
- life cycles of organisms (K–4).
- organisms and their environments (K–4).

Objectives for Students

1. Recognize and appreciate the wide variation in plant life.
2. Identify and describe different parts/structures of plants (roots, stems, leaves) and describe the functions of each.
3. Observe and describe the life cycles of plants.
4. Ask questions about plants that can be answered through investigations.
5. Design and carry out descriptive, classificatory, and explanatory investigations to gather information for answering questions about plants.
6. Use simple equipment and tools to gather data and extend the senses.
7. Through investigations, identify basic needs of plants: air, water, nutrients, and light.
8. Use evidence from investigations and science knowledge to answer questions about plant life, construct explanations, and make predictions.

NSES Concepts and Principles

Activities 1–4 address or provide preparation for learning these fundamental concepts and principles related to the *Science Standards* or *Benchmarks for Science Literacy*:

- Some animals and plants are alike in the way they look and the things they do, and others are very different from one another (K–2).
- A great variety of living things can be sorted into groups in many ways using various features to decide which things belong to which group (3–5).
- Features used for grouping depend on the purpose of the grouping (3–5).
- Each plant or animal has different structures that serve different functions in growth, survival, and reproduction (K–4).

---

[1]Adapted from National Research Council (1996). *National Science Education Standards*.

1. WHAT IS A TREE LIKE? (K–2)

ENGAGE: ASK A QUESTION ABOUT OBJECTS, ORGANISMS, OR EVENTS IN THE ENVIRONMENT.

a. Ask: *What are the properties of trees? How do trees differ? How are they similar?*

EXPLORE: PLAN AND CONDUCT SIMPLE INVESTIGATIONS TO COLLECT RELEVANT DATA.

b. Have students hug a tree trunk, feel its surface, and describe how it feels. Encourage students to smell the bark. Have them draw and give a name to their favorite tree or cut pictures of trees out of magazines.

EXPLAIN: USE DATA TO GENERATE INTERPRETATIONS, INCLUDING DESCRIPTIONS, CLASSIFICATIONS, PREDICTIONS, AND EXPLANATIONS.

c. Ask: *What was your favorite tree like? What did it look like? How did it smell? How did it differ from other trees?* Discuss children's findings with them.

2. HOW DO THE CHARACTERISTICS OF LEAVES VARY? (K–2)

Materials

Assortment of leaves
Magazines
Newspapers
Colored paper
Paintbrushes
Poster paint

ENGAGE: ASK A QUESTION ABOUT OBJECTS, ORGANISMS, OR EVENTS IN THE ENVIRONMENT.

a. Ask: *What are leaves like? What are the similarities in leaves from different trees? What are the differences in the leaves from different trees?*

EXPLORE: PLAN AND CONDUCT SIMPLE INVESTIGATIONS TO COLLECT RELEVANT DATA.

b. Invite students to take a walk through a nature area at home or school, collect a variety of fallen leaves, and bring them to class.

Safety Precautions

Stress collecting fallen leaves only. Do not allow students to pick from living trees and plants.

EXPLAIN: USE
DATA TO GENERATE
INTERPRETATIONS,
INCLUDING DESCRIPTIONS,
CLASSIFICATIONS,
PREDICTIONS, AND
EXPLANATIONS.

c. Instruct students to spread the leaves out and compare them. Ask: *How are the leaves alike? How are they different? How do the leaves differ in shape? size? color? number of points? arrangement of veins? How do they differ in other ways? Why do you think the leaves vary so much from one another?*

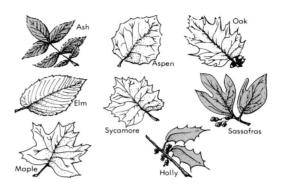

d. Tell the students to place the leaves in groups according to color, shape, size, or some other characteristic. Ask: *How many groups did you get?* Then tell them to rearrange the leaves according to other characteristics. Ask: *How many groups did you get?*

ELABORATE: EXTEND
CONCEPTS, PRINCIPLES,
AND STRATEGIES TO NEW
SITUATIONS AND
QUESTIONS.

e. Have students press some leaves between newspapers. Place books or something heavy on the newspapers. After several days, remove the weights and newspapers. Discuss how drying helps to preserve the leaves.

f. Tell students to place leaves on colored paper. Then show students how to dip brushes in poster paint and splatter it over the leaves to make a picture outline.

NSES   **Concepts and Principles**

Activity 3 addresses these fundamental concepts and principles related to the *Science Standards:*

- Organisms have basic needs. Plants require air, water, nutrients, and light (K–4).
- Organisms can survive only in environments in which their basic needs are met (K–4).
- Each plant or animal has different structures that serve different functions in growth, survival, and reproduction (K–4).

3. HOW CAN SOME PLANTS GROW WITHOUT SEEDS? (K–2)

Materials

Small tumblers (preferably clear plastic)
Small sweet potatoes, white potatoes, and carrot tops (with some root)
Toothpicks
Cuttings from coleus, philodendron, ivy, and other houseplants

ENGAGE: ASK A QUESTION ABOUT OBJECTS, ORGANISMS, OR EVENTS IN THE ENVIRONMENT.

a. Ask: *What is needed for new plants to grow? How can we get new plants to grow without planting them in soil? How can we take good care of our new plants?*

EXPLORE: PLAN AND CONDUCT SIMPLE INVESTIGATIONS TO COLLECT RELEVANT DATA.

b. Put three toothpicks each in a sweet potato, white potato, and carrot, as shown in the diagram. Place them in small tumblers of water. Take cuttings of houseplants and place them in small tumblers of water. Put all the tumblers in a well-lit place and make sure the water levels are maintained so that the water always touches the plants. Have students observe, measure, and record the changes in the plants, such as root development, height, number of leaves, and so on.

Coleus and philodendron   Sweet potato   White potato   Carrot

EXPLAIN: USE DATA TO GENERATE INTERPRETATIONS, INCLUDING DESCRIPTIONS, CLASSIFICATIONS, PREDICTIONS, AND EXPLANATIONS.

c. Ask: *Do new plants come only from seeds? What is your evidence?*
d. Ask: *What do plants need to grow?* Explain to students that plants require air, water, nutrients, and light. Plants can survive only in environments in which these basic needs are met. Ask: *How do you think these basic needs of plants are met when they are growing in water? How are the basic needs of plants met when they are growing in soil?*

NSES   **Concepts and Principles**

Activities 4–7 address these fundamental concepts and principles related to the *Science Standards:*

• Organisms have basic needs. Plants require air, water, nutrients, and light (K–4).
• Each plant or animal has different structures that serve different functions in growth, survival, and reproduction (K–4).

··

4. WHAT ARE ROOTS LIKE? (K–5)

Materials | Lima bean plants and radish plants growing in a germination bag
Magnifying lenses
Small, healthy coleus, geranium, or petunia plants
Potting soil
Planting containers (such as clean, empty milk cartons)

ENGAGE: ASK A QUESTION ABOUT OBJECTS, ORGANISMS, OR EVENTS IN THE ENVIRONMENT.

a. Ask: *What do the roots of a young plant look like? What could you do to find out?*

EXPLORE: PLAN AND CONDUCT SIMPLE INVESTIGATIONS TO COLLECT RELEVANT DATA.

b. Lead students to answer this question through their observations of the roots of bean plants and radish plants growing in a germination bag. Instruct students to use a magnifying lens and to record their observations, including drawings, of the structure of roots.

c. Continue the observation of the roots of plants for several days. Require students to make daily records of their observations in their journals.

EXPLAIN: USE DATA TO GENERATE INTERPRETATIONS, INCLUDING DESCRIPTIONS, CLASSIFICATIONS, PREDICTIONS, AND EXPLANATIONS.

d. After several days of observation, ask: *What do you notice about the roots? How are the roots of the bean plant and radish plant similar? How are they different? What are the small, fuzzlike projections coming from the roots?* (Root hairs.)

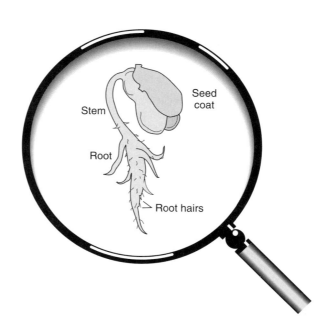

5. WHAT IS THE FUNCTION OF ROOTS? (K–5)

ENGAGE: ASK A QUESTION ABOUT OBJECTS, ORGANISMS, OR EVENTS IN THE ENVIRONMENT.

a. Ask: *What do you think is the function of the roots and the root hairs? What could you do to investigate to find out?* Lead students to suggest that functions of roots may be to absorb water and nutrients for plant growth and to provide support for plants. Ask: *How might you investigate these hypotheses?*

EXPLORE: PLAN AND CONDUCT SIMPLE INVESTIGATIONS TO COLLECT RELEVANT DATA.

b. Obtain two similar coleus, petunia, or geranium plants and remove all the roots from one plant. Fill the bottom half of two milk cartons or other planting containers with soil. Place the plant without roots down on top of the soil. Release the plant and observe what happens. Ask: *How might roots have helped this plant?* Explain that one function of the roots is to provide support for plants.

c. Push the bottom part of the stem of the plant without roots to a depth of about 5 cm into the soil. Water the plant daily. Observe the plant for 4 or 5 days. As a control, plant the other plant with roots in a container of soil.

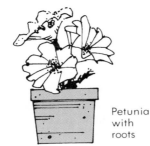

Petunia with roots

Petunia without roots

EXPLAIN: USE DATA TO GENERATE INTERPRETATIONS, INCLUDING DESCRIPTIONS, CLASSIFICATIONS, PREDICTIONS, AND EXPLANATIONS.

d. Ask: *What did you observe about the two plants? Why do you think this happens?* Explain that one function of the root hairs is to absorb water and nutrients for the plant. Because the root hairs are critical to the life of the plant, it is important that they not be damaged when a plant is pulled up or transplanted.

Gently pull the plant without roots from the soil. If this plant has developed new roots, discuss the function of the newly developed roots.

e. Ask: *Why do you think some roots grow comparatively shallow and others grow deep? What are some ways people use the roots of plants?*

6. DO PLANTS GET WATER THROUGH ROOTS OR LEAVES? (K–5)

ENGAGE: ASK A QUESTION ABOUT OBJECTS, ORGANISMS, OR EVENTS IN THE ENVIRONMENT.

a. Ask: *Do plants get water through their roots or leaves? What could we do to find out?*

EXPLORE: PLAN AND CONDUCT SIMPLE INVESTIGATIONS TO COLLECT RELEVANT DATA.

b. To gather evidence to answer this key question, lead children to set up a controlled investigation like the one illustrated. This investigation involves two plants. Water is added to the soil of one plant so that it can reach the roots. Water is sprinkled on the leaves of the second plant, with a plastic bib keeping the water from reaching the soil and roots. All other conditions are controlled.

plastic "bib"

dish

Pot A
Water soil

Pot B
Water leaves

c. Tell the children to keep daily records of their observations.

EXPLAIN: USE
DATA TO GENERATE
INTERPRETATIONS,
INCLUDING DESCRIPTIONS,
CLASSIFICATIONS,
PREDICTIONS, AND
EXPLANATIONS.

d. After about 2 weeks, lead a discussion of the children's findings. Ask: *What did you do in the investigation? What did you observe? How did your findings compare with your predictions? What can you infer about the role of leaves in taking in water? Did you actually see roots taking in water? What makes you confident in your inference that water is taken in by roots? What factors might have affected the results of your investigation?* (For example, watering might have damaged the leaves.)[2]

7. WHAT IS THE FUNCTION OF A STEM? (K–5)

Materials

Carnations
Geranium or celery stem
Red and blue food coloring
Drinking glass or clear plastic cup
Paper towel

Preparation

Place the stem of a white carnation in a cup containing water with blue food coloring. Leave the carnation in the water until it has turned blue.

ENGAGE: ASK A
QUESTION ABOUT OBJECTS,
ORGANISMS, OR EVENTS IN
THE ENVIRONMENT.

a. Ask: *Why is this carnation blue? Aren't carnations usually white? Do you think I planted a blue carnation seed? How does water get from the roots of a plant to the leaves? How do you think a florist produces blue carnations? If you wanted to change a white carnation into a blue carnation, what would you do? How could you find out if your idea was correct?*

[2]Adapted from National Gardening Association, 1990. *GrowLab: Activities for Growing Minds*. National Gardening Association, 180 Flynn Avenue, Burlington, Vermont 05401.

EXPLORE: PLAN AND
CONDUCT SIMPLE
INVESTIGATIONS TO
COLLECT RELEVANT DATA.

b. Fill a cup with water, tint with food coloring, and add a rolled paper towel, as in diagram (a).

   Ask: *What do you see happening to the paper towel? Why do you think this happens? How could this work in plants?*

c. Tell children to put some water in the drinking glass and add the food coloring. Cut a small slice off the bottom of the celery stem. Set the stem into the glass of colored water as in diagram (b). Allow it to sit in a sunny area for 2 hours. At the end of this period, cut open the stem. See diagram (c).

EXPLAIN: USE
DATA TO GENERATE
INTERPRETATIONS,
INCLUDING DESCRIPTIONS,
CLASSIFICATIONS,
PREDICTIONS, AND
EXPLANATIONS.

d. Ask: *What has happened to the celery stem? What parts of the stem appear to contain the colored water? How do you know? What can you conclude about the function of a stem?*

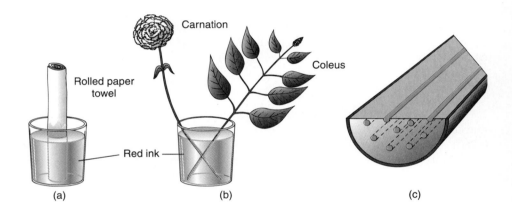

ELABORATE: EXTEND
CONCEPTS, PRINCIPLES,
AND STRATEGIES TO NEW
SITUATIONS AND
QUESTIONS.

e. Ask: *What do you think might happen if you put half of a split stem in one color of water and the other half in another color of water? Try it and see.*

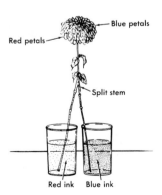

f. Ask: *What do you think might happen to the upward movement of water in a stem when the plant is in the dark or out of sunlight? How could you find out?*

NSES Concepts and Principles

Activities 8–10 address these fundamental concepts and principles related to the *Science Standards:*

• Organisms have basic needs. Plants require air, water, nutrients, and light (K–4).

8. HOW MUCH WATER IS ENOUGH FOR HEALTHY PLANT GROWTH? (K–5)

Materials

Young bean or radish plants
Milk cartons or plastic cups
Graduated cylinder or measuring cup

ENGAGE: ASK A QUESTION ABOUT OBJECTS, ORGANISMS, OR EVENTS IN THE ENVIRONMENT.

a. Ask: *How much water do you need each day? How much water do you think a plant needs to grow in a healthy way? How could you find out?*

EXPLORE: PLAN AND CONDUCT SIMPLE INVESTIGATIONS TO COLLECT RELEVANT DATA.

b. Guide students to design an investigation to determine how much water a plant needs to grow.
   1. Set up three young bean plants in small pots, labeled A, B, and C.
   2. Give the plant in pot A one tablespoon of water each week.
   3. Place pot B in a bowl of water as in the diagram.
   4. Water the plant in pot C as needed.

EXPLAIN: USE DATA TO GENERATE INTERPRETATIONS, INCLUDING DESCRIPTIONS, CLASSIFICATIONS, PREDICTIONS, AND EXPLANATIONS.

c. Ask: *How do the conditions of the plants differ? Which one seems healthiest? What are the indications of health?*

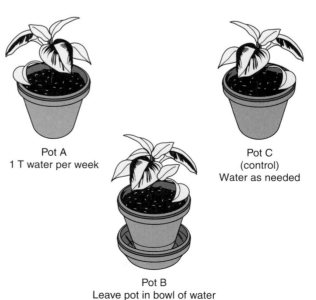

Pot A
1 T water per week

Pot C
(control)
Water as needed

Pot B
Leave pot in bowl of water

Children tend to overwater plants. Too much water can be as harmful as too little water. Lead students to observe plants to determine when they might need water.

9. HOW MUCH FERTILIZER IS ENOUGH FOR HEALTHY PLANT GROWTH? (K–5)

Materials

Young bean or radish plants
Milk cartons or plastic cups
Fertilizer
Graduated cylinder or measuring cup

ENGAGE: ASK A QUESTION ABOUT OBJECTS, ORGANISMS, OR EVENTS IN THE ENVIRONMENT.

a. Ask: *How much fertilizer do plants need?*

EXPLORE: PLAN AND CONDUCT SIMPLE INVESTIGATIONS TO COLLECT RELEVANT DATA.

b. Guide children to plan and set up an investigation similar to that in the illustration to determine how much fertilizer is enough for plants.

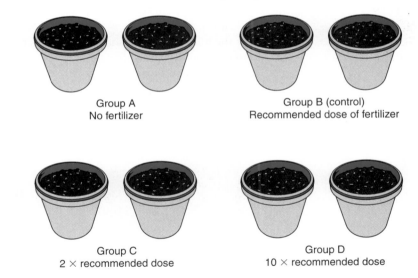

Group A
No fertilizer

Group B (control)
Recommended dose of fertilizer

Group C
2 × recommended dose

Group D
10 × recommended dose

c. Lead students to observe the plants and make records in their observation journals. They might observe, measure, and compare the height of each plant, leaf color, number of leaves, and leaf size.

EXPLAIN: USE DATA TO GENERATE INTERPRETATIONS, INCLUDING DESCRIPTIONS, CLASSIFICATIONS, PREDICTIONS, AND EXPLANATIONS.

d. Ask: *How do the conditions of the plants differ? Which one seems healthiest? What do you conclude about the amount of fertilizer a plant needs? What does fertilizer supply for plants?*

▶ *Teaching Background*

Plants require **mineral nutrients** for growth, repair, and proper functioning. Mineral nutrients are formed by the breakdown of rocks and other materials in the earth. Mineral nutrients can also be supplied by fertilizers applied by humans. Humans ordinarily obtain minerals from eating plants or animals. Nutrients can also be obtained from supplements.[3]

10. WHAT IS THE EFFECT OF LIGHT ON PLANT GROWTH? (3–5)

Materials

Germinated bean seeds
Sunny window or light source
Ruler
Potting soil
Clean milk carton
Shoe box with cover

ENGAGE: ASK A
QUESTION ABOUT OBJECTS,
ORGANISMS, OR EVENTS IN
THE ENVIRONMENT.

a. Ask: *What effect does light have on the way a plant grows? What do you think might happen to a plant if the amount of light from a light source is very limited? What do you think might happen if a plant is placed near a window? What could you do to find out?*

EXPLORE: PLAN
AND CONDUCT SIMPLE
INVESTIGATIONS TO
COLLECT RELEVANT DATA.

b. Plant four germinated bean seeds 3/4 inch to 1 inch (2 cm) deep in moist soil in a clean milk carton.

c. Place the milk carton in a shoe box that has only a single, 1 inch hole cut in the middle of one end. Cover the box and turn the opening toward bright sunlight or a strong lamp, as shown in the diagram.

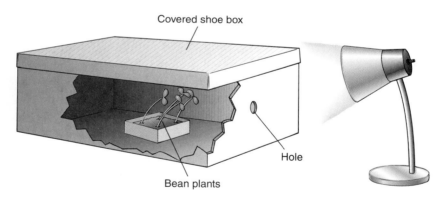

Covered shoe box

Hole

Bean plants

d. Lift the cover every 2 days and see how the bean plants are growing. Record observations. Add water as needed.

EXPLAIN: USE DATA TO
GENERATE INTERPRETATIONS,
INCLUDING DESCRIPTIONS,
CLASSIFICATIONS,
PREDICTIONS, AND
EXPLANATIONS.

e. Ask: *What is happening to the stems and leaves? Why do you think they are growing as they are? What do you think might happen if you turned the milk carton with the plants completely around in the shoe box?*

f. Try it and observe what happens in 2 days.

---

[3]Adapted from National Gardening Association, 1990. *GrowLab: Activities for Growing Minds.* National Gardening Association, 180 Flynn Avenue, Burlington, Vermont 05401.

▶ *Teaching Background*

Students should see that the beans grow toward the opening in the shoe box. When turned around, they reverse their direction of growth toward the opening again. Green plants need sunlight and are forced toward the light by **phototropism,** which causes the cells on one side of leaves to grow faster than the other. This causes the turning effect of the leaves toward the sunlight.

    g. Ask: *Knowing what you do about* **phototropism,** *the effect of light on plants, why is it necessary to turn your plants at the windowsill every few days? What might happen if you did not turn them?*

Concepts and Principles

Activities 11–15 address these fundamental concepts and principles related to the *Science Standards:*

- Organisms have basic needs. Plants require air, water, nutrients, and light (K–4).
- Each plant or animal has different structures that serve different functions in growth, survival, and reproduction (K–4).

11. WHAT MAKES LEAVES GREEN? (3–5)

Materials

Double boiler pot
Hot plate
Assorted green leaves
Rubbing alcohol

ENGAGE: ASK A QUESTION ABOUT OBJECTS, ORGANISMS, OR EVENTS IN THE ENVIRONMENT.

    a. Ask: *What color are most leaves? Why do you think this is so?*

Safety Precautions:

Caution children to stay away from boiling water.

EXPLORE: PLAN AND CONDUCT SIMPLE INVESTIGATIONS TO COLLECT RELEVANT DATA.

    b. Teacher should demonstrate this activity for the students.
        1. With water in the bottom and green leaves and rubbing alcohol in the top, set up the double boiler pot on the hot plate.
            Ask: *What color are the leaves as we put them in the rubbing alcohol?*
        2. Heat the double boiler so that water boils for 10 minutes. Review parts of plants and discuss leaves while the water boils.
        3. Remove leaves from the pot and observe.

EXPLAIN: USE DATA TO GENERATE INTERPRETATIONS, INCLUDING DESCRIPTIONS, CLASSIFICATIONS, PREDICTIONS, AND EXPLANATIONS.

c. Ask: *What color are the leaves now?*
What color is the rubbing alcohol now? Why?
What do we call the "green stuff" in leaves? (This is called **chlorophyll.**)

....

12. WHAT MAKES LEAVES GREEN? (METHOD TWO) (3–6)

Materials

Rock
1 inch by 4 inch strip of filter paper or white coffee filter
Clear plastic cup

ENGAGE: ASK A QUESTION ABOUT OBJECTS, ORGANISMS, OR EVENTS IN THE ENVIRONMENT.

a. Ask: *What color are most leaves? Why do you think this is so?*

EXPLORE: PLAN AND CONDUCT SIMPLE INVESTIGATIONS TO COLLECT RELEVANT DATA.

b. Another method to find "hidden" colors in plant leaves uses the following technique, which students can perform under your supervision:
   1. Use a rock to rub a leaf impression about 1 inch up on a 1 inch by 4 inch strip of filter paper or white coffee filter, as in diagram (a).
   2. Place enough water to cover the bottom of a clear plastic cup and fold the paper so it hangs from the edge of the jar, just touching the bottom. See diagram (b). What do you think will happen?
   3. Observe the changes.

EXPLAIN: USE DATA TO GENERATE INTERPRETATIONS, INCLUDING DESCRIPTIONS, CLASSIFICATIONS, PREDICTIONS, AND EXPLANATIONS.

c. Ask: *What happened? Why? What colors were revealed?*

ELABORATE: EXTEND CONCEPTS, PRINCIPLES, AND STRATEGIES TO NEW SITUATIONS AND QUESTIONS.

d. Try this activity with different leaves.

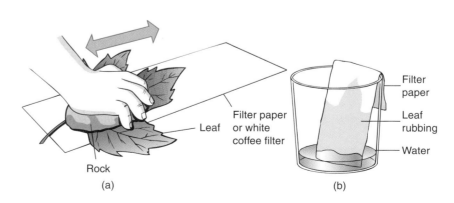

Leaf

Filter paper or white coffee filter

Rock

(a)

Filter paper

Leaf rubbing

Water

(b)

▶ *Teaching Background*

As the water slowly rises, it hits the plant leaf "stain" in the filter and separates out some of the pigments. This reveals the "hidden" colors of the leaf.

Note: Using acetone (nail polish remover) in place of the water will produce better results by separating pigments more effectively. If you use acetone, place it in a closed glass jar instead of an open plastic cup.

Safety Precautions

Acetone fumes can be harmful. Keep acetone in a closed container. Do not allow children to breathe the acetone fumes.

13. HOW DOES LIGHT AFFECT PLANTS? (K–2)

Materials

Two plants of the same type—one that has been growing in the dark for a week and the other in light
Healthy plant growing in pot
3M Post-it foil stars

ENGAGE: ASK A QUESTION ABOUT OBJECTS, ORGANISMS, OR EVENTS IN THE ENVIRONMENT.

a. Show students two plants of the same type—one that has been in the dark for a week and the other that has been in light. Ask: *How do you think they got this way?*

EXPLORE: PLAN AND CONDUCT SIMPLE INVESTIGATIONS TO COLLECT RELEVANT DATA.

b. Guide students to conduct this investigation:
   1. Select a healthy outdoor or indoor plant. Peel and stick a few foil stars on one or two leaves, while the plant is in the pot or ground and in growing conditions (has water, sun, etc.).
   2. Leave stars on for 1 week.
   3. Remove stars from leaves.

EXPLAIN: USE DATA TO GENERATE INTERPRETATIONS, INCLUDING DESCRIPTIONS, CLASSIFICATIONS, PREDICTIONS, AND EXPLANATIONS.

c. Ask: *What do you see? Why do you think this happened?*
d. Ask: *What do you think will happen to the spots that were under the stars if the plant is put back in the sun for 1 week?* Ask the children to try it, to observe what happens, and to record their data.
e. Ask: *What did you observe? Why did this happen?*

▶ *Teaching Background*

Plants are green because of **chlorophyll.** Chlorophyll absorbs light energy from the sun and helps plants make food. Without sunlight, plants use up the chlorophyll, the leaf starts to turn white, and the plant eventually dies.

14. WHAT COMES OUT OF LEAVES IN SUNLIGHT? (3–5)

Materials

Elodea water plants (obtained from classroom aquarium or pet store)
1 gallon widemouthed jar
Glass or plastic funnel
Test tube
Lamp or sunlight
Wooden splint
Matches
Magnifying lens

ENGAGE: ASK A QUESTION ABOUT OBJECTS, ORGANISMS, OR EVENTS IN THE ENVIRONMENT.

a. Ask: *What happens when your head is underwater and you let some air out of your mouth? What do you see?* (Remember from activities with air that bubbles indicate the presence of air.) *What do you think might happen to a plant if it is placed underwater in sunlight?*

EXPLORE: PLAN AND CONDUCT SIMPLE INVESTIGATIONS TO COLLECT RELEVANT DATA.

b. Do this activity:
 1. Put a water plant such as elodea in a 1 gallon widemouthed jar.
 2. Invert a glass or plastic funnel over the elodea and place a test tube completely full of water over the stem of the funnel, as shown in the diagram.
 3. Place the jar in direct sunlight for 3 days.

EXPLAIN: USE DATA TO GENERATE INTERPRETATIONS, INCLUDING DESCRIPTIONS, CLASSIFICATIONS, PREDICTIONS, AND EXPLANATIONS.

c. Ask: *What do you see coming up from the elodea plant?*
  What happened to the level of water in the test tube? Why do you think the water level changed?
  What do you think might be in the test tube?

ELABORATE: EXTEND CONCEPTS, PRINCIPLES, AND STRATEGIES TO NEW SITUATIONS AND QUESTIONS.

d. Ask: *How might you set up an experiment to find out what is in the test tube?*
e. *Note:* The teacher should perform this step as a demonstration: When most of the water in the test tube has been displaced, quickly remove the test tube and insert a glowing splint or lit match into the test tube, as shown in the diagram.

Ask: *What do you see happening to the wooden splint or lit match? Why do you think this happened?*

Guide students to understand that the splint burned brightly because of **oxygen** given off from the elodea plant in sunlight. Oxygen is given off by plants during photosynthesis.

Leaves have small pores called **stomata** through which air enters and gases escape (see drawings). Students can use magnifying lenses to view stomata as the oxygen is released from the green plant.

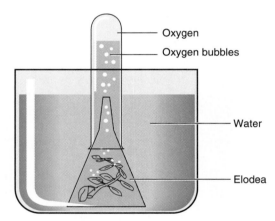

- Oxygen
- Oxygen bubbles
- Water
- Elodea

....

15. WHAT ELSE COMES OUT OF LEAVES IN SUNLIGHT? (3–5)

Materials

Two clear plastic bags
Two small, identical geranium plants
Plastic ties
Magnifying lenses

ENGAGE: ASK A QUESTION ABOUT OBJECTS, ORGANISMS, OR EVENTS IN THE ENVIRONMENT.

a. Ask: *What else might come out of leaves in sunlight?*

EXPLORE: PLAN AND CONDUCT SIMPLE INVESTIGATIONS TO COLLECT RELEVANT DATA.

b. Instruct students to do this activity:
   1. Place a clear plastic bag over one geranium and tie the bag around the stem, just above the soil level.
   2. Wave a second plastic bag through the air and tie it as well, as illustrated in the diagram.
   3. Put both plastic bags in direct sunlight for at least 3 hours.

EXPLAIN: USE DATA TO GENERATE INTERPRETATIONS, INCLUDING DESCRIPTIONS, CLASSIFICATIONS, PREDICTIONS, AND EXPLANATIONS.

c. After 3 hours, ask:
  - *What do you see forming on the top of the plant in the plastic bag? Where do you think the moisture came from?* (From the leaves of the plant.)
  - *What is your evidence that the moisture came from the leaves and not the soil?* (The plastic bag was tied off above the soil line.)
  - *How is the plastic bag without the plant different after 3 hours? Why do you think this happened? Why do you think the empty plastic bag was used in this activity?*
  - *What makes this investigation a controlled experiment?* (Two identical bags containing air are used, one with a plant and one without a plant. The condition varied—the manipulated variable—is whether or not a bag has a plant. The outcome or responding variable is the production of moisture.)

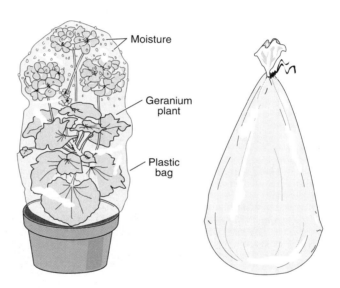

Moisture

Geranium plant

Plastic bag

▶ *Teaching Background*

Moisture is formed in the plastic bag with the plant as a by-product of **photosynthesis** in the leaves. The purpose of tying off the bag at the stem was to prevent moisture evaporating from the soil from entering the bag. The "empty" clear plastic bag is the control.

NSES **Concepts and Principles**

Activity 16 addresses these fundamental concepts and principles related to the *Science Standards:*

- Organisms can survive only in environments in which their basic needs are met (K–4).
- Each plant or animal has different structures that serve different functions in growth, survival, and reproduction (K–4).

16. WHAT IS THE EFFECT OF GRAVITY ON THE GROWTH OF ROOTS AND STEMS? (K–5)

Materials

Young, growing bean plants
Paper towels
Two pieces of glass or thick plastic to place growing plants between
Tongue depressors or applicator sticks
Small pebbles
Tape

ENGAGE: ASK A QUESTION ABOUT OBJECTS, ORGANISMS, OR EVENTS IN THE ENVIRONMENT.

a. Ask: *What do you think might happen to roots of a plant if they were planted facing up or sideways rather than facing down? What do you think might happen to roots if something were in their way? What could we do to find out? What do you think would happen to the stems of plants that are planted upside down or sideways?* Lead students to design an investigation in which the plant is planted upside down so that the progress of roots and stems can be observed.

EXPLORE: PLAN AND CONDUCT SIMPLE INVESTIGATIONS TO COLLECT RELEVANT DATA.

b. This investigation might be done as a class demonstration. Place four young bean plants between two moist paper towels. Put the paper towels with the seedlings between two pieces of glass or rigid, clear plastic. Put small pebbles under each root. Place the applicator sticks or tongue depressors between the pieces of glass or clear plastic, and tape as shown in the diagram.

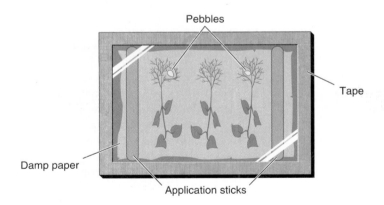

Pebbles

Tape

Damp paper

Application sticks

c. Stand the glass so the roots point up and the stems point down. Instruct the students to observe the plant growth for several days and record their observations.

EXPLAIN: USE DATA TO GENERATE INTERPRETATIONS, INCLUDING DESCRIPTIONS, CLASSIFICATIONS, PREDICTIONS, AND EXPLANATIONS.

d. Ask: *What did you observe about the roots? What did you observe about the stems? Why do you think this happened?* Through discussion, lead students to conclude that roots grow downward under the influence of gravity and that they grow around objects in the soil. Stems grow upward.

▶ *Teaching Background*

The roots will grow down (toward the earth), and the stems will grow up (away from the earth). The plant responses that cause this are called **tropisms. Geotropism** forces roots down as auxins (plant hormones) are concentrated by gravity along the bottom cells of stems and root tips. The bottom cells in the stem are stimulated by the hormones to grow faster than cells higher up; they get longer and curl upward. Root cells are more sensitive to these hormones than are stem cells, so the root cells inhibit cell growth. Root top cells elongate faster, and root tips curve downward.

C. INSECTS

▶ *Science Background*

Insects are the most successful group of animals on earth. Insects dominate the planet in terms of number of individuals and species. There are more kinds of insects than all other kinds of animals put together. All insects have six legs and three body parts: the head, thorax, and abdomen. Insects that may be familiar to children include dragonflies, crickets, lice, beetles, butterflies, flies, fleas, and ants.

Insects change in form through a process called metamorphosis as they grow and mature. Some insects progress from egg, to larva, to a pupal stage, and then to adults. Other insects look pretty much like adults when they hatch from eggs.[4]

NSES   Science Standards

All students should develop an understanding of

- characteristics of organisms (K–4).
- structure and function in living systems (5–8).
- life cycles of organisms (K–4).
- organisms and their environments (K–4).

Objectives for Students

1. Recognize the wide variation in insects.
2. Identify and describe different parts/structures of insects.
3. Define *metamorphosis* and name the stages in the metamorphosis of a mealworm.
4. Describe the sequence of stages in the development of a mealworm.
5. Ask questions about ants that can be answered through investigations.
6. Design and carry out descriptive investigations to gather information and answer questions about ants.

NSES   Concepts and Principles

Activity I addresses these fundamental concepts and principles related to the *Science Standards*:

- Plants and animals have life cycles that include being born, developing into adults, reproducing, and eventually dying. The details of this life cycle are different for different organisms (K–4).

---

[4]Adapted from FOSS (Full Option Science System), 1995. *Insects*. Lawrence Hall of Science, Berkeley, CA. (Published by Delta Education, Nashua, NH.)

1. WHAT STAGES DO INSECTS GO THROUGH? (K–5)

Materials

Jars with covers (clear plastic, if possible)
Mealworms (from pet shop)
Bran or other cereal flakes
Magnifying lenses
Spoons
Pictures of people and insects at different growing stages

ENGAGE: ASK A QUESTION ABOUT OBJECTS, ORGANISMS, OR EVENTS IN THE ENVIRONMENT.

a. Ask: *What are the stages people go through as they grow and change? Do insects, like mealworms, go through stages too? How could we find out?*

EXPLORE: PLAN AND CONDUCT SIMPLE INVESTIGATIONS TO COLLECT RELEVANT DATA.

b. Obtain some mealworms from a pet store, granary, or commercial supplier (see Appendix C). Introduce the mealworms and challenge students to predict how the mealworms will change as they grow. Using spoons, you or the students can transfer several mealworms and some bran or cereal flakes into a jar or other container with a lid. Provide a container for each student or group of two or three students. Punch several small holes in the lids for air.

c. Have students observe the mealworms several times a week and record on a chart or log any observed changes in appearance (color, length, stage, etc.) or behavior.

EXPLAIN: USE DATA TO GENERATE INTERPRETATIONS, INCLUDING DESCRIPTIONS, CLASSIFICATIONS, PREDICTIONS, AND EXPLANATIONS.

d. Using pictures of people and insects at different stages of growth, discuss how these living things grow. Help students make a chart comparing the stages of insects' lives with humans', like the one shown.

Stages	
People	*Insects*
Child	Larva
Teenager	Pupa
Adult	Adult

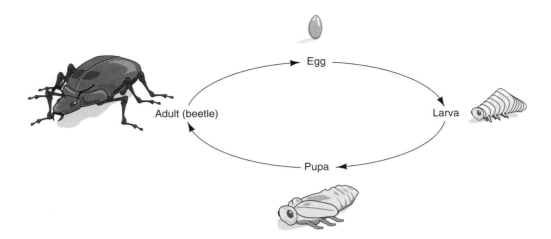

e. In addition, guide students to make a diagram, similar to the one shown, and include photos or drawings to visualize the stages of mealworm (and other insect) metamorphosis. Make the same kind of diagram for stages of human life (infant, child, teenager, and adult).

NSES   **Concepts and Principles**

Activity 2 addresses these fundamental concepts and principles related to the *Science Standards:*

- Organisms have basic needs. Animals need air, water, and food (K–4).
- Organisms can survive only in environments in which their basic needs are met (K–4).
- Each plant or animal has different structures that serve different functions in growth, survival, and reproduction (K–4).

2. HOW DO ANTS LIVE? (K–2)

Materials

Widemouthed glass jar (commercial mayonnaise or pickle jar) with screw top punctured with very small holes
Empty washed soup can
Soil to fill the jar two-thirds full
Small sponge
Pan large enough to hold the widemouthed glass jar
Sheet of black construction paper
Crumbs and bits of food such as bread, cake, sugar, seeds
Colony of ants (from pet shop, home, or school grounds)

ENGAGE: ASK A QUESTION ABOUT OBJECTS, ORGANISMS, OR EVENTS IN THE ENVIRONMENT.

a. Ask: *What do ants look like? Are all ants alike, or are there different kinds of ants? Where do ants make their homes?* Lead children to draw pictures of ants and to describe and explain their pictures.

EXPLORE: PLAN
AND CONDUCT SIMPLE
INVESTIGATIONS TO
COLLECT RELEVANT DATA.

b. Set up an ant colony following these directions:
    1. Place the soup can in the center of the widemouthed glass jar as in the diagram.
    2. Fill the jar two-thirds full of soil.
    3. Punch several airholes in the screw cover.
    4. Place a sheet of black construction paper around the outside of the jar.
    5. Add a small sponge with water. Add crumbs and bits of food (bread, cake, sugar, and seeds).
    6. Add ants.
    7. Place a cloth over the top of the jar and screw the jar lid in place.
    8. Place the jar in a pan of water.

Safety Precautions

Caution children not to handle the ants. As a defense, ants bite and sting. Sometimes after biting an enemy, ants will spray a chemical into the open wound.

c. Ask: *What effect will a sheet of black paper placed around the jar have on the ants?* (This simulates the dark underground so ants will tunnel close to the sides of the glass jar.) *Why place the soup can in the center of the jar with soil around it?* (So ants will not burrow into the center but will tunnel out to the jar's sides and be more visible.) *What is the purpose of placing the jar in a pan of water?* (So the ants cannot escape.)

d. Guide children to observe ants, including observing with magnifying lenses. Instruct students to make records, including drawings, of what ants look like and what the ants do. Students should observe body characteristics such as are shown in the diagram.[5] Ask: *Are all ants in the ant colony alike?*
    How many pairs of legs do ants have?

---

[5]Adapted and modified from *Ant Homes Under the Ground*, one of more than 75 teacher's guides in the Great Explorations in Math and Science (GEMS) series, available from the Lawrence Hall of Science, University of California at Berkeley. For more information, visit their website at www.lhsgems.org.

What are the antennae on the head used for?
How do ants move?
What does the egg of an ant look like?

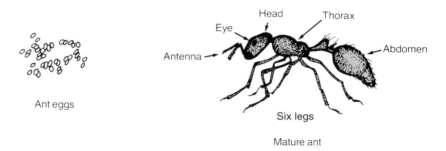

Ant eggs

Mature ant

e. Ask: *What do ants eat?*

Divide a paper plate into sections with a black marker. Place various food items on the plate (e.g., crackers, small seeds, sugar, lettuce). Set the plate outside near an ant trail on a nice warm day. Check back after 1 hour to see what has happened. Check back after 2 hours. What food have the ants taken? What is their favorite food?

EXPLAIN: USE DATA TO GENERATE INTERPRETATIONS, INCLUDING DESCRIPTIONS, CLASSIFICATIONS, PREDICTIONS, AND EXPLANATIONS.

f. Ask: *How do the ants connect their homes in the jar?*

What changes have the ants made in their environment since they were first placed in the jar?

In what ways are ants useful to people?
What are some other insects that live and work together?
What are some living things that are sometimes mistaken for insects?
What might happen if the ant colony were placed in a light, warm place?
How are ants different from spiders?
In what ways are ants social animals?

D. BIRDS

▶ *Science Background*

Birds are familiar animals in the child's environment. Birds differ in a variety of ways. Children can observe many different characteristics of birds, such as colors and sizes. Birds sing different songs, eat different kinds of food, and make different kinds of nests where they care for their young. The male bird may have a more colorful plumage than the female. Some birds change color with the season. Some birds migrate. Birds need trees and shrubs for protection from their predators, including small mammals, humans, and even other birds.

NSES **Science Standards**

All students should develop an understanding of

- characteristics of organisms (K–4).
- structure and function in living systems (5-8).
- organisms and their environments (K–4).

Objectives for Students

1. Recognize the wide variation in birds.
2. Identify and describe different characteristics of birds.
3. Ask questions about birds that can be answered through investigations.
4. Design and carry out descriptive and classificatory investigations to gather information for answering questions about birds.

NSES Concepts and Principles

Activities 1–4 address these fundamental concepts and principles related to the *Science Standards* and *Benchmarks for Science Literacy:*

- Some animals and plants are alike in the way they look and the things they do, and others are very different from one another (K–2).
- A great variety of living things can be sorted into groups in many ways using various features to decide which things belong to which group (3–5).
- Organisms have basic needs. Animals need air, water, and food (K–4).
- Organisms can survive only in environments in which their basic needs are met (K–4).

1. WHAT DO YOU KNOW ABOUT THE BIRDS AROUND YOU? (K–6)

Materials

Bird book (showing local birds)
Pictures of birds
Bird feeders (commercial or made in class)

ENGAGE: ASK A QUESTION ABOUT OBJECTS, ORGANISMS, OR EVENTS IN THE ENVIRONMENT.

a. Lead children in a discussion of what they know about birds.
  Ask: *How are birds alike? How are birds different?*
  Where do some birds go during the winter?
  What kinds of homes do birds live in?
  What do birds do that is different from what other animals do?
  What kinds of foods do birds eat?
  What are the names of some local birds?
  What do these birds look like?

EXPLORE: PLAN AND CONDUCT SIMPLE INVESTIGATIONS TO COLLECT RELEVANT DATA.

b. If the natural environment lends itself to feeding and observing birds, have students observe birds on the way to and from school, or take a class field trip to a local area, park, or zoo. In a city, you will probably see sparrows or pigeons, jays in picnic areas, ducks in ponds, geese on golf courses, and seagulls at the seashore. In addition, you may want to provide pictures of different birds, nests, and eggs for students to handle, observe, and discuss.

c. Record students' responses to this question on the board: *How could we attract birds to our school grounds?*
  Ask: *Where could we make a good bird feeding and observing area?* (Tree and shrub shelter that is free from predators and visible from the classroom.)

d. Set up a bird feeding and observing area.
  1. With your students, survey your school grounds and pick the best spot for a bird feeding and observing area.
  2. Find out what kinds of birds are common in your area, what their food preferences are, how they eat (on the ground or from feeders), and any other information that will make your feeding and observing most useful for birds.

3. Put up a bird feeder(s) and a water tray.
4. Design an experiment or follow the suggestions provided to investigate birds.

2. WHAT KINDS OF FOODS DO DIFFERENT BIRDS PREFER? (K–6)

Materials

Bird food (bread, popcorn, commercial birdseed)
Plastic cups
Small pieces of cloth

ENGAGE: ASK A QUESTION ABOUT OBJECTS, ORGANISMS, OR EVENTS IN THE ENVIRONMENT.

a. Ask: *What kinds of food do birds prefer?*

EXPLORE: PLAN AND CONDUCT SIMPLE INVESTIGATIONS TO COLLECT RELEVANT DATA.

b. Try offering small equal amounts of two kinds of food (e.g., bread and birdseed) to the birds at the same time.

Safety Precautions

Do *not* feed birds directly from your hand; instead, put some food in such places as a bird feeder on a tree limb or a pole, on the ground, in a plastic cup, and so on.

EXPLAIN: USE DATA TO GENERATE INTERPRETATIONS, INCLUDING DESCRIPTIONS, CLASSIFICATIONS, PREDICTIONS, AND EXPLANATIONS.

c. Ask: *Which food do birds prefer? What is your evidence?*
Where do birds prefer their food to be put?
Did different birds like different places?
What was the most popular feeding spot?

d. Ask: *Does one individual bird or kind of bird get the most food?*
   How does the bird do it?
   What happens when you try to give food to the other birds?
   Why do you think this happens?

3. HOW DO BIRDS INTERACT WITH THEIR SURROUNDINGS? (3–6)

ENGAGE: ASK A QUESTION ABOUT OBJECTS, ORGANISMS, OR EVENTS IN THE ENVIRONMENT.

a. Ask: *How do loud noises and sudden movements affect birds?*

EXPLORE: PLAN AND CONDUCT SIMPLE INVESTIGATIONS TO COLLECT RELEVANT DATA.

b. While birds are gathered, make a really loud noise, but remain perfectly still. Observe what happens. Next, make a sudden dramatic movement, but be very quiet. Observe what the birds do.

EXPLAIN: USE DATA TO GENERATE INTERPRETATIONS, INCLUDING DESCRIPTIONS, CLASSIFICATIONS, PREDICTIONS, AND EXPLANATIONS.

c. Ask: *What did the birds do when you made a loud noise?*
   What did the birds do when you made a sudden movement?
   Did the loud noise or the sudden movement scare the birds more?
   How do you know?
   Why do you think this is so?

How could you help children understand what scientists do?

d. Explain that when they observed birds and investigated how birds responded to noise and movement, they were acting like scientists. The investigation was a controlled experiment. Discuss with the children why it was important to control for movement when they were testing the effects of noise and why it was important to control for noise when they were testing the effects of movement.

4. HOW CAN YOU FIND OUT MORE ABOUT BIRDS? (3–6)

ENGAGE: ASK A QUESTION ABOUT OBJECTS, ORGANISMS, OR EVENTS IN THE ENVIRONMENT.

a. Ask: *Why is it so important to continue feeding birds and supplying water once we begin?*
   How are these "wild birds" the same and different from domestic (pet) birds like parrots and canaries?
   How do birds help people?
   How might birds harm people?
   What are some different ways birds in our neighborhood build their nests?

EXPLORE: PLAN AND CONDUCT SIMPLE INVESTIGATIONS TO COLLECT RELEVANT DATA.

b. The following types of questions can be asked about any of the local birds. These questions may have to be modified, however, depending on the kinds of birds that are found in your region.

- **Redheaded Woodpecker**. *Where does the woodpecker build its nest? How does it build its nest? What kind of food does the woodpecker eat? How does the woodpecker benefit and harm our environment? How does a woodpecker's beak aid it in getting food?*

- **Hummingbird**. *How does the male hummingbird differ in color from the female? Where do hummingbirds get their food? Are hummingbirds as big as cardinals or sparrows? Why do you have difficulty finding their nests? How do hummingbirds help in the pollination of plants? How does a hummingbird's beak aid it in getting food?*

- **Starling**. *Why do many other birds prefer not to live near starlings? What color is the starling? How does the starling vary in color compared with the hummingbird and woodpecker? Why do farmers dislike starlings during fruit harvesting season?*

 NSES

Concepts and Principles

Activity 5 addresses this fundamental principle related to the *Science Standards:*

- Each plant or animal has different structures that serve different functions in growth, survival, and reproduction (K–4).

5. HOW DO BIRD BONES DIFFER FROM MAMMAL BONES? (3–6)

Materials

Beef and chicken bones (one of each for every two students). If possible, these should be cut in half.

Wing bones of chickens (or any other bird).

ENGAGE: ASK A QUESTION ABOUT OBJECTS, ORGANISMS, OR EVENTS IN THE ENVIRONMENT.

a. Ask: *How do bird bones differ from the bones of mammals?*

EXPLORE: PLAN AND CONDUCT SIMPLE INVESTIGATIONS TO COLLECT RELEVANT DATA.

b. Allow students to help furnish beef and chicken bones.
1. Obtain a cut chicken bone, a cut beef bone, and a wing bone of a chicken.
2. *How did you know which bone was from a chicken and which was from a cow?*
3. Examine the centers of the two bones and record how the structure of the beef bone differs from that of the chicken bone.
4. Look at the chicken wing bone.
   How does its structure compare with the arm bones of a person?

EXPLAIN: USE DATA TO GENERATE INTERPRETATIONS, INCLUDING DESCRIPTIONS, CLASSIFICATIONS, PREDICTIONS, AND EXPLANATIONS.

c. Ask: *What advantages do you think bones of birds and mammals have for them?*
   What are some other structural differences between birds and mammals?

II. ORGANISMS AND THEIR ENVIRONMENTS

Organisms have basic needs. Animals need air, water, and food. Plants require air, water, nutrients, and light. Organisms can survive only in environments in which their basic needs are met.

A. AQUARIUM HABITATS

▶ *Science Background*

An aquarium is a wonderful context for studying aquatic life. There are many environmental factors important to life in aquarium habitats, including temperature, water transparency, nutrients, and concentrations of dissolved gases (oxygen and carbon dioxide).

Both plants and animals use oxygen and give off carbon dioxide through respiration. Plants also use carbon dioxide and give off oxygen in the process of photosynthesis. During daylight hours, aquatic plants produce more oxygen than plants and animals consume in respiration. At night, both plants and animals use accumulated oxygen.

When carbon dioxide dissolves in water, it makes the water acidic. Bromothymol blue (BTB) is a chemical indicator that can be used to monitor acid concentration in aquariums. BTB changes color, depending on the acidity of the water. A few drops of BTB in a

container of water that is neutral produces a pale blue. If the water is acidic, its color shifts to green or yellow when BTB is added. If the water is basic, the color turns to deep blue.

 Science Standards

All students should develop an understanding of

- organisms and their environments (K–4).

Objectives for Students

1. Define *habitat* and *ecosystem*.
2. Identify and describe the parts of aquarium and terrarium habitats and describe how the parts in each system interact.
3. Construct aquarium and terrarium habitats.
4. Ask questions and design and carry out investigations about components and interactions within ecosystems.

 Concepts and Principles

Activities 1–3 address these fundamental concepts and principles related to the *Science Standards:*

- Organisms have basic needs. Animals need air, water, and food. Plants require air, water, nutrients, and light. Organisms can survive only in environments in which their basic needs are met (K–4).
- An organism's patterns of behavior are related to the nature of that organism's environment, including the kinds and numbers of other organisms present, the availability of food and resources, and the physical characteristics of the environment (K–4).
- When the environment changes, some plants and animals survive and reproduce, and others die or move to new locations (K–4).

1. HOW CAN I CONSTRUCT AN AQUARIUM HABITAT? (1–3)

Materials

A 6 liter, clear plastic basin (used as the aquarium)
Five small aquatic plants (approximately 3 to 4 inches or 10 cm in height)
Freshwater fantailed guppy
Two water snails

ENGAGE: ASK A QUESTION ABOUT OBJECTS, ORGANISMS, OR EVENTS IN THE ENVIRONMENT.

a. Ask: *What is an aquarium? What lives in an aquarium? What are some of the things fish, plants, and other organisms need to survive in an aquarium? How must an aquarium be constructed and maintained to support living things?*

EXPLORE: PLAN AND CONDUCT SIMPLE INVESTIGATIONS TO COLLECT RELEVANT DATA.

b. It is preferable for each group of students to have their own aquarium. Teachers should guide and work with students to construct and maintain a freshwater aquarium, following these instructions:
   1. *Container.* Obtain a 4 to 6 liter (1 to 1.5 gallons), rectangular clear plastic container with strong walls. The container should have a large surface area to allow gas exchange with the atmosphere, but should not be too shallow. Wash the container well with water, but not soap.

2. *Sand*. Obtain a supply of coarse white sand. Rinse the sand in a bucket to remove debris. Add white sand to a depth of about 4 cm to the bottom of the aquarium container.

3. *Water*. Age tap water in an open container for 24 to 48 hours to allow chlorine in the water to escape. You may choose to use bottled spring water (but not distilled water). Gently pour the water into the container, perhaps over clean paper to prevent disturbing the sand.

4. *Plants*. Obtain water plants from a pond or purchase them from a science supply company or a local pet shop (see Appendix C and D). Root about two sprigs of waterweed (elodea) and two sprigs of eelgrass in the sand. Add some duckweed as a floating plant. Overplanting is better for your aquarium than underplanting. Allow 1 to 2 weeks for the plants to become acclimated to the water before adding animals.

5. *Fish*. Purchase small fish from a pet store or obtain some free from an aquarium hobbyist. Obtain male and female guppies or goldfish. Place the plastic bag containing the fish in your aquarium water for a few hours for the water temperatures in the bag and the aquarium to become equal. Use a dip net to add three to four fish to the aquarium. A rule of thumb is not to have more than 1 cm of fish (excluding tail) per liter of water. Dispose of the plastic container and water the fish came in.

6. *Snails*. Add several small pond snails to your aquarium.

7. *Care*. Add a plastic lid to your aquarium. Lift the corners of the lid to allow exchange of gases between the water and the atmosphere. Thus, you will not need a pump for aeration. Keep a supply of aged tap water available to replace evaporated water as necessary, keeping the water in the aquarium at a predetermined level.

8. *Temperature*. Place your aquarium in the room so that it can get light, but not direct sunlight. Too much light will promote the growth of algae (which can, if you desire, be observed and studied by students). The aquarium should be maintained at room temperature (70° to 78°F or 21° to 25°C; see Appendix H for conversions). A gooseneck lamp with a 60 to 75 watt bulb can be used to warm the water if necessary. Adjust the lamp so the bulb is a few centimeters above the water, until the temperature is maintained at the desired level. Check with your principal about school regulations concerning leaving the lamp on over the weekend.

9. *Food*. Feed the fish a small amount (a pinch) of commercial fish food every other day (or as instructed on the package). Do not overfeed. Uneaten food will decay, polluting the water. Fish can go as long as 2 weeks without food. Fish may supplement their diet by eating from the water plants. Snails do not require any special food. They eat water plants or the debris that collects on the bottom of the aquarium.

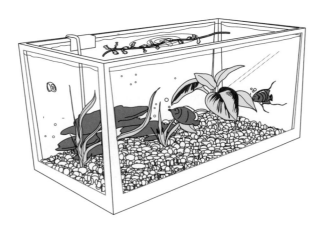

c. Two alternative containers for aquariums are shown in the following illustrations.

Food jar
aquarium

Soda bottle
aquarium

2. WHAT CAN I OBSERVE IN AN AQUARIUM? (1–3)

Materials

Aquarium
Plants
Fish
Snails

ENGAGE: ASK A QUESTION ABOUT OBJECTS, ORGANISMS, OR EVENTS IN THE ENVIRONMENT.

a. Ask: *What happens to the living things within an aquarium? How can we find out?*

EXPLORE: PLAN AND CONDUCT SIMPLE INVESTIGATIONS TO COLLECT RELEVANT DATA.

b. Let the children assist you in preparing one aquarium for each group of four students, following the instructions in Activity 1. Tell each group to observe their aquarium closely. Provide magnifying lenses to assist the students in their observations. Encourage them to talk freely about what they see. While the students are observing, move from group to group and listen to their discourse and questions. Do not answer their questions yet, but use them to help you plan class discussion.

c. Instruct the children to make records in their investigation journals of what they observe. Students might write about what they see and make labeled drawings with crayons, markers, pens, and pencils. Let children use their own terminology in their journals at first, gradually introducing (inventing) technical terms to supplement descriptions.

EXPLAIN: USE DATA TO GENERATE INTERPRETATIONS, INCLUDING DESCRIPTIONS, CLASSIFICATIONS, PREDICTIONS, AND EXPLANATIONS.

d. Take time on a regular basis to discuss with students what they are observing, changes they have noted, and questions they may have raised. Gather the students in a large group and ask such questions as: *What did you observe? Did anyone observe anything else? What is on the bottom of the aquarium?* (Sand.)

e. Explain that a **habitat** is a place where an animal or plant naturally lives or grows. A habitat provides the food, shelter, moisture, light, air, and protection the plants or animals need to survive. Ask: *Think of the aquarium as a habitat for fish; what components of the aquarium habitat support the fish and snails that live there?*

ELABORATE: EXTEND CONCEPTS, PRINCIPLES, AND STRATEGIES TO NEW SITUATIONS AND QUESTIONS.

f. Ask: *What do you wonder about fish and snails?* Lead the children to ask questions that can be answered through further observations or investigations. Children might ask such questions as: *What do the fish and snails eat? How much do they eat? Do the snails have mouths? What are those feelers on the snails?* (Antennae.) *What do they do?* (They contain the snails' eyes.) *What do the snails eat?* (Algae.) *Do the fish and snails sleep? Can they see me? What makes the water green? Will the fish have babies? Which is the mother fish and which is the daddy fish?* (The male guppies are more brightly colored than the females, plus, the females give birth to the baby guppies.) *What is the black stuff on the bottom of the aquarium?* (Detritus; waste products from fish.)

Do not answer the children's questions yet. Post their questions in the room for them to see, think about, and answer through further observation and investigation. Encourage them to observe carefully to try to answer the questions they have posed. Students should add to their journals and drawings regularly.

▶ *Teaching Suggestions*

Encourage children to look for changes in their aquariums. Point out that they will need their records to help them determine what is new in their aquariums.

- Children might observe clumps of transparent spheres on plants and the aquarium sides. These are eggs laid by the snails. Baby snails will hatch from the eggs. Mark the location of snail eggs on the outside of the aquarium with a marking pen. Ask students to observe the clumps regularly. Eventually, a small, black spot will appear in each sphere, becoming larger each day. After a week or 2 a small snail will hatch.
- If you are keeping guppies in your aquariums, children might also observe the birth of baby guppies. Female guppies carry their eggs in their bodies and deliver their young live. Children might note, with much amazement, that the baby guppies are eaten by the adults. To keep the young from being devoured, use a fish net to transfer the adults to another aquarium.

3. WHAT ENVIRONMENTAL FACTORS CAN AFFECT LIFE IN AN AQUARIUM HABITAT? (4–6)

Materials

Small container
BTB (bromothymol blue, obtained from science supply company, swimming pool supply company, or pharmacy)
Vinegar
Clean straws

ENGAGE: ASK A QUESTION ABOUT OBJECTS, ORGANISMS, OR EVENTS IN THE ENVIRONMENT.

a. Ask: *What environmental factors can affect life in an aquarium habitat?*

EXPLORE: PLAN AND CONDUCT SIMPLE INVESTIGATIONS TO COLLECT RELEVANT DATA.

b. Explain to students that the acidity of the water is one factor that needs to be controlled in an aquarium to support life. Explain that BTB is a chemical indicator, indicating whether a liquid is basic, neutral, or acidic. To demonstrate how BTB works, tell students to add two drops of BTB to 5 ml of water in a container. Ask: *What do you observe?* The water should be blue, indicating it is neutral.

Next, show your students a vial to which you have added 5 ml of water. Add two drops of BTB. Dip a straw in vinegar and then in the vial. Ask: *What do you observe?* Explain that the water turned green when the BTB was added because the vinegar was acidic.

Now, tell students to gently blow two or three breaths into the water in their own vials using a clean straw. Ask: *What do you observe now?* After a few breaths, the water usually turns yellow.

EXPLAIN: USE DATA TO GENERATE INTERPRETATIONS, INCLUDING DESCRIPTIONS, CLASSIFICATIONS, PREDICTIONS, AND EXPLANATIONS.

c. Ask: *What did you do? What did you see happen? Why do you think the water turned yellow when you breathed into it?* (The yellow color indicated that a weak acid formed from the interaction of the water in the vial and the carbon dioxide in your breath.)

ELABORATE: EXTEND CONCEPTS, PRINCIPLES, AND STRATEGIES TO NEW SITUATIONS AND QUESTIONS.

d. Explain to students that it is important to know the amount of acid in aquarium habitats because too much acid is harmful to the fish and other living organisms. Tell students to collect 5 ml of aged water and put it into a clean vial. Also tell them to add 5 ml of aquarium water to a second vial. Add two drops of BTB to each vial. Cap the vials and swirl the water in them. Usually the aquarium water will turn green or yellow, indicating acidity. Ask: *What do you think caused the acidity of the aquarium water?* Make a list of responses, such as something from the fish, too much food, chemicals from the air, something from the plants.

e. Ask how the students might investigate to find the source of the acid. Through discussion, allow the students to come up with the idea of running a controlled investigation. In the investigation, one factor is changed at a time, with everything else remaining the same.

B. TERRARIUM HABITATS

▶ *Science Background*

A terrarium is a habitat for plants and small animals, such as earthworms, pill bugs, and frogs. Terrariums must include everything a plant or animal needs to survive.

NSES **Science Standards**

All students should develop an understanding of

• organisms and their environments (K–4).

Objectives for Students

1. Define habitat and ecosystem.
2. Identify and describe the parts of aquarium and terrarium habitats and describe how the parts in each system interact.
3. Construct aquarium and terrarium habitats.
4. Ask questions and design and carry out investigations about components and interactions within ecosystems.

Concepts and Principles

Activities 1–5 address these fundamental concepts and principles related to the *Science Standards:*

- Organisms have basic needs. Animals need air, water, and food. Plants require air, water, nutrients, and light. Organisms can survive only in environments in which their basic needs are met (K–4).
- An organism's patterns of behavior are related to the nature of that organism's environment, including the kinds and numbers of other organisms present, the availability of food and resources, and the physical characteristics of the environment (K–4).
- When the environment changes, some plants and animals survive and reproduce, and others die or move to new locations (K–4).

1. WHAT IS IN SOIL? (K–5)

Materials

Soil
Magnifying lenses
Plastic spoons

ENGAGE: ASK A QUESTION ABOUT OBJECTS, ORGANISMS, OR EVENTS IN THE ENVIRONMENT.

a. Explain to students that soil is a very important natural resource that supports plant and animal life. Ask: *Where do you find soil? What do you think is in soil?*

EXPLORE: PLAN AND CONDUCT SIMPLE INVESTIGATIONS TO COLLECT RELEVANT DATA.

b. Instruct materials managers to pick up materials. Tell students to use the spoon to spread out their soil on a piece of white paper. Ask: *What do you observe about the soil?* Challenge students to use all of their senses except taste to observe the soil and to record at least three observations using each sense. To enhance the smell of soil, tell students to spray a bit of moisture on it.

EXPLAIN: USE DATA TO GENERATE INTERPRETATIONS, INCLUDING DESCRIPTIONS, CLASSIFICATIONS, PREDICTIONS, AND EXPLANATIONS.

c. Ask: *What did you observe? What was in your soil sample? Which senses was it easier to make observations with?*

2. WHAT IS AN EARTHWORM LIKE? (K–5)

Materials   Earthworms
                         Magnifying lenses

ENGAGE: ASK A
QUESTION ABOUT OBJECTS,
ORGANISMS, OR EVENTS IN
THE ENVIRONMENT.

    a. Ask: *What are earthworms like? How do they move? Where do they live? What do they eat? How could we find the answers to these questions?*

EXPLORE: PLAN
AND CONDUCT SIMPLE
INVESTIGATIONS TO
COLLECT RELEVANT DATA.

    b. Distribute an earthworm in a clear plastic cup to each group. Ask: *What do you observe about the earthworm?* Encourage students to use magnifying lenses to see details of the earthworms. If students wish, allow them to gently feel the earthworms or to hold them in their hands. Use the spoons to gently move the earthworms and see how they respond. Tell students to draw pictures of the earthworms in their investigation journals.

EXPLAIN: USE
DATA TO GENERATE
INTERPRETATIONS,
INCLUDING DESCRIPTIONS,
CLASSIFICATIONS,
PREDICTIONS, AND
EXPLANATIONS.

    c. Ask: *What did you observe about the earthworm? What were its characteristics? Did your earthworm have eyes and ears? How do you think it senses things, finds food, and finds its way around? What did your earthworm tend to eat? What did it do?*

▶ *Teaching Background*

Worms are segmented and have bristles on each segment. Worms have no eyes or ears, but their pointed head and round body is sensitive to vibrations and chemicals. Earthworms absorb water and oxygen through their skin. Remind students to keep an earthworm moist at all times when observing or it can dry out and die.

    Earthworms prefer to eat dried leaves and other organic matter, but will eat soil and extract the decomposing nutrients if nothing else is available. A worm's waste or casings contain nutrients that enrich the soil and provide the necessary nutrients for plant growth. An earthworm's tunneling mixes and aerates the soil.[6]

3. HOW CAN WE BUILD A TERRARIUM ENVIRONMENT FOR EARTHWORMS? (1–3)

Materials   Container for the terrarium (e.g., glass or plastic tanks, storage boxes, deli salad
                              containers, fish bowls, plastic bottles, or jars)
                         Soil
                         Sand
                         Small plants
                         Birdseed or grass seeds
                         Spray bottle for water
                         Litter (twigs, bark, and leaves)
                         Earthworms (obtained from digging in moist soil, from bait shop, or from commercial
                         supplier—see Appendix C)

---

[6]GEMS (Great Explorations in Math and Science), 1994. *Terrarium Habitats.* Lawrence Hall of Science, Berkeley, CA.

Safety Precautions

Collect soil from clean areas so that it is free from contaminants; wash your hands and have students wash their hands thoroughly after handling soil.

ENGAGE: ASK A QUESTION ABOUT OBJECTS, ORGANISMS, OR EVENTS IN THE ENVIRONMENT.

a. Explain that a **terrarium** is any enclosed container that has been set up to house plants and small animals. Terrariums must contain all the components the plants and animals need to survive.
b. Ask: *What do earthworms need to survive?* (Air, water, food, soil.) *Suppose we wanted to build a terrarium for earthworms. What components should the earthworm terrarium include?* (Soil with air and moisture, plants as a source of food.)

EXPLORE: PLAN AND CONDUCT SIMPLE INVESTIGATIONS TO COLLECT RELEVANT DATA.

c. Assist your students to construct a terrarium for each cooperative group in your classroom. To build a terrarium, follow these instructions:
    1. Obtain a container for your terrarium.
    2. Clean the container with water and rinse it well.
    3. Mix three parts soil with one part sand and fill the terrarium container one-third full of the mixture.
    4. Make small holes in the soil and plant two or three small plants in the holes. Cover the roots with soil and firmly press soil on all sides of the stems. Sprinkle some seeds over the soil.
    5. Add litter—twigs, bark, and leaves.
    6. Add moisture with a spray bottle. Limit the amount of moisture in a terrarium to about four squirts of water.
        Caution: Do not overwater the terrarium during this investigation.
    7. Carefully place an earthworm and a dry leaf for the earthworm to eat in the terrarium.
    8. Place a lid on the terrarium and put it in a cool place where it can get natural light, but no sunlight.
    9. Your terrarium should need no more than about two squirts of moisture per week.[7]

EXPLAIN: USE DATA TO GENERATE INTERPRETATIONS, INCLUDING DESCRIPTIONS, CLASSIFICATIONS, PREDICTIONS, AND EXPLANATIONS.

d. Ask: *What is a habitat?* Explain that a **habitat** is a place where an animal or plant naturally lives or grows. A habitat provides the food, shelter, moisture, light, air, and protection that the plants or animals need to survive. Your terrarium is a habitat for plants and earthworms. Ask: *How are the needs of earthworms met by the terrarium habitat? What other habitats do you observe regularly? What is the habitat for birds? fish? deer? humans?*

ELABORATE: EXTEND CONCEPTS, PRINCIPLES, AND STRATEGIES TO NEW SITUATIONS AND QUESTIONS.

e. Allow students to observe their terrarium habitats regularly for several weeks. Ask: *What changes have taken place in your terrarium? What do the earthworms do? What is your evidence about what earthworms eat? What happens to the plants? What happens to the seeds? Do you detect any moisture in your terrarium? How does the terrarium habitat supply the needs of the earthworms?*

    Students should keep written or pictorial records of their observations in their investigation journals.

---

[7]Adapted and modified from *Terrarium Habitats,* one of more than 75 teacher's guides in the Great Explorations in Math and Science (GEMS) series, available from the Lawrence Hall of Science, University of California at Berkeley. For more information, visit their website at www.lhsgems.org.

....

4. HOW CAN WE BUILD A DESERT TERRARIUM? (3–5)

Materials

Terrarium container
Cactus plant
Twig
Bottle cap
Desert animal, such as a lizard or horned toad

ENGAGE: ASK A QUESTION ABOUT OBJECTS, ORGANISMS, OR EVENTS IN THE ENVIRONMENT.

a. Ask: *What is a desert terrarium? What animals and plants might live there?* How can we build desert terrariums?

EXPLORE: PLAN AND CONDUCT SIMPLE INVESTIGATIONS TO COLLECT RELEVANT DATA.

b. A desert terrarium can be built out of a large mayonnaise jar, soda bottle, or other container, as in the illustrations.
   1. Select and clean a container for the terrarium.
   2. Place about 2 cups of sand onto the bottom of the jar or bottle.
   3. Place a small cactus plant, a twig, and a small bottle cap filled with water in the terrarium.
   4. Place a small desert animal, such as a lizard or horned toad, in the desert terrarium habitat.
   5. Place the terrarium so that it receives sunlight every day.
   6. Feed the animals live mealworms (see Appendix F for feeding requirements). These can be obtained from a local pet shop.
   7. Keep the bottle cap filled with water.
   8. Spray one or two squirts of water into the terrarium every 2 weeks, only if the terrarium is dry.
c. Regularly observe and keep records on how the desert animals interact with their terrarium habitat.

EXPLAIN: USE DATA TO GENERATE INTERPRETATIONS, INCLUDING DESCRIPTIONS, CLASSIFICATIONS, PREDICTIONS, AND EXPLANATIONS.

d. Ask: *Why do dryland animals have such scaly skin?*
   Why do you think ferns or mosses would not survive in this habitat?
   Would frogs or turtles be able to live in this habitat? Why or why not?

Food jar terrarium

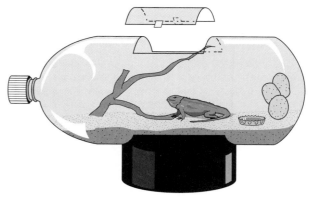

Soda bottle desert terrarium

5. HOW CAN WE BUILD A WETLAND TERRARIUM? (3–5)

Materials   Terrarium container with lid
Gravel
Ferns, mosses, lichens, and liverworts
Small water turtle or frog

ENGAGE: ASK A QUESTION ABOUT OBJECTS, ORGANISMS, OR EVENTS IN THE ENVIRONMENT.

a. Ask: *What is a wetland terrarium? What animals and plants might live there? How can we build wetland terrariums?*

EXPLORE: PLAN AND CONDUCT SIMPLE INVESTIGATIONS TO COLLECT RELEVANT DATA.

b. A wetland terrarium can be built in a large mayonnaise jar or other container, as in the illustrations.
   1. Select and clean a container for the terrarium.
   2. Spread gravel out on the bottom of the jar so it will be concentrated toward the back of the jar, as shown in the diagram.
   3. Place ferns, mosses, lichens, and liverworts over the gravel.
   4. Pour some water in the jar. (Do not put in so much that it covers the back portion of the arrangement.)
   5. Place a dried twig in the jar.
   6. Place a small water turtle or frog in the jar.
   7. Cover the jar with the punctured lid.
   8. Feed the turtle or frog insects or turtle food every other day (see Appendix F).
   9. Place the terrarium in an area where light is weak.

Lid

Gravel

Tape wood strips

Bog terrarium

c. Regularly observe and keep records on how the wetland animal interacts with its terrarium habitat.

EXPLAIN: USE DATA TO GENERATE INTERPRETATIONS, INCLUDING DESCRIPTIONS, CLASSIFICATIONS, PREDICTIONS, AND EXPLANATIONS.

d. Ask: *What kinds of conditions do the turtle, frog, or lizard need to survive in their particular habitats?*

What kinds of conditions do the bog plants require to grow well?

What kinds of food do the turtle, frog, or lizard eat?

What do you think would happen to the turtle if you left it in the desert habitat or to the lizard if you put it in the bog habitat?

What other kinds of environments or habitats could you make?

What does the environment have to do with the kinds of organisms found in it?

What might happen to a fern plant if it were transplanted to a desert region?

What might happen to a penguin if it were taken to live in a desert?

What would humans need to survive in an artic region?

ELABORATE: EXTEND CONCEPTS, PRINCIPLES, AND STRATEGIES TO NEW SITUATIONS AND QUESTIONS.

e. Complete the following chart for the aquarium and terrarium habitats you constructed, describing the food, water, shelter, and other conditions you provided for the organisms living there.

NAME OF HABITAT:	
Habitat Living Conditions	Description
Food	
Shelter	
Air	
Temperature	
Climate	
Water	
Others	

III. STRUCTURES AND FUNCTIONS OF HUMAN SYSTEMS

Each plant or animal has different structures that serve different functions in growth, survival, and reproduction. For example, animals, including humans, have body structures for respiration, protection from disease, and digestion of food. Warm-blooded animals have structures for regulating temperature. Humans have distinct body structures for walking, holding, seeing, and talking.

A. THE HUMAN SYSTEM FOR RESPIRATION

▶ *Science Background*

Humans, like other animals, need oxygen to survive. Oxygen is taken in through breathing. Breathing is controlled by movement of the diaphragm. When the diaphragm moves down, air is forced into the lungs. When the diaphragm moves up in the rib cage, air is forced out of the lungs. Gases and water vapor are exhaled from the lungs. When a person exercises, breathing rate increases. Breathing increases because more carbon dioxide is produced. Carbon dioxide causes the diaphragm to involuntarily work more rapidly. Lung capacity varies from person to person and can be increased by aerobic training.

 Science Standards

All students should develop an understanding of

- characteristics of organisms (K–4).
- structure and function in living systems (5–8).

Objectives for Students

1. Define *system* and apply the term to human systems.
2. Ask questions and design and carry out investigations to answer questions about structure and function in the human respiratory system.
3. Describe the form and function of the human system for respiration.

 Concepts and Principles

Activities 1–6 prepare students to understand these fundamental concepts and principles related to the *Science Standards*:

- Living systems at all levels of organization demonstrate the complementary nature of structure and function (5–8).
- The human organism has systems for digestion, respiration, reproduction, circulation, excretion, movement, control and coordination, and protection from disease. These systems interact with one another (5–8).

1. HOW DOES BREATHING CHANGE YOUR CHEST SIZE? (2–4)

Materials

Tape measure

ENGAGE: ASK A QUESTION ABOUT OBJECTS, ORGANISMS, OR EVENTS IN THE ENVIRONMENT.

a. Ask: *How does the size of your chest vary when you breathe? How might you find out?*

EXPLORE: PLAN AND CONDUCT SIMPLE INVESTIGATIONS TO COLLECT RELEVANT DATA.

b. Guide small cooperative groups of students to conduct this investigation.
   1. With a tape measure, check and record these measurements.

	Top of Chest	Lower Diaphragm
Inhale		
Exhale		

2. Construct a class graph to illustrate variations in measurement among students.

EXPLAIN: USE DATA TO GENERATE INTERPRETATIONS, INCLUDING DESCRIPTIONS, CLASSIFICATIONS, PREDICTIONS, AND EXPLANATIONS.

c. Ask: *How do inhale and exhale chest measurements vary for different students? for boys and girls? for tall and short students? Is there a pattern?*

2. WHAT IS IN OUR BREATH? (3–6)

Materials

Mirror (preferably metal)

ENGAGE: ASK A QUESTION ABOUT OBJECTS, ORGANISMS, OR EVENTS IN THE ENVIRONMENT.

a. Ask: *What do you see when you breathe outside on a very cold day?*
Why do you think that happens?
How might we find out?

EXPLORE: PLAN AND CONDUCT SIMPLE INVESTIGATIONS TO COLLECT RELEVANT DATA.

b. Assist students to do this activity:
   1. Obtain a mirror.
   2. Hold the mirror near your nose and mouth and exhale on it.
   What do you see on the mirror?

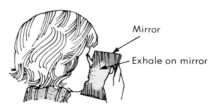

Mirror

Exhale on mirror

EXPLAIN: USE DATA TO GENERATE INTERPRETATIONS, INCLUDING DESCRIPTIONS, CLASSIFICATIONS, PREDICTIONS, AND EXPLANATIONS.

c. Ask: *Why does moisture collect on the mirror?* (Water vapor is exhaled. When the warm moist exhaled air comes in contact with the cooler mirror, water condenses on the surface of the mirror.) Ask: *Where does the moisture come from?* (From the exhaled air.) *What kinds of gases do you think you exhale?*

3. HOW CAN WE TEST THE GASES IN OUR BREATH? (3–6)

Materials

Three plastic cups
Turkey baster or large syringe
Plastic drinking straws
Calcium hydroxide tablets (obtain from a drugstore)

ENGAGE: ASK A
QUESTION ABOUT OBJECTS,
ORGANISMS, OR EVENTS IN
THE ENVIRONMENT.

a. Ask: *Is there a difference in the composition of the air around us and the air we exhale? How can we identify the gases contained in exhaled air?*

EXPLORE: PLAN
AND CONDUCT SIMPLE
INVESTIGATIONS TO
COLLECT RELEVANT DATA.

b. This investigation can be done as a teacher demonstration or by students in cooperative groups:
   1. Obtain two clear plastic cups, a turkey baster, a straw, and 100 cc of limewater made by dissolving a calcium hydroxide tablet in a large container of water. Mix half the limewater with regular water in each cup. Let the water settle.
   2. Put a straw in one cup and a turkey baster or large syringe in the other. Describe how the limewater in the cups looks.

(a) Breath in limewater   (b) Baster in limewater

   3. One student should blow through a straw into one cup of limewater while the other pumps the bulb of the turkey baster into the other cup of limewater.

EXPLAIN: USE
DATA TO GENERATE
INTERPRETATIONS,
INCLUDING DESCRIPTIONS,
CLASSIFICATIONS,
PREDICTIONS, AND
EXPLANATIONS.

c. Ask: *What happens to the limewater as you blow (exhale) through the straw into the water? Why does the water get "cloudy"?*
   What happens to the limewater when you squeeze the turkey baster into it?
   Why do you think the limewater did not change?
   Why is this a controlled experiment? What condition is varied?
   What is the responding variable? What do you think is controlled?

▶ *Teaching Background*

This investigation compares breathed air that is blown through a straw with regular air that is pumped from a turkey baster. The test results suggest that breathed air contains a significant amount of carbon dioxide gas. When carbon dioxide is added to limewater, the water changes to a milky color because the carbon dioxide combines with calcium hydroxide to form a white precipitate. You can see the white powder precipitate on the bottom of the cup. You can test the white powder that falls to the bottom by adding some vinegar; vinegar will cause calcium or carbonate to foam. Regular air may also contain carbon dioxide, but not enough to detect by this procedure.

4. WHAT MAKES YOU BREATHE FASTER? (3–8)

Materials

Stopwatch
Mirror

ENGAGE: ASK A QUESTION ABOUT OBJECTS, ORGANISMS, OR EVENTS IN THE ENVIRONMENT.

a. Ask: *How many times a minute do you breathe? How do you know? How would you go about finding out?*

EXPLORE: PLAN AND CONDUCT SIMPLE INVESTIGATIONS TO COLLECT RELEVANT DATA.

b. This activity should be done in groups of three: one student does the activity; the second student counts the number of breaths; the third student is the timekeeper. At the completion of each activity, the students should rotate in their tasks until all have completed the activity. Explain that students should count the number of exhaled breaths in a time interval. Students may use a mirror to see the exhaled breaths.

1. Student 1 should breathe normally. Student 2 should count the number of exhaled breaths in 15 seconds. Student 3 should use a stopwatch to start the count at an inhale phase and stop the count after 15 seconds. Do this three times, 1 minute apart.
2. Have the student being tested run in place for 1 minute and then repeat step 1.
3. Use this chart for recording your data.

Time	At Rest	After Exercise
1 minute		
2 minutes		
3 minutes		

4. When you finish three "at rest" and three "after exercise" data collections, rotate the jobs until all three of you have breathed, counted breaths, and kept time.
5. Graph your rest and exercise record on a diagram like the one shown.

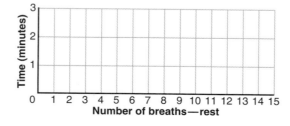

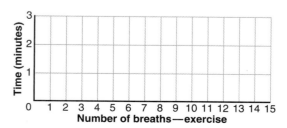

EXPLAIN: USE DATA TO GENERATE INTERPRETATIONS, INCLUDING DESCRIPTIONS, CLASSIFICATIONS, PREDICTIONS, AND EXPLANATIONS.

c. Ask: *What is the average number of times per minute a person breathes at rest? How would you figure that?* (Take the average of all nine readings, including three readings per person.)
   What is the average number of times per minute a person breathes after exercise?
   Why do you think exercise makes a person breathe faster?
   What is your evidence that you exhale or breathe out water vapor?

5. HOW CAN WE MAKE A MODEL OF LUNGS? (3–8)

Materials

For each group:

- Plastic cup
- Drinking straw
- Small plastic bag
- Small balloon
- Rubber band
- Scissors

ENGAGE: ASK A QUESTION ABOUT OBJECTS, ORGANISMS, OR EVENTS IN THE ENVIRONMENT.

a. Ask: *How do your lungs work to inhale and exhale gases?*

EXPLORE: PLAN AND CONDUCT SIMPLE INVESTIGATIONS TO COLLECT RELEVANT DATA.

b. Guide students to conduct this activity. You may wish to punch a hole in the plastic cups (see step 3) before students begin the activity. The heated tip of an ice pick will pierce the plastic easily.
   1. Obtain a plastic drinking straw, a small plastic bag, two rubber bands, a clear plastic cup, a small balloon, and scissors.
   2. Cut the straw in half.
   3. In the bottom of the cup, punch a hole the same width as the straw.
   4. Stretch and blow up the balloon a few times.
   5. Using a tightly wound rubber band, attach the balloon to the straw. Be sure the balloon does not come off when you blow into the straw, and that the rubber band does not crush the straw.

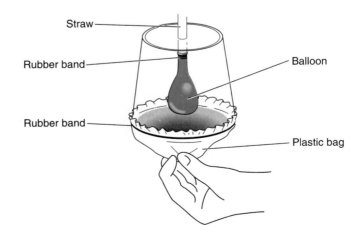

Straw
Rubber band
Balloon
Rubber band
Plastic bag

6. Push the free end of the straw through the cup's hole and pull until the balloon is in the middle of the cup. Seal the area around the hole and straw with modeling clay.
7. Place the open end of the cup into the small plastic bag and fold the bag around the cup, securing it tightly with a rubber band or masking tape. The plastic bag should be loose, not stretched taut, across the cup's opening.
8. Ask: *What do you think might happen to the balloon if you pull down on the plastic bag at the bottom of the cup?*
9. Pull down on the plastic bag. Record your observation. Ask: *What do you think might happen if you push up on the plastic bag?*
10. Push up on the plastic bag. Record your observation.

EXPLAIN: USE DATA TO GENERATE INTERPRETATIONS, INCLUDING DESCRIPTIONS, CLASSIFICATIONS, PREDICTIONS, AND EXPLANATIONS.

c. Ask: *What changes did you observe in the system? Why do these changes happen? Where in your body do you have something that works like this?*

Referring to a model or illustration of the chest cavity, guide students to identify the parts of the body used in breathing and describe how they function. Ask: *How is this physical model like the lungs?*

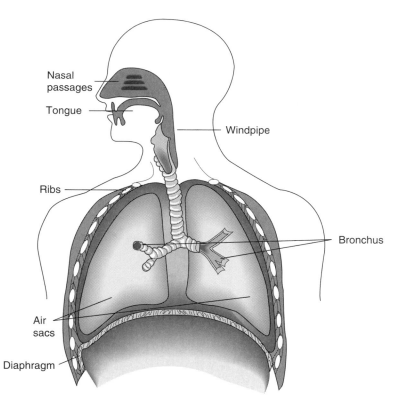

Nasal passages

Tongue

Windpipe

Ribs

Bronchus

Air sacs

Diaphragm

Respiratory system

6. HOW BIG ARE YOUR LUNGS? (3–5)

Materials

Dishpan
Drinking straws that are designed to bend (substitute plastic tubing obtained from
   aquarium shops)
Ruler
Measuring cup
Water
Gallon jug

ENGAGE: ASK A
QUESTION ABOUT OBJECTS,
ORGANISMS, OR EVENTS IN
THE ENVIRONMENT.

a. Ask: *How much air do your lungs hold? How could you measure the capacity of your lungs?
Do boys have bigger lungs than girls?*

EXPLORE: PLAN
AND CONDUCT SIMPLE
INVESTIGATIONS TO
COLLECT RELEVANT DATA.

b. Fill the dishpan about one-quarter full of water. Fill the jug to the very top with water. Put your hand tightly over the mouth of the jug and invert it in the dishpan, making sure not to let any air get into the jug. Put one end of the drinking straw in your
mouth, bend the straw gently, and slip the other end into the mouth of the jug. With
one continuous breath, keep blowing until you are completely out of air, as shown in
diagram (a).

Important: Make sure the mouth of the jug remains below water level.

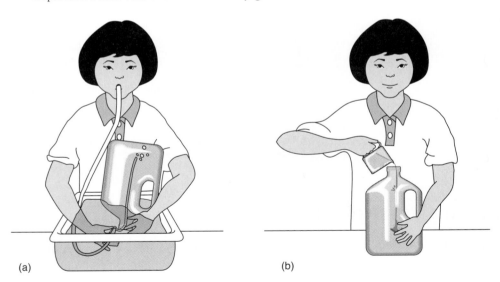

(a)   (b)

c. When you cannot blow any more water out of the jug, slide your hand over the jug's
mouth and turn it right side up. To measure how much air you exhaled, do this:
   1. Pour measuring cups filled with water into the jug until you have refilled the jug,
   as shown in diagram (b).
   2. The amount of water you use to refill the jug is the amount of air you exhaled.

Safety Precautions

For hygienic reasons, use separate drinking straws or plastic tubing for each student.

EXPLAIN: USE DATA TO GENERATE INTERPRETATIONS.

d. Ask: *Why does the water leave the jug when you blow into it?* (Air is a real material substance that forces the water out of the jug.) *How does this investigation show the capacity of your lungs? Who had the larger lung capacity, boys or girls? What is your evidence?*

B. THE HUMAN SYSTEM FOR REGULATING TEMPERATURE

▶ *Science Background*

Normal body temperature is 98.6°F. To maintain this temperature, the body converts food energy to heat energy. When the environment is very warm or through exercise, the temperature of the body may exceed the normal level. The body then cools itself through perspiring. When perspiration evaporates from the body, the body is cooled.

NSES   **Science Standards**

All students should develop an understanding of

• structure and function in living systems (5–8).

Objectives for Students

1. Describe how the evaporation of perspiration cools the body.

NSES   **Concepts and Principles**

Activity I addresses these fundamental concepts and principles related to the *Science Standards:*

• All organisms must be able to obtain and use resources, grow, reproduce, and maintain stable internal conditions while living in a constantly changing external environment (5–8).
• Regulation of an organism's internal environment involves sensing the internal environment and changing physiological activities to keep conditions within the range required to survive (5–8).

1. HOW DOES YOUR BODY COOL ITSELF? (K–5)

Materials

Two old socks (wool or cotton are best) for each student
Electric fan

ENGAGE: ASK A QUESTION ABOUT OBJECTS, ORGANISMS, OR EVENTS IN THE ENVIRONMENT.

a. Using a medicine dropper, place a few drops of water on the back of the hand of each student. Tell the students to gently blow across the water drop. Ask: *What happened to the water drop?* (It disappeared—evaporated.) *How did your hand feel?* (It got cooler.) Explain that evaporation is a cooling process. When water evaporates, the surface from which it evaporated gets cooler.
    Ask: *How does your body use evaporation to cool itself?*

EXPLORE: PLAN AND CONDUCT SIMPLE INVESTIGATIONS TO COLLECT RELEVANT DATA.

b. Have students place a dry sock on one hand and wet sock on the other hand. To improve the cooling effect, use a fan to blow air over the students' hands.

EXPLAIN: USE DATA TO GENERATE INTERPRETATIONS, INCLUDING DESCRIPTIONS, CLASSIFICATIONS, PREDICTIONS, AND EXPLANATIONS.

c. Invite students to share their findings from the exploration phase. Ask: *Which hand felt cooler, the one with the wet sock or the one with the dry sock? Why? What is the role of the moisture in cooling? What do you think happens when perspiration evaporates? Why does a fan cool us even on a hot day? Why do you feel cool on a hot summer day when you come out of the water after swimming?*

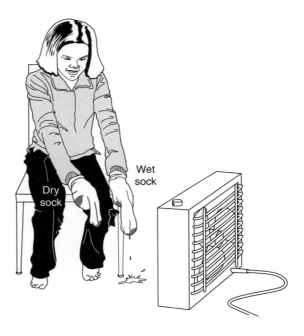

Dry sock

Wet sock

C. THE HUMAN SKIN AND PROTECTION FROM DISEASE

▶ *Science Background*

Our skin serves to protect us from microorganisms that cause disease. A cut or wound in the skin can let microorganisms enter the body. Microorganisms sometimes cause infection and disease. Cuts and wounds should be properly treated immediately to prevent infection. Antiseptics kill microorganisms; thus, they can be used for the treatment of cuts or wounds. Heat can also kill microorganisms.

NSES Science Standards

All students should develop an understanding of

• structure and function in living systems (5–8).
• regulation and behavior (5–8).

Objectives for Students

1. Describe how the skin functions to protect people.
2. Compare the human skin to skins on fruits.
3. Describe how cuts and wounds should be treated and why.

NSES Concepts and Principles

Activity I addresses these fundamental concepts and principles related to the *Science Standards:*

- The human organism has systems for digestion, respiration, reproduction, circulation, excretion, movement, control and coordination, and protection from disease (5–8).
- Disease is a breakdown in structure or function of an organism. Some diseases are the result of intrinsic failure of the system. Others are the result of damage by infection by other organisms (5–8).

---

1. HOW DOES OUR SKIN PROTECT US? (3–8)

Materials

Four unblemished apples
Three sewing needles
Book of matches
Candle on a pie tin
Rotten apple
Small sample of soil
Five small pieces of cardboard for labels
Rubbing alcohol

ENGAGE: ASK A QUESTION ABOUT OBJECTS, ORGANISMS, OR EVENTS IN THE ENVIRONMENT.

a. Ask: *How is the covering of an apple or an orange like your skin? What are the advantages of the covering on apples, oranges, and other types of fruit? How does the covering of your body, the skin, protect you?*

EXPLORE: PLAN AND CONDUCT SIMPLE INVESTIGATIONS TO COLLECT RELEVANT DATA.

b. The teacher should demonstrate the following steps for the students:
  1. Obtain five pieces of cardboard for labels, a candle in a pie tin, a match, three needles, and one rotten and four unblemished apples.
  2. Put the labels (a), (b), (c), and (d) on the four unblemished apples.
  3. Sterilize three needles by heating them in the flame of a candle. Ask: *What does it mean when a person says he or she wants to sterilize something? What does heat do to sterilize the needles?* (Discuss harmful microorganisms and disease. Explain that heat kills the microorganisms.) *In what other ways might you sterilize something?*
  4. With a sterile needle, puncture apple (a) in three places. Apply rubbing alcohol over two of the punctures. Explain that rubbing alcohol is an antiseptic that can also kill microorganisms.
  5. Push the second sterilized needle into the soil and then into three places in apple (b).
  6. Puncture apple (c) in three places with the third sterile needle, but do not apply any rubbing alcohol to the three punctures.
  7. Do nothing to apple (d) or to the rotten apple.

8. Place all four labeled apples in a warm place for several days.

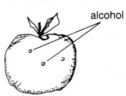

alcohol

(a) Three punctures with sterile needle; alcohol applied on two punctures

(b) Puncture with needle stuck in soil

(c) Puncture with needle but no alcohol

(d) Control (no holes)

Rotten

c. Ask: *What do you think might happen if the apples stand for a few days? In what ways do you think they will look alike? How will they be different? Why?*

d. Instruct each cooperative group to observe the apples daily. Every other day, students should make a diagram or illustration of the changes taking place. Changes should be discussed within lab groups.

EXPLAIN: USE DATA TO GENERATE INTERPRETATIONS, INCLUDING DESCRIPTIONS, CLASSIFICATIONS, PREDICTIONS, AND EXPLANATIONS.

e. Ask: *What has happened to some of the apples?*
   How are the apples alike? How are they different?
   How does the appearance of each apple relate to what was done to it in the investigation?
   What do you conclude about the observed changes in the apples?

f. Ask: *The skin of an apple is similar to what part of your body? Why did the rotten spots seem to grow a little larger each day?* (Microorganisms have a fantastic growth rate. As long as there is a substantial amount of food present and space enough for growth, they will continue to reproduce.) *What do you think might happen if your skin were punctured? What might a person do to a wound or puncture if he or she did not want to get an infection?* (The wound should be cleaned, an antiseptic applied, and the wound covered with a sterile bandage.) *What is the role of the sterile bandage? Should we have covered the "wound" of the apple with a sterile bandage?*

g. Ask: *How is this experiment a controlled experiment?*
   Be sure that students understand why this is a controlled experiment. The manipulated variable is the condition of the needle puncturing the apples. The responding variable is what happens to the apple. Apple (d), the apple that is not punctured, is the control in the experiment.

D. FOOD AND THE HUMAN SYSTEM FOR DIGESTION

▶ *Science Background*

Food provides energy and nutrients for growth, development, and normal functioning. Good nutrition is essential for good health. Foods contain starches, sugars, fats, and proteins that the body needs. During digestion, our body breaks down starches into glucose, a type of sugar, and the glucose then supplies energy for our muscles. Rice, corn, and potatoes are major sources of starch. Glucose itself is another major source of energy. Grapes, raisins, and bananas are natural sources of glucose. Soft drinks are another source of glucose. Fatty foods, such as fried foods, candy bars, cookies, and chips, can supply a great deal of energy per gram, but if the energy is not used, it is stored as fat within the body. During digestion, proteins are broken down into amino acids, substances our bodies need to build and repair tissues.

Specific chemical and physical tests can be conducted to determine which nutrients are in foods. Iodine can be used to test for starches. Tes-Tape can be used to test for glucose. Brown paper can be used to test for fats. Protein test papers (Coomassie blue test papers), purchased from a scientific supply company, can be used to test for proteins.

NSES Science Standards

All students should develop an understanding of

- structure and function in living systems (5–8).
- regulation and behavior (5–8).

Objectives for Students

1. Describe the structure and function of the human system for digestion.
2. Ask questions and design and carry out investigations about the contents of foods.
3. Describe and demonstrate tests of foods for water content, starch, sugars, fats, vitamins, and minerals.
4. Plan and commit to eating healthy diets that supply essential nutrients.

NSES Concepts and Principles

Activities 1–9 address these fundamental concepts and principles related to the *Science Standards*:

- The human organism has systems for digestion, respiration, reproduction, circulation, excretion, movement, control and coordination, and protection from disease (5–8).
- Behavior is one kind of response an organism can make to an internal or environmental stimulus (5–8).
- Behavioral response is a set of actions determined in part by heredity and in part from experience (5–8).

1. HOW MUCH WATER IS IN OUR FOODS? (5–8)

Materials

Blunt plastic knives
Scale for weighing
Lettuce, tomatoes, apples, oranges
Hand juicer
Paper plates
Small paper cups
Thick white bread
Bread toaster

ENGAGE: ASK A QUESTION ABOUT OBJECTS, ORGANISMS, OR EVENTS IN THE ENVIRONMENT.

a. Display a collection of foods. Ask: *How much water is in our foods? How could we find out?*

EXPLORE: PLAN
AND CONDUCT SIMPLE
INVESTIGATIONS TO
COLLECT RELEVANT DATA.

b. As a class or in cooperative groups, guide students to carry out these activities:
  1. Weigh each of the foods individually on a scale and record their weights in the "before" column of the chart.

WATER CONTENT CHART

Weight of Food in Grams or Paper Clips			
Food	Before	After	Weight of Water in Food
Lettuce			
Tomato			
Orange			
Apple			
Bread			

  2. Using a hand juicer, squeeze out all of the juice from the tomato. Weigh the tomato pulp (without the juice) and record the weight in the "after" column.
  3. Spread the lettuce leaves out on paper plates to dry overnight. The next day, weigh the lettuce leaves and record their weight in the after column.
  4. Repeat the previous step for the apple and the orange.
  5. Toast the bread in the toaster, weigh the bread, and record the number in the after column.
  6. Calculate the fractions of water in each food by dividing the weight of water in the food by the original weight of the food.

EXPLAIN: USE
DATA TO GENERATE
INTERPRETATIONS,
INCLUDING DESCRIPTIONS,
CLASSIFICATIONS,
PREDICTIONS, AND
EXPLANATIONS.

c. Ask: *What changes did you note in the foods? Why do you think the weight of each food changed? Which food initially had the highest fraction of water? Which food had the lowest fraction of water?*

ELABORATE: EXTEND
CONCEPTS, PRINCIPLES,
AND STRATEGIES TO NEW
SITUATIONS AND
QUESTIONS.

d. Ask: *What foods can you think of that are eaten in both fresh and dried form?* (Grapes/raisins, plums/prunes, and so on.) *What would you do to investigate what happens to raisins or prunes when they are soaked in water?* (Try it and see.)

▶ *Teaching Background*

Although water is not one of the basic nutrients, we must have it every day. We could not live without it. Besides drinking liquids, here are some common foods and the percentages of water by weight we get when we eat them. Students' test results may not agree with these. Even after students treat the various foods, they still will likely contain some water.

Lettuce	95%	Carrot	90%
Yogurt	90%	Apple	85%
Pizza	50%	Bread	35%

2. WHAT IS STARCH, AND HOW CAN WE TEST FOR IT? (5–8)

Materials

Paper plates
Dropper
Thin slices of banana, apple, potato, white bread, cheese, egg white, butter
Cracker
Cornstarch
Iodine solution
Granulated sugar

ENGAGE: ASK A QUESTION ABOUT OBJECTS, ORGANISMS, OR EVENTS IN THE ENVIRONMENT.

a. Some foods contain starch. Starch is a nutrient that provides energy for cells to use. Ask: *Which of these foods contains starch? How might we find out?*

EXPLORE: PLAN AND CONDUCT SIMPLE INVESTIGATIONS TO COLLECT RELEVANT DATA.

b. Explain that the chemical iodine can be used to test foods for starches. When iodine is placed on a starchy food, the food turns varying shades of purple-black in relation to the amount of starch present in it.

Safety Precautions

Iodine solution is poisonous, may cause burns if it is too strong, and can stain clothing. It must not be eaten. Because iodine is poisonous, do *not* eat any of the tested foods or give them to pets. Dispose of them properly.

c. Assist cooperative groups to carry out this investigation.
    1. On a paper plate, arrange and label each food sample as shown in the illustration.

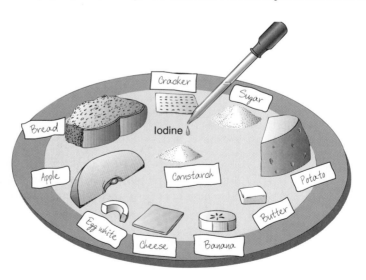

    2. Look at the colors of each food and record them on a chart.
    3. Place a drop of iodine solution on each sample of food.
    4. Look at the color of each food where the iodine drop touched it.

EXPLAIN: USE
DATA TO GENERATE
INTERPRETATIONS,
INCLUDING DESCRIPTIONS,
CLASSIFICATIONS,
PREDICTIONS, AND
EXPLANATIONS.

d. Ask: *How have some of the food colors changed?*
    Which foods have something in common after getting an iodine drop?
    If starch turns blue-black in iodine, which of your sample foods would you say contain starch?
    Which do not have starch?

▶ *Teaching Background*

Starch provides energy for cells to use. Major sources of starch are rice, corn, and potatoes. Like most starchy foods, these foods also contain vitamins and minerals. During digestion, the body breaks down starch into glucose, and the glucose provides energy for cells.

Some starchy foods are also high in fiber, indigestible material that helps move matter through the digestive tract. Fruits, vegetables, and whole grains are some sources of fiber.

Because they contain large amounts of starch, rice and flour turn purple-black when iodine is added. Certain vegetables and fruits contain little starch and may turn only a very faint purple-black during an iodine test.[8]

3. WHAT ARE FATS, AND HOW DO WE TEST FOR THEM? (5–8)

Materials

Paper plates
Water
Butter
Vegetable oil
Samples of common snack foods: peanuts, bread, margarine, celery, carrots, mayonnaise, lettuce, bacon, corn or potato chips, pretzels, cheese, cookies, cake, apple, whole milk, yogurt, chocolate
Brown paper bags or brown paper towels cut into 2 inch squares (enough so that there is one square for each food sample)
Source of light: sunlight or lamp
Dropper

ENGAGE: ASK A
QUESTION ABOUT OBJECTS,
ORGANISMS, OR EVENTS IN
THE ENVIRONMENT.

a. Fats also supply energy for the body.
    Ask: *How could we test to see if foods contain fat?*
b. Explain that fats leave greasy spots on brown paper, and this is a way to test for them. Assist students to carry out this test in cooperative groups:
    1. Put several drops of water on one square of brown paper, as in diagram (a). On a second square, put drops of oil as in diagram (b).

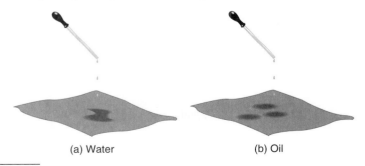

(a) Water   (b) Oil

8Science and Technology for Children (STC), *Food Chemistry*. Burlington, NC: Carolina Biological Supply Company, 1994.

2. Fats feel slippery when rubbed between the fingers.
   Ask: *How does the water stain feel? How does the oil stain feel?*
3. Ask: *How do the two stains look? What do you think will happen to the two stains after 10 minutes?*
4. After 10 minutes, check the two squares of paper.
   What happened to each stain?
   Where did the water drop go?
   How do the oil drops look?
   Explain that the water evaporated, but the oil stains remained shiny. This is the spot test for fats.

EXPLORE: PLAN AND CONDUCT SIMPLE INVESTIGATIONS TO COLLECT RELEVANT DATA.

c. Have groups of students conduct their own spot tests using the samples of snack foods.
   1. Get a paper plate containing samples of snack foods, squares of brown paper, and a copy of the lab sheet shown in the diagram.

FAT SPOT TEST LAB SHEET		
Food Samples	Predicted Fat	Contains Fat
Peanuts		
Bread		
Margarine		
Celery		
Carrots		
Mayonnaise		
Lettuce		
Bacon		
Corn/Potato chips		
Pretzels		
Cheese		
Cookies		
Cake		
Apple		
Whole milk		
Yogurt		
Chocolate		

2. Mark an X in the "predicted fat" column for foods you think contain fat.
3. Firmly rub each food sample 10 times on a separate square of brown paper, and label the paper with the food's name.
4. After 10 minutes, hold each paper square up to a source of light as in the illustration.

Safety Precautions

It is all right to use illumination from a window as a source of light, but caution children not to look directly into the sun.

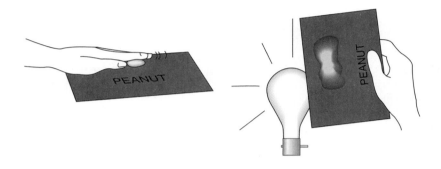

5. Mark an X in the "contains fat" column of your chart for each food that left a greasy spot.

EXPLAIN: USE DATA TO GENERATE INTERPRETATIONS, INCLUDING DESCRIPTIONS, CLASSIFICATIONS, PREDICTIONS, AND EXPLANATIONS.

d. Ask: *How did your predictions compare with your findings?*
   How would you summarize your test findings as to which foods contained fat?
e. Discuss with students the importance of reading food labels for ingredients. Also discuss how they might select foods with less fat.
   Ask: *Why might it be healthier to eat such foods as skim milk, low-fat cottage cheese, and nonfat ice cream?*
   How could we have a party, serving good-tasting foods, and still cut down on the amount of fat we eat?

▶ *Teaching Background*

Some foods have a lot of fat, and others have little or no fat. Fats that are thick (solid) at room temperature usually come from animals like cows, pigs, and sheep. These fats are called **saturated fats**. Fats that are soft (semisolid) at room temperature usually are made from animals (e.g., lard and butter) or are manufactured (e.g., margarine). Fats that are liquid at room temperature usually come from plants (e.g., peanut oil, olive oil, corn oil).

4. WHAT IS GLUCOSE, AND HOW DO WE TEST FOR IT? (5–8)

Materials

Tes-Tape (get in drugstore)
Bananas (fairly ripe)
Milk
Different kinds of apples (McIntosh, Delicious, Rome)

Granular sugar, moistened with water
Oranges
Maple syrup
Honey
Paper plates
Small paper cups

Preparation

For efficiency in distribution, the teacher or designated students should prepare the following beforehand for each group of two to four students: paper plate containing cut samples of foods and small cups with very small samples of honey, milk, and maple syrup; 1 inch Tes-Tape strip for each food to be tested; data collection sheet.

ENGAGE: ASK A QUESTION ABOUT OBJECTS, ORGANISMS, OR EVENTS IN THE ENVIRONMENT.

a. Explain that glucose is one kind of sugar. Many foods contain glucose. Glucose is a major source of energy for our bodies. Ask: *How can we test foods for glucose?*

EXPLORE: PLAN AND CONDUCT SIMPLE INVESTIGATIONS TO COLLECT RELEVANT DATA.

b. Explain to students that they will use Tes-Tape to test different foods for glucose. Tes-Tape is a special chemically treated paper designed for use by people who have diabetes. Guide cooperative groups of students to conduct this investigation:
    1. Get a paper plate that contains food samples, Tes-Tape strips, and a data collection sheet.
    2. Assign one group member to each of the following tasks: tester, observer, and recorder.
    3. The tester should number each food, then write the numerals 1 through 10 on separate Tes-Tape strips.

4. Using the appropriately numbered strip that corresponds to the food being tested, the tester should touch a 1 inch strip of the Tes-Tape to each food separately, until the strip is wet, and hand the Tes-Tape to the observer.
5. The observer should look at the wet end of the Tes-Tape to see *what color it is.*
6. The observer gives the following information to the recorder:
    a. Number of the sample Tes-Tape strip
    b. Name of the food sample
    c. Color of the wet end of the Tes-Tape strip
7. The students should repeat the preceding procedures with all of the food samples.
8. As each food is tested, the recorder notes on the Tes-Tape data collection sheet the data that the observer provides. The recorder attaches each Tes-Tape strip in the appropriate place on the chart.

TES-TAPE SUGAR TEST DATA COLLECTION SHEET		
Food Samples	Tape Color after Test	Tape Strip
Orange		
Banana, ripe		
Banana, green		
Maple syrup		
Milk		
Honey		
McIntosh apple		
Yellow Delicious apple		
Rome apple		
Granulated sugar		

EXPLAIN: USE DATA TO GENERATE INTERPRETATIONS, INCLUDING DESCRIPTIONS, CLASSIFICATIONS, PREDICTIONS, AND EXPLANATIONS.

c. Ask: *From the data collected, which foods contain glucose? What evidence do you have to support this?*

From the changes in the Tes-Tape color, which foods appear to have the most glucose? the least?

Which foods, if any, did not change the color of the Tes-Tape? Why do you think this happened?

ELABORATE: EXTEND CONCEPTS, PRINCIPLES, AND STRATEGIES TO NEW SITUATIONS AND QUESTIONS.

d. Have students bring in labels from food packages, read the ingredients list, and list all the forms of sugar each food contains, such as honey, brown sugar syrup, sweeteners, corn sugar, corn sweeteners, molasses, invert sugar, sucrose, fructose, dextrose, maltose, lactose, and so on.

Find out the amounts of sugar (both labeled and "hidden") in the common foods you eat. For example, soft drinks can contain about 8 teaspoons per 12 ounces, and many breakfast cereals contain about 2 1/2 teaspoons (10 g) of sugar plus 3 teaspoons (13 g) of other carbohydrates for a total of 5 1/2 teaspoons (23 g) per 1 ounce serving.

Ask: *What do you think might happen if you tested artificial sweeteners (saccharin, aspartame, etc.) with Tes-Tape?*

Why would it be healthier to eat fresh fruit as a snack rather than cakes, candy, and soft drinks, even though all of these contain sugar?

▶ *Teaching Background*

There are several types of sugars, including sucrose, lactose, fructose, and glucose. Glucose is a major source of energy for the body. Starches consist of long linked chains of glucose. Much of the glucose the body needs comes from the breakdown of starches. There are also natural sources of glucose, including apples, grapes, raisins, and bananas. Soft drinks are another source of glucose. Sweets ordinarily contain other types of sugars.[9]

5. HOW CAN YOU SEE WHICH SODA HAS MORE SUGAR? (5–8)

Materials

Three pairs of 12 ounce cans of soft drinks, unopened, assorted flavors and brands (each pair should contain one diet and one regular of same flavor and brand)
Aquarium filled with water
Scale for weighing

ENGAGE: ASK A QUESTION ABOUT OBJECTS, ORGANISMS, OR EVENTS IN THE ENVIRONMENT.

a. Place a can of regular cola and a can of diet cola in an aquarium filled with water. The regular can of cola sinks, but, surprisingly, the can of diet cola floats.

Ask: *Why do you think the can of diet cola floated while the can of regular cola sank?*

EXPLORE: PLAN AND CONDUCT SIMPLE INVESTIGATIONS TO COLLECT RELEVANT DATA.

b. When students suggest that the can of diet cola was lighter, ask: *How could we test this hypothesis?*

c. Instruct students to
   1. weigh each of the six cans of diet and regular soft drinks;
   2. record the weights in a table like the one illustrated;

[9]Science and Technology for Children (STC), *Food Chemistry*. Burlington, NC: Carolina Biological Supply Company, 1994.

3. test each of the six cans to determine if it floats or sinks; and

4. record their observations about floating or sinking in the table.

SUGAR CONTENT OF DIET AND REGULAR SOFT DRINKS

Pair	Brand	Diet Weight	Regular Weight	Float or Sink?
1				Diet
				Regular
2				Diet
				Regular
3				Diet
				Regular

EXPLAIN: USE DATA TO GENERATE INTERPRETATIONS, INCLUDING DESCRIPTIONS, CLASSIFICATIONS, PREDICTIONS, AND EXPLANATIONS.

d. Ask: *What did you determine in your tests? Did your data support the hypothesis that the cans of regular soft drinks were heavier than the cans of diet soft drinks?*

e. Ask: *Why do you think a can of diet cola is lighter than a can of regular cola of the same brand and flavor?* When students suggest that the cans of regular soft drink contain more liquid than the cans of diet soft drink, lead them to examine labels to compare the volumes of liquid in the regular and diet soft drink cans. Students might also open the cans and measure the volume using a graduated cylinder.

If students do not suggest it, also ask them to compare the ingredients of the regular and diet soft drinks. The weight of a diet soft drink is usually about 10 to 15 g less than the weight of a regular soft drink. The difference is usually sugar or corn syrup.

6. WHAT ARE PROTEINS, AND HOW DO WE TEST FOR THEM? (5–8)

Materials

For each group:

- Six Coomassie blue protein test strips in a clean envelope
- Test tray
- Forceps
- Petri dish
- Toothpicks
- Paper towels

(Protein test strips and other materials are available from Carolina Biological Supply— see Appendix C for address.)

For the class:

- Half liter (1 pint) white vinegar
- Half liter (1 pint) rubbing alcohol
- 1 liter plastic bottle to mix and store developing solution
- Medicine droppers
- Plastic spoons
- One carton skim milk, 237 ml (one-half pint)
- Unshelled peanuts
- Rice grains

Preparation

To test for proteins, students immerse a Coomassie blue test strip in a liquid or food, and then place the test strip in a developing solution for several minutes. To prepare the developing solution, mix together half a liter of white vinegar and half a liter of rubbing alcohol in a 1 liter plastic mixing bottle. Close the bottle and store the developing solution.

ENGAGE: ASK A QUESTION ABOUT OBJECTS, ORGANISMS, OR EVENTS IN THE ENVIRONMENT.

a. Ask: *What nutrients have we tested for so far?* Starch, fat, and glucose (sugar). *What do you know about proteins? What foods contain proteins? How can we test liquids and foods for proteins?*

EXPLORE: PLAN AND CONDUCT SIMPLE INVESTIGATIONS TO COLLECT RELEVANT DATA.

b. Hold up a strip of protein test paper. Handle the test strip only with forceps so as not to contaminate it with your hands. Explain to students that the strip has a special chemical—Coomassie blue—on it that reacts to proteins. During testing, the paper must be developed in a special solution. When developed, the color of the paper will stay deep blue if the protein content of the food being tested is high; the blue color will fade if there is a medium amount of protein in the food; and the blue color will disappear if the food contains little or no protein.

c. To test liquids or foods for proteins, have students follow these directions:
   1. Put three drops of milk in section 1 of the test tray.
   2. Put three drops of water in section 2 of the test tray.
   3. Using a spoon, put a few grains of rice in section 3 of the test tray. Put two or three drops of tap water on the rice and stir for about a minute with a toothpick.
   4. Shell a peanut (without touching the nut itself) and place it in section 4 of the test tray. Use a plastic spoon to crush the peanut. Add two or three drops of water and stir with a new toothpick.
   5. Using a spoon, put a small amount of crushed granola bar in section 5 of the test tray. Add two or three drops of water and stir with a new toothpick.
   6. Obtain six test strips and number them 1 to 6 on the white end of the strips. Be careful not to touch the test strips. Holding a test strip by its white end with forceps, immerse the blue end in the liquid or food just long enough to wet the strip—test strip 1 in the milk, test strip 2 in water, test strip 3 in the moistened rice, test strip 4 in the moistened peanut, and test strip 5 in the moistened granola bar. Place test strip 6 in the empty section 6 of the test tray as a control. Use clean toothpicks to make sure each food is in contact with the test paper. Be sure the white end of each test strip is not in contact with the liquid or food being tested.

7. Leave the test strips in the tray sections just long enough to wet the strips. Using forceps, remove each of the numbered test strips from the tray sections and place them on a paper towel. Use clean toothpicks to clean any food particles from them and use a paper towel to blot off any excess liquid.

8. Ask your teacher to pour a little developing solution in the bottom of your petri dish. Using forceps, transfer each of the test strips to the developing solution. Make sure the blue tip of the test strip is immersed.

9. Leave the test strips in the developing solution for about 5 minutes. Keep stirring the solution with a toothpick.

10. After 5 minutes, remove the protein test papers from the developing solution and place them on a paper towel.

11. Note and record the color of each test strip in the following chart. Based on the color observed, determine the protein content of each food—high, medium, or low.

PROTEIN TEST RESULTS

Liquid or Food	Color of Protein Test Strip	Protein Content (High, Medium, or Low)
1. Milk		
2. Tap water		
3. Rice		
4. Peanut		
5. Granola bar		
6. Control		

EXPLAIN: USE DATA TO GENERATE INTERPRETATIONS, INCLUDING DESCRIPTIONS, CLASSIFICATIONS, PREDICTIONS, AND EXPLANATIONS.

d. In a class-sized group, invite students to discuss their procedures and share their results.

Ask: *What happened to the protein test strips in each liquid or food? Which food or liquids were high in proteins? Which had a medium protein content? Which foods had a low amount or no proteins?* Share the following master chart of protein test results with students.

PROTEIN TEST RESULTS

Liquid or Food	Color of Protein Test Strip	Protein Content (High, Medium, or Low)
1. Milk	Remains blue	High
2. Tap water	Blue disappears	Low
3. Rice	Blue disappears	Low
4. Peanut	Remains blue	High
5. Granola bar	Blue almost disappears	Medium
6. Control	Blue disappears	Low or none

▶ *Teaching Background*

Protein is one group of food nutrients that the body uses for building tissues and repairing broken-down cells. Proteins are vital for children's proper physical and mental growth and development. Because protein cannot be made by or stored in the body, it must be eaten regularly to promote the repair of used body cells. Eggs, cheese, meat, fish, and legumes are some foods that contain large proportions of protein.

In a protein test, the chemical Coomassie blue actually binds to protein. Because of this chemical reaction, the protein and Coomassie blue will remain on the test paper after it has been in the developing solution. In the absence of protein, the Coomassie blue will dissolve in the developing solution.[10]

7. WHAT ARE MINERALS, AND HOW DO WE TEST FOR THEM? (5–8)

Materials

Two chicken leg bones stripped of all meat
Two covered jars large enough to hold the chicken bones
Soap
Water
Paper towels

ENGAGE: ASK A QUESTION ABOUT OBJECTS, ORGANISMS, OR EVENTS IN THE ENVIRONMENT.

a. Ask: *What do bones do for our bodies?*
    Why must bones be strong and hard?
    What do we eat that might make bones strong and hard?
    What might cause bones to get soft and weak?
    How might we test for calcium?

EXPLORE: PLAN AND CONDUCT SIMPLE INVESTIGATIONS TO COLLECT RELEVANT DATA.

b. Demonstrate this activity for your students:
    1. Wash both chicken leg bones and dry them with paper towels.
    2. Pass both chicken bones around the classroom.
    3. Ask: *How do the bones feel? Are they hard or soft?*
    4. Place a chicken bone in each jar.
    5. Pour vinegar in one jar only and water in the other, cover both jars, and let stand for several days.

[10]Activities on proteins are based on activities in *Food Chemistry*, Science and Technology for Children (STC), National Science Resources Center, Smithsonian Institution, Washington, D.C. STC guides and materials are available from Carolina Biological Supply (see Appendix C for address). Reprinted with permission from the National Science Resources Center, Washington, DC.

6. After several days, remove the bone from the jar of vinegar, rinse it thoroughly with water, and dry it well with a paper towel. Remove the other bone from its jar of water, and dry it with a paper towel.
7. Pass both bones around the classroom and ask: *Do both bones feel the same? If not, how are they different?*

Safety Precautions

Because vinegar is a mild acid, you should wash your hands with soap and water after conducting the activity.

EXPLAIN: USE DATA TO GENERATE INTERPRETATIONS, INCLUDING DESCRIPTIONS, CLASSIFICATIONS, PREDICTIONS, AND EXPLANATIONS.

c. Ask: *Why do you think the bone that was in vinegar is soft and rubbery?*

Lead students to understand that the bone that was in vinegar is soft and rubbery because its calcium has been removed. Vinegar (acetic acid) reacts with calcium and can be used as a test for it. Minerals make up a large part of bones and teeth, which is why minerals are so important for children. Although we need small amounts of many minerals (called *trace elements*), calcium is needed in larger quantities for bone and teeth formation.

Ask: *Why do you think it is so important for students to eat a lot of milk products?* (Calcium is found in large quantities in milk and milk products and in smaller quantities in green leafy vegetables and oranges.)

What might happen if you did not eat enough milk products?

8. WHAT ARE VITAMINS, AND HOW DO WE TEST FOR THEM? (5–8)

Materials

To make vitamin C indicator liquid for the class:

- Teaspoon
- Cornstarch
- Measuring cup
- Water
- Pan
- Hot plate
- Empty plastic gallon jug
- Iodine

For each group:

- Ruler
- Six clean baby food jars
- Variety of at least six different juices that are canned, frozen, or fresh (e.g., orange, apple, grape, pineapple, etc.)
- Six droppers
- Six wooden stirrers

Preparation

A simple vitamin C indicator liquid can be made ahead of time and will keep for several days. You will know when it is time to dispose of it, because it will lighten from its optimum color of royal blue to a very pale blue. To make 1 gallon of vitamin C indicator:

1. Boil 1 1/2 teaspoons (6 ml) of cornstarch in 1 cup (250 ml) of water for 2 minutes.

2. Put 10 full droppers of the cornstarch mixture into a gallon jug of water, use a clean dropper to add 1 dropper full of iodine, cover the jug, and shake it until you have a uniform blue color.

ENGAGE: ASK A QUESTION ABOUT OBJECTS, ORGANISMS, OR EVENTS IN THE ENVIRONMENT.

a. Ask: *What do you know about vitamins? What are vitamins? How can we test foods for vitamins?*

EXPLORE: PLAN AND CONDUCT SIMPLE INVESTIGATIONS TO COLLECT RELEVANT DATA.

b. Tell students that we can test for vitamin C by testing how it reacts with a special mixture of cornstarch, iodine, and water. Explain that the fewer drops of juice needed to make the blue color disappear, the more vitamin C that juice contains. Instruct students to follow these directions to test foods for vitamin C:

1. Using your ruler to measure, pour 1 cm of vitamin C indicator liquid into each of six clean baby food jars. Label each jar with the name of the juice you will test for vitamin C.
2. Using a clean dropper for each juice, add one kind of juice to each jar of indicator liquid, one drop at a time, and count the number of drops. (See the diagram.) Stir the liquid indicator with a clean wooden stirrer as you add drops.
3. When the indicator is no longer blue, the test is finished.
4. Record the number of drops of each juice needed to clear up the blue vitamin C indicator liquid.

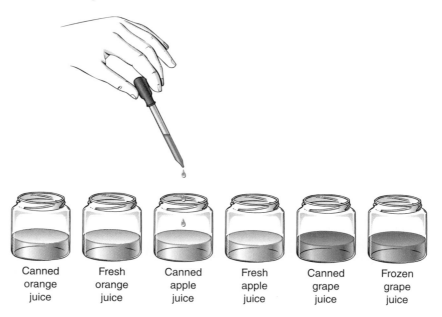

| Canned orange juice | Fresh orange juice | Canned apple juice | Fresh apple juice | Canned grape juice | Frozen grape juice |

EXPLAIN: USE DATA TO GENERATE INTERPRETATIONS, INCLUDING DESCRIPTIONS, CLASSIFICATIONS, PREDICTIONS, AND EXPLANATIONS.

c. Invite students to discuss their procedures and results.

Ask: *Which juice(s) caused the blue color to disappear with the least number of drops? Which juice(s) caused the blue color to disappear with the most drops?*

Explain that scientists have discovered more than 26 vitamins our bodies need. The lack of one vitamin could result in a vitamin deficiency disease. Vitamin C is probably the best known vitamin. It is found in citrus fruits, tomatoes, raw cabbage, strawberries, and cantaloupe.

Ask: *From these tests, which juice(s) had the most vitamin C?*

ELABORATE: EXTEND CONCEPTS, PRINCIPLES, AND STRATEGIES TO NEW SITUATIONS AND QUESTIONS.

d. Ask: *How do you think the following conditions could affect the vitamin C content of foods: heat, sunlight, air, age of food, and so on? How could you design experiments to test these variables?*

9. HOW MUCH OF EACH NUTRIENT DOES YOUR BODY NEED, AND HOW CAN YOU FIND OUT WHAT IS IN EACH FOOD? (5–8)

Materials

Food labels from a large variety of packaged foods. Collect food labels yourself, and ask students to collect and bring in empty food packages or labels from the packages. You will need at least one food label for each pair of students.

ENGAGE: ASK A QUESTION ABOUT OBJECTS, ORGANISMS, OR EVENTS IN THE ENVIRONMENT.

a. Ask: *Can you think of another way, besides testing, to determine the nutritional content of foods?* If students do not suggest reading food labels, raise the idea.

EXPLORE: PLAN AND CONDUCT SIMPLE INVESTIGATIONS TO COLLECT RELEVANT DATA.

b. Pass out food labels and a copy of the food label record sheet to pairs of students. Ask: *What kind of information is given on the food labels?* Discuss the information given on the food labels. Explain that starch and sugar are carbohydrates. The labels give the total amount of carbohydrates in one serving of the food, but not the specific amounts of starch or sugar. Also explain that people who study nutrients (called **nutritionists**) suggest the average amount of each nutrient a person should consume. This amount is called the recommended daily allowance, or RDA. Answer questions students might have, for example, about serving sizes or grams and milligrams.

Nutrition Facts

Serving Size 2/3 cup (55g)
Servings Per Container 12

Amount Per Serving

Calories 210
  Calories from Fat 25

% Daily Value*

Total Fat 3g	**5%**
Saturated Fat 1g	**4%**
Polyunsaturated Fat 0.5g	
Monounsaturated Fat 1.5g	
Cholesterol 0mg	**0%**
Sodium 140mg	**6%**
Potassium 190mg	**5%**
Total Carbohydrate 44g	**15%**
Other Carbohydrate 23g	
Dietary Fiber 3g	**13%**
Sugars 18g	
Protein 5g	
Vitamin A	0%
Vitamin C	0%
Calcium	2%
Iron	6%
Thiamine	10%
Phosphorus	10%
Magnesium	10%

* Percent Daily Values are based on a 2000 calorie diet. Your daily values may be higher or lower depending on your calorie needs.

	Calories	2,000	2,500
Total Fat	Less than	65g	80g
Sat Fat	Less than	20g	25g
Cholesterol	Less than	300g	300g
Sodium	Less than	2400mg	2400mg
Potassium		3500mg	3500mg
Total Carbo		300g	300g
Dietary Fiber		25g	30g

Calories per gram:

Fat 9   •   Carbohydrate 4   •   Protein 4

c. Tell students to examine the food labels and record on their record sheet the information given about carbohydrates (starch and sugar), fats, proteins, calcium (a mineral they have tested), and vitamin C (the type of vitamin they have tested).

Food Label Record Sheet

Name of Food _____

Serving Size _____

Nutrient	Weight per Serving	Percentage of U.S. RDA
Carbohydrates		
Fats		
Proteins		
Minerals-calcium		
Vitamins-vitamin C		

EXPLAIN: USE DATA TO GENERATE INTERPRETATIONS, INCLUDING DESCRIPTIONS, CLASSIFICATIONS, PREDICTIONS, AND EXPLANATIONS.

d. Bring pairs of students together in groups of eight. Ask students to compare the nutrition facts from their food labels and record sheets and to complete the facts chart illustrated:

FOOD GROUP FACTS CHART

Calories	Food highest in calories per serving:	Food lowest in calories per serving:
Carbohydrates	Food highest in carbohydrates per serving:	Food lowest in carbohydrates per serving:
Fats	Food highest in fats per serving:	Food lowest in fats per serving:
Proteins	Food highest in proteins per serving:	Food lowest in proteins per serving:
Calcium	Food highest in calcium per serving:	Food lowest in calcium per serving:
Vitamin C	Food highest in vitamin C per serving:	Food lowest in vitamin C per serving:

e. Assemble the class as a whole and discuss which kinds of food are high and low in basic nutrients.

ELABORATE: EXTEND
CONCEPTS, PRINCIPLES,
AND STRATEGIES TO NEW
SITUATIONS AND
QUESTIONS.

f. Sometimes nutritionists recommend selecting foods from the basic food groups, such as meats, fruits, vegetables, breads and cereals, and dairy products. Introduce the *Food Guide Pyramid.* Ask:

> *Which food group relates to carbohydrates?*
> *Which food group relates to proteins?*
> *Which food group relates to fats?*
> *Which food group relates to vitamin C?*
> *Which food group relates to calcium?*

Through discussion, develop a typical day's menu for students in your class.

Ask: *How close are the daily food choices in the menu to the recommendations of the pyramid? In the menu, is there more food in one group than is recommended? Is there less food than recommended for one group?*

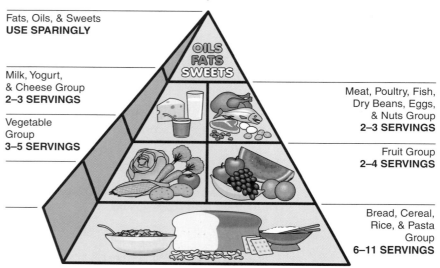

Food Guide Pyramid
A Guide to Daily Food Choices

Fats, Oils, & Sweets
USE SPARINGLY

Milk, Yogurt,
& Cheese Group
2–3 SERVINGS

Vegetable
Group
3–5 SERVINGS

OILS
FATS
SWEETS

Meat, Poultry, Fish,
Dry Beans, Eggs,
& Nuts Group
2–3 SERVINGS

Fruit Group
2–4 SERVINGS

Bread, Cereal,
Rice, & Pasta
Group
6–11 SERVINGS

IV

Earth and Space Science Activities

Earth is the home planet of human beings, the only planet in the universe known to support life. Life is possible on the earth largely because of a set of linked factors, including the earth's position within the solar system, its size and mass, its structure and resources, its range of temperatures, its atmosphere, and its abundance of water.

Students in grades K–8 can begin to develop understanding of the earth as a set of closely interrelated systems by studying the geological structure of the earth; the atmosphere, climate, and weather of the earth; the earth's oceans; and the earth in the solar system.

I. STRUCTURE OF THE EARTH

Children explore the complexities of the earth as they study the properties of rocks and minerals, the crystalline structure of minerals, and the structure of the earth's surface.

A. PROPERTIES OF ROCKS AND MINERALS

▶ *Science Background*

A mineral is a solid element or compound that has a specific composition and a crystalline structure. There are many different minerals in and on the earth—for example, talc, calcite, quartz, fluorite, and diamond. Minerals can be distinguished by such properties as hardness, texture, luster, streak color, cleavage, density, crystalline structure, and chemical properties.

Rocks are usually composed of minerals. Waves, wind, water, and ice cause erosion, transport, and deposit of earth materials. Sediments of sand and smaller particles are gradually buried and are cemented together with dissolved minerals to form solid rock. Rocks buried deep enough may be re-formed by pressure and heat, melting and recrystallizing into different kinds of rock. Layers of rock deep within the earth may be forced upward to become land surfaces and even mountains. Eventually, this new rock will erode under the relentless, dynamic processes of the earth.

Rocks bear evidence of the minerals, temperatures, and forces that created them. Through studies of thousands of layers of rocks, geologists have described the long history of the changing face of the earth.[1]

 Science Standards

All students should develop an understanding of

- properties of the earth's systems (K–4).
- structure of the earth's systems (5–8).

Objectives for Students

1. Describe properties of rocks and minerals, including texture, luster, color, cleavage, hardness, density, and crystalline structure.
2. Perform tests to determine the hardness of minerals and rocks.
3. Construct charts of the properties of a variety of minerals and rocks, and use the charts to identify specific minerals and rocks.

 Concepts and Principles

Activities 1–9 address these fundamental concepts and principles related to the *Science Standards*:

- The earth's materials are solid rocks and soils, water, and gases of the atmosphere (K–4).
- The varied materials have different physical and chemical properties (K–4).

1. WHAT ARE ROCKS AND MINERALS LIKE? (2–5)

Materials for Activities 1–9

Kits of rock samples, including such rocks as basalt, granite, limestone, marble, pumice, sandstone, shale, and slate
Kits of mineral samples, including such minerals as feldspar, calcite, fluorite, gypsum, graphite, hematite, hornblende, magnetite, mica, and quartz
Streak plates
Nails
Pennies

(Kits of rocks and minerals can be obtained from scientific supply houses such as Delta Education or Carolina Biological. For addresses, see Appendix C.)

ENGAGE: ASK A QUESTION ABOUT OBJECTS, ORGANISMS, OR EVENTS IN THE ENVIRONMENT.

a. Ask: *Where do you find different kinds of rocks?* (At home, on the school campus, on the way to school.) *How are the different rocks alike? How are they different? Where do you think the rocks originally came from?*

---

[1]American Association for the Advancement of Science (1993). *Benchmarks for Science Literacy* (New York: Oxford University Press); F. J. Rutherford and A. Ahlgren (1990). *Science for All Americans* (New York: Oxford University Press).

EXPLORE: PLAN
AND CONDUCT SIMPLE
INVESTIGATIONS TO
COLLECT RELEVANT DATA.

b. Initially refer to both rocks and minerals as "rocks." Provide each small group with a mixture of samples of several different rocks. For example, select large and small samples of calcite, quartz, feldspar, talc, granite, sandstone, and magnetite. Let each student in the cooperative groups examine each rock. Ask the groups to discuss what is the same and what is different about the rocks. Students often describe rocks in imaginative detail: "This rock weighs three and a half crayons. This rock is shiny and has little ripples. This one is shaped like a loaf of bread and you can stand it on its end."

c. Select four rocks that are similar in color, such as four black rocks. Place the rocks on a tray so that each student in the group can observe them. Tell each student to write down descriptions of the four rocks, without letting the other students in the group know which rocks they are describing. Ask them to take turns reading their description of one rock, while the other students try to determine which rock is being described.

EXPLAIN: USE
DATA TO GENERATE
INTERPRETATIONS,
INCLUDING DESCRIPTIONS,
CLASSIFICATIONS,
PREDICTIONS, AND
EXPLANATIONS.

d. Ask: *What were some of the property words you used to describe the rocks?* (Words related to color, texture, relative shininess, relative weight, shape, etc.)

e. Explain that rocks and minerals are different kinds of objects. A mineral has a specific composition and a *crystal* structure. Rocks are made up of minerals.

2. WHAT IS MEANT BY THE STREAK OF A MINERAL AND HOW CAN WE TEST FOR IT? (2–5)

ENGAGE: ASK A
QUESTION ABOUT OBJECTS,
ORGANISMS, OR EVENTS IN
THE ENVIRONMENT.

a. Ask: *How can we identify different minerals? What properties of minerals can we use to identify them?*

When students suggest color as a property that can be used to identify minerals, provide this information:

Color was probably one of the first properties you used to describe the minerals. Observable color of a mineral is not a conclusive clue to its identity, because different samples of the same mineral may have different colors. The color of the powdered form of the mineral is more consistent than its observable color. Geologists obtain powdered forms of minerals by wiping them across a *streak plate*.

EXPLORE: PLAN
AND CONDUCT SIMPLE
INVESTIGATIONS TO
COLLECT RELEVANT DATA.

b. Provide each small group with a mineral kit and two streak plates. Tape identifying numbers, 1–12, to each mineral. Do not reveal the names of the minerals yet.

c. Demonstrate how one stroke of the mineral across the porcelain plate will usually produce a streak.

d. Point out to students three or four similarly colored minerals. Tell them to test the streak of each one. Instruct students to note the streak color for each mineral and to compare it with the observable color of the mineral.

e. Have the students begin a mineral properties chart as in the illustration. Children should start with a blank chart and fill in all parts of it, including the labeling of each column, as they make observations and tests of each mineral. Use observed color and streak color as the first two properties on the chart.

EXPLAIN: USE DATA TO GENERATE INTERPRETATIONS, INCLUDING DESCRIPTIONS, CLASSIFICATIONS, PREDICTIONS, AND EXPLANATIONS.

f. Interact with cooperative groups to assess their color and streak descriptions of different minerals.

With the children in a class-sized group, ask: *Why should we record descriptions of rocks and minerals in a chart?* Explain that building a chart of mineral properties is a way to organize data. Charts of mineral properties help us to summarize observations and identify unknown minerals. Other ways to organize data and information include data tables, graphs, and classification systems.

MINERAL PROPERTIES CHART

Number of Mineral	Observed Color	Streak Color	Feel	Hardness	Luster		
1	green to white	grayish					
2			soapy	softer than a penny			
3					metallic		
4					dull		
5							
6							
7							
8							
9							
10							
11							
12							

3. HOW CAN MINERALS BE IDENTIFIED BY FEEL? (2–5)

ENGAGE: ASK A QUESTION ABOUT OBJECTS, ORGANISMS, OR EVENTS IN THE ENVIRONMENT.

a. Ask: *How can the feel of a mineral be used to identify the mineral? What are some words that describe the feel of a mineral?* (Smooth, rough, rounded edges, and soapy.)

EXPLORE: PLAN AND CONDUCT SIMPLE INVESTIGATIONS TO COLLECT RELEVANT DATA.

b. Have students feel each mineral and record their descriptions in their charts.

EXPLAIN: USE DATA TO GENERATE INTERPRETATIONS, INCLUDING DESCRIPTIONS, CLASSIFICATIONS, PREDICTIONS, AND EXPLANATIONS.

c. As you work with groups, assess students' chart entries. With the whole class, review the meaning of *feel* and words they have used to describe the feel of each mineral.

4. WHAT IS MEANT BY THE HARDNESS OF A MINERAL AND HOW CAN WE TEST FOR IT? (2–5)

ENGAGE: ASK A QUESTION ABOUT OBJECTS, ORGANISMS, OR EVENTS IN THE ENVIRONMENT.

a. Ask: *Are the minerals in your kit equally hard? Which one seems hardest? Which one seems softest? How can you tell?*

Explain that the relative hardness of a mineral can be determined by a scratch test. The harder of two minerals will scratch the softer.

EXPLORE: PLAN AND CONDUCT SIMPLE INVESTIGATIONS TO COLLECT RELEVANT DATA.

b. Demonstrate how to use a penny to gently scratch a soft mineral and a nail to gently scratch a mineral of medium hardness. Explain that students will classify minerals as *soft*, *medium*, and *hard* using a copper penny and a steel nail as standards:
   * A soft mineral can be scratched by a penny.
   * A mineral of medium hardness can be scratched by a nail.
   * A hard mineral cannot be scratched by a nail.
   To prevent damage to minerals, encourage students to scratch gently.

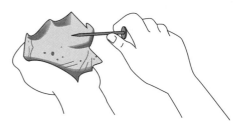

c. Have students test the hardness of each mineral in their charts. Tell students to add a "hardness" column to the mineral properties chart and to record the hardness of each mineral.

EXPLAIN: USE DATA TO GENERATE INTERPRETATIONS, INCLUDING DESCRIPTIONS, CLASSIFICATIONS, PREDICTIONS, AND EXPLANATIONS.

d. In a large group, ask students to report the results of their hardness tests. Work toward agreement in hardness test results. Students may have to retest some mineral samples.

5. WHAT IS MEANT BY LUSTER AND HOW CAN IT BE USED IN IDENTIFYING MINERALS? (2–5)

ENGAGE: ASK A QUESTION ABOUT OBJECTS, ORGANISMS, OR EVENTS IN THE ENVIRONMENT.

a. Tell students that *luster* refers to the way a mineral's surface reflects light.

Ask: *What are some words you can use to describe the luster of a mineral?*

Explain that some minerals have a metal-like luster and are called metallic. Other minerals are nonmetallic. Some terms you could use to describe the nonmetallic luster of a mineral might be *dull*, *glassy*, *waxy*, *pearly*, and *shiny*.

b. Have students hold each of their minerals up to the light or shine a flashlight on each one and describe its luster. Tell them to add the luster descriptions to their mineral properties charts.

c. In a large group, ask students to report the results of their luster tests. Work toward agreement in test results. Students may have to retest some mineral samples.

1. Pick up mineral A. Shine the penlight on it.

2. Describe how the rock looks in the light. Dull? Shiny? Glassy?

3. Using the terms you have agreed on in class, record results in the space labeled "Light" on your mineral profile sheet.

4. Repeat steps 1, 2, and 3 for the other 11 minerals.

6. HOW CAN THE TRANSMISSION OF LIGHT THROUGH A MINERAL BE USED TO IDENTIFY THE MINERAL? (2–5)

ENGAGE: ASK A QUESTION ABOUT OBJECTS, ORGANISMS, OR EVENTS IN THE ENVIRONMENT.

a. Hold common transparent (e.g., clear plastic), translucent (e.g., wax paper), and opaque (e.g., aluminum foil) materials to the lens of an overhead projector or flashlight. Ask: *How do these materials differ in the way they transmit light?* Explain that materials can be *transparent*, with a lot of light shining through them; *translucent*, with a little light shining through; or *opaque*, with no light shining through. Ask: *How can the amount of light a mineral transmits help us in identifying it?*

EXPLORE: PLAN AND CONDUCT SIMPLE INVESTIGATIONS TO COLLECT RELEVANT DATA.

b. Have students shine a flashlight on each mineral and look to see how much light is transmitted. Students should record their findings for each of the numbered minerals in their mineral properties charts.

7. WHAT CAN THE SHAPE OF A MINERAL TELL US? (2–5)

ENGAGE: ASK A QUESTION ABOUT OBJECTS, ORGANISMS, OR EVENTS IN THE ENVIRONMENT.

a. Ask: *Do any of your minerals seem to have a characteristic shape?*
b. Tell students that the shape of a mineral is often a clue to its crystal-like structure. The shape of minerals might be described as like a cube, like a box that is bent over (calcite), having crystals, having masses that are not fully crystals, having thin layers (e.g., biotite), or having no special shape.

EXPLORE: PLAN AND CONDUCT SIMPLE INVESTIGATIONS TO COLLECT RELEVANT DATA.

c. Have students describe the shape of each mineral and add their descriptions to the mineral properties chart. Circulate among cooperative groups to assess the descriptions of shape entered in the chart.

EXPLAIN: USE DATA TO GENERATE INTERPRETATIONS, INCLUDING DESCRIPTIONS, CLASSIFICATIONS, PREDICTIONS, AND EXPLANATIONS.

d. Work with individuals and small groups to suggest procedures and answer questions related to the shape property. Spot-check their mineral charts to assess understanding.

8. WHAT SPECIAL PROPERTIES DO DIFFERENT MINERALS HAVE? (2–5)

ENGAGE: ASK A QUESTION ABOUT OBJECTS, ORGANISMS, OR EVENTS IN THE ENVIRONMENT.

a. Ask: *What other special properties of your minerals have you observed?*

EXPLORE: PLAN
AND CONDUCT SIMPLE
INVESTIGATIONS TO
COLLECT RELEVANT DATA.

b. Have students list other special properties of each mineral on their mineral properties charts. For example, they should use a magnet to test each mineral for magnetic properties or use a batteries and bulb test circuit to see if the mineral conducts electricity.

EXPLAIN: USE
DATA TO GENERATE
INTERPRETATIONS,
INCLUDING DESCRIPTIONS,
CLASSIFICATIONS,
PREDICTIONS, AND
EXPLANATIONS.

c. Supply the name of each of the minerals numbered 1–12. Provide students with a master chart of mineral properties and have them compare their charts with the master chart. If discrepancies occur with any of the minerals, encourage students to make some fresh observations.

9. HOW CAN YOU IDENTIFY AN UNKNOWN MINERAL? (2–5)

ENGAGE: ASK A
QUESTION ABOUT OBJECTS,
ORGANISMS, OR EVENTS.

a. Ask: *How can you use your mineral properties chart to identify a mineral sample?*

EXPLORE: PLAN
AND CONDUCT SIMPLE
INVESTIGATIONS.

b. Give students one or more of minerals 1–12 with the identifying number labels removed. Have students use their mineral properties charts to identify each mineral.

c. Ask: *What have you concluded about the identity of your unknown samples? How did you use observation and your charts to identify the unknown samples?*

EXPLAIN: USE
DATA TO GENERATE
INTERPRETATIONS.

B. THE STRUCTURE OF MINERALS: CRYSTALS AND CRYSTAL FORMATION

▶ *Science Background*

Crystals are nonliving substances that form into rocklike bodies of various shapes. Crystals grow in size when more layers of the same substance are added on; the basic crystal shape, however, remains the same. The size of crystals is determined by differences in the rate of crystallization. If crystals are disturbed in the forming process, they will break apart into hundreds of microscopic pieces. Crystalline form is important in determining some of the properties of substances.

NSES Science Standards

All students should develop an understanding of

- properties of the earth's systems (K–4).
- structure of the earth's systems (5–8).

Objectives for Students

1. Demonstrate and describe different kinds of investigations to grow crystals.
2. Describe how crystal size is affected by conditions during formation.
3. Distinguish between and describe the formation of stalactites and stalagmites.

NSES   **Concepts and Principles**

Activities 1–4 address these fundamental concepts and principles related to the *Science Standards:*

• Earth materials are solid rocks and soils, water, and gases of the atmosphere (K–4).
• The varied materials have different physical and chemical properties (K–4).

1. HOW CAN SALT CRYSTALS BE GROWN? (3–6)

Materials

Salt
Tablespoon
Jar lid
Small glass
Magnifying lens

ENGAGE: ASK A QUESTION ABOUT OBJECTS, ORGANISMS, OR EVENTS IN THE ENVIRONMENT.

a. Guide students to examine a grain of salt through a magnifying lens. Ask: *What do you see? What does a salt grain look like? What are crystals? How are crystals formed?*

EXPLORE: PLAN AND CONDUCT SIMPLE INVESTIGATIONS TO COLLECT RELEVANT DATA.

b. Guide students to conduct these activities within their cooperative groups:
   1. Obtain a tablespoon of salt, a jar lid, and a small glass of water. Mix the salt into the glass of water. Stir the water well. Let the solution stand for a few minutes until it becomes clear.
      Ask: *What happens to the salt?*
   2. Very gently pour some of the salt solution into the jar lid. Put a piece of string in the solution, letting one end hang out, as in diagram (a). Let the solution stand for several days where the lid will not be disturbed.
      Ask: *What do you predict will happen to the salt solution?*

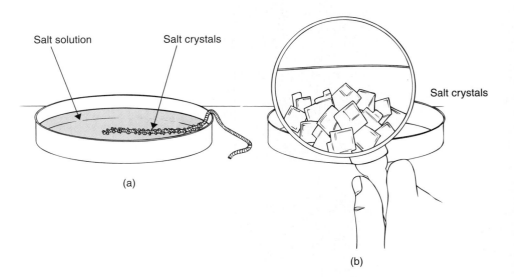

Salt solution   Salt crystals

Salt crystals

(a)

(b)

3. After several days have passed, use your magnifying lens to look at the materials in the lid. Lift the string out of the jar lid. Examine the string with your magnifying lens. Describe what you see with the hand lens. See diagram (b).

EXPLAIN: USE DATA TO GENERATE INTERPRETATIONS, INCLUDING DESCRIPTIONS, CLASSIFICATIONS, PREDICTIONS, AND EXPLANATIONS.

c. Ask: *How are the materials in the lid different from your original salt solution?*
   Why do you now have a solid when you started out with a liquid?
   What name could you give to the formations in the lid?

d. Explain to the students that the salt dissolved in the water. When the salt water stood for several days, the water evaporated, leaving behind crystals of salt. Crystals are nonliving substances found in nature that are formed in various geometrical shapes.

2. HOW CAN SUGAR CRYSTALS BE GROWN? (3–6)

Materials | Tablespoon | Jar lid
Granulated sugar | Small glass

ENGAGE: ASK A QUESTION ABOUT OBJECTS, ORGANISMS, OR EVENTS IN THE ENVIRONMENT.

a. Instruct students to examine grains of sugar through a magnifying lens. Ask: *What do you observe? How are sugar crystals different from salt crystals? How can we grow crystals of sugar?*

EXPLORE: PLAN AND CONDUCT SIMPLE INVESTIGATIONS TO COLLECT RELEVANT DATA.

b. Students should conduct these activities in their cooperative groups:
   1. Obtain a tablespoon of sugar, a jar lid, and a small glass of water. Be sure the tablespoon is clean. Mix a tablespoon of sugar into the glass of water. Stir the water well. Let the solution stand for a few minutes until it becomes clear. Ask: *What happens to the sugar?*
      How is the sugar solution similar in appearance to the salt solution?
   2. Very gently pour some of the sugar solution into the lid and let the solution stand undisturbed for several days. Ask: *What do you think might happen to the sugar solution?*
   3. After several days have passed, use your magnifying lens to look at the materials in your lid.

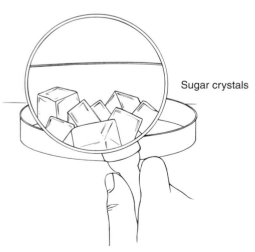

Sugar crystals

EXPLAIN: USE DATA TO GENERATE INTERPRETATIONS, INCLUDING DESCRIPTIONS, CLASSIFICATIONS, PREDICTIONS, AND EXPLANATIONS.

c. Ask: *How are the materials in this lid different from the salt crystals? How are they alike? What happened to the sugar solution?*
  Explain that when the sugar water stood for several days, the water evaporated, leaving behind sugar crystals.

3. HOW DOES THE RATE OF COOLING DURING CRYSTAL FORMATION AFFECT CRYSTAL SIZE? (3–6)

Materials

Pyrex beaker   Clean jar lid
Alum   String
Tablespoon   One smooth, sanded washer
Hot plate   Pencil
Cooking mitt

ENGAGE: ASK A QUESTION ABOUT OBJECTS, ORGANISMS, OR EVENTS IN THE ENVIRONMENT.

a. Ask: *What determines how large a crystal is?*

EXPLORE: PLAN AND CONDUCT SIMPLE INVESTIGATIONS TO COLLECT RELEVANT DATA.

b. Demonstrate the following steps for your students:
  1. Heat 200 ml of water in a Pyrex beaker. Add 3 tablespoons of alum. Heat and stir the mixture until the alum fully dissolves, as in diagram (a).

(a)   (b)   (c)

2. Using an insulated cooking mitt, remove the beaker and put it on a solid surface where it cannot be moved or struck.
3. Carefully pour a small amount of the alum solution into a clean jar lid as in diagram (b). Place the lid in a secure, dry place away from heat sources or direct sunshine.
4. Sand a washer and tie it to one end of a piece of string. Wind and tie the other end to a pencil so that when the pencil is suspended across the top of a jar, the washer hangs down about 1 cm from the bottom of the jar as in diagram (c). Place the jar in a secure, dry place next to the jar lid.
5. Have students observe the jar and lid every day. Caution students not to shake or move the containers.

EXPLAIN: USE DATA TO GENERATE INTERPRETATIONS, INCLUDING DESCRIPTIONS, CLASSIFICATIONS, PREDICTIONS, AND EXPLANATIONS.

c. Have students record their observations and use their data to answer these questions:
Where did the first crystals form: bottom of jar, sides of jar, or string?
How does the size of crystals in the jar compare with that in the jar lid?
Why do some rocks have large crystals and some have small crystals?

d. Through discussion, explain that minerals are crystalline in structure. The form of the crystals is important in determining some of the properties of minerals. Differences in the rate of crystallization determine differences in crystal size. Crystals in the jar lid are smaller than those in the jar due to the differences in cooling times. Slower cooling (jar) produces larger crystals, whereas faster cooling (lid) produces smaller crystals.
Ask: *Why would the liquid in the jar cool slower than the liquid in the jar lid?*

4. WHAT ARE STALACTITES AND STALAGMITES, AND HOW ARE THEY FORMED? (3–6)

Materials

Paper towel
Epsom salt
Spoon
30 cm (1 ft) of thick string
Large tin can
Two small jars or clear plastic cups
Two heavy washers

ENGAGE: ASK A QUESTION ABOUT OBJECTS, ORGANISMS, OR EVENTS IN THE ENVIRONMENT.

a. Ask: *How are some rocks formed in caves?*
What is a stalactite, and how is it formed?
What is a stalagmite, and how is it formed?

EXPLORE: PLAN AND CONDUCT SIMPLE INVESTIGATIONS TO COLLECT RELEVANT DATA.

b. Allow students to carry out this investigation in cooperative groups:
1. Fill the large tin can about three-quarters full of water. Add Epsom salt one spoonful at a time, stirring vigorously after each addition, until no more will dissolve.

Note: Epsom salt crystals will fall to the bottom of the can when no more will dissolve.

2. Fill the two small jars or plastic cups with the Epsom salt solution and place the containers 5 cm (2 in.) apart on the paper towel. Tie a heavy washer to each end of the string. Place one washer in each of the small jars or paper cups.

Note: Arrange the string in the cups so that you have at least 5 cm (2 in.) between the string and the paper towel.

3. Observe the jars or cups, the paper towel, the string, and the washer daily. Record the observations on a record sheet or in your science journals.

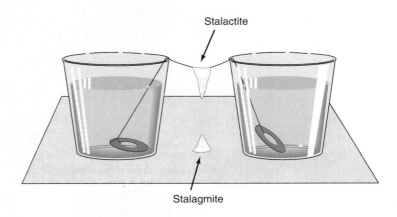

Stalactite

Stalagmite

EXPLAIN: USE DATA TO GENERATE INTERPRETATIONS, INCLUDING DESCRIPTIONS, CLASSIFICATIONS, PREDICTIONS, AND EXPLANATIONS.

c. Ask: *What do you observe? What is the substance deposited on the string and on the paper towel? How did they get there? What is your evidence?*

d. Help students learn the difference between stalactites and stalagmites. Point out that the deposits that hang down are called **stalactites** (*c* for ceiling), while those that point up are called **stalagmites** (*g* for ground).

Ask: *Is the crystal formed on the string like a stalactite or a stalagmite? Why do you think so? Is the crystal formed on the paper towel like a stalactite or a stalagmite? Why do you think so?*

How could you help children understand what scientists do?

e. Children sometimes fail to understand the link between causes and effects because they think of an investigation in terms of its component parts rather than its interactions. Scientists use the notion of *system* to help them think in terms of components and interactions. Explain that a system is a collection of components that interact to perform some function. Examples of systems are a school system and the city water system.

Thinking of an investigation as a **system** made up of parts that interact with one another can help to broaden children's thinking. Ask: *What are the components of our investigation system?* (Containers, Epsom salt, water, string, washers, paper towels.) *How does each component interact with other components? What is your evidence?*

By observing small systems, we can draw inferences about what happens in larger systems of the world. Ask: *How is what we observed like what might happen in a cavern in the earth?*

Stalactites and stalagmites in Mammoth Cave, Mammoth Cave National Park, Kentucky.

C. STRUCTURE OF THE EARTH'S SURFACE

▶ *Science Background*

The earth's surface is always changing. Waves, wind, water, and ice shape and reshape the earth's land surface by eroding rock and soil in some areas and depositing it in other areas, sometimes forming seasonal layers. Smaller rocks come from the breaking and weathering of bedrock and larger rocks. Soil is made partly from weathered rock, partly from plant and animal remains. Soil also contains many living organisms.

Source: American Association for the Advancement of Science (1993). *Benchmarks for Science Literacy.* New York: Oxford University Press.

NSES   **Science Standards**

All students should develop an understanding of

- properties of the earth's systems (K–4).
- structure of the earth's systems (5–8).

Objectives for Students

1. Describe how germinating seeds and plants can naturally break up rocks and soil.
2. Demonstrate a procedure for determining the composition of soils.

3. Describe what might be found in soils.
4. Demonstrate a procedure to illustrate how the earth's surface forms layers.
5. Demonstrate, describe, and explain a procedure to illustrate how layers in the earth's surface might be observed.

NSES   **Concepts and Principles**

Activities 1–3 address these fundamental concepts and principles related to the *Science Standards:*

- Soils have properties of color and texture, capacity to retain water, and ability to support the growth of many kinds of plants (K–4).
- Soils consist of weathered rocks and decomposed organic material from dead plants, animals, and bacteria. Soils are often found in layers, with each having a different chemical composition and texture (5–8).
- The surface of the earth changes. Some changes are due to slow processes, such as erosion and weathering, and some changes are due to rapid processes, such as landslides, volcanic eruptions, and earthquakes (K–4).

1. HOW CAN LIVING THINGS PRODUCE FORCES THAT CAN CHANGE THE EARTH'S SURFACE? (K–2)

Materials

Two plastic vials or medicine bottles with snap lids
Dry bean seeds
Water

ENGAGE: ASK A QUESTION ABOUT OBJECTS, ORGANISMS, OR EVENTS IN THE ENVIRONMENT.

a. Ask: *How can germinating seeds produce forces that can change rocks and soil?*

EXPLORE: PLAN AND CONDUCT SIMPLE INVESTIGATIONS TO COLLECT RELEVANT DATA.

b. Fill both of the vials or medicine bottles with as many dry beans as will fit. Add as much water as you can to one vial of beans. Snap the lids on both vials.
    Ask: *What do you think might happen to the two vials?*

A Water   **B** No water

EXPLAIN: USE DATA TO GENERATE INTERPRETATIONS, INCLUDING DESCRIPTIONS, CLASSIFICATIONS, PREDICTIONS, AND EXPLANATIONS.

c. Observe both vials the next day.

Ask: *What do you observe? Why did it happen?*

Lead students to understand that in the container with water, the beans expanded and lifted the lid off. In the vial without water, there was no observable change. Ask: *How could the force of germinating seeds and growing plants produce changes in the earth's surface?* Help students infer that swelling and growing plants change the land by breaking up rocks and soil just as the swelling beans lifted the vial's lid off. Ask students to find places on the school grounds or on concrete walks where plants grow through and crack rocks like this:

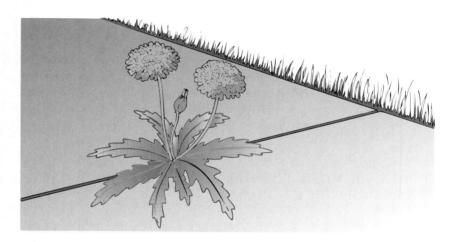

2. WHAT IS IN SOIL? (3–6)

Materials

Soil (from backyard)
Alum
Clear plastic vial with lid

ENGAGE: ASK A QUESTION ABOUT OBJECTS, ORGANISMS, OR EVENTS IN THE ENVIRONMENT.

a. Ask: *What is in soil? How can we find out?*

EXPLORE: PLAN AND CONDUCT SIMPLE INVESTIGATIONS TO COLLECT RELEVANT DATA.

b. To observe different kinds of materials in backyard soil:
1. Add about 1 inch of soil to a clear plastic vial with a lid (approximately 1 inch in diameter and 3 inches high).
2. Add a pinch of alum to the soil. Tell the students that alum is a chemical used in making pickles. It is safe, but caution the students not to taste it.
3. Fill the vial to the top with water, cover it, and shake it vigorously.
4. Place the vial on the table and leave it there for the duration of the investigation.
5. After several minutes, observe and record observations. The alum acts as a dispersing agent, helping the soil particles to break into smaller parts and settle out into layers. Students should observe sand at the bottom of the vial, silt above the sand, clay above the silt, water, and organic matter floating on the water.

Organic matter
Water
Clay
Silt
Sand

Soil + alum + water

EXPLAIN: USE DATA TO GENERATE INTERPRETATIONS, INCLUDING DESCRIPTIONS, CLASSIFICATIONS, PREDICTIONS, AND EXPLANATIONS.

c. Ask: *From the results of your investigation, what do you conclude is in soil? Which particles do you think are larger: sand, clay, or silt? Why do you think so?*

Source: GEMS (Great Explorations in Math and Science), 1994. *Terrarium Habitats.* Lawrence Hall of Science. University of California at Berkeley.

3. WHAT IS CORE SAMPLING, AND HOW CAN WE USE IT TO INFER LAYERS IN THE EARTH? (K–5)

Materials

Cupcakes
Clear plastic straws
Plastic knives

Preparation

In this activity, straws will be used to take core samples of layered cupcakes. Layered cupcakes may be made by the teacher or a parent volunteer as follows:

1. Use either different flavors or white batter mixed with food coloring.
2. Put batter in four layers in foil or paper cups.
3. Bake the cupcakes. Add frosting if desired.

ENGAGE: ASK A QUESTION ABOUT OBJECTS, ORGANISMS, OR EVENTS IN THE ENVIRONMENT.

a. Ask: *How do geologists study what is below the earth's surface?*
Provide students this background information:

> **Geologists** study the earth and use many devices to discover what is under the surface. **Core sampling** is done by putting hollow drilling tubes into the ground and extracting a sample of what the tubes went through.

b. Show students a cupcake. Ask: *What do you think is inside the cupcake? How could we find out without eating it or cutting into it? How can scientists learn what's underground?*

EXPLORE: PLAN AND CONDUCT SIMPLE INVESTIGATIONS TO COLLECT RELEVANT DATA.

c. Provide groups of students one cupcake on a paper plate, five clear plastic straws cut into thirds, a plastic knife, drawing paper, and markers. Do *not* remove the foil or paper cup from the cupcake.
d. Instruct students to draw what they think the inside of the cupcake looks like.

e. Explain and demonstrate to students how to take side "core samples," as in diagram (a):
   1. Carefully insert a straw into the side of the cupcake, rotate slightly, remove, and place sample on paper plate.
   2. Repeat with another straw.
f. Instruct students to take two side core samples of their cupcake. Ask: *Can you determine what the entire cupcake looks like with these two core samples? If not, what must you do?*
g. Instruct students to take three samples by inserting the straw straight down into the cupcake, as in diagram (b).

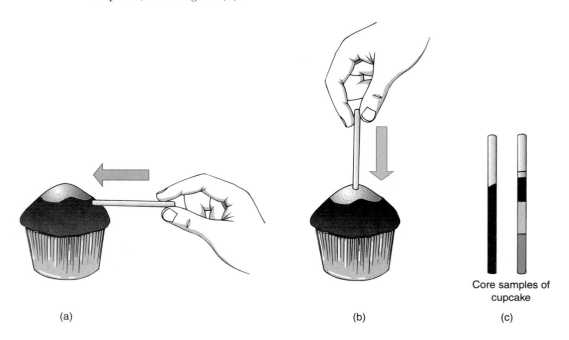

Core samples of cupcake

(a) (b) (c)

h. Compare these samples with those taken from the side, as in diagram (c).

EXPLAIN: USE DATA TO GENERATE INTERPRETATIONS, INCLUDING DESCRIPTIONS, CLASSIFICATIONS, PREDICTIONS, AND EXPLANATIONS.

i. Ask: *How are they different? Based on your core samples, what do you infer is inside the cupcake?*
   Instruct students to make drawings of what they now think the inside of the cupcake looks like.
j. Tell students to use the plastic knives to cut down and separate the cupcakes into halves. Ask: *How do your direct observations compare with your inferences and your drawings? How could geologists use core sampling to infer what is inside the earth?*

Source: Cupcake Geology activity in the Mesa Public Schools Curriculum Unit "Earthquakes" by JoAnne Vasquez.

II. THE ATMOSPHERE, WEATHER, AND CLIMATE OF THE EARTH

Our spherical earth consists mostly of rock, with three-fourths of the planet covered by a thin layer of water and the entire planet blanketed by a thin layer of air called the atmosphere. Weather (in the short run) and climate (in the long run) involve the transfer of heat energy from the sun in and out of the atmosphere. The earth has a variety of climatic patterns, which consist of different conditions of temperature, precipitation, humidity, wind, air pressure, and other atmospheric phenomena. Water continuously circulates in and out of the atmosphere—evaporating from the surface, rising and cooling, condensing into clouds and then rain or snow, and falling again to the surface. The water cycle plays an important part in determining climatic patterns.

Children can begin to understand the atmosphere, water cycle, weather, and climate by engaging in inquiry activities related to evaporation and condensation, and observing and recording the weather on a regular basis. Emphasis should be on developing observation and description skills and forming explanations based on observable evidence.[2]

A. THE WATER CYCLE

▶ *Science Background*

In the **water cycle**, water evaporates into the air as **water vapor**.

As the air becomes laden with water vapor, the **relative humidity** of the air increases. When warm, moist air cools, it condenses as liquid water on available surfaces such as an iced tea glass, a bathroom mirror, or dust particles in the air.

NSES Science Standards

All students should develop an understanding of

- changes in the earth and sky (K–4).
- structure of the earth's systems (5–8).

Objectives for Students

1. Observe and describe the disappearance of water that is left uncovered.
2. Define *evaporation* and explain that evaporated water has not disappeared but has changed into water vapor (a gaseous state) and has gone into the air.
3. Use the cohesive bond model of water developed in previous activities to explain what happens when a liquid evaporates.
4. Explain how interactions between a liquid and its environment may affect evaporation.
5. Define *condensation* and *dew point*.
6. Describe and demonstrate the conditions for condensation.
7. Construct and explain a model of the water cycle.

NSES Concepts and Principles

Activities 1–9 address these fundamental concepts and principles related to the *Science Standards:*

- Water, which covers the majority of the earth's surface, circulates through the crust, oceans, and atmosphere in what is known as the "water cycle" (5–8).
- Water evaporates from the earth's surface, rises and cools as it moves to higher elevations, condenses as rain or snow, and falls to the surface where it collects in lakes, oceans, soil, and rocks underground (5–8).

---

[2]*Science for All Americans, Benchmarks for Science Literacy,* and the *National Science Education Standards.*

1. HOW MUCH WATER EVAPORATES FROM AN OPEN AQUARIUM? (K–2)

Materials   Aquarium or other large, open container

Safety Precautions   When children work with water, cover their work tables, perhaps with newspapers. Have plenty of paper towels on hand to clean up water spills.

ENGAGE: ASK A QUESTION ABOUT OBJECTS, ORGANISMS, OR EVENTS IN THE ENVIRONMENT.

a. Ask: *How can we determine the amount of water that evaporates from an aquarium?*

EXPLORE: PLAN AND CONDUCT SIMPLE INVESTIGATIONS TO COLLECT RELEVANT DATA.

b. Assist students to conduct this investigation:
    1. Using masking tape or marking pens, mark the beginning water levels of a classroom aquarium.
    2. Check the water levels each morning. Using a measuring cup, add enough water to the containers to bring the water levels back up to the original marks you made. Be sure the water added to the aquarium sits in a large open container for at least 24 hours.
    3. Keep a record of how much water was added to your containers each week.

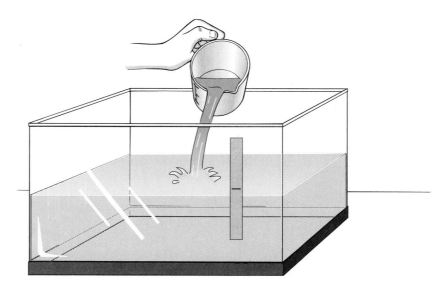

EXPLAIN: USE DATA TO GENERATE INTERPRETATIONS, INCLUDING DESCRIPTIONS, CLASSIFICATIONS, PREDICTIONS, AND EXPLANATIONS.

c. Ask: *How much water evaporated from the aquarium each day?*

2. WHERE DOES WATER GO WHEN IT EVAPORATES? (K–2)

Materials

Aquarium with water, fish, and sand
Empty aquarium container
Sand

ENGAGE: ASK A QUESTION ABOUT OBJECTS, ORGANISMS, OR EVENTS IN THE ENVIRONMENT.

a. Ask: *When water evaporates, where does it go?*

EXPLORE: PLAN AND CONDUCT SIMPLE INVESTIGATIONS TO COLLECT RELEVANT DATA.

b. Lead children to form hypotheses about where the water in an aquarium or other container went when it disappeared. Possible hypotheses include the following:
   - The missing water soaked into the sand.
   - The fish drank it.
   - The custodian spilled it.
   - It went into the air.

c. Help the children design and conduct controlled investigations to test each hypothesis. In a controlled investigation, all variables are kept the same except one.
   1. To test if the water soaked into the sand, observe two aquariums with water and fish, one with and one without sand.
   2. To test if the fish drank the water, compare one container with fish and one without (both containers should be identical in every other way except one has no fish).
   3. To test if the water went into the air, observe one container covered and one uncovered.

EXPLAIN: USE DATA TO GENERATE INTERPRETATIONS, INCLUDING DESCRIPTIONS, CLASSIFICATIONS, PREDICTIONS, AND EXPLANATIONS.

d. Ask: *What did you observe in your investigations? What can you conclude?* Discuss with the students how they can interpret the data from each of their experiments. For example, explain that the amount of the evaporated water was the same in aquariums with and without sand, so the water must not have soaked into the sand. There was a difference in the evaporated water only in the experiment in which one aquarium was covered and the other was not covered. Therefore, the cover must have prevented water from evaporating.

Discuss with the children how these experiments provide evidence that the water went into the air. Explain that the missing water does not just disappear; it changes into water vapor (a gaseous state) and goes into the air.[3]

3. HOW CAN YOU PROMOTE THE EVAPORATION OF WATER? (K–2)

Materials

Shallow containers such as jar lids
Lamp with 60 watt bulb

Safety Precautions

Caution the children not to touch the light bulb and electrical connections. For safety reasons, you may choose to demonstrate that water evaporates more quickly when it is heated.

---

[3]Adapted from a variation of an SCIS activity developed by Herbert Thier.

ENGAGE: ASK A QUESTION ABOUT OBJECTS, ORGANISMS, OR EVENTS IN THE ENVIRONMENT.

a. Ask: *What can you do to speed up the evaporation of water?*

EXPLORE: PLAN AND CONDUCT SIMPLE INVESTIGATIONS TO COLLECT RELEVANT DATA.

b. Place water in two shallow containers, such as jar lids. Lead the students to try different things to promote evaporation. Eventually they should focus on (1) fanning the air above the liquid and (2) heating the liquid with the light from an unshaded 60 watt light bulb in a lamp. Emphasize that students should do something to the liquid in one jar lid and do nothing to the liquid in the other. For example, the liquid in one container is fanned; the other is not. The liquid in one container is heated by the light source; the other is not. This way, they can compare the water levels in the two containers and see whether evaporation is affected by fanning or heating.

EXPLAIN: USE DATA TO GENERATE INTERPRETATIONS, INCLUDING DESCRIPTIONS, CLASSIFICATIONS, PREDICTIONS, AND EXPLANATIONS.

c. Ask: *Does fanning water speed up its evaporation? What is your evidence? Does shining light on water speed up its evaporation? What is your evidence? Why do you think fanning the water or shining light on it speeded up the evaporation?*

4. WHICH EVAPORATES MORE QUICKLY, WATER OR RUBBING ALCOHOL? (4–6)

Materials

Rubbing alcohol
Droppers

Safety Precautions

Do not allow students to handle or touch the rubbing alcohol.

ENGAGE: ASK A QUESTION ABOUT OBJECTS, ORGANISMS, OR EVENTS IN THE ENVIRONMENT.

a. Ask: *Which evaporates more quickly, water or rubbing alcohol?*

EXPLORE: PLAN AND CONDUCT SIMPLE INVESTIGATIONS TO COLLECT RELEVANT DATA.

b. The teacher should place drops of water and drops of rubbing alcohol near one another on wax paper for each cooperative group. The students then observe the two liquids to determine what happens to them over time. (To speed up evaporation, children may gently fan both of the drops of liquid.)

EXPLAIN: USE DATA TO GENERATE INTERPRETATIONS, INCLUDING DESCRIPTIONS, CLASSIFICATIONS, PREDICTIONS, AND EXPLANATIONS.

c. Ask: *What happened to each liquid? Where did each liquid go when it disappeared? Which liquid evaporated more quickly? Using what you know of the bonding of drops in a liquid, why do you think the drops of alcohol evaporated more quickly?*

▶ *Teaching Background*

The cohesive force of drops for one another is greater in water than in alcohol. Thus, the alcohol drops can escape the cohesive forces holding them in the liquid more easily than the water can. That is the reason alcohol evaporates more quickly than water.

5. HOW FAST DOES WATER IN A WET SPONGE EVAPORATE? (3–6)

Materials	Meterstick or wire coat hanger Paper clips Sponge Masking tape or marking pens

ENGAGE: ASK A QUESTION ABOUT OBJECTS, ORGANISMS, OR EVENTS IN THE ENVIRONMENT.

a. Ask: *How can we determine the rate of evaporation of water in a wet sponge?*

EXPLORE: PLAN AND CONDUCT SIMPLE INVESTIGATIONS TO COLLECT RELEVANT DATA.

b. Assist students to set up and conduct this investigation:
1. Using a meterstick or wire coat hanger, and paper clips, build either of the balances shown.
2. Soak a piece of sponge until it is very wet, but not dripping. Hang the sponge with an S-shaped paper clip or string to one end of the balance. Add paper clips to the other end until the balance is level.
    How many clips did it take?
3. Every 15 minutes, check to see if the balance is level.
    What do you see happening after several observations?
    Why do you think the paper clip end of the balance is lower?
4. Keep a written record of what happens.
5. At each 15 minute observation, take off and record how many paper clips must be removed to keep the balance level.
6. When the sponge is dry, take your written observations and plot a line graph with the data. Set up your graph like the one that follows.

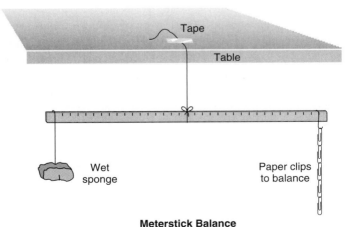

Meterstick Balance

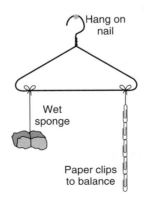

Wire Coat Hanger Balance

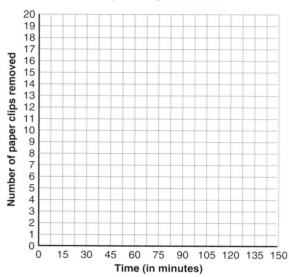

EXPLAIN: USE DATA TO GENERATE INTERPRETATIONS, INCLUDING DESCRIPTIONS, CLASSIFICATIONS, PREDICTIONS, AND EXPLANATIONS.

c. Ask: *What does the graph tell you about the rate of evaporation of the water in a wet sponge?*

6. WHAT VARIABLES AFFECT HOW QUICKLY WATER EVAPORATES IN A WET SPONGE? (3–6)

ENGAGE: ASK A QUESTION ABOUT OBJECTS, ORGANISMS, OR EVENTS IN THE ENVIRONMENT.

a. Ask: *What are some variables that might affect how quickly the water in the sponge of Activity 5 evaporates? How could you set up an experiment to test the effect of these variables on evaporation?*

EXPLORE: PLAN AND CONDUCT SIMPLE INVESTIGATIONS TO COLLECT RELEVANT DATA.

b. Some variables that might affect the rate of evaporation are type of liquid (water vs. alcohol), temperature of the liquid (hot vs. cold), air temperature (hot vs. cold), wind velocity (no wind, moderate wind, strong wind), and relative humidity (dry day vs. moist day). Guide students in designing investigations, gathering data, and recording and graphing the results in the same way as was done in the previous activity.

EXPLAIN: USE DATA TO GENERATE INTERPRETATIONS, INCLUDING DESCRIPTIONS, CLASSIFICATIONS, PREDICTIONS, AND EXPLANATIONS.

c. Ask: *What did you observe in your investigations? What do you conclude?*

ELABORATE: EXTEND CONCEPTS, PRINCIPLES, AND STRATEGIES TO NEW SITUATIONS AND QUESTIONS.

d. Ask: *How do your findings from your investigation relate to each of these situations?*
   - Water evaporates faster from your hands when you vigorously rub them together.
   - A blow dryer can be used to dry your hair faster.
   - Your hair dries faster on a dry day than on a wet one.
   - A wet towel dries faster if it is spread out rather than crumpled in a ball.

7. WHAT IS CONDENSATION? HOW DOES IT OCCUR? (3–6)

Materials

Clean, empty vegetable or fruit cans
Ice

ENGAGE: ASK A QUESTION ABOUT OBJECTS, ORGANISMS, OR EVENTS IN THE ENVIRONMENT.

a. Ask: *What is condensation? What conditions are needed for condensation?*

EXPLORE: PLAN AND CONDUCT SIMPLE INVESTIGATIONS TO COLLECT RELEVANT DATA.

b. Provide each group two identical, empty vegetable cans. Give students these instructions:
   1. Add the same amount of water to each can so that they are about three-fourths full.
   2. Place ice in one of the cans so that the water is almost to the top of the can.
   3. Stir the water in each can.
   4. Observe the outside of each can.

EXPLAIN: USE DATA TO GENERATE INTERPRETATIONS, INCLUDING DESCRIPTIONS, CLASSIFICATIONS, PREDICTIONS, AND EXPLANATIONS.

c. Ask: *What happened to the outside of each can as you stirred the water?* (Moisture collected on the outside of the container with ice water.) *What conditions were necessary for the water to appear on the outside of the can?* (The can had to be cool.) *Where did the water come from?*

d. If students suggest that cold water soaked through the can, ask: *How could we test this hypothesis?*

   Hint: You might put food dye in the water and then observe to see if any of the food coloring actually soaked through the can.

   Ask: *People often say that a glass of ice water is sweating; why is this explanation incorrect?*

e. Provide this explanation of condensation:

   > When water evaporates, it goes into the air as water vapor. If moisture-laden air comes into contact with a surface that is cool enough, then water vapor condenses (changes from a gas to a liquid) from the air and collects on the cool surface.

ELABORATE: EXTEND CONCEPTS, PRINCIPLES, AND STRATEGIES TO NEW SITUATIONS AND QUESTIONS.

f. Ask: *What is the source of the warm, moist air in each of these examples of condensation? What is the surface on which water condenses in each case?*
   - *Formation of clouds.* (Warm, moist air in the atmosphere rises and cools. As the water vapor cools, it condenses on dust particles.)
   - *Dew.* (Warm, moist air is cooled as it mixes with cooler air near the surface of the earth. As the water vapor cools, it condenses on the grass and other surfaces.)
   - *Vapor trails.* (Warm, moist air from the exhaust of a jet mixes with cooler air high in the atmosphere. As the water vapor cools, it condenses on dust particles in the atmosphere.)
   - *Moisture on bathroom mirrors after a hot shower.* (Warm, moist air produced during the hot shower condenses on the cooler bathroom mirror.)

8. HOW CAN EVAPORATION AND CONDENSATION BE USED TO DESALINATE SALT WATER? (3–5)

Materials

Salt
Water
Tablespoon
Small weight (rock)
Large sheet of black construction paper
Large clear plastic bowl
Plastic wrap
Large rubber band
Small glass custard cup

ENGAGE: ASK A QUESTION ABOUT OBJECTS, ORGANISMS, OR EVENTS IN THE ENVIRONMENT.

a. Ask: *How can evaporation and condensation be used to remove the salt from salt water?*

EXPLORE: PLAN AND CONDUCT SIMPLE INVESTIGATIONS TO COLLECT RELEVANT DATA.

b. This activity may be done individually or in groups of two to four:
   1. Pour 3 tablespoons of salt into a large clear plastic bowl, add water to a depth of about 2 to 3 cm, and stir until all the salt is dissolved.
   2. Place the small glass cup in the water in the center of the bowl, as in the diagram.
   3. Cover the large bowl with plastic wrap and fasten the wrap with a large rubber band.
   4. Place a weight (small pebble) on top of the plastic wrap directly above the custard dish, as shown in the diagram.
   5. *Caution:* Make certain that the plastic wrap sticks tightly to the sides of the bowl and that the large rubber band keeps it sealed when the pebble is placed on the wrap.
   6. Carefully place the bowls in direct sunlight on a sheet of black construction paper, making sure the custard cup is directly under the weight pushing down on the plastic wrap.

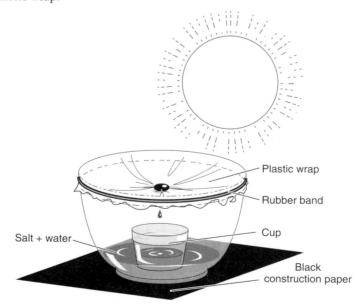

Plastic wrap

Rubber band

Salt + water

Cup

Black construction paper

7. *What do you think might happen to the salt water?*
8. *Why do you think you were told to cover the salt water with plastic wrap?*
9. *Why do you think you were told to put the bowl on black construction paper?*
10. Record your observations every day.
11. Take off the plastic wrap and taste the water in the custard cup.

EXPLAIN: USE DATA TO GENERATE INTERPRETATIONS, INCLUDING DESCRIPTIONS, CLASSIFICATIONS, PREDICTIONS, AND EXPLANATIONS.

c. Ask: *How does the water taste?*
   Where did the water in this dish come from?
   What happened to your salt solution?
   Where did the water in the bowl go?
   Why did the water "disappear"?
   What is left in the bottom of the large bowl?

▶ *Teaching Background*

Water in a saline solution absorbs the sun's energy and evaporates, leaving the salt behind.

9. WHAT IS THE TEMPERATURE AT WHICH CONDENSATION TAKES PLACE? (3–6)

Materials

Clean, empty cans
Ice
Thermometers

ENGAGE: ASK A QUESTION ABOUT OBJECTS, ORGANISMS, OR EVENTS IN THE ENVIRONMENT.

a. Ask: *How can we find out how cold a surface has to be before water vapor condenses on it?*

EXPLORE: PLAN AND CONDUCT SIMPLE INVESTIGATIONS TO COLLECT RELEVANT DATA.

b. Give students these instructions:
   1. Fill an empty can about three-fourths full of tap water at room temperature.
   2. Place a thermometer in the water and read the temperature.
   3. Add about one-fourth can of ice to the water.
   4. Stir the ice and water and read the temperature every 2 minutes.
   5. Carefully observe the outside of the can. At the first sign of condensation, read the temperature of the cold water. Wiping the outside of the can occasionally with a brown paper towel will aid in determining when condensation first forms on the can.

EXPLAIN: USE DATA TO GENERATE INTERPRETATIONS, INCLUDING DESCRIPTIONS, CLASSIFICATIONS, PREDICTIONS, AND EXPLANATIONS.

c. Instruct groups to record on the board the temperature at which condensation first occurred. Note discrepancies among the data collected. According to the *Benchmarks for Science Literacy*, when students arrive at very different measurements of the same thing, "it is usually a good idea to make some fresh observations instead of just arguing about who is right" (American Association for the Advancement of Science, 1993, *Benchmarks For Science Literacy*. New York: Oxford University Press, p. 10).

d. Explain that the temperature at which condensation will form on a cool surface is called the *dew point*. The dew point depends on the relative humidity of the air, that is, on the relative amount of moisture already in the air.

B. WEATHER

▶ *Science Background*

The components of weather are temperature, precipitation, humidity, wind, air pressure, clouds, and other atmospheric phenomena. These weather conditions can be readily observed and recorded by children. By keeping a weather journal during the year, students can discover weather patterns and trends, though they may not be consistent. Younger students can draw daily weather pictures of what they see; older students can make charts and graphs from the data they collect using simple weather instruments.

Science Standards

All students should develop an understanding of

- properties of the earth's systems (K–4).
- structure of the earth's systems (5–8).

Objectives for Students

1. Name and measure such components of weather as temperature, wind direction and speed, air pressure, and precipitation.
2. Describe patterns and trends in local weather conditions.
3. Construct a variety of weather instruments.
4. Name and describe different types of clouds, and explain how clouds are formed.

Concepts and Principles

Activities 1–7 address these fundamental concepts and principles related to the *Science Standards*:

- Water circulates through the crust, oceans, and atmosphere in what is known as the water cycle (5–8).
- The atmosphere is a mixture of gases that include water vapor (5–8).
- Clouds, formed by the condensation of water vapor, affect weather and climate (5–8).
- Global patterns of atmospheric movement influence local weather (5–8).

1. HOW CAN WE DESCRIBE THE WEATHER? (K–3)

Materials   Thermometers

ENGAGE: ASK A QUESTION ABOUT OBJECTS, ORGANISMS, OR EVENTS IN THE ENVIRONMENT.

a. Ask: *What is our weather like today?* Record the words students use to describe the weather (*cold, hot, warm, muggy, cloudy, rainy, windy,* etc.).

Ask: *If we wanted to compare the weather today with the weather on another day, what would we record about today's weather?* Most children see weather forecasts on television. They are beginning to learn that weather controls much of their lives, from the clothes they wear to the games they play. Through discussion, lead children to consider these variables related to weather: temperature, cloud cover, wind, humidity, and rain or snow (precipitation).

EXPLORE: PLAN AND CONDUCT SIMPLE INVESTIGATIONS TO COLLECT RELEVANT DATA.

b. Construct a bulletin board depicting a large weather chart similar to the one shown in the diagram on page A-248. Encourage children to make daily observations of weather conditions and to make entries on the class weather chart.

c. Examine the weather chart with the children. Discuss the kinds of things children might do that would be affected by the weather. If they play outside, what would they wear: warm clothes, rain gear? Discuss the weather conditions for several days in a row.

EXPLAIN: USE DATA TO GENERATE INTERPRETATIONS, INCLUDING DESCRIPTIONS, CLASSIFICATIONS, PREDICTIONS, AND EXPLANATIONS.

d. Ask: *What patterns in the weather do you see? How has the temperature changed from day to day? How is the weather today different from last summer? last winter?* Count the number of cool days, warm days, cloudy days, clear days, rainy days, and dry days to help find patterns in the weather.

ELABORATE: EXTEND CONCEPTS, PRINCIPLES, AND STRATEGIES TO NEW SITUATIONS AND QUESTIONS.

e. Ask: *What is the weather like in other regions? How would weather conditions affect life in other regions?* Using the Internet, find and chart daily weather conditions in other regions and countries around the globe.

2. HOW DOES OUTSIDE TEMPERATURE CHANGE THROUGHOUT A DAY AND FROM DAY TO DAY? (2–4)

Materials   Thermometers

ENGAGE: ASK A QUESTION ABOUT OBJECTS, ORGANISMS, OR EVENTS IN THE ENVIRONMENT.

a. Ask: *How does the temperature vary from place to place? Is the temperature the same inside and outside the classroom? Is the temperature the same everywhere on the school grounds? Is the temperature the same in the shade and the sun?*

EXPLORE: PLAN AND CONDUCT SIMPLE INVESTIGATIONS TO COLLECT RELEVANT DATA.

b. Guide students to measure and compare the temperature at various locations: inside and outside the classroom, in the sun and in the shade, and at different places on the school grounds. Discuss the differences in the temperatures at different locations and why the differences might occur.

Day Date	MON	TUES	WED	THURS	FRI	MON	TUES	WED	THURS	FRI	MON	TUES	WED	THURS	FRI
Temperature															
Clouds	○	○	○	○	○	○	○	○	○	○	○	○	○	○	○
Wind	—	—	—	—	—	—	—	—	—	—	—	—	—	—	—
Other	☐	☐	☐	☐	☐	☐	☐	☐	☐	☐	☐	☐	☐	☐	☐
Student's Name															

A-248

EXPLAIN: USE
DATA TO GENERATE
INTERPRETATIONS,
INCLUDING DESCRIPTIONS,
CLASSIFICATIONS,
PREDICTIONS, AND
EXPLANATIONS.

c. Ask: *Is the temperature the same throughout the day?* Allow students to measure the outside temperature every hour. Discuss the temperature differences that are observed. Emphasize that how the temperature changes is very important to judging the weather.

3. HOW ARE CLOUDS AND FOG FORMED? (3–6)

Materials

Ice cubes
Two clear, narrow-mouthed bottles
Hot and cold water
Matches

ENGAGE: ASK A
QUESTION ABOUT OBJECTS,
ORGANISMS, OR EVENTS IN
THE ENVIRONMENT.

a. Ask: *What is a cloud and how is it formed?*
    What is fog and how is it formed?

EXPLORE: PLAN
AND CONDUCT SIMPLE
INVESTIGATIONS TO
COLLECT RELEVANT DATA.

b. Fill a bottle with very hot water and let it sit for a few minutes. Then pour out most of the water, leaving about 2 cm of water in the bottom of the bottle. For comparison, set up an identical bottle with an equal amount of cold water. Place an ice cube on the top of each bottle as shown in the diagram.

EXPLAIN: USE
DATA TO GENERATE
INTERPRETATIONS,
INCLUDING DESCRIPTIONS,
CLASSIFICATIONS,
PREDICTIONS, AND
EXPLANATIONS.

c. As students observe the two bottles, ask:
    What do you see happening in each bottle?
    Why did the cloud or fog form in the bottle?
    Why do you think clouds or fog formed in the bottle with hot water and not in the bottle with cold water?

ELABORATE: EXTEND
CONCEPTS, PRINCIPLES,
AND STRATEGIES TO NEW
SITUATIONS AND
QUESTIONS.

d. Set up the bottle with hot water as in step *b*. Light a match, extinguish it, and blow some of the smoke from the match into the bottle. Place an ice cube on the bottle. Ask: *What differences do you observe with and without the smoke? What was the purpose of the smoke?* (To provide particles on which water vapor might condense.)

e. Ask: *How do clouds and fog form in nature?*

HOW CAN YOU MAKE A WIND VANE, AND HOW IS IT USED TO DETERMINE WIND DIRECTION? (3–6)

4. HOW CAN YOU MAKE A WIND VANE, AND HOW IS IT USED TO DETERMINE WIND DIRECTION? (3–6)

Materials

Scissors
Construction paper
Drinking straw
Pencil with eraser
Straight pin
Glass bead
Empty thread spool
A 30 cm square piece of corrugated cardboard

ENGAGE: ASK A QUESTION ABOUT OBJECTS, ORGANISMS, OR EVENTS IN THE ENVIRONMENT.

a. Ask: *How can you tell the direction the wind is blowing?*
    How does knowing wind direction help us understand weather and weather prediction?
    What instruments can be used to find wind direction and speed?
    How can we make and use these instruments?

EXPLORE: PLAN AND CONDUCT SIMPLE INVESTIGATIONS TO COLLECT RELEVANT DATA.

b. To make a wind vane, follow these directions:
    1. Cut an arrow-shaped point and tail fin from construction paper, as shown in the diagram.
    2. Attach the point and tail fin to the straw by cutting notches in both ends of the straw and gluing the cutouts in place.
    3. Attach the straw to a pencil by sticking the straight pin through the middle of the straw, through a glass bead, and into the pencil eraser. Make sure the straw can swing easily in all directions and is balanced.

    Note: Move the pin in the straw until it balances with arrow and tail attached.

    4. Glue the empty thread spool to the center of the corrugated cardboard. Mark north, south, east, and west on the cardboard as shown in the diagram.

5. When the glue has dried, push the pencil into the hole of the spool and check to see that the straw moves easily. You now have a wind vane.

c. Carefully take your wind vane outdoors and line up the north label on your wind vane with the north on a magnetic compass. If the wind is strong, tape the cardboard to a horizontal surface or weight it down with something heavy.

EXPLAIN: USE DATA TO GENERATE INTERPRETATIONS, INCLUDING DESCRIPTIONS, CLASSIFICATIONS, PREDICTIONS, AND EXPLANATIONS.

d. Ask: *What do you see happening to the arrow?*
   From which direction is the wind blowing? How do you know?
   How would you name this wind?
   The arrow will swing around until the point faces the direction from which the wind is blowing. This direction then becomes the wind's name.
   Ask: *Does the wind always blow from the same direction? How could we find out?*

e. Keep a record of wind observations three times a day for 1 week. Make sure to record the data on a chart.
   After 1 week, do you detect
   any pattern of winds during the day?
   any pattern of winds from day to day?
   any prevailing or consistent direction from which the wind blows?
   any correlation between wind direction and weather conditions, such as temperatures, humidity, clouds, and so on?

f. Check local TV weather and newspapers for wind direction. *How do your data compare? If they differ, why do you think so?*

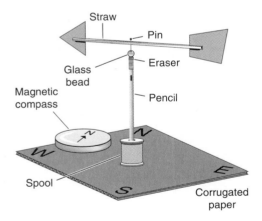

▶ *Teaching Background*

Wind, or moving air, brings about changing weather conditions. A **wind vane** is an instrument that shows the direction from which the wind is blowing. Winds are named for the direction from which they blow. For example, a north wind is blowing from the north to the south. An **anemometer** is an instrument that measures wind speed.

5. HOW CAN YOU MEASURE HOW FAST THE WIND BLOWS? HOW DOES WIND SPEED VARY WITH LOCATION AND TIME? (3–6)

Materials

Long sewing needle
30 cm of monofilament nylon line
Ping-Pong ball
Glue
Cardboard

Red marking pen
Protractor
Bubble level (hardware store)
Tongue depressor

Preparation

Thread a sewing needle with a 30 cm monofilament line, push the needle through the Ping-Pong ball, and knot and glue the end of the line to the Ping-Pong ball.

Safety Precautions

Use caution when pushing the needle through the Ping-Pong ball.

ENGAGE: ASK A QUESTION ABOUT OBJECTS, ORGANISMS, OR EVENTS IN THE ENVIRONMENT.

a. Ask: *How can we measure how fast the wind blows?*

EXPLORE: PLAN AND CONDUCT SIMPLE INVESTIGATIONS TO COLLECT RELEVANT DATA.

b. Either the teacher or students should follow these directions to make an anemometer:
   1. Glue the other end of the line that is attached to the Ping-Pong ball to the center of a protractor. With the marking pen, color the line red.
   2. Glue a bubble level to the protractor as shown in the diagram.
   3. Glue a tongue depressor to the protractor as a handle. You now have an anemometer to measure wind speed.
   4. When the glue is dry, carefully take your anemometer outside to test it in the wind.
c. To take readings of the wind's speed, follow these directions:
   1. In the wind, hold the protractor level using the tongue depressor handle.
   2. Keep the protractor level by making sure the bubble is centered in the bubble level.
   3. Observe any swing of the Ping-Pong ball and string and see what angle the string makes on the protractor. For instance, in the diagram the string moved to approximately 65 degrees.

Bubble level

Tongue depressor

Bubble level

Glue

Protractor

Colored line

Wind

Ping Pong ball

d. Use your anemometer in various spots on your school grounds, and then refer to the following chart to find the wind speed.

Protractor Anemometer Wind Speeds

String Angle	Wind Speed (Miles per Hour)	String Angle	Wind Speed (Miles per Hour)
90	0	50	18.0
85	5.8	45	19.6
80	8.2	40	21.9
75	10.1	35	23.4
70	11.8	30	25.8
65	13.4	25	28.7
60	14.9	20	32.5
55	16.4		

After you have tested the wind speed in different places on your school grounds, record the data on a chart like this one.

Date								
Time								
Protractor angle								
Wind speed								
Wind direction								

EXPLAIN: USE DATA TO GENERATE INTERPRETATIONS, INCLUDING DESCRIPTIONS, CLASSIFICATIONS, PREDICTIONS, AND EXPLANATIONS.

e. Invite students to describe their anemometers and explain how they work. Guide students to use their charts to answer these questions:
Where does the wind blow the fastest on your school grounds?
Does wind blow faster at ground level or at higher levels?
Is there a place where wind blows faster, such as between two buildings or at a corner of two wings of a building? Why?

6. HOW CAN YOU MEASURE AIR PRESSURE CHANGES, AND HOW DO AIR PRESSURE CHANGES AFFECT WEATHER? (3–6)

Materials

Large can (e.g., coffee can)
Large balloon and rubber band
Straw
Glue
Straight pin
Index card

ENGAGE: ASK A
QUESTION ABOUT OBJECTS,
ORGANISMS, OR EVENTS IN
THE ENVIRONMENT.

a. Blow up a balloon.

Ask: *What is in the balloon?* (Air.) *How do you know there is air in the balloon?* (The air pushes back when we press on the balloon.)

Lead students to understand that we live at the bottom of an ocean of air that presses on us at all times. The pressure of the atmosphere (air pressure) is a variable that affects weather conditions. A barometer is an instrument that measures the pressure of the air.

EXPLORE: PLAN
AND CONDUCT SIMPLE
INVESTIGATIONS TO
COLLECT RELEVANT DATA.

b. To make a barometer, follow these directions:
1. Obtain a can, such as a coffee can, a balloon, a rubber band, a straw, glue, a straight pin, and a card.
2. Cover the can with a piece of a large balloon and use a tight rubber band to seal the can.
3. Place a small amount of glue in the center of the balloon on the can and attach a straw, as shown in the diagram. Place another drop of glue on the other end of the straw and attach the pin.
4. Mark an index card with lines that are the same distance apart. Tape the card on the wall as shown in the diagram. Set the can so the pin points to one of the middle lines on the card.

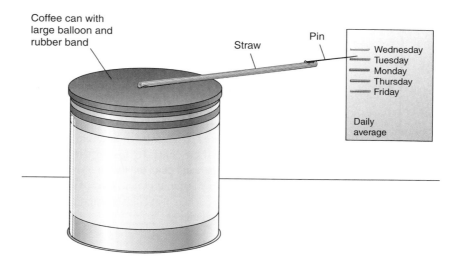

c. Ask: *What happens to the balloon on top of the can if the air pressure on it increases? What happens to the position of the pin on the end of the straw?*

What happens to the balloon if the air pressure outside the can decreases? What happens to the position of the pin on the end of the straw?

Lead students to understand that when air pressure increases, it pushes down on the balloon, causing the straw to indicate a high reading. When the air pressure is low, the opposite will happen. A falling barometer reading may indicate that a storm is approaching.

d. Record the readings of the barometer three times a day for a week. Observe and record the type of weather (temperature, cloud conditions, humidity, wind) that exists at the time of each barometer reading.

EXPLAIN: USE
DATA TO GENERATE
INTERPRETATIONS,
INCLUDING DESCRIPTIONS,
CLASSIFICATIONS,
PREDICTIONS, AND
EXPLANATIONS.

e. Ask: *How do the readings of the barometer differ during the day?*
How do the readings differ from day to day?
What might cause the readings to vary?
What kind of air pressure generally existed during your fair-weather readings?
What kind of air pressure generally existed during your stormy-weather readings?

Note: Room temperature will affect the barometer students make in this activity. This barometer does not, therefore, measure only air pressure differences. You may want to have some students keep their barometers outside class and then compare the readings from the different locations.

7. HOW CAN YOU MEASURE RELATIVE HUMIDITY AND HUMIDITY CHANGES? (3–6)

Materials

Two thermometers
Wide cotton shoelace
Small dish of water
Empty milk carton
Thread
Piece of cardboard

ENGAGE: ASK A
QUESTION ABOUT OBJECTS,
ORGANISMS, OR EVENTS IN
THE ENVIRONMENT.

a. Ask: *What instrument is used to measure the amount of water, or humidity, in the atmosphere?*
How can this instrument be made, and how does it work?

b. Give students these instructions:

1. Obtain an empty milk carton, two identical thermometers, a cotton shoelace, and some thread.
2. Cut a 10 cm section from the cotton shoelace and slip the section over the bulb of one of the thermometers. Tie the shoelace section with thread above and below the bulb to hold the shoelace in place. Thread the other end of the 10 cm section through a hole in the milk carton and allow it to rest in a small bottle or dish of water inside the milk carton.

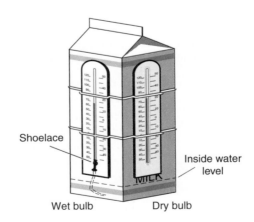

Shoelace

Inside water level

Wet bulb   Dry bulb

FINDING RELATIVE HUMIDITY IN PERCENT

Difference in degrees between wet-bulb and dry bulb thermometers

Air temperature (reading of dry-bulb thermometer) in degrees fahrenheit

	1	2	3	4	5	6	7	8	9	10	11	12	13	14	15	16	17	18	19	20	21	22	23	24	25	26	27	28	29	30
30°	89	78	68	57	47	37	27	17	8																					
32°	90	79	69	60	50	41	31	22	13	4																				
34°	90	81	72	62	53	44	35	27	18	9	1																			
36°	91	82	73	65	56	48	39	31	23	14	6																			
38°	91	83	75	67	59	51	43	35	27	19	12	4																		
40°	92	84	76	68	61	53	46	38	31	23	16	9	2																	
42°	92	85	77	70	62	55	48	41	34	28	21	14	7																	
44°	93	85	78	71	64	57	51	44	37	31	24	18	12	5																
46°	93	86	79	72	65	59	53	46	40	34	28	22	16	10	4															
48°	93	87	80	73	67	60	54	48	42	36	31	25	19	14	8	3														
50°	93	87	81	74	68	62	56	50	44	39	33	28	22	17	12	7	2													
52°	94	88	81	75	69	63	58	52	46	41	36	30	25	20	15	10	6													
54°	94	88	82	76	70	65	59	54	48	43	38	33	28	23	18	14	9	5												
56°	94	88	82	77	71	66	61	55	50	45	40	35	31	26	21	17	12	8	4											
58°	94	89	83	77	72	67	62	57	52	47	42	38	33	28	24	20	15	11	7	3										
60°	94	89	84	78	73	68	63	58	53	49	44	40	35	31	27	22	18	14	10	6	2									
62°	94	89	84	79	74	69	64	60	55	50	46	41	37	33	29	25	21	17	13	9	6	2								
64°	95	90	85	79	75	70	66	61	56	52	48	43	39	35	31	27	23	20	16	12	9	5	2							
66°	95	90	85	80	76	71	66	62	58	53	49	45	41	37	33	29	26	22	18	15	11	8	5	1						
68°	95	90	85	81	76	72	67	63	59	55	51	47	43	39	35	31	28	24	21	17	14	11	8	4	1					
70°	95	90	86	81	77	72	68	64	60	56	52	48	44	40	37	33	30	26	23	20	17	13	10	7	4	1				
72°	95	91	86	82	78	73	69	65	61	57	53	49	46	42	39	35	32	28	25	22	19	16	13	10	7	4	1			
74°	95	91	86	82	79	74	70	66	62	58	54	51	47	44	40	37	34	30	27	24	21	18	15	12	9	7	4	1		
76°	96	91	87	83	78	74	70	67	63	59	55	52	48	45	42	38	35	32	29	26	23	20	17	14	12	9	6	4	1	
78°	96	91	87	83	79	75	71	67	64	60	57	53	50	46	43	40	37	34	31	28	25	22	19	16	14	11	9	6	4	1
80°	96	91	87	83	79	76	72	68	64	61	57	54	51	47	44	41	38	35	32	29	27	24	21	18	16	13	11	8	6	4
82°	96	91	87	83	79	76	72	69	65	62	58	55	52	49	46	43	40	37	34	31	28	25	23	20	18	15	13	10	8	6
84°	96	92	88	84	80	77	73	70	66	63	59	56	53	50	47	44	41	38	35	32	30	27	25	22	20	17	15	12	10	8
86°	96	92	88	84	80	77	73	70	66	63	60	57	54	51	48	45	42	39	37	34	31	29	26	24	21	19	17	14	12	10
88°	96	92	88	85	81	78	74	71	67	64	61	58	55	52	49	46	43	41	38	35	33	30	28	25	23	21	18	16	14	12
90°	96	92	88	85	81	78	74	71	68	64	61	58	56	53	50	47	44	42	39	37	34	32	29	27	24	22	20	18	16	14

Example:
Temperature of dry-bulb thermometer 76°
Temperature of wet-bulb thermometer 68°
The difference is 8°

Find 76° in the dry-bulb column and 8° in the difference column. Where these two columns meet, you read the relative humidity. In this case, it is 67%.

3. Attach both thermometers to the milk carton as shown in the diagram. You now have a **hygrometer**—an instrument that measures the relative humidity in the atmosphere.

Note: The two thermometers should register the same temperature before the shoelace is placed over one of them; otherwise, the difference in readings must be considered a constant that is part of all computations.

4. When the shoelace is wet, fan it with a piece of cardboard for 1 minute.
5. Ask: *What do you think might happen to the thermometer with the wet shoelace? Why do you think so?*
6. Check the temperature readings of the two thermometers.
7. Ask: *How do you account for the difference in readings between the thermometer with the shoelace (called the "wet bulb") and the one without the shoelace (called the "dry bulb")?*
8. Explain that when the shoelace is wet, the evaporation of the water results in a cooling of the wet-bulb thermometer, whereas the dry-bulb thermometer will continue to read the temperature of the air around it.

Note: This is the same phenomenon that occurred in a previous activity where students placed one dry wool or cotton sock and one wet wool or cotton sock on their hands to show the cooling effect of evaporation.

9. Look at the relative humidity table provided. To locate the relative humidity on the table, find the temperature of the dry-bulb thermometer on the *y* axis (vertical axis) and the difference between the readings of the two thermometers on the *x* axis (horizontal axis). The example below the table shows a dry-bulb temperature of 76°F, a difference of 8°F (wet-bulb, 68°F), and a relative humidity of 67%.

10. Take readings on your hygrometer every day for 2 weeks and record your findings. Also try readings in different places.

EXPLAIN: USE DATA TO GENERATE INTERPRETATIONS, INCLUDING DESCRIPTIONS, CLASSIFICATIONS, PREDICTIONS, AND EXPLANATIONS.

c. Invite students to share their records from the exploration phase. Ask: *What reasons can you give for different readings?*
Using your hygrometer, can you predict which days are better for drying clothes outside?
How is relative humidity used by weather forecasters to predict weather?
Why were you asked to fan the wet-bulb thermometer?

▶ *Teaching Background*

Air contains moisture (from evaporated water from the ground, rivers, lakes, and oceans). Air pressure and temperature affect the amount of moisture air can hold at any given time. Relative humidity is the amount of water vapor actually contained in volume of air divided by the maximum amount that could be contained in the same volume.

III. THE EARTH'S OCEANS

Our earth has been called *the water planet*. Children are naturally drawn to water. "Whether they are playing in a pond, chasing waves at the beach, or splashing in a rain puddle on a city street, children are entranced by water" (Valerie Chase, 1997, *Living in Water*. Baltimore: National Aquarium in Baltimore, p. 1).

The earth's water is found in oceans, lakes, rivers, ponds, and streams; in ground water systems; and in ice and water vapor forms. Water circulates through the crust, atmosphere, and oceans of the earth in the *water cycle*. Rain falling on land collects in rivers and lakes, soil, and porous layers of rock, and much of it flows back to the oceans.

More than 97% of all the water on the earth is salt water in ocean basins. Oceans, as well as the land, are contained within the crust of the earth. Oceans cover 71% of the earth's surface, with land covering 29%. There are four oceans on the earth: Pacific Ocean, Atlantic Ocean, Indian Ocean, and Arctic Ocean. The Antarctic Ocean is included with the Pacific, Atlantic, and Indian Oceans. Seas, gulfs, and bays are all parts of oceans that are partially enclosed by land.

Ocean floors are typically 2 to 3 miles deep in the Pacific, Atlantic, and Indian Oceans. The Mariana Trench, stretching in the western Pacific from New Guinea toward the sea of Japan, reaches depths of 6.5 miles below sea level and about 3 miles below the level of the sea floor flanking it. In comparison, the Grand Canyon is about 1 mile deep and Mount Everest is about 5.5 miles above sea level.

Shores are places where land and sea meet, where we can take quiet walks and lose ourselves in thought or search for shells, driftwood, and strange creatures.

For plants and animals to survive in the ocean, on the ocean floor and ocean trenches, or on rocky shores they need to be able to adapt to tremendously varied conditions. For example, plants and animals on the seashore must resist battering ocean waves or find security in crevices and fissures. Most of the animals on sandy shores live below the surface. A sandy beach may appear lifeless, but when the tide rolls in, the inhabitants spring into action and an astounding variety of life is revealed.

 Science Standards

All students should develop an understanding of

- structure of the earth's systems (5–8).

Objectives for Students

1. Demonstrate that the water pressure in a body of water increases with depth.
2. Demonstrate and explain that the buoyant force of salt water is greater than the buoyant force of fresh water.
3. Compare the surface area of the earth that is ocean with that which is land.
4. Compare the amount of water in the oceans with the total amount of water in the earth system.
5. Identify a variety of foods that contain nutrients from ocean organisms.
6. Describe and explain the effects of pollution on life in water.

 Concepts and Principles

Fundamental concepts and principles that underlie the standards and relate to oceans include the following:

- In the course of the water cycle, water evaporates from the earth's surface, rises and cools as it moves to higher elevations, condenses as rain or snow, and falls to the surface where it collects in lakes, oceans, soils, and underground (5–8).
- Water is a solvent. As it passes through the water cycle it dissolves minerals and gases and carries them to the oceans (5–8).
- Oceans have a major effect on climate, because water in the ocean holds a large amount of heat (5–8).

1. WHAT PART OF THE EARTH'S SURFACE IS COVERED BY OCEANS? (3–6)

Materials

Inflatable globe (preferably showing natural land features rather than political boundaries)

ENGAGE: ASK A QUESTION ABOUT OBJECTS, ORGANISMS, OR EVENTS IN THE ENVIRONMENT.

a. Hold up the inflatable globe. Ask: *What is this globe a model of?* (Earth.) *How is it like the real earth and how is it different? What is shown on the globe's surface?* (Land and oceans.) *About how much of the earth is covered by oceans? How could we use the globe to find out?*

EXPLORE: PLAN AND CONDUCT SIMPLE INVESTIGATIONS TO COLLECT RELEVANT DATA.

b. Tell the class we need to collect data by using a sampling method. Help the student follow these steps:
   1. Show the class a two-column table with the headings "Ocean" and "Land."
   2. Select a student to be the record keeper.
   3. Instruct one student to toss the inflatable globe to another student.
   4. The person who catches the globe will look to see if his or her right thumb is on an ocean or land part of the globe's surface and report this information to the record keeper.
   5. The record keeper will make a tally mark in the appropriate column on the table.
   6. Then the inflatable globe should be tossed to another student and the process repeated.
   7. Continue for a total of 100 tosses.

EXPLAIN: USE THE DATA TO GENERATE INTERPRETATIONS, INCLUDING DESCRIPTIONS, CLASSIFICATIONS, AND EXPLANATIONS.

c. Ask: *How many times out of 100 tosses was the catcher's right thumb on an ocean area?* (Approximately 70 times.) *How many times out of 100 tosses was the catcher's right thumb on a land area?* (Approximately 30 times.)
d. Ask: *Why do you think the catcher's right thumb was on an ocean area more often than on a land area?* (Because more of the surface of the inflatable globe is ocean area so there is more chance of the catcher's right thumb being on an ocean.) Discuss the term *percent* with the class. *What percent of the times was the catcher's thumb on an ocean area?* (The answer should be close to 70%.) *What percent of the times was the catcher's thumb on a land area?* (Answer should be close to 30%.)
e. Challenge the class to find out what percent of the earth's surface is covered by oceans using their textbook or other references. (70%.) Ask the class to explain how well and why this sampling technique worked to estimate the relative amount of land and ocean on the earth's surface.

2. WHAT PART OF THE EARTH'S WATER IS IN THE OCEANS? (3–8)

Materials·
Six 2-liter bottles
Graduated cylinders
Permanent marker
Colored water

ENGAGE: ASK A QUESTION ABOUT OBJECTS, ORGANISMS, OR EVENTS IN THE ENVIRONMENT.

a. Ask: *What part of the earth's water is in the oceans? How could we make a model to show this?*
b. Conduct this teacher demonstration:
   1. Show the class a 2-liter bottle labeled "All Earth's Water" filled with 2,000 ml of colored water. Tell them this represents all the water on the earth.
   2. Then display five other 2-liter bottles containing the following volumes of colored water on a table in front of a sheet of chart paper: Bottle A, 1,944 ml; Bottle B, 1,750 ml; Bottle C, 1,400 ml; Bottle D, 1,000 ml; Bottle E, 700 ml.
   3. Tell the students that one of these bottles represents the amount of water in the earth's oceans.
   4. Ask students to vote for the one they think represents the water in the earth's oceans by writing the letter of their choice on a Post-it note. Have the students stick their Post-it in a column above the bottle that matches the letter they chose.
   The class has just created a histogram of their ideas.

EXPLORE: PLAN
AND CONDUCT SIMPLE
INVESTIGATIONS TO
COLLECT RELEVANT DATA.

c. Ask: *How could we find out which bottle best represents the amount of water in the earth's oceans?*

d. Ask groups of students to decide what information they would need and how they would make the bottle that represents the water in the earth's oceans. After they have had some discussion time, provide the information that 97.2% of the earth's water is in the oceans. You might also reveal that the bottle labeled "All Earth's Water" contains 2,000 ml of colored water. Allow groups to use colored water, graduated cylinders, and a 2-liter bottle to create a model that represents the amount of water in the oceans.

EXPLAIN: USE THE
DATA TO GENERATE
INTERPRETATIONS,
INCLUDING DESCRIPTIONS,
CLASSIFICATIONS, AND
EXPLANATIONS.

e. Encourage groups to compare their completed model with the "All Earth's Water" bottle. Ask each group to explain to the class how they decided how much water to put in the bottle and how they carried out their idea.

f. Based on the models constructed by the groups, ask them to vote again (this time by a show of hands) for the lettered bottle that they think best represents the amount of water in the earth's oceans. (They should select bottle A.) Ask: *Are you surprised by how much of the earth's water is in the oceans? Do you think that the oceans are an important part of our planet? Why?*

ELABORATE: EXTEND
CONCEPTS, PRINCIPLES,
AND STRATEGIES TO NEW
PROBLEMS AND
QUESTIONS.

g. Ask students to list the places that water is found in the earth's system. Answers might include lakes, rivers, ponds, oceans, puddles, in the soil, underground, in the air as water vapor, in clouds as water droplets, frozen in ice caps and glaciers, and so on. Challenge them to find out how much of the earth's water is found in each and to create a visual representation of their findings. They might make a model or a circle graph.[4]

3. DO OBJECTS FLOAT DIFFERENTLY IN SALT WATER THAN IN FRESH WATER? (4–6)

Materials

Two raw eggs
Two clear glass containers
Box of Kosher or pickling salt, which can be purchased in many supermarkets. When dissolved in water, this salt produces a clear solution. Table salt can be substituted, but it makes a cloudy rather than a clear solution
Large container for mixing concentrated salt water

ENGAGE: ASK A
QUESTION ABOUT OBJECTS,
ORGANISMS, OR EVENTS IN
THE ENVIRONMENT.

a. For this teacher demonstration you will need a mixture of concentrated salt water for one container and an equal amount of fresh water for the other container. Then follow these steps:
   1. Prepare the salt water by mixing one part salt with four parts cool water in a large container. For example, if you use 300 ml cups (10 oz), add half a cup of salt to 2 cups of water. Stir the salt-water mixture thoroughly until the salt dissolves.
   2. Pour concentrated salt water into one container and put an equal amount of fresh water in the other container.

b. Show the students the two containers of water without discussing their contents. Ask: *Do you think an egg will float in water?*

---

[4]Data relating to this investigation is available at http://www.sea.edu/k12lessonplans/ K12WatersEarth.htm.

EXPLORE: PLAN
AND CONDUCT SIMPLE
INVESTIGATIONS TO
COLLECT RELEVANT DATA.

c. Put an egg in each container and ask: *What did you observe?* Discuss students observations with them.

EXPLAIN: USE DATA TO
GENERATE INTERPRETATIONS,
INCLUDING DESCRIPTIONS,
CLASSIFICATIONS,
PREDICTIONS, AND
EXPLANATIONS.

d. Ask: *Why do you think the egg floated in one container of water and sank in the other one?* Through questioning and discussion, lead students to understand that salt water is denser than fresh water. The denser salt water was able to support the egg. Ask: *Would it be easier for you to float in a fresh water lake or in the ocean? Why?*

ELABORATE: EXTEND
CONCEPTS, PRINCIPLES,
AND STRATEGIES TO NEW
SITUATIONS AND
QUESTIONS.

e. Ask: *How much salt will need to be added to fresh water to increase its density so that it will support an egg?*

f. Place an egg in the fresh water. Add salt a spoonful at a time, stirring the water, until the egg rises and floats. Count the number of spoonfuls of salt needed. Measure the volume of salt added and compare it to the original volume of the water.[5]

4. WHAT AFFECTS THE PRESSURE OF A STREAM OF WATER? (3–5)

Materials

Plastic gallon milk jug

ENGAGE: ASK A
QUESTION ABOUT OBJECT,
ORGANISMS, OR EVENTS IN
THE ENVIRONMENT.

a. Ask: *If the side of a plastic milk jug were punctured with very small holes (one above another) and the jug were then filled with water, what do you think would happen to the water? How would the water pour out of the holes?*

EXPLORE: PLAN
AND CONDUCT SIMPLE
INVESTIGATIONS TO
COLLECT RELEVANT DATA.

b. Prepare and perform this teacher demonstration for students:
   1. Obtain a clean, plastic, 1-gallon milk jug.
   2. About 4 cm from the bottom of the milk jug, puncture a *very small hole* with a pencil or nail. Puncture three additional small holes 1 cm apart, vertically, above the first hole as in the diagram. Put masking tape over the holes.

Note: Do not make the holes too large.

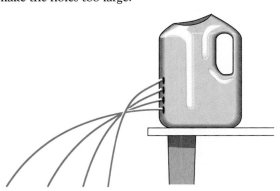

[5]For additional information on this activity, see Science and Technology for Children. (1995). *Floating and Sinking: Teacher's Guide*. Burlington, NC: Carolina Biological Supply.

3. Fill the container half full with water. Hold the plastic jug over a sink, large basin, or tub, and remove the masking tape as shown.

c. Ask: *What do you notice about the way the water comes out of the holes? Which stream went the greatest distance? Which stream went the least distance?*

EXPLAIN: USE DATA TO GENERATE INTERPRETATIONS, INCLUDING DESCRIPTIONS, CLASSIFICATIONS, PREDICTIONS, AND EXPLANATIONS.

d. Ask: *Why do you think the water comes out of the holes like this?*

e. Ask: *If the jug were filled closer to the top with water, do you think there would be a difference in the way the water comes out? Tape over the holes, refill the jug until the water is within a centimeter of the top, and remove the tape. Ask: What do you notice about the way the water comes out of the holes? What difference did you notice in the way the water came from the holes of the jug when there was less water and when there was more water in it?*

f. Ask: *What can you conclude about how water pressure varies with depth?*

ELABORATE: EXTEND CONCEPTS, PRINCIPLES, AND STRATEGIES TO NEW SITUATIONS AND QUESTIONS.

g. Ask: *What results do you think you would get if you used a quart, half-gallon, or 2-gallon container? Try it and record your findings.*

5. WHAT FOODS CONTAIN PRODUCTS FROM THE OCEAN? (4–6)

Materials

Food product labels
Grocery store advertisements
Sorting mats and transparency with a Venn diagram as shown

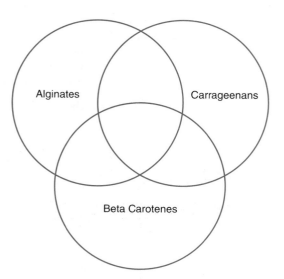

Preparation

Several weeks before this lesson, ask your students and colleagues to collect the ingredient lists from the following products they might use at home: brownie mix, cheese, chocolate milk, coffee creamer, cottage cheese, egg substitute, evaporated milk, frozen foods and desserts, frozen yogurt, ice cream, infant formula, margarine, mayonnaise, multiple vitamins, pet food, pudding, relishes, salad dressing, sauces and gravies, sour cream, toothpaste, whipped topping, whipping cream, and yogurt. Provide a box for collection of the labels and containers in your classroom.

ENGAGE: ASK A QUESTION ABOUT OBJECTS, ORGANISMS, OR EVENTS IN THE ENVIRONMENT.

a. Distribute the grocery store advertisements to the class and encourage them to look them over. Ask: *Do you eat anything that comes from the ocean?* (Students will probably suggest fish, shrimp, clams, etc.) *What do these products eat?* (Students will probably say other smaller animals in the ocean.) *Are there plants in the ocean?* (Students will probably say seaweed or algae.) *Do some of the animals in the ocean eat the ocean plants? Do you eat any of the ocean plants?* (Some students may know that seaweed is used to wrap sushi.)

EXPLORE: PLAN AND CONDUCT SIMPLE INVESTIGATIONS TO COLLECT RELEVANT DATA.

b. Guide students to collect data following these procedures:
   1. With students working in small groups (4 students per group is best), distribute to each group at least 10 ingredient lists from different products from the collection box. The groups do not need to have the same assortment of ingredient lists.
   2. Provide each group with a copy of the Venn diagram. Give the students a few minutes to look at their materials. Suggest that they use the Venn diagram to organize their ingredient lists based on the presence of alginates, carrageenans, and beta-carotenes.
   3. If students need assistance, display the transparency of the Venn diagram on the overhead projector and model the procedure. Ask a student to read an ingredient list to look for any or all of these ingredients. Then write the name of the product in the appropriate segment of the Venn diagram. Do several more examples if necessary.
   4. Each group should write the names of each of the products for which they have an ingredients list on their Venn diagram. If you want them to include more product names, they can switch label sets with another group.

EXPLAIN: USE DATA TO GENERATE INTERPRETATIONS, INCLUDING DESCRIPTIONS, CLASSIFICATIONS, AND EXPLANATIONS.

c. Ask the groups to share their findings with the class. Have them describe what the product names in each segment of the Venn diagram have in common.
d. Ask if anyone knows what these ingredients are. Then tell the students that each of these ingredients comes from seaweeds, which are large forms of marine algae that grow in coastal waters around the world. The three terms on the Venn diagram refer to compounds extracted from each of the three main kinds of marine algae: brown, red, and green. Alginates come from brown algae. They make water-based products thicker, creamier, and more stable. In ice cream, they prevent the formation of ice crystals. Carrageenans come from red algae. They are used in stabilizing and gelling foods, cosmetics, pharmaceuticals, and industrial products. Beta-carotene comes from green algae. It is a natural pigment that is used as yellow-orange food coloring and may help prevent certain types of cancers.

ELABORATE: EXTEND CONCEPTS, PRINCIPLES, AND STRATEGIES TO NEW PROBLEMS AND QUESTIONS.

e. Challenge students to find other products that contain these ingredients in their pantries or at the grocery store. Bring samples of edible seaweed such as nori, kombu, dulse, and kelp to class for students to observe. Explain that these marine algae are used in many Asian cuisines, often as wrappers for rice, meat, and vegetables (sushi). Using proper sanitation precautions, offer samples of the edible seaweed to students who wish to try it.

Source: This activity is based on two lessons from the internet: "There Are Algae in Your House!" from the Ocean Planet Website of the Smithsonian (http://seawifs. gsfc.nasa.gov/OCEAN_PLANET/HTML/education-lesson . . .) and "Is there Seaweed/Algae in your food?" from Neptune's Website: Oceanography lesson plans (http://pao.cnmoc. navy.mil/educate/Neptune/lesson/social/algae.htm).

6. WHAT ARE SOME EFFECTS OF WATER POLLUTION? (3–8)

Materials

For each group, 4 quart-sized or 2-liter clear containers (plastic soda bottles, food jars with covers, etc.)
Tap water aged for 3 to 4 days
Soil and/or gravel from an aquarium or pond
Water with algae and other aquatic microorganisms from a freshwater aquarium or a pond
Measuring cups and spoons
Plant fertilizer
Hand lenses for each group
Liquid laundry detergent (not green)
Motor oil
Vinegar

Preparation

Two weeks in advance of conducting this activity, four jars should be set up by you and designated student helpers for each cooperative group of students:
1. Fill four containers one-third full with aged tap water, add 4 cm of pond soil or aquarium gravel, and then fill the rest of the jar with pond water and algae.
2. Add 1 teaspoon of plant fertilizer to each jar, stir well, and loosely screw on the jar covers.
3. Put the jars near the window in good, indirect light or under a strong artificial light.
4. Label the jars A, B, C, and D.

ENGAGE: ASK A QUESTION ABOUT OBJECTS, ORGANISMS, OR EVENTS IN THE ENVIRONMENT.

a. Ask: *What things do people do, sometimes unknowingly, that result in water pollution? How can water pollution affect water environments in ways that are detrimental to the organisms that live in or depend on the water?*

EXPLORE: PLAN AND CONDUCT SIMPLE INVESTIGATIONS TO COLLECT RELEVANT DATA.

b. Guide students to conduct this investigation:
1. Provide each group of students the four jars that were set up 2 weeks earlier. The jars contain pond water, algae, pond soil or aquarium gravel, and fertilizer.
2. Instruct the groups to observe and describe on their record sheets how each jar looks. Make sure students use hand lenses.

RECORDING OBSERVATIONS		
Date _____ Observers'/Recorders' Names _____		
Jar	Observation Before Additive	Observation after Additive
A		
B		
C		
D		

3. Students should add 2 tablespoons of detergent to jar A; enough motor oil to cover the surface of jar B; and 1/4 to 1/2 cup (250 mL) of vinegar to jar C. Jar D will not have any additive and will be the control. See the diagram.

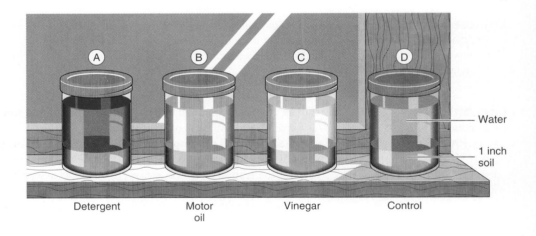

4. Students should loosely cover the jars and return them to the light as before.
5. Ask: *What do you think might happen in each of the jars?*
6. Provide time for students to observe and record their observations two to three times a week. After 4 weeks, groups should summarize their observations.

EXPLAIN: USE DATA TO GENERATE INTERPRETATIONS, INCLUDING DESCRIPTIONS, CLASSIFICATIONS, PREDICTIONS, AND EXPLANATIONS.

c. Ask: *What changes did each jar go through? Why do you think jars A, B, and C went through such changes?*

ELABORATE: EXTEND CONCEPTS, PRINCIPLES, AND STRATEGIES TO NEW SITUATIONS AND QUESTIONS.

   d. Ask: *How could you apply these findings?*
      How might you set up activities to try to reverse the effects of the pollutants used in jars A, B, and C?
      Where in everyday life do we see the effects of water pollution like that in jars A, B, and C?
      How could these effects be prevented?

....

7. HOW CAN WE TRY TO REVERSE THE EFFECTS OF AN OIL SPILL? (3–8)

Materials

Aluminum pan
Motor oil
Feathers
Paper towels
Dishwashing liquid
Four hard-boiled eggs
Paper plate
Very large rubber band
Turkey baster

ENGAGE: ASK A QUESTION ABOUT OBJECTS, ORGANISMS, OR EVENTS IN THE ENVIRONMENT.

   a. Ask: *How difficult do you think it is to clean up an oil spill? How do you think it could be done?*
      What is the most effective way to clean up an oil spill?
      What devastating effects does an oil spill have on the environment?

EXPLORE: PLAN AND CONDUCT SIMPLE INVESTIGATIONS TO COLLECT RELEVANT DATA.

   b. Fill an aluminum pan half full of water, cover the water surface with motor oil, and use it for the following parts of the activity.

   c. Feathers in an oil–water mix. Leave feathers in the oil–water mix for several minutes. Remove the feathers. Ask: *How do you think we might remove oil from the feathers?* Try wiping the feathers with paper towels. Ask: *Did wiping with paper towels remove all the oil?* Try cleaning the feathers with dishwashing liquid. Ask: *Which method of cleaning the oil off the feathers was better? What other ways might we try to remove the oil from feathers?* Try them.

   d. Eggs in an oil–water mix. Put four hard-boiled eggs (with shells on) into the oil–water mix and then remove one egg at a time after each of these intervals: 15 minutes, 30 minutes, 60 minutes, and 120 minutes. Ask: *What happens to the eggs?* Try removing the oil from the eggs with the methods you used for the feathers. After cleaning the oil off the eggs, crack and remove the shells. Ask: *Did the oil get inside the egg that was in the oil for 15 minutes? the one for 30 minutes? the one for 60 minutes? the one for 120 minutes?* Record your findings. Ask: *If oil did get into the egg, can it be removed?*

   e. Removing or containing oil. Using the following materials, how might you remove or keep the oil from spreading: paper towel, dishwashing liquid, turkey baster, large rubber band? Lay a paper towel on the surface of the oil and let it stay for 3 minutes. Remove the paper towel and put it on the paper plate. Ask: *What do you see happening to the paper towel and oil?* Add more motor oil, if needed, and spread a very large rubber band on the top of the oil. Ask: *What happens to the oil?* Using the turkey baster, try to remove the oil. Ask: *What happens to the oil?* Replace the oil into the pan of water. Add several drops of dishwashing liquid. Ask: *What happens to the oil?* Ask: *Which method was best for removing the oil? Which method was best for keeping the oil together in one place?*

EXPLAIN: USE DATA TO GENERATE INTERPRETATIONS, INCLUDING DESCRIPTIONS, CLASSIFICATIONS, PREDICTIONS, AND EXPLANATIONS.

    f. Ask: *What possible problems and adverse effects might result when chemicals are used to remove oil from animals in a real oil spill? How might an oil spill in Alaska affect people in the continental United States? Sometimes oil spills are purposely set on fire. What adverse effects might this have on the environment?* Lead students to understand that oil spills adversely affect land and water plants and animals directly by coating them with oil, often leading to their deaths. In addition, an oil spill affects future plant and animal life by destroying eggs and interfering with plant reproduction. Sometimes, the procedures used to reverse oil spills can interfere with environmental interrelationships, especially when chemicals are used.

Additional Activities Related to Oceans

Scientific study of the oceans bridges many science disciplines. Marine biologists monitor animals and plants that live in ocean habitats. Some chemists investigate mineral content and salinity levels of oceans. Physical oceanographers study wave and tidal action. Meteorologists observe weather systems affected by ocean currents. Therefore, many of the activities from previous sections could be included in a study of the oceans.

- Activities on the water cycle, such as "How Much Water Evaporates from an Open Aquarium?" (p. A-238), "Where Does Water Go When It Evaporates?" (p. A-239), "How Can You Promote the Evaporation of Water?" (p. A-239), and "What Is Condensation? How Does It Occur?" (p. A-243) can contribute to an understanding of how water circulates between land, the atmosphere, and bodies of water.
- Activities on aquariums, including "How Can I Construct an Aquarium Habitat?" (p. A-178), "What Can I Observe in an Aquarium?" (p. A-180), and "What Environmental Factors Affect Life in an Aquarium Habitat?" (p. A-181) involve simulations of marine environments.
- "How Can Salt Crystals Be Grown?" (p. A-227) could help to explain formation of sea salt and the increased salinity of some tidal pools. "How Can Evaporation and Condensation Be Used to Desalinate Salt Water?" (p. A-244) further explores the nature of salt water.

IV. VIEWING THE SKY FROM EARTH

A. POSITIONS AND MOTIONS OF THE SUN, MOON, AND STARS

▶ *Science Background*

Beyond the earth's atmosphere, other objects are visible in the earth's sky. The brightest and most noticeable of these is our sun, the star at the center of our solar system. Energy from the sun heats both the ocean and land, drives the process of photosynthesis enabling plants to produce food, and illuminates our world during the daytime. Our moon appears about the size of the sun in our sky, though it does not shine as brightly. Rather than producing its own light, the moon is visible because of reflected sunlight. Other planets in our solar system are also visible in the earth's sky. Mercury, Venus, Mars,

Jupiter, and Saturn appear at times in the night sky, looking like bright, non-twinkling stars. The other, more distant planets can be viewed through telescopes, but cannot be located with just the naked-eye. A clear night sky also reveals patterns of stars, known as constellations.

Objects in our sky appear to move because the earth rotates on its axis once every 24 hours, the period known as 1 day. Though it appears that the sun, moon, planets, and most of the stars rise in the east and set in the west, it is really the earth's turning that is responsible for this apparent motion. Polaris, the North Star, because of its unique location directly above the earth's north pole, appears to remain stationary in the sky for viewers in the northern hemisphere.

Through the following activities, discussion, and expository teaching you will help the students begin to develop an understanding of these fundamental principles about distant objects in the sky:

1. The sun, moon, and stars all have properties, locations, and movements that can be observed and described.
2. The sun has a pattern of movement through the sky. It appears to move across the sky in the same way every day, but its path slowly changes during the seasons.
3. The moon appears to move across the sky much like the sun.
4. The observable shape of the moon changes from day to day in a cycle that lasts about a month.
5. Stars, in their constellations, appear to move in the sky during the night.
6. Most objects in the solar system are in regular and predictable motion. Those motions explain such phenomena as the day and the phases of the moon.

Understanding of these principles can be developed from an early age, beginning with observations over time, and progress at higher grade levels to the development of explanations for the observed phenomena.

NSES Science Standards

As a result of their science activities, all students should develop an understanding of

- objects in the sky (K–4).
- changes in the earth and sky (K–4).
- the earth in the solar system (5–8).

Objectives for Students

1. Observe and describe properties, locations, and movements of the sun, moon, and stars in the sky.
2. Describe the apparent daily motion of the sun across the sky and discuss how this motion varies during the year.
3. Compare and contrast the apparent motion of the sun across the sky with the apparent motion of the moon across the sky.
4. Observe, describe, and name the moon's phases as they change during the month, and explain why this happens.
5. Use compass directions and angles to describe the position of objects in the sky.

NSES **Concepts and Principles**

Activities 1–4 are daytime astronomy activities involving the observation of shadows. They address these fundamental concepts and principles related to the *Science Standards:*

- The sun, moon, and stars all have properties, locations, and movements that can be observed and described (K–4).
- The sun has a pattern of movement through the sky. It appears to move across the sky in the same way every day, but its path slowly changes during the season (K–4).

1. WHAT CAUSES SHADOWS? (K–2)

Materials
Overhead projector
Projection screen or blank wall

ENGAGE: ASK A QUESTION ABOUT OBJECTS, ORGANISMS, OR EVENTS IN THE ENVIRONMENT.

a. Turn on the overhead projector so that it illuminates the projection screen or blank wall. Select several students to stand between the projector and the screen (facing the screen). Ask: *What do you see on the screen?* (Shadows.) *What causes these shadows?*

EXPLORE: PLAN AND CONDUCT SIMPLE INVESTIGATIONS TO COLLECT RELEVANT DATA.

b. Ask: *What is necessary for a shadow to form? If we didn't have the light from the overhead or the students standing here would there be a shadow on the screen? How could we find out?* Students may suggest having the volunteer students move out of the light, or turning off the overhead. Try these things and other suggestions they may come up with.

EXPLAIN: USE DATA TO GENERATE INTERPRETATIONS, INCLUDING DESCRIPTIONS, CLASSIFICATIONS, AND EXPLANATIONS.

c. Ask: *When were shadows produced? What did they look like? What two things must you have to create a shadow?* Lead the children to the realization that in order to have a shadow there must be a light source and an object to block the light. Encourage them to develop an operational definition of a shadow. (A dark area caused by the blocking of light.)

2. HOW CAN SHADOWS BE CHANGED? (K–2)

Materials
Flashlight
Two large sheets of white paper
Scissors
Plastic funnel
Pencil or crayon

ENGAGE: ASK A QUESTION ABOUT OBJECTS, ORGANISMS, OR EVENTS IN THE ENVIRONMENT.

a. Ask: *Are shadows of the same object always the same size and shape?* Encourage students to share their ideas.

EXPLORE: PLAN
AND CONDUCT SIMPLE
INVESTIGATIONS TO
COLLECT RELEVANT DATA.

b. Working with a partner, students should put a funnel on a large sheet of white paper. Suggest that they use the flashlight to make a shadow of the funnel on the paper. Encourage them to try shining the flashlight from different positions. Ask: *How does the shadow change?*

c. Suggest that students do the following to record the size and shape of two shadows. One student should shine the flashlight on the funnel while the other one traces and cuts the shadow shape out with the scissors, in this sequence:

1. First, while holding the flashlight low and to the side, trace and cut out the shadow of the funnel. Label it "low."

2. Next, switch roles with your partner. Put a new piece of white paper under the funnel, hold the flashlight high, and then trace and cut out the shadow of the funnel. Label it "high."

3. Compare the size and shape of the two cutout shadows.

EXPLAIN: USE
DATA TO GENERATE
INTERPRETATIONS,
INCLUDING DESCRIPTIONS,
CLASSIFICATIONS, AND
EXPLANATIONS.

d. Ask: *Are both of your shadow shapes the same?* (No.) *How are they different?* (They are different sizes and shapes.) *Which one is longer?* (The one labeled "low" is longer.) *Which one is shorter?* (The one labeled "high" is shorter.) *What caused the difference in shapes?* (The position of the light source.) Try to lead the students to the conclusion that the position of the light source affects the shadow's size and shape. When the light source is low, shining on the object from the side, the shadow is long and when the light source is high, shining down on the object from above, the shadow is short.

ELABORATE: EXTEND
CONCEPTS, PRINCIPLES,
AND STRATEGIES TO NEW
PROBLEMS AND
QUESTIONS.

e. Ask: *What happens to the shadow if you move the light source in an arc from one side of the object, over it, and to the other side of the object?* This simulates the apparent motion of the sun in the sky and provides background experience for future activities.

3. HOW DO SHADOWS CAUSED BY THE SUN CHANGE DURING THE DAY? (K–4)

Materials

Flagpole or fence post
Sidewalk chalk
Paint stirrers (to use as stakes in the lawn)

ENGAGE: ASK A QUESTION ABOUT OBJECTS, ORGANISMS, OR EVENTS IN THE ENVIRONMENT.

a. Ask: *Do you think that shadows outdoors change during the day? How might we find out?*

EXPLORE: PLAN AND CONDUCT SIMPLE INVESTIGATIONS TO COLLECT RELEVANT DATA.

b. On a sunny day, take the class outside to the flagpole or a fence post early in the morning. Ask: *Does the flagpole or fence post have a shadow? How could we mark the position of this shadow?*

c. Show the students the sidewalk chalk and paint stirrers if they need a hint. Have the students identify the "end" of the shadow, that is, the part cast by the top of the flagpole or the fence post. If the end of the shadow falls on concrete, sidewalk chalk can be used to mark its position. If the end of the shadow falls on grass, a paint stirrer can be used as a stake to mark its position. Record the time of the observation either in chalk on the concrete or with pencil on the paint stirrer. Throughout the day, about once each hour if possible, return to the flagpole or fence post with the class to mark the shadow's current position.

EXPLAIN: USE DATA TO GENERATE INTERPRETATIONS, INCLUDING DESCRIPTIONS, CLASSIFICATIONS, AND EXPLANATIONS.

d. After making the final afternoon observation, ask: *What did you find out about how the shadow changed during the day?* (It started out long on that side, then got shorter, then got longer on the other side.) *Why do you think the shadow changed in this way?* (Because the sun seemed to move across the sky.) *How did the position of the sun change during our observations today?* (Indicating directions, lead students to understand that it started out low over there in the morning, moved higher in the sky around noon, then kept moving that way in the afternoon.) Develop the concept that the sun appeared to move from east to west in the sky during the day and that caused the size, shape, and direction of the shadow to change over time.

ELABORATE: EXTEND CONCEPTS, PRINCIPLES, AND STRATEGIES TO NEW PROBLEMS AND QUESTIONS.

e. Ask: *Do you think the flagpole or fence post shadow will change the same way tomorrow? next week? next month? How could we find out?* Assist the students in continuing their investigation of shadow positions throughout the school year and help them look for patterns in their findings.

4. HOW CAN SHADOWS TELL YOU WHEN IT IS LOCAL NOON? (4–6)

Materials (For each small group of students)

Long nail
Hammer
Sheets of white paper (8.5 × 11 inches)
Rectangular board big enough to hold the paper
Pencil
Clock or watch
Metric ruler

ENGAGE: ASK A QUESTION ABOUT OBJECTS, ORGANISMS, OR EVENTS IN THE ENVIRONMENT.

a. Ask: *On a sunny day, at what time are shadows the shortest? How could we find out? How does the position of the sun in the sky relate to the length of the shadow cast by an object?*

EXPLORE: PLAN AND CONDUCT SIMPLE INVESTIGATIONS TO COLLECT RELEVANT DATA.

b. Put a piece of paper in the middle of the board. Hammer the nail into the board and paper as shown, making sure the nail will not easily come out of the board.

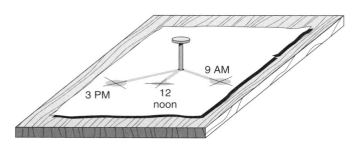

c. Late in the morning about 10:30, place the board where it will get sunlight until about 2:00 in the afternoon. Do not move the board during your observations. Every half hour or at shorter intervals, draw an X at the end of the shadow cast by the nail. Beside the X, note the time of each observation.

d. Upon returning to the classroom, carefully measure the distance between each X and the nail to the nearest millimeter. Create a data table that shows the time of the observation and the length of the corresponding shadow. Construct a line graph to represent these data. The manipulated or independent variable, "time of observation," should be plotted on the x axis; the responding or dependent variable, "shadow length," should be plotted on the y axis.

EXPLAIN: USE DATA TO GENERATE INTERPRETATIONS, INCLUDING DESCRIPTIONS, CLASSIFICATIONS, AND EXPLANATIONS.

e. Ask: *Did the shadow length change during your observation period? When was it shortest? When would you expect to have the shortest shadow?* (When the sun was highest in the sky.) Explain that "local noon" occurs when the sun is at its highest point above the horizon for a given day. Local noon does occur in the middle of the day at a given location, but because time zones cover large geographic areas, local noon probably does not occur exactly at 12:00 noon according to your accurately set clock. Daylight savings time, which shifts the time by 1 hour during certain months of the year, also affects the clock time that local noon occurs. Ask: *Is local noon exactly at 12:00 noon on the clock at our location? How do you know?*

ELABORATE: EXTEND CONCEPTS, PRINCIPLES, AND STRATEGIES TO NEW PROBLEMS AND QUESTIONS.

f. Ask: *Do you think local noon will occur at the same time tomorrow at this location? How could we find out? How could you modify your observations to be more certain of the actual time of local noon? Do you expect students in other towns to find the same time for local noon at their location? Why or why not? How could you find out?* (Students might suggest sharing data electronically with schools in other geographic areas.)

NSES **Concepts and Principles**

Activities 5–7 relate to the relative positions and motions of the sun, earth, and moon. They address these fundamental concepts and principles related to the *Science Standards:*

• The sun, moon, and stars all have properties, locations, and movements that can be observed and described (K–4).

• The sun has a pattern of movement through the sky. It appears to move across the sky in the same way every day, but its path slowly changes during the season (K–4).

5. WHY IS THERE DAY AND NIGHT? (2–4)

Materials

Styrofoam ball (about the size of a baseball)
Craft stick and brad for each small group
Lamp with a bright bulb (at least 100 watts)
Globe
Room that can be darkened
Small lump of sticky tack

ENGAGE: ASK A QUESTION ABOUT OBJECTS, ORGANISMS, OR EVENTS IN THE ENVIRONMENT.

a. Ask: *What do you think causes day and night? Does every place on earth have daytime or nighttime at the same time?*

EXPLORE: PLAN AND CONDUCT SIMPLE INVESTIGATIONS TO COLLECT RELEVANT DATA.

b. Distribute a ball, craft stick, and brad to each small group. Demonstrate how to assemble these parts as shown.

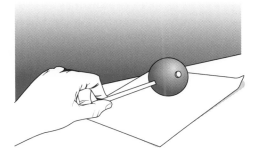

c. Have the students hold the ball by the craft stick. Then darken the room lights and turn on the bright light. Tell students to discover what they can about the way the ball is lit and record observations about their ball. The following questions might guide their thinking: *How much of the ball is lit up? Is the brad in the lit part? If not, what can you do to the ball to move the brad to the lit part? If you became tiny and were on the brad on the lit side of the ball, would you be able to see the bright light bulb? If you were tiny and were on the brad on the unlit side of the ball, would you be able to see the bright light bulb?*

EXPLAIN: USE DATA TO GENERATE INTERPRETATIONS, INCLUDING DESCRIPTIONS, CLASSIFICATIONS, AND EXPLANATIONS.

d. Ask the class to share their observations of the balls in the bright light.

e. Show the globe to the class. Ask: *What is the globe a model of?* (earth.) *How is the globe like the earth? How is it different?* Place the lamp several meters from the globe and darken the room. Then, turn on the bright bulb. Ask: *What do you think the bright bulb is a model of?* (The sun.) *How is the bright bulb like the sun? How is it different? Is the entire globe lit by the bright light? How much of it is lit?* (One half.) *Which half?* (The half toward the bright light.) *How does this model now show day and night?* (The lit side of the earth is having daytime, and the unlit side is having nighttime.) *What happens when I turn the globe?* (The places that are lit change.) *Are the same places on the earth having daytime when the globe is turned?* (No.)

f. Stick the small lump of sticky tack on the globe to mark the location of your school. Ask: *Is it day or night where the sticky tack is? What could I do to the globe so that the sticky tack is having daytime, then nighttime, then daytime, and so on?*

g. Slowly spin the globe on its axis in a counterclockwise direction as viewed from above the north pole. As the sticky tack moves from darkness into the light, explain to the students that this is sunrise for the people at that location. When the sticky tack is in the center of the lit side of the globe, with the light shining directly onto it, it is noon for the people at that location. When the sticky tack moves from the lit to the unlit area, it is sunset. When the sticky tack is in the center of the unlit area, on the side of the earth away from the sun, it is midnight.

6. HOW DOES THE APPEARANCE OF THE MOON'S SHAPE CHANGE OVER TIME? (2–4)

Materials

Black construction paper
Soft white chalk

ENGAGE: ASK A QUESTION ABOUT OBJECTS, ORGANISMS, OR EVENTS IN THE ENVIRONMENT.

a. Distribute materials to the students. Give them 5 minutes to draw the shape of the moon. Post the pictures for all to see. Ask: *Are all the drawings the same shape?* (No.) Sort them so that similar shapes are grouped together. Ask representatives from each group to tell why they drew the moon the way they did. Ask: *Can everyone's drawing be correct even if they are different shapes?* (Yes.) *How can this be?* (The moon doesn't always appear the same shape.) *How could we find out how the appearance of the moon's shape changes over time?* (Hopefully, someone will suggest observing and recording the moon's appearance in the sky for a week or so.)

EXPLORE: PLAN AND CONDUCT SIMPLE INVESTIGATIONS TO COLLECT RELEVANT DATA.

b. Have the students take home a large sheet of black construction paper and some white chalk, then observe the moon daily for a week. They should divide their paper into eight equal rectangles as shown.

Moon Calendar by Suzy	11/5	11/6	11/7
11/8	11/9	11/10	11/11

Students can use the first rectangle for the title and their name and the remaining seven spaces for their daily observations. It is best to begin this assignment several days after new moon when fair weather is expected—the waxing crescent moon should be visible in the western sky shortly after sunset. Assuming it is clear, the moon should be visible in the evening sky for the next week. If there is an overcast night, students should indicate on their chart that the sky was cloudy.

EXPLAIN: USE DATA TO GENERATE INTERPRETATIONS, INCLUDING DESCRIPTIONS, CLASSIFICATIONS, AND EXPLANATIONS.

c. At the end of the observation period, students should bring their moon calendars to class to share and compare. Ask: *How did the moon's shape seem to change during the week?* Have them see if everyone's observations supported the same conclusions. Ask: *Did more of the moon appear to be illuminated each night?* Tell the students that the apparent shape of the moon is known as its phase. Use a chart like this to introduce the names of the phases. Challenge the students to identify which phases they observed.

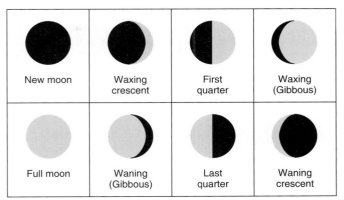

Phases of the Moon as Seen from the Earth

ELABORATE: EXTEND CONCEPTS, PRINCIPLES, AND STRATEGIES TO NEW PROBLEMS AND QUESTIONS.

d. Ask students to predict what the moon will look like for the next few days, then make observations to check their predictions.

An ongoing Moonwatch Bulletin Board[6] could be maintained in your classroom. Each night, have three students draw the shape of the moon on an index card. Have the three students compare their drawings and arrive at one drawing that represents their observations. Post the drawing on the appropriate month/date cell on the bulletin board calendar. As a pattern develops, have the class predict the next day's moon phase.

7. WHY DOES IT APPEAR THAT THERE ARE PHASES OF THE MOON? (4–6)

Materials

Styrofoam ball (about the size of a baseball) and a craft stick for each student
Lamp with a bright bulb (at least 100 watts)
A room that can be darkened

ENGAGE: ASK A QUESTION ABOUT OBJECTS, ORGANISMS, OR EVENTS IN THE ENVIRONMENT.

a. Ask: *What are moon phases? Why does the moon have phases?*

EXPLORE: PLAN AND CONDUCT SIMPLE INVESTIGATIONS TO COLLECT RELEVANT DATA.

b. Use some simple objects to create a model that shows the cause of the moon's phases as viewed from the earth. In this model a styrofoam ball represents the moon, a bright light bulb represents the sun, and your head represents the earth. Your eyes will see the view of the moon phase from the earth.

---

[6]For additional details on moon watches, see G. Robert Moore, "Revisiting Science Concepts," *Science and Children 32*(3), November/December 1994, 31–32, 60.

c. Insert the craft stick into the styrofoam ball to act as a handle. Hold the moon ball in your left hand with your arm outstretched. Ask: *How much of the moon ball can you see at one time?* Darken the room. Ask: *Is it easy to see the moon ball? Is any part of it illuminated?* Turn on the bright light bulb to represent the sun. Look at the moon ball from several angles. Ask: *Is part of it illuminated now? How much of the moon ball is illuminated at the same time?* Describe the location of the lit part in relation to the bright light.

d. The moon orbits around the earth each month. To simulate this in your model, stand facing the bright light, hold the moon ball in your left hand so that the moon ball appears to be a little to the left of the light bulb. Ask: *Is a lit area visible on the moon ball when it is in this position?* Describe it. (The right edge of the moon ball is illuminated in a narrow crescent shape.) Slowly turn to your left, keeping your arm holding the moon ball outstretched. Watch how the illuminated part of the moon ball varies as its position changes. If the moon ball goes into the shadow cast by your head, just lift the moon ball a little higher so the light can reach it. Move the moon ball around its orbit several times. Look for patterns in the way it is illuminated.

EXPLAIN: USE DATA TO GENERATE INTERPRETATIONS, INCLUDING DESCRIPTIONS, CLASSIFICATIONS, AND EXPLANATIONS.

e. Have a class discussion about the questions posed in the explore phase of the lesson. Lead the students to an understanding of the following concepts.
   1. The moon does not produce its own light, it reflects light from the sun.
   2. Half of the moon, that half facing the sun, is illuminated at any given time.
   3. We can only see half of the moon's surface at any given time, the half that is facing the earth.
   4. Depending on the relative positions of the earth, sun, and moon, only part of the illuminated moon's surface may be facing the earth, so we see phases of the moon.

ELABORATE: EXTEND CONCEPTS, PRINCIPLES, AND STRATEGIES TO NEW PROBLEMS AND QUESTIONS.

f. Have the students complete an illustration showing the apparent moon phase when the moon is at various positions in its orbit around the earth. This illustration is really a two-dimensional model to explain why the moon appears to have phases. A completed illustration might look something like the following diagram.

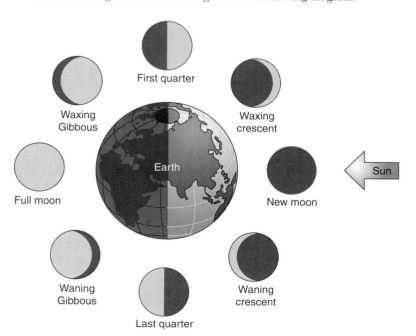

NSES **Concepts and Principles**

Activity 8 introduces an easy way for students to describe the location in the sky of celestial objects. It addresses this fundamental principle related to the Science Standards:

- The sun, moon, and stars all have properties, locations, and movements that can be observed and described.

8. HOW CAN WE DESCRIBE POSITIONS OF OBJECTS IN THE SKY? (4–6)

Materials

Cardinal direction signs
Ten index cards each labeled with a large number from 1 to 10
Masking tape or sticky tack
Adding machine tape
"Handy Angle Measurements" sheet

ENGAGE: ASK A QUESTION ABOUT OBJECTS, ORGANISMS, OR EVENTS IN THE ENVIRONMENT.

a. Post cardinal directions—north, south, east, and west—on the classroom walls. Post the 10 index cards at various locations on the walls and ceiling of the classroom. Put a strip of adding machine tape all the way around the room at the students' seated eye level. This represents the horizon.

b. Ask: *How could you explain to someone where to look for a particular object in the sky? What kinds of measurements and units might be helpful?* Ask several students to describe the location of something in the classroom. Discuss alternative approaches.

EXPLORE: PLAN AND CONDUCT SIMPLE INVESTIGATIONS TO COLLECT RELEVANT DATA.

c. Point out the cardinal directions signs posted in the room. Distribute copies of the "Handy Angle Measurements" sheet shown in the diagram on page A-278. Demonstrate how to extend your arm, and discuss the angles represented by the different parts of the hand. Mention that the adding machine tape around the room represents the horizon, the starting point for their angle measurements. Ask the students to try to measure the angle from the horizon line to the point straight overhead using an outstretched arm and clenched fist. It should take approximately nine fists, since the angle from the horizon to the point overhead (zenith) is 90 degrees and each fist represents about 10 degrees.

d. Have the students number from one to ten on a sheet of paper. Ask them to use cardinal directions and angle measurements to describe the position of each index card number posted in the room, from their seat.

Note: Because the cards are relatively close to the observers, the observing position will affect the results. Do not expect students in different parts of the room to have the same direction and angle measurement for each card.

EXPLAIN: USE DATA TO GENERATE INTERPRETATIONS, INCLUDING DESCRIPTIONS, CLASSIFICATIONS, AND EXPLANATIONS.

e. Ask: *How were you able to describe the positions of the index cards?* (By finding the direction to look and measuring how high above the horizon with my outstretched hand.)
   Could you use this same technique to describe the position of objects in the sky? What would you need to know to be successful? (Cardinal directions.)

Safety Precautions

Caution students to never look directly at the sun. The sun is very bright. Looking at it could cause blindness. Only use this technique to describe the location of the moon, stars, planets, and so on.

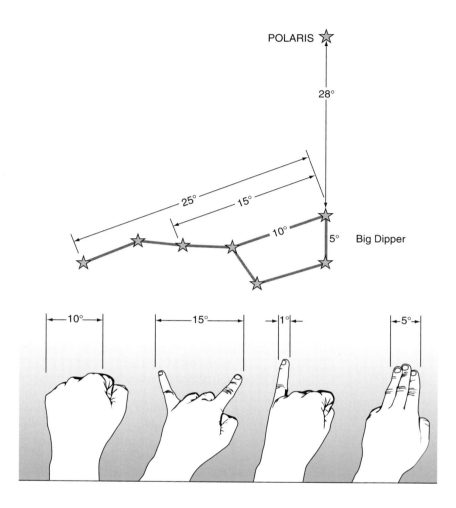

ELABORATE: EXTEND CONCEPTS, PRINCIPLES, AND STRATEGIES TO NEW PROBLEMS AND QUESTIONS.

f. Apply this measuring technique to describing the position of the moon in the sky. Find out how the moon moves across the sky during the night. Determine the cardinal directions around your observation point. A compass, street map, or locating Polaris (the North Star) should help.

g. Record your observations in a data table like the one shown.

Time of Observation	Direction	Angle above the Horizon
7:30 PM		
8:00 PM		
8:30 PM		
9:00 PM		
9:30 PM		
10:00 PM		

Observe and record the position of the moon at half-hour intervals. Describe how the moon moves during the night. Develop an investigation to determine how the position of the moon at a given hour changes from night to night. Ask: *What did you find?*

h. If you live in the northern hemisphere, you can determine your latitude by measuring the position of Polaris above the horizon. Polaris is the end star in the handle of the Little Dipper. The pointer stars of the Big Dipper are helpful in finding Polaris. Polaris is *not* the brightest star in the sky. To find it, face the northern horizon. Look for the patterns shown in the handy angle measurement diagram. The orientation of the Big Dipper will vary, but its pointer stars always point toward Polaris. Decide which star is Polaris. Determine how many degrees it is above the horizon using the Handy Angle Measurement technique. That number of degrees should be the same as the latitude of your observation position. Note the position of Polaris relative to objects on the ground (trees, houses, etc.). Try finding Polaris several hours later. Ask: *Is it still in the same angle above the horizon? Is it still in the same place relative to the objects on the ground?*

You might notice that while Polaris is in the same location, the nearby star patterns have seemed to move in a counterclockwise direction around Polaris. Activity 5, Making a Star Clock in the GEMS (Great Explorations in Math and Science) Module *Earth, Moon, and Stars*, is a very good activity related to the motion of the circumpolar constellations (those around the pole).[7]

B. MODELS OF THE SOLAR SYSTEM AND THE EARTH-MOON SYSTEM

▶ *Science Background*

Our solar system includes the sun (our star), nine planets, and numerous smaller bodies including asteroids and comets that orbit around the sun. The four planets closest to the Sun—Mercury, Venus, Earth, and Mars—are known as the inner planets. They are relatively small, rocky bodies. The other five planets—Jupiter, Saturn, Uranus, Neptune, and Pluto—are known as the outer planets. All of the outer planets except Pluto are large and gaseous. Pluto is small and believed to be icy. The orbits of the planets lie roughly in the same plane and are elliptical in shape.

The earth-moon system is unique in the solar system. Other planets have moons, but the earth is the only planet with just one very large moon. Although much smaller than the sun, our moon appears about the same size in our sky. This is because it is much closer to the earth.

Scale models are an obvious strategy for helping students develop the concepts of relative sizes and distances in space.

Through the following activities, discussion, and expository teaching, you will help the students begin to develop an understanding of the relative sizes and distances in our solar system and in the earth-moon system.

 NSES **Science Standards**

All students should develop an understanding of

- the earth in the solar system (5–8).

---

[7]For many good astronomy activities see Sneider, Cary I. (1986). *Earth, Moon, and Stars*. Great Explorations in Math and Science (GEMS). Berkeley: Lawrence Hall of Science, University of California.

Objectives for Students

1. Demonstrate and describe a scale model of our solar system.
2. Name the planets in order of size.
3. Name the planets in order of distance from the sun.
4. Demonstrate and describe a model of the earth-moon system.

 Concepts and Principles

Activities 1–3 relate to the use of models to represent the vast sizes and distances found within our solar system. The activities address these fundamental concepts and principles that support the *Science Standards:*

- The earth is the third planet from the sun in a system that includes the moon, the sun, eight other planets and their moons, and smaller objects, such as asteroids and comets (5–8).
- The sun, an average star, is the central and largest body in the solar system (5–8).
- Models can represent the real world, making abstract concepts more concrete (5–8).

1. HOW SPREAD OUT ARE THE PLANETS IN OUR SOLAR SYSTEM? (3–6)

Materials

Ten sentence strips, each labeled with one of the solar system bodies (Sun, Mercury, Venus, Earth, Mars, Jupiter, Saturn, Uranus, Neptune, Pluto)

ENGAGE: ASK A QUESTION ABOUT OBJECTS, ORGANISMS, OR EVENTS IN THE ENVIRONMENT.

a. Ask students to draw a picture showing what they know about the orbits of the planets around the sun in our solar system. To assess students' prior knowledge, ask: *How many planets did you include? Could you name the planets? Do you think you placed the planets in the right order from the sun? Are the orbits of the planets all the same distance apart? What is a scale model? Was your drawing a scale model? Why or why not?*

EXPLORE: PLAN AND CONDUCT SIMPLE INVESTIGATIONS TO COLLECT RELEVANT DATA.

b. Select 10 students to represent the major bodies in the solar system. Give each of them a labeled sentence strip to hold.

Select a starting place at one edge of the playground or at the end of a very long hall. Instruct the sign holding students to follow these instructions for constructing the model solar system.

1. The "sun" stands at one end of the area.
2. Mercury takes 4 small steps from the sun.
3. Venus takes 3 small steps outward from Mercury.
4. Earth takes 2 small steps beyond Venus.
5. Mars takes 5 small steps beyond Earth.
6. Jupiter takes 34 small steps beyond Mars.
7. Saturn takes 40 small steps beyond Jupiter.
8. Uranus takes 90 small steps beyond Saturn.
9. Neptune takes 100 small steps beyond Uranus.
10. Pluto takes 88 small steps beyond Neptune.

c. Tell the class that the positions of the students with the signs represent the average distance between the planets' orbits. With the holders remaining in their places and holding up their signs all the students should observe the spacing and think about these questions: *Which planets' orbits are closest together? Which ones are really spread out? Are the planets' orbits spaced at equal distances from the sun?*

EXPLAIN: USE DATA TO GENERATE INTERPRETATIONS, INCLUDING DESCRIPTIONS, CLASSIFICATIONS, AND EXPLANATIONS.

d. Upon returning to the classroom, discuss the students' responses to the questions. Important ideas to emerge from the discussion include the following:

- The first four planets—Mercury, Venus, Earth, and Mars—do not have much distance between their orbits. These planets are known as the inner planets.
- The rest of the planets—Jupiter, Saturn, Uranus, Neptune, and Pluto—have rather large distances between their orbits. These planets are known as the outer planets.

Explain that the planets are not usually lined up as in our model. The model does not show the actual positions of the planets, but the relative spacing of their orbits.

2. HOW DO THE PLANETS IN OUR SOLAR SYSTEM COMPARE IN SIZE? (5–8)

Materials

Butcher paper
Pencils
Markers
Scissors
Metersticks
Metric rulers or metric tapes

ENGAGE: ASK A QUESTION ABOUT OBJECTS, ORGANISMS, OR EVENTS IN THE ENVIRONMENT.

a. Cut out a circle with a diameter of 5.6 cm to represent Earth. Show the circle to the class. Ask: *If we made a scale model of the planets in our solar system, how big would each planet be if Earth was this big?*

b. Have the class count off by eights. Tell each of the "ones" to draw a circle to represent Mercury in this model. Each of the "twos" should draw Venus to this scale, and so on. When the models showing student's prior knowledge are cut out, ask all the "ones" to bring their Mercury circles to the front of the room. Compare the range of sizes represented and how these circles compare with the Earth circle. Ask: *What does this tell us about what these people know about the size of Mercury compared to Earth?* Repeat this procedure with each of the other number groups and their cutout planets. You will probably be able to conclude that as a class we really are not sure how the planets compare in size.

EXPLORE: PLAN AND CONDUCT SIMPLE INVESTIGATIONS TO COLLECT RELEVANT DATA.

c. Tell the class that the diameter of the Earth circle in our model is 5.6 cm. Measure its diameter so they can confirm its size. Tell them that you will give each person the diameter measurement of their planet, so that they can make an accurate scale model for our solar system models. The following table includes the data:

Group Number from Counting Off	Planet	Diameter in Centimeters
Ones	Mercury	2.1
Twos	Venus	5.3
Threes	Mars	3.0
Fours	Jupiter	62.6
Fives	Saturn	52.8
Sixes	Uranus	22.4
Sevens	Neptune	21.7
Eights	Pluto	1.0

It may be necessary to review the meaning of the term *diameter*—the distance across the circle through the center. If students are reminded that diameter = 2 × radius, they might realize that if they find the radius (half of the diameter) of their circle and swing the radius around a center point, they will get a circle of the proper diameter. This technique is especially useful for the big planet circles.

d. After each circle is cut out, it should be labeled with the name of the planet it represents. Students should have the diameter of their planet circle checked for accuracy by at least two other students and make any necessary corrections.

e. Encourage students to get into solar system groups of eight so that there is one model of each planet in their group. Provide each group with a 5.6 cm diameter Earth circle. Challenge the groups to use their models to make a list of the planets in order of size from smallest to largest.

EXPLAIN: USE DATA TO GENERATE INTERPRETATIONS, INCLUDING DESCRIPTIONS, CLASSIFICATIONS, AND EXPLANATIONS.

f. Ask: *How did you compare the planets' sizes?* (We made scale models.) *Are our models the actual sizes of the planets?* (No. They are much smaller, but are "to scale" so they can be compared.) You may want to explain that in our model 1 cm = approximately 2,285 km. At this scale, the diameter of the sun would be approximately 6 meters. Perhaps you could draw a circle with a diameter of 6 meters on the playground so they could see how big the sun is compared to the planets. Ask: *Do our models show the actual shapes of the planets?* (No. Planets are spheres, not circles. We made a two-dimensional rather than a three-dimensional model.)

g. Ask: *What did you learn about the relative sizes of planets?* (They vary greatly in size.) *What was the order of the planets from smallest to largest diameter?* (Pluto, Mercury, Mars, Venus, Earth, Neptune, Uranus, Saturn, Jupiter.)

ELABORATE: EXTEND CONCEPTS, PRINCIPLES, AND STRATEGIES TO NEW PROBLEMS AND QUESTIONS.

h. Ask students to make up comparison questions about the relative diameters of the planets, for example: *Which planet has a diameter about half Earth's diameter?* (Mars.) *How many Earth diameters would fit in one Jupiter diameter?* (Eleven.) Have them challenge each other to find the answers using the scale models as an aid.

3. HOW COULD YOU MAKE A SCALE MODEL OF THE EARTH AND MOON? (5–8)

Materials

Basketball
Volleyball
Softball
Baseball
Tennis ball
Golf ball
Ping-Pong ball
Piece of rope 7.28 meters long
Metric rulers

ENGAGE: ASK A QUESTION ABOUT OBJECTS, ORGANISMS, OR EVENTS IN THE ENVIRONMENT.

a. Hold up the basketball. Tell the class that in our model of the earth and moon, it will represent Earth. Display the other balls. Ask: *Which ball would you select to represent the size of the moon in our model?* Record responses on a histogram on the board. *What would we need to know to determine which ball best represents the size of the moon when the earth is the size of a basketball?* (The actual diameter of the earth and the moon.)

EXPLORE: PLAN AND CONDUCT SIMPLE INVESTIGATIONS TO COLLECT RELEVANT DATA.

b. The diameter of the earth is 12,756 km and the diameter of the moon is 3,475 km. Ask: *What information do we need to collect about the balls to select the best ball to represent the moon?* Have the students get into small groups to come up with a plan to determine which ball would represent the moon. Carry out your plan.

EXPLAIN: USE DATA TO GENERATE INTERPRETATIONS, INCLUDING DESCRIPTIONS, CLASSIFICATIONS, AND EXPLANATIONS.

c. Ask: *Which ball did your group select to be the best moon ball if the earth is the size of the basketball?* (The tennis ball is best, because the earth's diameter is about 3.7 times the diameter of the moon, and the basketball's diameter is about 3.7 times the diameter of the tennis ball.)

   Ask: *What procedures did your group use to solve this problem?* (Measured the balls, used ratios, etc.) This might be an appropriate time for a review about ratios and proportions. *What is the scale of this model?* (1 cm on this model = approximately 530 km in reality.)

ELABORATE: EXTEND CONCEPTS, PRINCIPLES, AND STRATEGIES TO NEW PROBLEMS AND QUESTIONS.

d. Ask: *If we use the basketball to represent the earth and the tennis ball to represent the moon, how far apart should they be held to represent the actual distance between the earth and the moon?* Ask a student to hold the basketball to represent the earth. Start with the tennis ball close to the basketball and slowly walk away. Ask the students to tell you when you should stop. As different groups of students or individuals tell you the distance is right, stick a piece of tape on the wall or floor to show the distance they predicted. After all have expressed their ideas, move back close to the basketball. Give the student holding the basketball one end of the 7.28 meter rope. Slowly unwrap the rope as you retrace your steps away from the basketball. When you get to the end of the rope, hold up the tennis ball. Now the model represents the relative sizes of the earth and the moon and how far they are apart. The actual distance from the earth to the moon is approximately 384,000 km. The moon is approximately 30 Earth-diameters from the earth.

Appendixes

Sixty Years of Elementary School Science: A Guided Tour

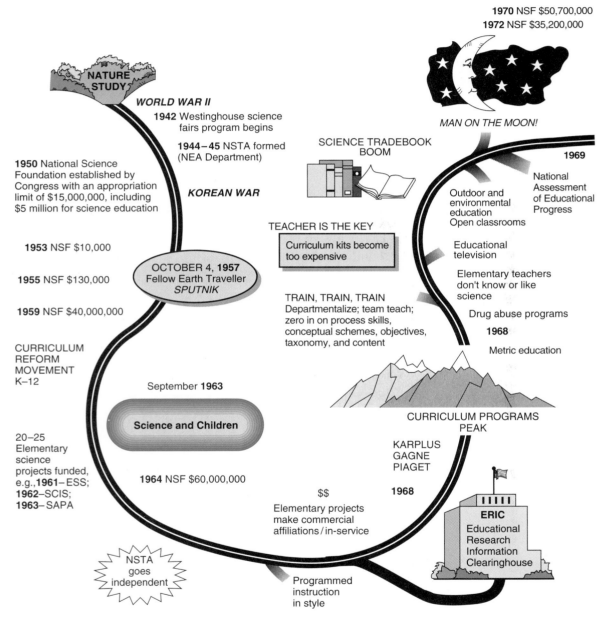

1970 NSF $50,700,000
1972 NSF $35,200,000

MAN ON THE MOON!

NATURE STUDY

WORLD WAR II

1942 Westinghouse science fairs program begins

1944–45 NSTA formed (NEA Department)

SCIENCE TRADEBOOK BOOM

1969

National Assessment of Educational Progress

1950 National Science Foundation established by Congress with an appropriation limit of $15,000,000, including $5 million for science education

KOREAN WAR

Outdoor and environmental education Open classrooms

1953 NSF $10,000

TEACHER IS THE KEY

Curriculum kits become too expensive

Educational television

1955 NSF $130,000

OCTOBER 4, **1957**
Fellow Earth Traveller
SPUTNIK

Elementary teachers don't know or like science

Drug abuse programs

1959 NSF $40,000,000

TRAIN, TRAIN, TRAIN
Departmentalize; team teach; zero in on process skills, conceptual schemes, objectives, taxonomy, and content

1968

Metric education

CURRICULUM REFORM MOVEMENT K–12

September **1963**

Science and Children

CURRICULUM PROGRAMS PEAK

KARPLUS
GAGNE
PIAGET

20–25 Elementary science projects funded, e.g.,**1961**– ESS; **1962**–SCIS; **1963**– SAPA

1964 NSF $60,000,000

$$
Elementary projects make commercial affiliations / in-service

1968

ERIC
Educational Research Information Clearinghouse

NSTA goes independent

Programmed instruction in style

Source: Modified from Phyllis R. Marcuccio "Forty-Five Years of Elementary School Science: A Guided Tour" as it appeared in *Science and Children 24,* no. 4 (January 1987): 12-14. Copyright 1987 by the National Science Teachers Association. Reproduced with permission.

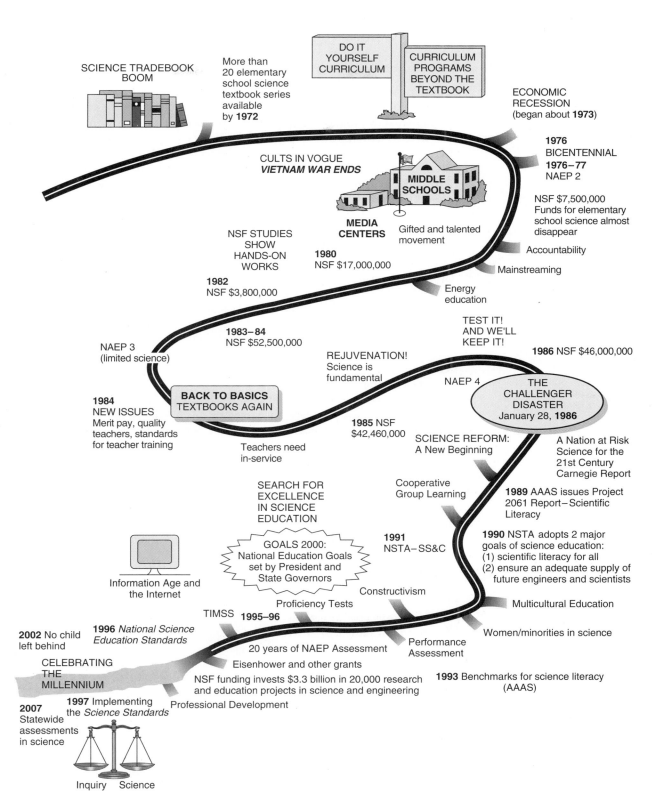

SCIENCE TRADEBOOK BOOM

More than 20 elementary school science textbook series available by **1972**

DO IT YOURSELF CURRICULUM

CURRICULUM PROGRAMS BEYOND THE TEXTBOOK

ECONOMIC RECESSION (began about **1973**)

1976 BICENTENNIAL
1976–77 NAEP 2

CULTS IN VOGUE
VIETNAM WAR ENDS

MIDDLE SCHOOLS

NSF $7,500,000 Funds for elementary school science almost disappear

MEDIA CENTERS

Gifted and talented movement

Accountability

Mainstreaming

NSF STUDIES SHOW HANDS-ON WORKS

1980 NSF $17,000,000

Energy education

1982 NSF $3,800,000

1983–84 NSF $52,500,000

TEST IT! AND WE'LL KEEP IT!

1986 NSF $46,000,000

NAEP 3 (limited science)

REJUVENATION! Science is fundamental

NAEP 4

THE CHALLENGER DISASTER January 28, **1986**

1984 NEW ISSUES Merit pay, quality teachers, standards for teacher training

BACK TO BASICS TEXTBOOKS AGAIN

1985 NSF $42,460,000

SCIENCE REFORM: A New Beginning

A Nation at Risk Science for the 21st Century Carnegie Report

Teachers need in-service

Cooperative Group Learning

1989 AAAS issues Project 2061 Report – Scientific Literacy

SEARCH FOR EXCELLENCE IN SCIENCE EDUCATION

1991 NSTA–SS&C

1990 NSTA adopts 2 major goals of science education:
(1) scientific literacy for all
(2) ensure an adequate supply of future engineers and scientists

Information Age and the Internet

GOALS 2000: National Education Goals set by President and State Governors

Constructivism

Multicultural Education

Proficiency Tests

Performance Assessment

Women/minorities in science

TIMSS **1995–96**

1996 *National Science Education Standards*

2002 No child left behind

20 years of NAEP Assessment

Eisenhower and other grants

1993 Benchmarks for science literacy (AAAS)

CELEBRATING THE MILLENNIUM

NSF funding invests $3.3 billion in 20,000 research and education projects in science and engineering

1997 Implementing the *Science Standards*

Professional Development

2007 Statewide assessments in science

Inquiry   Science

Notes on the Guided Tour

Notable Achievements

- Elementary school science now has a niche in elementary schools: It is accepted as important for all students, it is integrated with other subjects in the curriculum, and it is supported by principals and other administrators led by a government that expects all of its citizens to be scientifically literate.
- There is a new breed of elementary science specialists.
- Hands-on teaching is giving rise to inquiry and technology to foster creativity, intuition, and problem-solving skills. (Hands-on teachers are "guides" rather than "tellers.") The popularity of hands-on inquiry teaching is also creating a need for more in-service training and for more science centers and labs.
- Nonschool settings, such as outdoor education centers and museums, have increased their support, often introducing subject matter that includes issues of social concern like pollution, ecology, and energy education.
- Teaching tools—books, software, videos, and other multimedia products—drive the changing curricula.
- Up-to-date research in science education is readily available through the Eisenhower Clearinghouse.
- Recent and projected certification programs subject teachers to more rigorous standards.
- Studies and testing, forums and conferences exist to deal specifically with the concerns of elementary science.
- The business and industry communities, concerned about the interrelationships of science, technology, and society, have sought a role in science education. Organizations like the American Chemical Society, the National Academy of Science, and the American Association for the Advancement of Science have also cooperated to forward the cause of science education.
- SI metric measure has been generally adopted to in science education.
- A teamwork approach to curriculum building now exists among teachers, scientists, administrators, community, and government.
- There are established pockets of commitment to science, and programs have been developed to point out excellent science teaching throughout the country.

Familiar Road Signs

- Surges in National Science Foundation funding
- Efforts following crisis situations
- The continuing presence of textbooks
- National Assessment of Educational Progress reports
- Calls for new curricula
- Calls for in-service programs

Some Remaining Problems

- Teachers continue to be educated in the same way.
- No comprehensive, agreed-upon scope and sequence has been established.
- Progress depends on funds from the National Science Foundation.

- The pool of students interested in science is shrinking—nearly half the current ninth grade class in urban high schools will not even graduate, let alone seek science-related careers.
- Despite millions of dollars spent on curriculum studies, teachers still depend on textbooks.
- The United States continues to lag behind other countries in the amount of science being taught to children.
- The best science students are not attracted to science teaching careers.
- Average Americans care more for pseudoscience than science.
- Teachers do not apply educational research.
- Attaining proficiency for all students on statewide assessments in science is a continuing challenge for students, teachers, and schools.

Science Supplies, Equipment, and Materials Obtainable from Community Sources

This is only a partial list of possible community sources for science program materials in elementary and middle schools. Other sources that should not be overlooked include parents, the janitor or custodian of the school, the school cafeteria, radio and television repair shops, florists' shops, other teachers in the school, junior and senior high school science teachers, and so on. The materials are there; it just takes a little looking.

There are times, though, when in spite of the most careful searching, certain pieces of equipment or supplies are not obtainable from local sources; there are also many things that schools should buy from scientific supply houses. A partial list of some selected, reliable scientific supply houses is provided in Appendix C.

Dollar Store or Department Store

balloons
balls
compasses (magnetic)
cotton (absorbent)
flashlights
food coloring
glues and paste
inks
magnifying glasses
marbles
mechanical toys
mirrors
mousetraps
paper towels
scissors
sponges
staples
thermometers

Drugstore

adhesive tape
alcohol (rubbing)
bottles
cigar boxes
cold cream
corks
cotton
dilute acids, preferably 1–5%
dilute H_2O_2 (1.5%)
forceps or tweezers
limewater
medicine droppers
pipe cleaners
rubber stoppers
soda bicarbonate

spatulas
straws
sulfur
Tes-Tape™
tincture of iodine, diluted to straw color

Electrical Appliance Shop

bell wire
dry cells
electric fans
flashlight bulbs
flashlights
friction tape
magnets (from old appliances)
soldering iron

Fabric Shop

cardboard tubes
cheesecloth
flannel
knitting needles
leather
needles
netting
scraps of different kinds of fabrics
silk thread
spools

Farm or Dairy

birds' nests
bottles
clay
containers
gravel

hay or straw
humus
insects
leaves
loam
lodestone
rocks
sand
seeds

Fire Department

samples of materials used to extinguish various types of fires
water pumping equipment

Plant Nursery or Garden Supply Store

bulbs (tulips, etc.)
fertilizers
flowerpots
garden hose
garden twine
growing plants
labels
lime
peat pots
seed catalogs
seeds
spray guns
sprinkling cans
trowels and other garden tools

Service Station

ball bearings
cans
copper tubing

gears
gear transmissions
grease
inner tubes
jacks
maps
pulleys
tools
valves from tires
wheels

Grocery Store

aluminum foil
aluminum pie tins
ammonia
baking soda
borax
cellophane
clothespins
cornstarch
corrugated cardboard boxes
food storage bags
fruits
granulated sugar
paper bags
paper towels
paraffin
plastic wrap
salt
sandwich bags
sealable plastic bags
sponges
vegetables
vinegar
wax
wax paper

Hardware Store

brace and bits
cement
chisels
clocks
corks
dry-cell batteries
electric push buttons, lamps, and
    sockets
extension cords
files

flashlights
fruit jars
glass cutters
glass friction rods
glass funnels
glass tubing
hammers
hard rubber rods
insulated copper wire
lamp chimneys
metal and metal scraps
metersticks
nails
nuts and bolts
paints and varnishes
plaster of paris
pulleys
sandpaper
saws
scales
scrap lumber
screening
screwdrivers
screws
steel wool
thermometers (indoor and outdoor)
3–6 volt toy electric motors
tin snips
turpentine
wheelbarrow
window glass (broken pieces will do)
wire
yardsticks

Machine Shop

ball bearings
iron filings
iron rods
magnets
nuts and bolts
scrap metals
screws
wire

Medical Centers, Dental Offices, or Hospitals

corks
flasks

funnels
glass tubing
lenses
litmus paper
microscopes
models, such as teeth
rubber sheeting
rubber stoppers
rubber tubing
test tube holders
test tubes
thermometers
tongue depressors

Music Shop

broken string and drumheads
musical instruments
pitch pipes
tuning forks

Pet Shop

air pumps
animal cages
ant houses
aquariums
cages
fish
insects
nets (butterfly, fish, etc.)
plastic tubing
strainers
terrariums

Restaurant or Fast-Food Outlet

beverage stirrers
bones (chicken, etc.)
bottles
cans (coffee, 5-gallon size)
drums (ice cream)
five-gallon cans (oil)
food coloring
gallon jars (widemouthed, pickles, mayon-
    naise, etc.)
gallon jugs (vinegar)
pie tins
plastic spoons
plastic trays
soda straws

Note: For additional sources of common, easily obtained supplies and apparatus suitable for your elementary or middle school science program, see *The NSTA Guide: Science Education Suppliers* (Arlington, VA: National Science Teachers Association, published annually).

Selected Sources of Scientific Supplies, Models, Living Things, Kits, and Software

Brock Optical

Microscopes—rugged enough for small children
E-mail: magiscope@aol.com
URL: http://www.magiscope.com

Carolina Biological Supply Company

Instructional materials for all sciences; Science and Technology for Children (STC) guides and materials
E-mail: carolina@carolina.com
URL: http://www.carolina.com

Delta Education

Materials, kits, and activities for hands-on science programs, including FOSS, SCIS 3 + , and DSMII (Delta Science Modules)
E-mail: ecurran@delta-edu.com
URL: http://www.delta-education.com

Discovery Scope

Small, hand-held microscopes
E-mail: dscopes@aol.com
URL: http://www.discoveryscope.net

Educational Innovations

Heat-sensitive paper, UV-detecting beads, Cartesian diver, super-absorbent polymers, and other science supplies
E-mail: info@teachersource.com
URL: http://www.teachersource.com

Educational Products, Inc.

Science fair display boards and materials
E-mail: kdavis@educationalproducts.com
URL: http://www.educationalproducts.com

Estes Industries

Model rockets
E-mail: agrimm@centurims.com
URL: http://www.esteseducator.com

ETA/Cuisenaire

Hands-on science materials
E-mail: info@etacuisenaire.com
URL: http://www.etacuisenaire.com

Fisher Science Education

Instructional materials for all sciences
E-mail: info@fisheredu.com
URL: http://www.fisheredu.com

Forestry Suppliers, Inc.

Orienteering compasses, water, soil, and biological test kits, tree borers, soil sieves, rock picks, weather instruments, and other materials for interdisciplinary science teaching
E-mail: fsi@forestry-suppliers.com
URL: http://www.forestry-suppliers.com

Ken-A-Vision Manufacturing Co., Inc.

Microscopes
E-mail: info@ken-a-vision.com
URL: http://www.ken-a-vision.com

Lab-Aids, Inc.

Single-concept hands-on kits for chemistry, biology, environmental science, and earth science
E-mail: customerservice@lab-aids.com
URL: http://www.lab-aids.com

Learning Technologies, Inc.

Portable planetariums and other materials for astronomy teaching
E-mail: starlab@starlab.com
URL: http://www.starlab.com

Mountain Home Biological

Living materials, barn owl pellets, skull sets
E-mail: mtnhome@gorge.net
URL: http://www.pelletlab.com

NASCO

Science, materials and supplies
E-mail: info@enasco.com
URL: http://www.nascofa.com

National Gardening Association

GrowLab guides for kids' gardening, professional development materials on plant science
E-mail: MK@garden.org
URL: http://www.kidsgardening.com

NSTA Science Store

Books, posters, software, CD-ROMs
URL: http://www.nsta.org

Ohaus Corporation

Balances and measurement aids
E-mail: cs@ohaus.com
URL: http://www.ohaus.com

Pitsco LEGO Educational Division

LEGO construction kits, model hot air balloons, educational technology products
E-mail: pitsco@pitsco.com
URL: http://www.pitsco-legodacta.com

Rainbow Symphony, Inc.

Lesson kits for the study of light and color, specialty optics materials, diffraction gratings, 3-D lenses, solar eclipse safe-viewing glasses
E-mail: kathy@rainbowsymphony.com
URL: http://www.rainbowsymphony.com

Sargent-Welch

GEMS materials, materials for all sciences
E-mail: Sarwel@Sargentwelch.com
URL: http://www.Sargentwelch.com

TOPS Learning Systems

Science lessons using simple available materials
E-mail: tops@canby.com
URL: http://www.topsscience.org

Source: Compiled from advertisements and Web searches.

Noncommercial Sources and Containers for Living Things

Organisms	Noncommercial Source	Culture Containers
POND SNAILS	Freshwater ponds, creeks	Aquaria, large battery jars, gallon glass jars
LAND SNAILS	Mature hardwood forests: on rocks, fallen logs, damp foliage	Terraria, large battery jars
DAPHNIA	Freshwater ponds: at water's edge, and associated with algae	Gallon glass or plastic jars
ISOPODS AND CRICKETS	Under rocks, bricks, and boards that have lain on the ground for some time; between grass and base of brick buildings	Glass or plastic terraria, plastic sweater boxes (Provide vents in cover.)
MEALWORM BEETLES	Corn cribs, around granaries	Gallon glass jars with cheesecloth
FRUIT FLIES	Trap with bananas or apple slices. (Place fruit in a jar with a funnel for a top.)	Tall baby food jars, plastic vials (Punch hole in jar lids, cover with masking tape, and then prick tiny holes in tape with a pin.)
WINGLESS PEA APHIDS*	Search on garden vegetables (e.g., English peas)	On pea plants potted in plastic pots, milk cartons (keep aphids in a large terrarium so they cannot wander to other plants in the school.)
GUPPIES	Obtain free from persons who raise guppies as a hobby. (They are usually glad to reduce the population when they clean tanks.)	Aquaria, large battery jars
CHAMELEONS*	Dense foliage along river banks or railroad tracks. (Catch with net or large tea strainer.)	Prepare a cage using a broken aquarium. (Broken glass can be replaced by taping cloth screening along sides.)
FROGS*	Along edges of ponds, ditches, creeks (Catch with large scoop net.)	Large plastic ice chest (Set near a sink so a constant water supply can be provided.)
CHLAMYDOMONAS AND EUGLENA	Freshwater pond	Gallon glass jars, aquaria, battery jars
ELODEA (ANARCHARIS)*	Ponds, creeks: usually along edge or in shallows	Aquaria, large battery jars
EELGRASS*	Wading zone or brackish water	Aquaria, large battery jars

DUCKWEED	Edge of ponds or freshwater swamps	Aquaria, large battery jars
COLEUS AND GERANIUM	Persons who raise them (Start by rooting cuttings in 1 part sand, 1 part vermiculite, in plastic bags.)	Clay pots, milk cartons, tin cans

Source: Carolyn H. Hampton and Carol D. Hampton. "The Establishment of a Life Science Center." Reproduced with permission by *Science and Children 15* (7), (April 1978), 9. Copyright 1978 by The National Science Teachers Association, 1840 Wilson Blvd., Arlington, VA 22201–3000.

*These species are difficult to obtain from their natural habitats. Unless you have a convenient source, it is better to buy them commercially. Try a local aquarium, pet shop, or science supply house.

Note: For additional excellent articles on raising and using living things in elementary school classrooms, see Carol Hampton, Carolyn H. Hampton, and David Kramer, *Classroom Creature Culture: Algae to Anoles,* rev. ed., 1994, Arlington, VA: National Science Teachers Association.

Constructing Storage Areas for Supplies and Houses for Living Things

Your classroom has unused space that can be used for storage, such as spaces below window ledges, countertops, sinks, above and around heating units (radiators), and even under student desks.

You can purchase excellent commercially made cabinets that fit any of these spaces, or your students and/or your custodian and you can construct them. With some creativity, you and your students can arrange these cabinets in a variety of ways.

Small Items Storage

With an inquiry-based science program, you will constantly need to store many small items. Shoe, corrugated cardboard, cigar, and other small boxes provide space for collecting, organizing, and storing small, readily available materials for particular science areas. The following diagrams illustrate how to construct and store shoe boxes for small science items. Cardboard or clear plastic shoe boxes may be used. You may also use large cardboard boxes for storage, placing them in easily obtained wood or steel shelving units especially designed for this purpose. Your custodian can help with this.

SHOE BOX COLLECTION

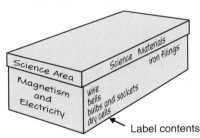

Living Things Storage

Encourage your students to bring small animals (including insects) and plants into your classroom. To be well prepared, have the following kinds of containers available:

- Insect cages
- Small animal cages
- Aquariums
- Terrariums

Insect Cages.[1]

Use small cake pans, coffee can lids, or covers from ice cream cartons for the cage cover and base. Roll wire screening into a cylinder to fit the base and then lace the screening together with a strand of wire.

---

[1] For additional information about insects in the classroom, see: Laurel D. Hansen, Roger D. Akre, and Elizabeth A. Myhre, "Homes Away from Home: Observe Insects Indoors with These Creature Containers," *Science and Children* 31(1), September 1993, 28–31; Rebecca Olien, "Worm Your Way Into Science—Experiments with These Familiar Creatures Promote a Better Understanding of the Natural World," *Science and Children* 31(1), September 1993, 25–27.

STORAGE OF SHOE BOX COLLECTIONS

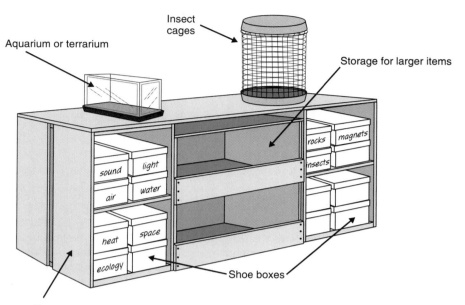

Insect cages

Aquarium or terrarium

Storage for larger items

rocks magnets

insects

sound light

air water

heat space

ecology

Shoe boxes

Four orange crates, two vertical, two horizontal

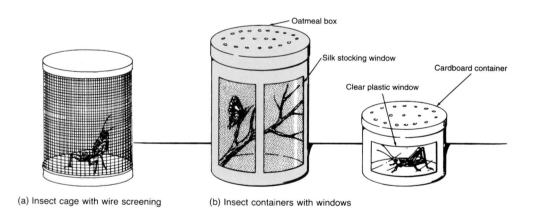

Oatmeal box

Silk stocking window

Cardboard container

Clear plastic window

(a) Insect cage with wire screening

(b) Insect containers with windows

You can cut windows in a paper coffee container, oatmeal box, or another suitable cardboard or Styrofoam container. Cut out the window and glue clear plastic wrap, cellophane, silk, a nylon stocking, or some other thin fabric over the opening as shown.

Another home for insects such as ants that live in the soil can be made by filling a widemouthed quart or gallon pickle or mayonnaise jar with soil up to 2 inches from the top. Cover the jar with a nylon stocking and place it in a pan of water. Put the insects in and cover the jar with black construction paper to simulate the darkness of being underground.

Small Animal Cages.

You can also use some of the insect cages for other small animals. Larger animals can be housed in cages that you and your students construct from window screening. Cut and fold the screening as shown in the diagram. Use nylon screening or be very careful of the sharp edges of wire screening. Tack or staple three sides of the screening to a wooden base and hook the other side for a door.

For housing *nongnawing* animals, you will need a wooden box and sleeping materials such as wood shavings. *Gnawing* animals need a wire cage. A bottle with a one-hole stopper and tubing hung on the side of the cage will supply water. Before proceeding, consult publications such as *Science and Children* and read some of the articles on the care and maintenance of various animals.

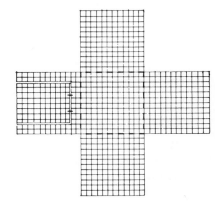

Terrariums.

The word *terrarium* means "little world." In setting up a terrarium for any animal, you should try to duplicate in miniature the environment in which the animal originally lived. You can make a terrarium with five pieces of glass (four sides and bottom) taped together. The top should be made of glass as well, but should have a section cut out to allow for access to the terrarium. Place the finished glass terrarium in a large cookie or cake pan. Commercially made terrariums are also available.

Another simple terrarium can be made from a 2-liter plastic pop bottle, charcoal, pebbles, topsoil, small plants, and scissors (see the diagram).

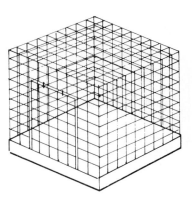

Constructing a 2-liter bottle terrarium

Soak the bottle in warm water to remove labels and glue. Carefully pry the bottom (a) from the bottle (b) so the bottom remains intact. Turn the bottle on its side. Rub your hand over it to find the ridge. With scissors, make a slit about 1.5 cm above the ridge. Cut all the way around the bottle at that level, staying above the ridge. Discard the top of the bottle and the cap.

Put layers of charcoal, pebbles, and topsoil into part (a). Select and arrange the plants in the soil. You can add moss, bark, or small ornaments to your terrarium. Moisten, but do not saturate, the soil. Invert bottle (b) upside down into (a). Push down gently to seal. Your terrarium is ready!

Source: Virginia Gilmore, "Helpful Hints—Coca-Cola® Bottle Terrarium." Reproduced with permission by *Science and Children* 16(7), April 1979, 47. Copyright 1979 by the National Science Teachers Association, 1840 Wilson Blvd., Arlington, VA 22201.

Food Requirements for Various Animals

Food and Water	Guinea Pigs	Hamsters	Mice	Rats
Daily				
pellets or		large dog pellets: 1 or 2		
grain	corn, wheat, or oats		canary seeds or oats	
green or leafy vegetables, lettuce, cabbage, and celery tops or	2 leaves	1 1/2 T 1 leaf	2 tsp 1/8–1/4 leaf	3–4 tsp 1/4 leaf
grass, plantain, lambs' quarters, clover, alfalfa or	1 handful	1/2 handful	—	—
hay, if water is also given				
carrots	1 medium			
Twice a week				
apple (medium)	1/4 apple	1/8 apple	1/2 core and seeds	1 core
iodized salt (if not contained in pellets)		sprinkle over lettuce or greens		
corn, canned or fresh, once or twice a week		1 T or 1/3 ear	1/4 T or end of ear	1/2 T or end of ear
water	1/4 ear	necessary only if lettuce or greens are not provided		

Food and Water	Water Turtles	Land Turtles	Small Turtles
Daily			
worms or night crawlers or	1 or 2	1 or 2	1/4 inch of tiny earthworm
tubifex or bloodworms and/or raw chopped beef or meat and fish-flavored dog or cat food	1/2 tsp	1/2 tsp	enough to cover half the area of a dime
fresh fruit and vegetables		1/4 leaf lettuce or 6–10 berries or 1–2 slices peach, apple, tomato, melon or 1 T corn, peas, beans	
dry ant eggs, insects or other commercial turtle food			1 small pinch
water	always available at room temperature; should be ample for swimming and submersion		
	3/4 of container	large enough for shell	1/2 to 3/4 of container

Food and Water Plants (for Fish)	Goldfish	Guppies
Daily dry commercial food	1 small pinch	1 very small pinch; medium-size food for adults; fine-size food for babies
Twice a week shrimp—dry—or another kind of dry fish food	4 shrimp pellets or 1 small pinch	dry shrimp food or other dry food: 1 very small pinch
Two or three times a week tubifex worms	enough to cover 1/2 area of a dime	enough to cover 1/8 area of a dime
add enough "conditioned" water to keep tank at required level	allow 1 gallon per inch of fish; add water of same temperature as that in tank—at least 65°F	allow 1/4–1/2 gallon per adult fish; add water of same temperature as that in tank —about 70° to 80°F
Plants: cabomba, anarcharis, etc.	should always be available	

Food and Water	Newts	Frogs
Daily small earthworms or mealworms or	1–2 worms	2–3 worms
tubifex worms or	enough to cover 1/2 area of a dime	enough to cover 3/4 area of a dime
raw chopped beef water	enough to cover a dime should always be available at same temperature as that in tank or at room temperature	enough to cover a dime

Note: See also: *Using Live Insects in Elementary Classrooms for Early Lessons in Life,* available from Center for Insect Science, Education Outreach, 800 E. University Blvd., Suite 300, Tucson, AZ 85721.
Source: Grace K. Pratt, *How to . . . Care for Living Things in the Classroom,* Arlington, VA: National Science Teachers Association, 11.

Safety Suggestions for Elementary and Middle School Inquiry Activities

1. Review science activities carefully for possible safety hazards.
2. Eliminate or be prepared to address all anticipated hazards.
3. Post appropriate safety rules in the classroom, review specific applicable safety rules before each activity, and provide occasional safety reminders during the activity.
4. Do not allow students to handle equipment, supplies, and chemicals until they have been given specific information on their use.
5. Maintain fair, consistent, and strictly enforced discipline during science activities.
6. Be particularly aware of possible eye injuries from chemical reactions, sharp objects, small objects such as iron filings, and flying objects such as rubber bands.
7. Require students to wear American National Standards Institute approved safety goggles (with Z87 printed on the goggles) whenever they do activities in which there is a potential risk to eye safety.
8. Consider eliminating open flames; use hot plates where possible as heat sources.
9. Prevent loose clothing and hair from coming into contact with any chemicals, equipment, flame, or other sources of heat.
10. Consider eliminating activities in which students taste substances; do not allow students to touch or inhale unknown substances.
11. Warn students of the dangers of handling glassware; be sure proper devices for handling hot objects are available.
12. Warn students of the dangers of electrical shock; use small dry cells in electrical activities; be aware of potential problems with the placement of extension cords.
13. Instruct students in the location and proper use of specialized safety equipment, such as fire extinguishers, fire blankets, or eye baths, when that equipment might be required by the science activity.
14. Instruct students in the proper care and handling of classroom pets, fish, or other live organisms used as part of science activities.
15. For students with disabilities, ensure safe access and use of equipment and materials.
16. Instruct students to report immediately to the teacher
    - any equipment in the classroom that appears to be in an unusual or improper condition,
    - any chemical reactions that appear to be proceeding in an improper way, or
    - any personal injury or damage to clothing caused by a science activity, no matter how trivial it may appear.
17. Provide practice sessions for safety procedures.

Sources: The University of the State of New York, *Elementary Science Syllabus,* 49, 1985, Albany, NY: The State Education Department, Division of Program Development; Ralph E. Martin, Colleen Sexton, Kay Wagner, and Jack Gerlovich, *Teaching Science for All Children,* 1994, Boston: Allyn & Bacon.

Measuring Tools, Measuring Skills

In elementary and middle school science and mathematics, students should have many opportunities to

- use a variety of types of measuring instruments;
- measure length, area, volume, mass, and temperature; and
- make comparisons using different systems of units.

Metric Prefixes

milli = .001 (one thousandth)
centi = .01 (one hundredth)
kilo = 1000 (one thousand)

Measuring Length
Length is a linear measure.

Metric Units

millimeter = 0.001 meter (one-thousandth of a meter; the thickness of about 20 pages)
centimeter = 0.01 meter (one-hundredth of a meter; width of a little fingernail)
kilometer = 1000 meters (about 10 city blocks)

Some Conversions

1 inch = 2.54 centimeters
1 centimeter = 10 millimeters
100 centimeters = 1000 millimeters = 1 meter
1 meter = 39.37 inches = 3.28 feet
1000 meters = 1 kilometer = 0.621 mile
100 meters = 109 yards
1 yard = 3 feet

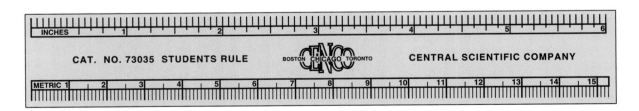

Use the ruler to convert lengths between units.

1 in.   = _____ cm   = _____ mm
3 in.   = _____ cm   = _____ mm
10 cm   = _____ mm   = _____ in.
140 mm = _____ cm   = _____ in.

Use the ruler to measure lengths.

Length of dollar bill   = _____ in. = _____ cm = _____ mm
Diameter of quarter   = _____ in. = _____ cm = _____ mm
Thickness of quarter   = _____ in. = _____ cm = _____ mm

Measuring Area
Area is a surface measure.

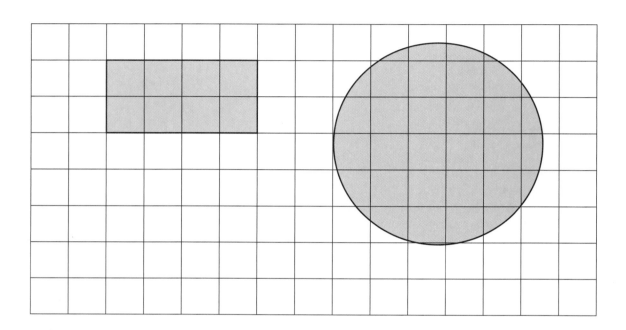

The area of each small square in the figure is 1 square centimeter = 1 cm^2.

Determine the area of the shaded rectangle

• by counting squares. _____
• by formula ($A = L \times W$). _____

Determine the area of the shaded circle

• by counting squares. _____
• by formula ($A = \pi r^2$). _____

Measuring Volume
Volume is three-dimensional.

1 cubic centimeter (cm^3 or cc) is the volume of a cube that is 1 centimeter on each side.

Some Conversions

$1 \text{ cm}^3 = 1 \text{ cc} = 1 \text{ milliliter (ml)}$
$1000 \text{ cm}^3 = 1000 \text{ ml} = 1 \text{ liter}$
$1 \text{ liter} = 1.06 \text{ quarts}$

Determine the volume of the large solid in the figure

- by counting unit cubes.
- by using the formula, $V = L \times W \times H$. _____

Estimate the volume of a golf ball in cubic centimeters. A golf ball has a diameter of about 4 cm.

[*Answer:* Estimate how many unit cubes (1 cm^3) might fit inside a golf ball if it were hollow. A good estimate of its volume might be between 25 and 40 unit cubes. By formula, the volume of a golf ball is about 33.5 cm^3.]

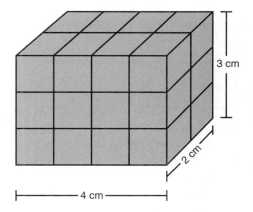

3 cm

2 cm

4 cm

Measuring Mass and Weight

Mass is a measure of the amount of matter in an object and, also, a measure of the inertia of an object. Mass is measured in grams, milligrams, or kilograms using a balance. Weight is a measure of the gravitational pull on an object, measured with a spring scale. Mass and weight are not the same thing, but the weight of an object can be found from its mass.

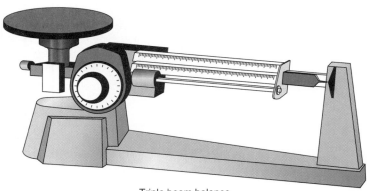

Triple beam balance

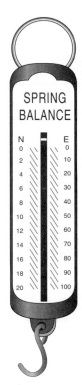

SPRING BALANCE

Spring scale

Some Conversions

1000 grams (g) = 1 kilogram (kg)
1 milligram = 0.001 gram (one-thousandth of a gram)
1 gram = 1000 milligrams (mg)
1 kg-mass weighs 2.2 pounds on the surface of the earth

Nutrition Facts

Serving Size 2/3 cup (55g)
Servings Per Container 12

Amount Per Serving

Calories 210
   Calories from Fat 25

% Daily Value*

Total Fat 3g	**5%**
Saturated Fat 1g	**4%**
Polyunsaturated Fat 0.5g	
Monounsaturated Fat 1.5g	
Cholesterol 0mg	**0%**
Sodium 140mg	**6%**
Potassium 190mg	**5%**
Total Carbohydrate 44g	**15%**
Other Carbohydrate 23g	
Dietary Fiber 3g	**13%**
Sugars 18g	
Protein 5g	

Vitamin A	0%
Vitamin C	0%
Calcium	2%
Iron	6%
Thiamine	10%
Phosphorus	10%
Magnesium	10%

* Percent Daily Values are based on a 2000 calorie diet. Your daily values may be higher or lower depending on your calorie needs.

		Calories	2,000	2,500
Total Fat	Less than		65g	80g
Sat Fat	Less than		20g	25g
Cholesterol	Less than		300g	300g
Sodium	Less than		2400mg	2400mg
Potassium			3500mg	3500mg
Total Carbo			300g	300g
Dietary Fiber			25g	30g

Calories per gram:
Fat 9   •   Carbohydrate 4   •   Protein 4

Some Masses and Weights

Mass of nickel = 5 g

Mass of small child weighing about 60 pounds on earth = 27.3 kg (divide 60 by 2.2)

Weight on moon of small child of mass 27.3 kg = 10 pounds (1/6 of weight on earth)

Food labels tell how many grams and milligrams of different substances are in a food product.

Measuring Temperature

Temperature is a measure of how hot or cold a substance is. Temperature is measured with a thermometer in degrees Celsius or degrees Fahrenheit.

Some Equivalent Temperatures: Use the Fahrenheit/Celsius thermometer to convert from one temperature unit to the other.

Boiling point of water	100°C = _____°F	
Normal body temperature	_____°C = 98.6 °F	
Room temperature	22°C = _____°F	
Freezing point of water	0°C = _____°F	
Slush of crushed ice, water, and ice cream salt	_____°C = 10°F	
A really cold day in Alaska	_____°C = −15°F	

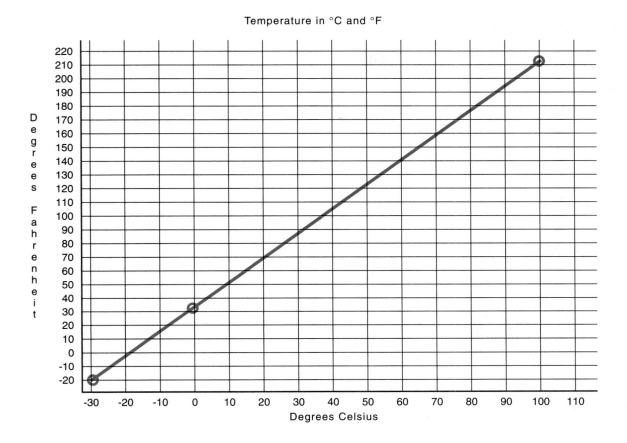

Temperature in °C and °F

Use the graph to find equivalent temperatures.

0°C   = _____ °F
212°F = _____ °C
40°F   = _____ °C
180°F = _____ °C
50°C   = _____ °F

Selected Science Education Periodicals for Teachers and Children

American Biology Teachers

National Association of Biology Teachers
http://www.nabt.org/

Audubon Magazine

National Audubon Society
http://www.Audubon.org/nas/

Discover Magazine

http://www.discover.com/

Journal of Research in Science Teaching

National Association for Research in Science Teaching
http://www.narst.org

National Geographic

National Geographic Society
http://www.nationalgeographic.com/

National Geographic Kids

National Geographic Society
http://www.nationalgeographic.com/kids/

Natural History

American Museum of Natural History
http://www.amnh.org/naturalhistory/

Ranger Rick

National Wildlife Federation
http://www.nwf.org

School Science and Mathematics

School Science and Mathematics Association
http://www.ssma.org

Science

American Association for the Advancement of Science
http://www.aaas.org

Science and Children

National Science Teachers Association
http://www.nsta.org

Science Education

John Wiley & Sons
http://www.wiley.com

Science Scope

National Science Teachers Association
http://www.nsta.org

Scientific American

http://www.sciam.com

Sky and Telescope

Sky Publishing Corp.
http://www.skyandtelescope.com

Super Science (for grades 3–6)

Scholastic
http://teacher.scholastic.com

The Science Teacher

National Science Teachers Association
http://www.nsta.org

Your Big Backyard

National Wildlife Federation
http://www.nwf.yourbigbackyard.com/

Professional Societies for Teachers, Supervisors, and Science Educators

American Association for the
Advancement of Science (AAAS)

http://www.aaas.org

American Association of Physics
Teachers (AAPT)

http://www.aapt.org/

American Chemical Society (ACS)

http://www.acs.org/

Association for Educators of Teachers of
Science (AETS)

http://www.aets.chem.pitt.edu/

Association for Supervision and
Curriculum Development (ASCD)

http://www.ascd.org/

Council for Elementary Science
International (CESI)

http://unr.edu/homepage/crowther/
cesi.html

International Society for Technology in
Education (ISTE)

http://www.iste.org/

National Association of Biology
Teachers (NABT)

http://www.nabt.org/

National Association of Geoscience
Teachers (NAGT)

http://www.nabt.org/

National Geographic Society (NGS)

http://www.nationalgeographic.com

National Science Teachers Association
(NSTA)

http://www.nsta.org

National Wildlife Federation (NWF)

http://www.nwf.com/

School Science and Mathematics
Association (SSMA)

http://www.ssma.org

Contemporary Elementary Science Projects and Programs

Name	Grades	Address	Characteristics
AIMS	K–10	AIMS Educational Foundation http://www.aimsedu.org/	*Activities for Integrating Math and Science Project:* Integration of math skills with science processes into a series of enjoyable investigatory activities; accompanying teacher booklets.
Bottle Biology	K–8	Department of Plant Pathology College of Agricultural and Life Sciences, University of Wisconsin, Madison. Available from NSTA Science Store http://www.nsta.org	*Bottle Biology* is an ideas book for exploring the world through soda bottles and other recyclable materials. The book contains over 20 scientific investigations using bottle constructions, including the Ecocolumn, the Predator-Prey Column, the Niche Kit, and the TerrAqua Column.
BSCS	K–6	BSCS http://www.bscs.org/	*Biological Science Curriculum Study:* Name of project, "Science for Living: Integrating Science, Technology, and Health." Integrated curriculum designed to relate what children know with their exploration and evaluation of new knowledge. Designed around concepts and skills for each grade level: order and organization (grade 1); change and measurement (grade 2); patterns and prediction (grade 3); systems and analysis (grade 4); transformation and investigation (grade 5); balance and decisions (grade 6). Each investigatory lesson has five sequenced phases: engagement, exploration, explanation, elaboration, and evaluation.
ESS	K–6	Available from: Delta Education http://www.delta-education.com	*Elementary Science Study:* A program of 56 nonsequential, open-ended exploratory activities that are not grade-level specific. Student worksheets, booklets, and teacher's guides. Most units are accompanied by kits of materials. Films and film loops also available. Although designed for regular students, ESS units have been shown to be useful in teaching science to children who have language deficiencies, learning difficulties, or other learning disadvantages.
FOSS	K–6	Lawrence Hall of Science http://www.lhs.Berkeley.edu/ Available from: Delta Education http://www.delta-education.com	*Full Option Science System:* Designed for both regular and special education students, 12 modules with lab kits are available. Lessons are in earth, life, and physical sciences with extension activities in language, computer, and math. Can be integrated with textbook programs and state frameworks.

Name	Grades	Address	Characteristics
GEMS	1–10	Lawrence Hall of Science http://www.lhs.Berkeley.edu/	*Great Explorations in Math and Science:* Developed at the Lawrence Hall of Science, this is a series of more than 30 teacher's guides for activities using easily obtained materials.
GrowLab	K–8	National Gardening Association http://www.kidsgardening.com	*GrowLab: Activities for Growing Minds* is a K–8 curriculum guide for use with an indoor classroom garden. Many delightful activities with catchy titles and graphics are included.
PEACHES	Preschool	Lawrence Hall of Science http://www.lhs.Berkeley.edu/	*Preschool Explorations for Adults, Children, and Educators in Science.* The PEACHES program consists of 10 teacher's guides for children's activities and teacher workshops. Teacher's guides on such topics as *Ant Homes under the Ground, Homes in a Pond, Ladybugs,* and *Elephants and Their Young* are available.
SAVI/SELPH (Designed for students with disabilities)	2–10	Available from: Sargent-Welch http://www.Sargentwelch.com Lawrence Hall of Science http://www.lhs.Berkeley.edu/	*Science Activities for the Visually Impaired/Science Enrichment Learning for the Physically Handicapped:* Teacher activity guides in nine modules, student equipment kits.
SCIS 3+	K–6	Available from: Delta Education http://www.delta-education.com	*Science Curriculum Improvement Study:* Originally developed by a team at the University of California, Berkeley, there have been several generations of SCIS developed, with the most recent being SCIS 3+. The SCIS programs are built around a hierarchy of science concepts. Science process skills are integrated into the materials-centered programs, which use an inductive instructional approach and a three-phase learning cycle: (1) student exploration, (2) teacher explanation of concepts, and (3) student application of the old with new.
STC	1–6	National Science Resources Center Smithsonian Institution Available from: Carolina Biological Supply Co. http://www.carolina.com	*Science and Technology for Children:* This program consists of units of hands-on instruction that integrate science and mathematics with other disciplines. A primary focus of program developers is to interest more females and minority children in science.

Source: Modified from Richard D. Kellough, *Integrating Mathematics and Science for Kindergarten and Primary Children,* 1996, Upper Saddle River, NJ: Merrill/Prentice Hall, 396–397.